OPERATION FIREDOG

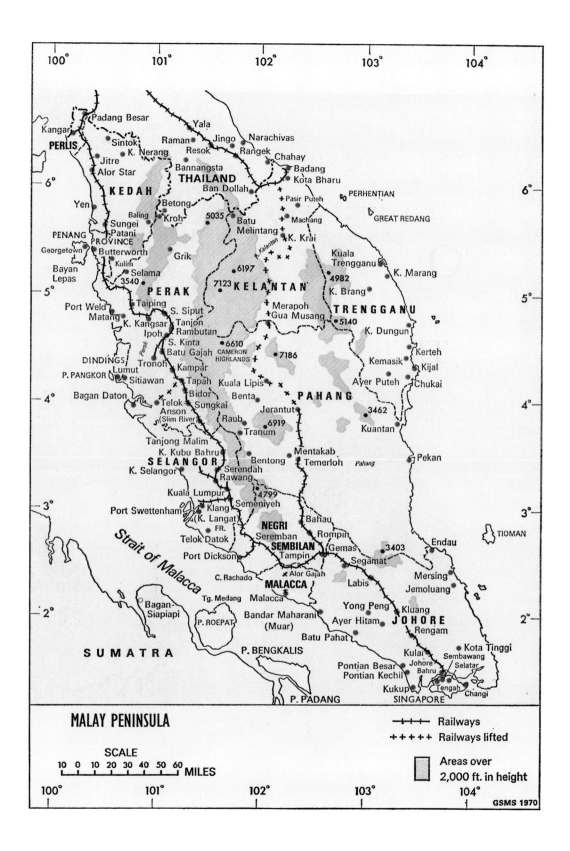

MALAY PENINSULA

SCALE
10 0 10 20 30 40 50 60 MILES

━┼┼┼━ Railways
╋╋╋╋╋ Railways lifted

Areas over
2,000 ft. in height

GSMS 1970

MINISTRY OF DEFENCE
AIR HISTORICAL BRANCH (RAF)

Operation Firedog

Air Support In
The Malayan Emergency
1948 – 1960

Malcolm Postgate

London: HMSO

ISBN 0 11 772724 5

CONTENTS

INTRODUCTION

CHAPTER 1. BACKGROUND TO THE EMERGENCY

CHAPTER 2. THE ORGANIZATION AND OPERATION OF THE AIR
FORCES IN MALAYA

CHAPTER 3. OFFENSIVE AIR SUPPORT IN THE MALAYAN
CAMPAIGN

Foreword

by Air Chief Marshal Sir David Lee GBE CD

Although this is the first published edition of this book it was written almost 20 years ago, shortly after the events which it narrates. It was written for official purposes and though it came out in book form it had a restricted circulation and has remained inaccessible to the public until now.

The manuscript was researched and written under the auspices of the Air Historical Branch, Ministry of Defence, and the author, Malcolm Postgate, had free access to official and classified sources. Some of these will now be in course of release to the Public Record Office, but there will be many no doubt which will not have survived. Thus this treatment of the Malayan Emergency is unique, and the book itself must now serve as the only authority for many of the sources which it quotes.

The Malayan Emergency was a very important chapter in the history of South-East Asia, and in British Military and Diplomatic history too. It lasted for 12 years and at its height it was occupying over a quarter of a million men, in the armed services and the police. It was a success story and it deserves to be better remembered. The ingredients of the Emergency were not particular to Malaya but were common to all the post-colonial territories of the region, among them Indo-China, Indonesia and the Philippines. All of them had been under some form of colonial status before World War II, whether British, French, Dutch or American, and all had been occupied by the Japanese. As the war came to an end the indigenous resistance movements, if not communist inspired already, were exploited by those which were. They transformed themselves into so-called independence movements, but movements whose purpose sought to usurp any democratic change-over to national independence and to impose their own totalitarian ideologies.

The subsequent history of the region cannot be said to have been a happy one, and parts of it are still suffering from the pernicious influences of those days or their after-effects. Only in the Malaysian peninsular is the story more heartening, and that is the story narrated in this book.

Ostensibly the book deals only with the air side of the campaign, which involved units from the Royal Air Force, Royal Australian Air Force, Royal New Zealand Air Force and the Malayan Auxiliary Air Force, as well as from the Royal Navy. But as will be seen, it is not possible to extricate the air story from the whole, and all aspects are touched upon. That indeed was the key lesson from this campaign, namely the intimate collaboration between army, navy and air forces, the police, the civil government and the local communities. It is a lesson which, unfortunately, was not fully learned elsewhere.

This book is very well researched and is an important one. The peace, prosperity and stability now enjoyed by Malaysia and Singapore owe themselves to the successes and sacrifices of this campaign. The author is to be congratulated for producing a splendidly researched and most valuable account of the Emergency.

ABBREVIATIONS

The use of abbreviations has been avoided as far as possible but some have had to be used and the following explanation is provided to clarify their meaning.

ACC	Aircraft Control Centre
ACFE	Air Command Far East
AHQ(M)	Air Headquarters, Malaya
AIS	Aeronautical Inspection Service
AM	Air Ministry
AMES	Air Ministry Experimental Station
AOC	Air Officer Commanding
AOP	Air Observation Post
APC	Armament Practice Camp
APIS	Army Photographic Interpretation Centre
B	Bomber
CT	Communist Terrorist
CTO	Communist Terrorist Organization
DCM	District Committee Member
Det	Detachment
DF/GA	Day Fighter/Ground Attack
DO(M)	Director of Operations (Malaya)
DWEC	District War Executive Committee
F	Fighter
FB	Fighter Bomber
FE	Far East
FEAF	Far East Air Force
FECS	Far East Communication Squadron
FEFBW	Far East Flying Boat Wing
FETW	Far East Transport Wing
FR	Forest Reserve
	Fighter Reconnaissance
GHQ	General Headquarters
GOC	General Officer Commanding
HAA	Heavy Anti-Aircraft
H/C	Helicopter
HE	High Explosive
HQ	Headquarters
JAPIC	Joint Air Photographic Intelligence Centre
JOC	Joint Operations Centre
LAA	Light Anti-Aircraft
LB	Light Bomber
LL	Light Liaison
LR/GR	Long Range/General Reconnaissance
LZ	Landing Zone
MAAF	Malayan Auxiliary Air Force
MB	Medium Bomber
MCP	Malayan Communist Party

MPAJA	Malayan Peoples' Anti-Japanese Army
MR	Maritime Reconnaissance
MRLA	Malayan Races' Liberation Army
MR/TPT	Medium Range Transport
N/AWF	Night/All Weather Fighter
OCAJA	Overseas Chinese Anti-Japanese Army
ORS	Operational Research Section
PR	Photographic Reconnaissance
PW	Psychological Warfare
RAF	Royal Air Force
RAAF	Royal Australian Air Force
RASC	Royal Army Service Corps
RMAF	Royal Malayan Air Force
RNAS	Royal Naval Air Station
RNZAF	Royal New Zealand Air Force
Recce	Reconnaissance
R/P	Rocket Projectile
SACEUR	Supreme Allied Commander Europe
SAP	Semi-Armour Piercing
SAS	Special Air Service
SCM	State Committee Member
SEP	Surrendered Enemy Personnel
SF	Security Forces
SR/TPT	Short Range Transport
SWEC	State War Executive Committee
TDP	Target Director Post
UE	Unit Equipment
VHF	Very High Frequency
VR	Visual Reconnaissance

Introduction

The aim of this narrative is to summarize the part played by the air forces in the campaign against the Communist terrorists in Malaya between 1948 and 1960. Chapter 1 deals with the rise of the Communist threat in Malaya and the measures that were taken by the Federal Government to counter it and concludes with a brief chronological summary of the military campaign. This summary of the Emergency serves as a background to the analysis of the various roles that were played by the air forces during the campaign that is contained in the remaining chapters of the narrative.

Geography of Malaya*

In 1952 the Federation of Malaya covered an area of 53,240 square miles, a little larger than England, and was 400 miles from north to south with a maximum width of 200 miles. It was a country ideally suited to the techniques of guerilla warfare, with a spinal range of mountains that rises to over 7,000 feet and four-fifths of its area covered by jungle, whose topmost storey provides an almost unbroken canopy at an average height of 150 feet from the ground and whose lower layers are so dense that visibility is limited to 25 yards or less in most places. The remaining one fifth of the country comprises rubber and coconut palm plantations, tin mines, rice fields, native villages and towns.[1] In 1952 there were 5,337,000 inhabitants of Malaya, of whom 2,631,000 were Malays, 2,044,000 were Chinese and 586,000 were of Indian or Pakistani stock. The population was widely dispersed, mostly down the western littoral of the country and included $1\frac{1}{4}$ million Chinese who had no citizenship rights, of whom half a million were squatters, and 100,000 indigenous aborigine Malays who lived in remote parts of the jungle on the lower slopes of the central mountain range. Both these groups were an easy prey to intimidation by the terrorists and the former provided most of the recruits to their ranks.

---

* At the beginning of the Emergency Malaya consisted of two separate political entities, the Federation of Malaya (*ie* the Malay Peninsula) and the Colony of Singapore (*ie* Singapore Island). In this narrative, except where otherwise stated, the mention of 'Malaya' refers only to the Federation of Malaya.

CHAPTER 1

BACKGROUND TO THE EMERGENCY

THE OPPOSING FORCES

Origins of the Communist Threat[1]

Communist infiltration in South-East Asia began in the early 1920's with the establishment at Shanghai of a Far Eastern Bureau of the Comintern, Russia's organization for the dissemination of Communism abroad. After six years of preparatory work by Chinese agents the Malayan Communist Party (MCP) was formed in 1929 with the intention of overthrowing the Malayan Administration and establishing a Communist controlled democratic republic. From its inception the MCP was a subversive organization whose revolutionary aims met with little response among the Malays but which did succeed in penetrating the schools and craft guilds of the Hainanese section of the Chinese community. During the late 1920's and the early 1930's the MCP increased its hold on certain sections of the labour force and, by 1937, despite being declared illegal, the party was strong enough to foment a serious wave of strikes with the intention of crippling the economy of the country. In the same year a truce was called in China between the ruling Kuomintang party and the Chinese Communist Party in order to present a united front against the Japanese invader. This enabled the MCP, under the disguise of patriotism, to increase its strength by forming anti-Japanese groups amongst the Chinese and the Malays who were not otherwise interested in Communism. Early in 1940 the Kuomintang faction in Malaya, realizing that it was being engulfed by the MCP, withdrew its support. By then, however, the Communists had acquired an experienced underground organization with several thousand members which was capable of fomenting serious anti-British strikes and demonstrations.

When the Japanese invasion of the Malay Peninsula became imminent late in 1941 it was considered necessary to establish a network of subversive agents who would work for the Allied cause in the event of the country being overrun. In the light of later events it is ironical that the only organization capable of carrying out this task was the MCP and, despite some misgivings, expediency prevailed and 200 of their members retired into the jungle under British instructors after the fall of Singapore to serve as the mainspring of the resistance movement.[2] This band formed the nucleus of the Malayan Peoples' Anti-Japanese Army (MPAJA), a guerilla formation which received arms and ammunition from the Allies in order to harass the enemy's supply lines in return for providing intelligence concerning Japanese movements. After some initial aggression the MPAJA was forced on to the defensive and became hard pressed to maintain its existence. However, when the British re-established contact with the peninsula in February 1943, this force still provided the only effective instrument of strengthening internal resistance to the Japanese. British officers of Force 136, a specialist group of ex-residents of Malaya that had been raised in Ceylon, were infiltrated into the country to co-ordinate further supplies of arms to the MPAJA and to direct their activities in order to assist the Allied invasion forces.[3] The utility of this force was hampered during the last two years of the war, however, by the trial of strength which took place between the MPAJA and a rival organization, the Overseas Chinese Anti-Japanese Army (OCAJA) which the Kuomintang had organized under the direction of the Chinese Nationalist Government.[4] By the time the Japanese capitulated the OCAJA had been driven into a salient in Northern Perak and resistance activities over the remainder of the peninsula were directed by the MPAJA, a highly organized and well-armed force of about 4,000 guerillas and 6,000 ancillary personnel that was deployed in seven independent groups which operated from three to five separate jungle camps.[5]

After the Japanese surrender the MPAJA was kept in being by the occupation forces for a further six months in order to afford some control over the disorderly elements that were scattered throughout the country, but it was finally disbanded in December 1945. At this point the MCP, which had been willing to co-operate with the British during the Japanese occupation, revived its original aim of overthrowing the administration and establishing a Communist state in Malaya. All members of resistance movements were required to come forward and surrender their arms for a gratuity and a promise of rehabilitation in civil employment and, although some 6,000 did so and the majority of the arms issued by Force 136 were recovered, several hundred armed guerillas remained in the jungle as the nucleus of a clandestine military force under the control of the MCP. This force afforded a serious threat to the stability of Malaya but the swift establishment of a British Military Administration frustrated any attempt at a *coup d'état* by the Communists. The MCP, therefore, reverted to a policy of apparent co-operation with the authorities while furthering their revolutionary aims by covert means such as fomenting labour unrest and infiltrating public organizations, by means of which they hoped to paralyse the country's economy and undermine the authority of the Government. However, by the beginning of 1948 it was clear that public support for their movement had not materialized and that they could not succeed in disrupting the administration by peaceful means alone. Therefore, following instructions propagated at the Russian sponsored conference of the World Federation of Democratic Youth at Calcutta in February 1948,[6] the MCP embarked on a more violent programme of labour unrest and demonstrations. When these were aborted by rigorous Government prohibitions their campaign took a more vicious turn with the outbreak of a planned series of murders and sabotage during the first week of June 1948 that was extravagantly acclaimed in the Communist press throughout the world as the spontaneous expression of the suppressed peoples of South-East Asia arising from beneath the yoke of British Imperialism. By mid-June 1948 the scale of insurrection throughout the newly-created Federation of Malaya called for the strongest counter-measures and Emergency Powers were invoked by the Federal Government on 16 June and the military authorities were called in to assist the civil administration in restoring law and order.

Having openly committed itself to armed resistance against the Government the MCP adopted a three-stage strategic plan; firstly to cause terror and economic chaos in rural areas by a programme of assassination and sabotage with the aim of undermining confidence in the administration, secondly to 'liberate' selected rural areas and establish local Communist administration there to serve as the nucleus for the third and final phase of the rebellion during which the urban areas would be 'liberated' and a Communist republic declared. The MCP estimated that six months would suffice to complete each of these stages and that two years at the most would see Malaya transformed into a Communist state. In the event the measures that were taken by the Government and the Security Forces during the twelve year campaign against the Communist terrorists prevented them from completing even the first stage of their plan, which underwent progressive modification as the MCP was compelled to recognize the failure of its attempt to seize the country by force until finally it was abandoned altogether.

Strength and organization of the Communist Terrorists[7]

The Communist Terrorist Organization (CTO) in Malaya consisted of two main branches, the military and the civilian, whose activities were controlled and co-ordinated by the political body of the MCP. The MCP was organized on a state basis with an orthodox Communist chain of command from the Central Executive Committee, which only met at intervals of a year or so, through the State Committees, which met every six months, the District Committees, which met every two or three months and selected and co-ordinated all terrorist attacks within their area, to the branch and sub-branch committees, whose members were attached to and exercised political control over the smallest military units. Between the Central Executive Committee and the State Committees were three 'Bureaux' that were responsible for co-ordinating the MCP's policy in the North, Centre and South of Malaya. One of these, in Central Malaya, was abolished in 1952 owing to the elimination of an increasing number of terrorists who were responsible for executive control.[8]

The field army of the insurgents was formed out of veterans of the MPAJA and was restyled the Malayan Races Liberation Army (MRLA) on 1 February 1949 in order to elicit popular support for their cause under the guise of nationalism.[9] This force was divided into ten regiments that were deployed approximately on a state basis (*see* Annex D),[10] each of which contained between 200 and 500 terrorists divided between four or five companies and ten or twelve platoons. In addition an Independent Platoon of 60 or 70 terrorists was attached to each regiment.[11] The strongest regiments were deployed in the western states of Malaya where the main inhabited areas were located. At the beginning of the Emergency this insurgent army numbered about 2,500 with a further 600 organized into highly mobile 'killer' squads as the spearhead of the initial campaign of assassination and violence. By 1951 the strength of the MRLA had reached its maximum of about 8,000, after which it fell to less than 5,000 in 1953, less than 3,000 in 1955, to a final total of about 500 at the end of the Emergency in 1960. Losses were partly offset by recruiting during the early years of the insurrection and altogether some 11,000 terrorists were eliminated during the Emergency. 95 per cent of the armed terrorists were Chinese, the majority of whom were born in China and owed little allegiance to the country of their adoption, with Indians and a few extremist Malays comprising the remaining 5 per cent.

At the start of the Malayan campaign there were only a few hutted camps in the jungle fringes and many of the insurgents lived in their own houses in the district from which they were recruited and were difficult to distinguish from the innocent local populace. By 1951, however, almost all the MRLA lived in well camouflaged and guarded camps in relatively inaccessible parts of the jungle. Here they were trained in the arts of guerilla warfare and became familiar with the use of standard firearms and even automatic weapons and explosives. The supply of arms and ammunition, however, was a constant factor limiting recruitment to their forces, although it did not interfere with their activities to any great extent. The legacy of

the Japanese occupation provided them with sufficient arms for their initial requirements but, as the campaign progressed, their armouries dwindled as arms captured
from the Security Forces or leaked from ordnance stores failed to replace those that
were lost. Nevertheless, by practising stringent economies the number of terrorists
who were armed remained at about 75 per cent of their total number although most
of the ammunition which they carried was old and unreliable. At no time in the
Emergency were the MRLA able to organize external supply lines for there plenish-
ment of arms or recruits, partly as a result of the Security Forces' blockade of the
borders and partly because the Chinese Communists were involved in the Korean
War during the period when the terrorists held the initiative in Malaya and were
thus in no position to help. This isolation of the Malayan insurrection from external
aid was a major factor in its ultimate defeat.

The insurgent army could not have survived without the assistance of the underground 'Masses Organization', with whom they were linked by the civilian branch
of the CTO, the 'Min Yuen' or 'Peoples 'Movement'. The 'Min Yuen' provided the
MRLA with food, funds, clothing, medical supplies, recruits and intelligence concerning the movements of the Security Forces, all of which they levied from the
populace partly by extortion or intimidation, as well as being responsible for the
dissemination of Communist propaganda amongst the unfortunate villagers on whom
they battened. They were deployed in a static district and branch organization and
in general played a non-combative role. During 1952, however, a number of the
'Min Yuen' were armed as their contact with the populace made them the chief
target for the Security Forces and, when the maintenance of their essential service
eventually made it necessary to draft members of the MRLA into this body, it became
increasingly difficult to distinguish them from the real insurgent army. Many of the
'Min Yuen' were enrolled in ancillary units of this army such as the 'Local Defence
Corps', 'Self Protection Corps', 'Armed Work Forces' or 'District Units', whose
only difference from the MRLA was that they were under the control of District
and not State Committees of the MCP.[12] By September 1957 it was estimated that
only 200 of the remaining 1,830 terrorists were still serving in the MRLA.[13] No
figures are available of the strength of the 'masses organization' on which the 'Min
Yuen' relied, since many gave only casual or unwilling support to the Communist
cause, but it is probable that at the height of the Emergency in 1951 over one
million of the Chinese population were at least potential supporters of the MCP and
adopted a passive attitude of non-co-operation with the Security Forces until the
dwindling fortunes of the terrorists and the realization that the forces of law and
order could offer them adequate protection from intimidation inspired a change of
heart.

Strength and organization of the Security Forces[14]

Deployed against the CTO was a composite force, drawn from the various
branches of the civilian and military services, which contained about 9,000 Police
and ten infantry battalions at the start of the campaign but was then rapidly expanded
until it included 67,000 Police, 300,000 Home Guards and 23 infantry battalions at
the height of the Emergency in 1951.

Whilst the main task of the military forces was the destruction of the insurgent
army, the main commitment of the Federal Police was to protect the local populace
from intimidation by the terrorists and it is some indication of the difficulties which
this entailed that the strength of the Regular Police rose from 9,000 at the start of

the Emergency to 16,814 in January 1951 and a maximum of 24,427 in January 1954. From 1950 onwards this total included the Special Field Force, numbering 2,915 in January 1957, which included trained Jungle Companies for active operations against the terrorists, for patrolling across the Thailand border and for manning the deep jungle forts that were established after 1952. In addition to the Regular Police a Special Constabulary, comprised mostly of Malays, was raised in each state to guard plantations, mines and other vital installations and to enforce food control regulations. The strength of this force rose from 10,000 in August 1948 to a maximum of 44,878 in January 1952, after which their establishment was reduced to 23,857 by the end of 1955 and their role was changed from static defence duties to active patrolling by five to six hundred Area Security Units and 40 to 50 Special Squads which operated outside their own localities. All Police units, Regular and Special, were controlled from the Federal Police Headquarters at Kuala Lumpur through State, District and Circle Headquarters, each of which included operational, CID and Special Branch Staffs.

As well as a force of up to 50,000 full time Police, various local part-time units were raised to relieve the Regular Police from duties which did not require special qualifications and also to identify the local populace with the anti-terrorist campaign. In 1949 Kampong Guards, armed with shotguns, were formed to defend Malay villages against terrorist attacks and, together with the Auxiliary Police that were formed in urban areas for traffic control and similar duties, they totalled 47,000 by the end of 1950. In September 1951 the Chinese Home Guard was formed to carry out similar duties, especially in resettled areas, and their strength had risen to 30,000 by the end of the year. Following the reorganization of civil defence in July 1951 the Kampong Guards and the Chinese Home Guard were amalgamated into a composite Home Guard with a maximum strength of 300,000. Thereafter greater selectivity and improved training weeded out the unreliable members, who were largely responsible for the loss of shot guns to the terrorists, and the strength of the Home Guard fell to 152,000 in 1955 and continued to decline with the removal of Emergency restrictions from certain areas. In 1956 8,500 Home Guards were relieved of the static defence duties for which they had been formed and were organized into operational platoons for active patrolling against the terrorists outside their parent states. Other non-military units that were employed by the Security Forces during the Malayan campaign were the Civil Liaison Corps, a body of Europeans and Chinese with local knowledge whose members were attached to Army units in order to facilitate contact with the local populace, and the Special Operations Volunteer Force, a uniformed force of ex-terrorists that was formed in 1953 and deployed in ten platoons for operations against selected targets under Police Special Branch direction.[15]

Complementary to the civilian security services was a composite military force in which infantry was the predominant arm. The number of battalions that were available for anti-terrorist operations in Malaya rose from ten at the start of the Emergency to 26 in June 1950 after which it dropped to 21 in August 1957. The strength of each battalion and the number of battalions in each brigade varied according to the needs of each state but, by the end of 1951, all British battalions contained five companies and approximately 1,000 men[16] and the total strength of the Army in Malaya had increased from 10,000 in June 1948 to a maximum of 30,000, of whom half were non-operational. The provision of troops for this force was a truly Commonwealth effort as, among the units serving in Malaya at the end of 1955, were six British, six Gurkha, seven Malay, one Fijian, one African and one

Australian battalion, besides a New Zealand squadron of the Special Air Service Regiment.[17] Supporting the infantry at various stages during the campaign were two armoured car regiments, each containing up to six squadrons, one or two field batteries and one field regiment of artillery, two field engineer regiments, one Commando brigade, three squadrons of the 22nd Special Air Service Regiment and one squadron of the Parachute Regiment.[18]

As with the Police, the control of the Army in Malaya was decentralized along geographical lines. The four Sub-Districts that existed in Malaya and Singapore in 1948 were reorganized into three Districts in November 1949; South Malaya District, responsible for operations in Johore, Negri Sembilan, Malacca and Selangor, Malaya District, responsible for operations in Pahang, and North Malaya District, responsible for operations in Perak, Kedah and Perlis, Kelantan, Province Wellesley and Penang.[19] After the success of anti-bandit operations in Central Malaya in 1956, only North and South Malaya Districts were left to control operations against the bulk of the remaining terrorists in Perak and Johore.[20] Within each District a Brigade Headquarters, commanding a number of battalions, was normally located at Police Headquarters in each state capital, while Battalion Headquarters were located with Police District Headquarters at the administrative centre of each Civil District and Company Headquarters with each Police Circle Headquarters. This decentralization of control to company or even platoon level was designed to ensure that there existed a framework of troops in support of the Police throughout the Federation, onto which reinforcements could be superimposed when necessary, and was well suited to a campaign against an enemy that was deployed along similar lines.

Operating in concert with the ground forces was a composite force of aircraft provided by the RAF, the RAAF, the RNZAF, and the local auxiliary and national air forces, as well as the Navy and the Army. The strength of the air forces that were available for operations in support of the ground forces against the terrorists increased from three fighter, four medium range transport, one photographic reconnaissance and one flying boat squadron in July 1948 to a maximum potential in July 1954 of two medium bomber, three fighter, three flying boat, three medium range transport, four equivalent short range transport and one photographic reconnaissance squadron, with a combined establishment of 166 aircraft.[21] In addition to these air forces various units of the Royal Navy operated in conjunction with the Royal Malayan Navy in intercepting illegal seaborne traffic and carrying out several bombardments of shore targets, while one squadron of naval helicopters carried out the major part of the trooplifting commitment between 1954 and 1956.[22]

Command and Control of the Anti-Terrorist Campaign[23]

The primary task of the military forces in Malaya during the Emergency was to assist the government in restoring law and order and to this end their activities were closely co-ordinated with those of the Police to enforce the regulations that were devised by the civil administration to end the insurrection and prevent its recurrence. Not the least successful manifestation of this co-operation between the military and civil authorities was the joint system of control that was developed to meet the exigencies of the campaign against the terrorists. Before April 1950 the campaign was controlled by the Commissioner of Police, advised by members of the three Armed Services, but he had insufficient powers to ensure its effective direction and in that month Lieutenant-General Sir Harold Briggs was appointed Director of Operations to co-ordinate, on behalf of the High Commissioner, the activities of all the Security Forces, to enforce the administrative measures that were considered necessary to deal with the situation and to allot his resources accordingly. The instrument of his direction was the Federal War Council, whose members included the Chief Secretary of the Federation, the General and Air Officers Commanding in Malaya, the Commissioner of Police and the Secretary for Defence. In November 1950, in order to simplify procedure and to create a greater sense of urgency in the campaign against the terrorists, the High Commissioner agreed to preside over the War Council, which thus assumed overriding powers on all matters affecting the Emergency. In order to associate responsible opinion in Malaya with the conduct of the Emergency, representatives of the Malay, Chinese and Planters' Associations were added to this council while, in November 1951, the original Armed Services and Government members formed a Director of Operations Committee to handle detailed operational planning.

General Sir Robert Lockhart succeeded General Briggs as Director of Operations on 3 December 1951 but, following the murder of the High Commissioner, Sir Henry Gurney, by the terrorists, General Sir Gerald Templer was appointed Director of Operations and High Commissioner on 7 February 1952 and thus became responsible for all Government activities including the conduct of the Emergency. Under his administration, which lasted until April 1954, the Director of Operations Committee remained responsible for directing the campaign against the terrorists while the Federal Executive Council, successor to the Federal War Council, served as the Cabinet to ensure that every activity of the Government was bent on ending the Emergency. At State or Settlement and District levels, War Executive Councils, containing influential members of the local community as well as local military and police commanders, had been set up in September 1950 and continued to prosecute and co-ordinate the campaign against the terrorists according to the priorities established by the Director of Operations Committee. In January 1955 wider racial representation was also provided on these local war councils and Operations Sub-Committees were formed to handle the daily conduct of anti-terrorist operations.

In March 1956, as part of the agreed sequence for the progressive handover of responsibilities to the Federal Government prior to Independence on 31 August 1957, the Minister for Internal Defence and Security became responsible to the Federal Executive Council for the overall direction of the Emergency, for which purpose an Emergency Operations Council was formed that contained various Ministers representing the Malay, Chinese and Indian communities as well as Service and Police Chiefs. When Independence was achieved the Director of Operations became responsible to this council, and not to the British Government, for the conduct of the anti-terrorist campaign and this system of control was maintained until the end of the Emergency.

THE CAMPAIGN AGAINST THE COMMUNIST TERRORISTS[24]

The Briggs Plan

When the Emergency was declared in June 1948 the Federation of Malaya had only been in existence for four months and the Government was ill-prepared to deal with the threat of the Communist terrorists, the magnitude of which was not at first appreciated as its impact was felt mainly in rural areas and not in the centres of administration. Deficiencies in the constitution, in the command structure of the armed forces, in the civil administration and in the Police were gradually rectified as the seriousness of the insurrection was realized, but it was not until the end of 1950 that the British Government were fully convinced of the gravity of the situation and accorded to the Federal Government the full degree of financial and military support without which real progress against the terrorist threat was not possible.

Improvements in the strength and organization of the Administration and the Security Forces were of little use, however, without an overall plan to direct their operations in the offensive against the terrorists. Such a plan was propounded by General Briggs, the first Director of Operations, in April 1950. This plan, on which the campaign was largely fought and won, was two-pronged, combining civil and military action with the intention of destroying the terrorists and preventing a recurrence of their activities. It was designed to exploit the fact that the CTO could not exist without receiving money, supplies and recruits from the local population and could not operate effectively without information from them. Its primary aim was, therefore, to cut off the CTO from the populace and this depended on the Administration's success in controlling and protecting vulnerable sections of the community, especially in isolated areas, in eradicating Communist cells from the populated areas and in controlling the supply and distribution of vital commodities to prevent them from getting into terrorist hands. Once effective control had been established over the populace and their confidence in the Government's ability to control the situation had been restored then a military offensive could be launched in order to seek out and destroy the armed element of the CTO.

Measures taken by the Civil Administration[25]

Various measures were taken by the Federal Government in order to control the population and to separate the terrorists from their source of supplies and information, most of which were invoked under the Emergency Regulations Bill that was passed on 5 July 1948 and periodically revised thereafter. Heavy penalties were imposed for assisting the terrorists and wide and diverse powers were given to the Government, including the right to issue detention orders, declare protected or prohibited areas, to seize property, control movement on the roads, disperse assemblies, impose curfews and to control businesses and the distribution of food. Many of these edicts were rescinded or modified after 1953 as the situation improved but the Emergency Regulations Bill remained in force throughout the Emergency as the basis for all the important measures that were taken by the Administration to combat the terrorist threat.

The most notable contribution that was made towards the severance of communications between the terrorists and their supporters amongst the local inhabitants was the resettlement of a large part of the Chinese squatter population. The assistance which they gave to the Communist cause was recognized as early as December 1948 and during 1949 various regulations were promulgated which empowered State or Settlement authorities to resettle squatter communities in areas that could be satisfactorily administered and policed. During the first nine months of 1949 6,343 persons were detained under this regulation, of which 1,226 were released to live in places where they would be free from terrorist intimidation.[26] With the appointment of General Briggs as Director of Operations in 1950 the problem of resettlement was tackled with increased energy and by the end of that year 117,198 persons had been moved into 140 New Villages, most of which were protected by barbed wire and perimeter lights and defended by the Malay Police and the Chinese Home Guard. By the end of 1951 385,000 persons had been resettled in 429 New Villages and a year later there were 509 such settlements with a population of 461,822. In the space of two years nearly half a million Chinese squatters had been brought under effective administrative control and the Communist terrorists had been virtually cut off from their major source of support. The cost of the resettlement programme was high, over 41 million dollars,[27] and it inevitably suffered from the urgency with which it was carried out. At first discontent was rife amongst those who had been forcibly resettled and they were extremely susceptible to Communist infiltration. The Government made great efforts, however, to develop a proper community spirit in the New Villages and the provision of social amenities, education facilities and the solution of the problem of land tenure helped to improve the lot of their inhabitants and fostered their conversion to the Government's cause, which was a major factor in bringing the Emergency to a successful conclusion.

As resettlement progressed the terrorists turned their attention to scattered labour lines on isolated rubber estates and tin mines, which provided an easy target for intimidation. From January 1951 onwards, therefore, these lines were regrouped and brought within defended perimeters under the protection of the Auxiliary Police, while restrictions on the hours and places of work were imposed in order to afford some protection to the labour force during the hours of daylight.

One of the Police Special Branch's strongest weapons against the 'Masses Organization' on which the CTO depended was the regulation that was enacted early in the Emergency which gave them the power to arrest and detain a person for up to two years without trial, a law that was strengthened in January 1949 when the Government was empowered to detain whole villages that were known to be consorting with the terrorists. By the end of 1949 detention centres had been established at seven places in the Federation and 5,575 persons had been detained.[28] By the end of 1950, 9,035 persons were under detention, but this number declined to 2,234 by the end of 1953 as popular support for the terrorists dwindled. At the end of 1955 less than 1,000 persons were detained, by which time the general limitation of detention periods to six months had taken much of the sting out of this measure.

As it was felt that many of the detainees were victims of circumstance, whose legitimate desire for self-government had been exploited by the Communists, Rehabilitation Centres were opened at Taiping, Morib near Kluang, Majeedi near Johore Bahru and Telok Mas between 1949 and 1952,[29] in order to provide vocational training for male and female Chinese and Malay detainees with the aim of re-educating them for unconditional release into a free and democratic society.

Further relief to the problem of accommodating detainees was provided by the Emergency Regulation that was gazetted in November 1948, which made provision for the deportation of undesirable persons with their consent. Nine thousand and sixty-two detainees and their dependants were deported to China during 1949 and a further 460 to India.[30] Some difficulty was then encountered, however, in reaching agreement with the receiving countries, especially with China where repatriation to the mainland was interrupted altogether in 1950 with the southward advance of the Communists in that country. By November 1950, however, limited disembarkation was resumed through the port of Swatow and a record number of 7,099 Chinese were repatriated during 1951, together with 73 Indians. A further 5,277 persons were repatriated during 1952 but the numbers fell thereafter to under 1,000 in 1954 and the practice of deportation had virtually ceased by the end of 1956. By September 1957 a total of 12,190 persons had been deported and a further 2,717 had been repatriated at their own request.[31]

Besides the Chinese squatters, another section of the populace that was subject to Communist intimidation were the 60,000 aborigines who inhabited remote jungle areas of the central mountain range, especially in Perak, Pahang and Kelantan. From 1952 onwards the terrorists withdrew into these remote areas in order to conserve their dwindling strength and their exploitation of these primitive people intensified as they compelled them to provide porters, guides, couriers, purchasing agents, a labour force for cultivating their vegetable plots and an intelligence screen against the approach of Security Force patrols. As it was considered impolitic as well as impracticable to resettle these aboriginal jungle dwellers, a plan was put into effect in 1953 to bring them under Government control and protection in their own habitat. Eleven deep jungle forts were established, manned by the Police Field Force, which served as centres of administration as well as medical and trading centres and bases for offensive operations by the Security Forces.[32] An intelligence service, using aborigines, was formed and some of them were enrolled as Auxiliary Police. So effective were these measures that it was estimated that only 300 or 400 aborigines were still under terrorist domination at the end of 1956.[33]

Other Emergency measures that were taken by the Government to underline the schism between the terrorists and their supporters amongst the civilian population were National Registration, which was completed by April 1949 and helped in identifying terrorists and hindering their movement by public transport, and the power of excluding any person from a Police District by an order signed by the officer in charge of that district.

The terrorists proved most vulnerable, however, through their supply organization. Their chief weakness lay in their inability to live off the natural food products of the jungle, which were scarce and did not form a balanced diet. Jungle cultivations were susceptible to discovery and destruction from the air and were never developed enough to make the terrorists self-sufficient. Food had to be obtained from the populated areas, therefore, as well as money, clothing, medicines, printing materials and other items essential to the terrorists' campaign, and it was the supply points between the centres of population and the jungle fringes that provided the most prolific killing grounds for the Security Forces. In order to restrict and identify these supply points an intensive food-denial campaign was put into effect in June 1951 when resettlement and the regrouping of labour had progressed far enough to justify its application. The control of food and essential supplies was carried out at District level and its main features were the strict rationing of rice, enforced by ration cards, the declaration of Food Restricted and Prohibited Areas, the control and protection of restricted articles while in transit, the licensing of shops entitled to sell them and the limitation and careful accounting of their stock. After 1953 this programme was combined with a sustained military effort to find and destroy terrorist cultivations in the jungle and between them these measures forced the bandits to split into smaller units in order to survive and thereby deprived them of much of their offensive power. Slow but progressive starvation had a cumulative effect on terrorist morale and food denial operations became the basis of all Security Force operations during the last few years of the Emergency. In recognition of the role played by these operations in reducing the terrorists' will to continue the struggle, an Emergency Food Denial Organization was formed in 1956 to supervise this campaign throughout the Federation.

Besides helping to starve out the terrorists the food denial programme also elicited vital intelligence material as it increased the chances of identifying the terrorists' food suppliers and pressure could be brought against them to become informers or police agents. Information gathered in this way was of vital importance for knowledge of terrorist locations and movements was the key to the whole offensive campaign against them. At the beginning of the Emergency, however, the intelligence services in Malaya were in a poor state. The Malayan Security Service had suffered losses during the Japanese occupation that had not been made up, the Police were undermanned and not mobile, poor telephonic communications hindered the transmission of information and a dearth of trained interpreters prevented the exploitation of such terrorists and Communist literature that were captured.[34] Worst of all, in view of the lack of police protection in the face of terrorist intimidation, no information about the insurgents was forthcoming from the public.

On his appointment as Director of Operations in April 1950, General Briggs realized that intelligence was the prerequisite of all successful anti-terrorist operations and in May of that year he established a Federal Joint Intelligence Advisory Committee to examine means of strengthening intelligence and Police Special Branch techniques. In August 1950 a Director of Intelligence Services was appointed to co-ordinate the various intelligence agencies of the Security Forces and the Civil Departments, to supervise the collation, evaluation and dissemination of both strategic and tactical information and to advise the Director of Operations on Emergency intelligence matters. By 1953 the Director of Intelligence Services was co-ordinating the work of the Federal Intelligence Committee and the Combined Intelligence Staff, which included representatives of the Police, the Armed Services and the civil Administration, the Police Special Branch, with officers at Federal, Contingent, Circle and District Headquarters who advised the Government on all subversive activities and produced operational intelligence for the Security Forces, and special Military Intelligence Officers who worked at all levels in liaison with the Police Special Branch.

The main sources of information about terrorist locations were police agents, normally former Communist supporters who remained in touch with the terrorists, informers, usually members of the public reporting suspicious movements, reconnaissance by the ground forces and by aircraft searching for terrorist camps, food dumps and courier routes, and surrendered enemy personnel, who proved surprisingly willing to give information. Not the least important factor in the successful outcome of the campaign against the terrorists was the fact that, quite early in the Emergency, the Police Special Branch knew the names and identities of all of them and also their approximate spheres of operation. The flow of information concerning their detailed movements, however, depended primarily on the current successes achieved by the Security Forces, both in killing terrorists and in protecting the public from their depredations. It was important, therefore, to disseminate news of these successes to both the public and the terrorists in order to raise the morale of the former and to undermine that of the latter. This task was the responsibility of the Information and Psychological Warfare Services.

At the start of the Emergency information and directives to the public were disseminated through the Emergency Publicity Committee of the Department of Public Relations but, in June 1950, this task, as well as that of propaganda against the terrorists, was taken over by the Emergency Information Services at Federal Police Headquarters in Kuala Lumpur, with representatives at State or Settlement and District levels. In October 1952 the Emergency Information Service was separated from the Director of Operations Staff and placed under the Director General of Information Services. In March 1954, however, responsibility for the psychological offensive against the terrorists was reinvested with that part of the Director of Operations Staff known as the Psychological Warfare Section, while the Director of Information Services became responsible to the Home Affairs Department of the Government for disseminating Emergency propaganda and information to the public.[35]

Propaganda was conveyed to the terrorists either directly, through the media of leaflets, Information Services newspapers and broadcast messages, all of which were distributed on the ground as well as from the air, or indirectly by hearsay from the general public. Advice, exhortation, directives and general information on Emergency matters that were aimed at the public were promulgated in posters, leaflets, newspapers, Press communiqués, touring loudspeaker vans, Radio Malaya programmes, films and aerial and ground broadcasts. Leaflets and broadcasts were prepared in simple vernacular languages for distribution to the scattered native villages and estates where the majority of the plural society of Malaya lived and some impression of the effort that was put into the information and propaganda services is given by the fact that the number of leaflets that were distributed by all methods rose from 30 million in 1948 to 53 million in 1950, to 77 million in 1953 and to over 100 million in every year between 1954 and 1957.[36] The 12 mobile public address and cinema units that addressed $1\frac{1}{4}$ million people in 1948 were expanded to a fleet of 91 units by 1953, whose combined messages reached an audience of of over one million people every month.

The importance of the contribution made by the propaganda and information services to the successful outcome of the campaign cannot be underestimated. In the long run only the people of Malaya themselves could have defeated Communism and that is the reason why the Emergency remained largely a civil campaign to elicit the support of the uncommitted masses. The crux of the problem lay in winning the confidence and loyalty of the bulk of the Chinese population and to stimulate amongst them a positive reaction against Communism. The formation of the Malayan Chinese Association in February 1949 went some way towards rallying Chinese support for the Government's cause and by the middle of 1951 it was clear that the cumulative effect of Security Force measures had increased public confidence in them, with a resultant improvement in co-operation and an increase in the flow of information concerning terrorist whereabouts. Continuous efforts were made to foster the public's support for the anti-terrorist campaign through such means as the 'Anti Bandit Month' of February 1950 and the formation of the Home Guard and other self-protection units. In 1955 Good Citizens Committees were formed in many villages and the public anti-Communist rallies which they organized assured the populace that it was safe to give information to the authorities and also helped to convince both the terrorists and the people that Communism was a lost cause in Malaya. The preliminary to the final collapse of a terrorist unit in any locality was usually the realization that they had lost all public support and it was at this point that they were particularly susceptible to psychological warfare techniques and were most liable to defect. Largely as a result of the offensive mounted by the Psychological Warfare Department 254 terrorists surrendered during 1952 and this number increased to a maximum of 372 in the following year.[37] In 1954 and 1955 over 200 defections a year were recorded but thereafter the number declined as the Psychological Warfare Department was faced with a smaller and more obstinate hardcore of terrorists who were not so susceptible to their blandishments.

So successful were the propaganda and information services in encouraging defections from the Communist cause and stimulating the confidence of the people in the ultimate victory of the Government forces that it became possible to progressively lift Emergency restrictions from the whole country through the creation of 'White Areas' in which the inhabitants were responsible for their own defence against any resurgence of Communist activity. However, the task of providing these services with exploitable material, in the form of terrorist eliminations, remained the major commitment of the armed forces, both military and civilian.

Military Plan of Action

As the Malayan campaign remained the responsibility of the Government all military action was closely co-ordinated with that of the police and was directed initially towards enforcing regulations that were designed to protect the populace and prevent the insurrection from getting out of hand. Only when stability was restored and the local administration was capable of taking over static defence duties were the military forces deployed for offensive operations to search out and destroy the terrorists. In fact, for the first two years of the Emergency, the initiative lay entirely with the terrorists and the combined operations of the Police and the Army were directed solely towards dealing with outbreaks of insurrection as and when they occurred and were not based on any premeditated plan of campaign. The armed forces during this period were largely restricted to static guard duties and such jungle patrols as were undertaken were not subject to any overall design and generally proved fruitless. It is true that two carefully planned and methodical sequences of military operations were undertaken to restore order in parts of Johore during 1949[38] but the success which they achieved was only temporary as the machinery of civil administration was not yet adequate to prevent a resurgence of terrorist activity.

Under the Briggs Plan that was initiated on 1 June 1950, however, steps were taken to enhance the strength and efficiency of the Police and civil administration in order to consolidate the gains achieved by military action. So far unco-ordinated military operations, largely dictated by the unpredictable activities of the insurgents, had yielded little permanent result, but now an overall military plan was devised to rectify this situation. Under this plan the minimum number of troops that were necessary to guarantee security against terrorist attacks were deployed in close conjunction with the Police in populated areas throughout the Federation. On to this defensive framework the surplus military forces were superimposed in selected areas to dominate the jungle up to five hours journey from potential terrorist supply areas, thus forcing them to run this gauntlet if they wished to remain active in these areas. Either they would do so and face elimination or they would be forced to move on to another locality. In this way it was planned to eradicate the terrorist threat progressively throughout the country by starting 'area domination' operations in Johore on 1 June 1950 and then working steadily northwards. It was hoped to clear Johore of all terrorists by 1 November 1950 and to start clearing up operations in Negri Sembilan and Malacca on 1 August 1950 and in South West Pahang on 1 September 1950.[39] To this end six of the 19 infantry battalions then in Malaya were deployed in Johore in May 1950,[40] but the terrorists' foothold in that state proved too firm and hopes of a quick victory over them were too sanguine. The programme of military operations had to be revised and in the end Malaya was cleared of the terrorist threat from the central states outwards, Johore not being declared 'White' until the end of 1958. Nevertheless, with certain modifications, the policy of clearing each State or Settlement in turn of the Communist menace remained the overall strategic plan for the remainder of the campaign and, since the MRLA regiments were deployed largely on a State basis, it proved well suited to local conditions.

The usual technique for offensive operations against the terrorists was to mount a pre-planned combined operation which involved constant patrolling, with full aerial support, in order to keep the enemy on the move and force him to split up into small groups that were more susceptible to ambush, while associated food denial measures compelled him to make contact with the civilian population and increased his chances of encountering a Security Force patrol. Within the area of one of these large scale operations each battalion was allotted a particular locality and these were divided in turn between its constituent companies, of which two platoons were operational at any time and the third was held in reserve.[41] During 1951 and 1952 most of these operations lasted for a maximum of two or three months but experience showed that merely beating through an area once or twice in the hope of driving the enemy into ambushes on the far side had little chance of success as the areas were too large and the cover too thick. Besides which, food control measures had to be maintained for at least three months to have any real effect and so, from the middle of 1953 onwards, an era of protracted operations, each of which lasted from six months to a year or more, was inaugurated which ultimately proved successful in systematically eradicating the terrorist units.

Summary of the Campaign against the Terrorists[42]

The course of the twelve year campaign against the terrorists in Malaya was influenced by the changing policy of the MCP, by Government counter-measures and Security Force operations and by the effect of these developments and Communist fortunes elsewhere in Asia on the attitude of the public. The statistical information that is collated and represented in Annexes H and J gives details of the number of terrorist inspired incidents, the number of contacts made between the Security Forces and the terrorists and the number of casualties that were inflicted on both sides and provides a fair picture of the general trend of the campaign and the relative successes of the opposing forces.

The fluctuating fortunes of the terrorists and the Security Forces during the Emergency fell roughly into four periods; firstly from June 1948 to October 1949, when the initial Communist attempt to seize power in Malaya was checked and they withdrew into the jungle to reorganize their forces for a prolonged war; secondly from October 1949 to August 1951, when the terrorists, encouraged by Communist successes all over Asia, launched a second offensive which brought the level of violence to a peak in 1951; thirdly from August 1951 to July 1954, when the counter-measures that were instigated by the Director of Operations appointed in 1950 began to take effect, the back of the revolt was broken, the terrorists lost over half their strength and the remnant was compelled to retire to deep jungle hideouts in order to survive; fourthly from July 1954 to July 1960 when, the crisis being over, the strength of the terrorists dwindled steadily before Security Force pressure, as did the number of incidents, contacts and casualties to both sides, until the point was reached when the Emergency could be declared over.

At the start of the Emergency the initiative lay entirely with the terrorists as the Malayan Government and the Security Forces were ill-equipped to deal with a situation whose gravity was not fully appreciated. During the first few months of the campaign, therefore, the Security Forces were largely committed to the task of stabilizing civilian morale and affording some degree of protection to the public and to essential utilities and industrial installations. Despite their efforts, however, the terrorist inspired incident rate averaged 212 a month until the end of 1948, by which time they had killed and wounded over 900 people for the loss of 700 of their own number. However, despite the static role played by most of the Security Forces during this period, a few limited offensive operations were mounted against the terrorists. In May and June 1948, prior to the declaration of the Emergency, Operations 'Pepper' and 'Haystack' were launched in the North Perak valley against the remnants of the anti-Communist OCAJA, a Kuomintang faction now calling themselves the Malayan Overseas Chinese Self-Protection Corps who had taken the law into their own hands because of the lack of Government protection against the Communists in that area.[43] Further south, during July and August 1948 'Shawforce' and the 'Ferret Forces', small independent units formed largely from Malay and Gurkha regiments,[44] were sent out against the Communist terrorists in Perak but achieved little success owing to the lack of information about their location. These operations did, however, give the ground forces experience of jungle operations while the air support that was provided for these patrols introduced the air forces to most of the techniques of their commitments throughout the remainder of the campaign.

By the end of 1948 the measures taken by the civil administration were beginning to have an effect and the Security Forces had been reinforced to the point where the Police could take over many of the static defence duties and release the Army for jungle operations against the terrorists. The initial object of the insurgents, to subvert the Government by a reign of terror and establish a 'liberated' area in Pahang by 3 August 1948,[45] had been decisively defeated and sanguine hopes were expressed that the situation could soon be brought under control. The MCP leaders, however, remained unshaken by these reverses and the problem of eliminating the forces which they controlled was rendered infinitely more difficult when they withdrew into the jungle and, from April to October 1949, set about reorganizing their army and its supply force for a protracted guerilla campaign, leaving behind small 'killer' squads in the populated areas to continue their policy of terrorism, intimidation and extortion and to occupy the attention of the Security Forces.

This withdrawal of the terrorists into the jungle was reflected in a marked decline in the rate of the incidents which they inspired from an average of 50 a week at the end of 1948 to 26 a week from mid-February to December 1949. The nature of terrorist attacks also changed as they showed a marked reluctance to attack targets that were well guarded or where they were deprived of the element of surprise and the total number of casualties which they inflicted on the civilian population during the whole of 1949 was less than during the first six months of the campaign. In contrast, the Security Forces were able to take limited offensive actions as their numbers increased and their organization improved and during 1949 they succeeded in killing 618 terrorists, mostly in Pahang and Northern Selangor, for the loss of 229 of their own number. In the Cameron Highlands area of North West Pahang and the neighbouring parts of Perak and Selangor, Operation 'Gargoyle' was launched in January 1949[46] and was followed by a series of operations from April to July, 'Ramillies', 'Blenheim', 'Spitfire' and 'Sarong', against the 300 or more terrorists associated with No 5 Regiment MRLA in this region. The terrorists fled before the advancing columns of the Security Forces but their escape northwards was blocked by Operations 'Pintail', 'Widgeon', 'Pathfinder' and 'Overall' which were mounted in Perak and Kedah between July and September 1949. Meanwhile Operations 'Triangle', 'Snow White', 'Lemon' and 'Plunder' had been mounted further south in South West Pahang, Northern Negri Sembilan and Selangor between April and September 1949, particularly against No 1 Regiment MRLA, during which a notable success was achieved with the elimination of 37 out of 45 terrorists in the Kuala Langat Forest Reserve of Selangor in April, largely owing to the use of offensive air support.[47] Further south Operations 'Constellation' and 'Leo' were mounted against No 3 Regiment MRLA, in North West Johore and Malacca in September and October 1949, during which 32 terrorists were killed, 23 were captured and a further 28 surrendered. While these operations were in progress in Central and Southern Malaya Operations 'Holiday' and 'Pussycat' were launched in the extreme north, on the borders of Kedah and Perlis with Thailand, in conjunction with the Thai Police in order to prevent infiltration across the border and to flush the terrorists out of this area.

While these operations were being launched against the armed terrorists, operations such as Operation 'London' in Selangor were designed to increase the pressure on their 'Min Yuen' support force and a further attempt to win the support of the uncommitted Chinese populace was made in February 1949 with the formation of the Malayan Chinese Association.[48] To counteract their waning influence the insurgents adopted the title of the MRLA on 1 February 1949 in order to disguise their insurrection as a nationalist movement and, to foster the impression that it included all races, No 10 Regiment was formed of dissident Malays in Pahang.[49] This unit, however, was so harried by the Security Forces that it had virtually disintegrated by the end of the year and the rebellion continued as it had started to be based almost entirely on the alien Chinese element of the population.

By 6 September 1949 the pressure of Security Force operations and the progress made in the control of the dissident element of the population by detention, repatriation and re-education made it appear that the revolt was under control and the first surrender terms were offered to the terrorists. At first this offer achieved notable results and 116 of the 216 terrorists who surrendered during 1949 did so under its terms.[50] It soon became clear, however, that these were only the waverers who regretted taking to the jungle in the first place and the surrender rate soon fell to a low level as the bulk of the MRLA remained intact, training and reorganizing. Optimistic hopes of a quick termination to the Emergency were dampened and public confidence in its outcome was not enhanced by Communist successes in China, Korea and Indo-China in 1949 and 1950 and the subsequent recognition of Mao Tse-tung by Britain and of Ho Chi Minh by Russia. The Communist star in Asia appeared to be waxing strongly, providing a considerable fillip to the morale of the MRLA and giving serious food for thought to the Chinese community of Malaya who began to show a marked reluctance to co-operate with the authorities in case they jeopardized their safety under a future Communist government.

This deterioration in the Emergency situation marked the advent of its second phase, which witnessed the peak of terrorist activity and which began when they launched a second offensive in October 1949 with considerably more forethought and skill than in June 1948. The incident rate rose sharply to an average of over 500 a month throughout 1950 and the number of civilian and military casualties also increased to nearly 200 a month—figures that were three times the number recorded during 1949. The situation appeared to be getting out of hand and it was clear that urgent action was needed by both civilian and military authorities to stem the tide. This was forthcoming with the appointment of General Briggs as Director of Operations in April 1950 to co-ordinate the efforts of the civilian and military authorities and to ensure that the maximum effort was afforded to anti-terrorist operations. He realized that there was no quick or easy way to end the Emergency and that it was not sufficient to eliminate the terrorists as replacements were readily available. It was necessary to break their morale and to isolate them from their supply lines, notably the 'Min Yuen'. To this end the programme of resettling the Chinese squatter population was intensified and the effect of the extension of effective administration to outlying communities was immediately apparent in the increased amount of intelligence information that was received by the Police Special Branch. To rouse the populace from its apathetic attitude towards the prosecution of the Emergency an 'Anti-Bandit Month' was held in February 1950, during which civilians took over many of the normal duties of the Police and released them for active operations against the terrorists,[51] and the Government Information and Propaganda services were expanded.

In the military sphere the bulk of the Security Forces were withdrawn from fruitless jungle patrols to protect the towns and villages and to dominate the ground between them and the jungle fringes in which the terrorists would be compelled to contact their supporters for essential supplies. The arrival of two more infantry brigades and offensive aircraft reinforcements[52] enabled the Security Forces to concentrate in Johore in the latter half of 1950 while retaining a defensive framework throughout the Federation and several combined food denial and offensive patrolling operations were mounted in that state, notably Operation 'Moccasin', which had achieved 30 terrorist eliminations by the beginning of August, Operation 'Asbab', during which 62 'Min Yuen' were arrested in the Yong Peng area, where 25 terrorists had been killed by a patrol of the 1st Battalion 2nd Gurkha Rifles during Operation 'Thor' in January, and Operations 'Kohat', 'Jackal' and 'Letter', which were mounted between October and December 1950 and seriously disrupted the 6th Company of No 4 Regiment MRLA. Further north at least 30 terrorists were eliminated during Operations 'Thandiani', 'Baxaul' and 'Butlin', which were mounted in the Jerantut and Sungei Sembing areas of Pahang between January and April 1950, while two notably successful operations were carried out on the borders of Negri Sembilan, Selangor and Pahang in April and October 1950— Operation 'Jackpot',[53] during which 29 members of No 2 Regiment MRLA were killed, 10 were captured, 15 surrendered and 74 of their agents were arrested, and Operation 'Autumn Double', during which 11 terrorists were killed and 17 of their camps destroyed. No results were forthcoming from Operation 'Foxhound' in this area in August 1950, however, and a similar lack of contact with the terrorists rewarded a series of Operations, 'Carp', 'Albemarle', 'Rabbit' and 'Cleaver II', which were mounted against No 5 Regiment MRLA in Perak between April and November 1950, although five terrorists were killed in an air strike south west of Tapah during Operation 'Hotspur' in October 1950. Operation 'Rose' against elements of No 8 Regiment MRLA in the Kulim area of Kedah in September also proved abortive but three operations on the eastern side of the Federation during 1950, 'Walkover' and 'Trek' in Trengganu and 'Kota' in Kelantan succeeded in their object of destroying isolated terrorist cultivation plots and establishing the local Home Guard.

By the end of 1950 Security Force pressure had forced the terrorists to split into smaller groups for survival and the incident rate had been reduced by nearly 200 a month. The terrorists, despite killing nearly 1,000 civilian and military personnel during the year, lost over 800 of their own forces. The improvements in the Emergency situation that were caused by the measures introduced under the Briggs Plan continued into 1951 and, with the receipt of additional intelligence material, the

Security Forces increased their rate of contact with the terrorists to more than double the rate of 1950 and the number of eliminations rose accordingly. Realizing their danger the terrorists launched an all-out offensive of violence and intimidation in order to disrupt the Briggs Plan. The incident rate rose to 606 a month in June 1951, the highest for the whole Emergency, and only fell below 500 a month on one occasion during the year. However, most of this outburst of violence was represented by 'nuisance' attacks against 'soft' or undefended targets that were designed to intimidate the local populace and the number of civilian casualties in 1951 actually showed a slight decrease over the previous year. In general the terrorists continued to avoid contact with the Security Forces as far as possible but, especially in North Johore and North Perak, they began concentrating in large gangs again towards the end of the year and adopted more aggressive tactics, including several well-planned attacks on ground patrols. In one ambush they killed 11 members of the 1st Battalion, The Queen's Own Royal West Kent Regiment for the loss of only six of their own number.[55] Altogether the Security Forces suffered 505 killed and 663 wounded during 1951, an increase of over 50 per cent on the casualties suffered during 1950. In return, however, they achieved a similar increase in terrorist eliminations, killing 1,025, wounding 650 and capturing a further 121.

Many of these eliminations were achieved by combined police and military action in the jungle fringe areas, which testified to the tactical success of the 'framework' deployment of the Security Forces under the Briggs Plan. With the formation of Police Jungle Companies, however, the Army was able to hand over their commitment in the whole of Kelantan and the Kuantan area of East Pahang in March and July 1951 in order to concentrate on combined operations in South West Pahang, Selangor and Negri Sembilan. Operations 'Kick Off,' 'Cathedral' and 'Hustle' had failed to make contact with the terrorists in this area in January 1951 but six members of the 24th Company, No 6 Regiment MRLA were killed during Operation 'Stymie' in the Raub area of Pahang in February and another six from the 28th Company of the same regiment were killed near Temerloh in March during Operation 'Sabai'. During Operations 'Valetta', 'Mantrap' and 'Tansing' in the Rawang and Bentong areas of Selangor and Pahang in February and March six terrorists had been killed and the remainder of a gang of 250 or more had been dispersed. Further pressure was put on the terrorists in the Labis area of Johore during Operations 'Dagger' and 'Target' in March and in the same month, during Operation 'Prosaic' in South East Pahang, the Special Air Service were used for the first time in the campaign for deep jungle operations. Between June and August 1951 a general intensification of effort was made in North West Johore and Negri Sembilan and Operations 'Warbler', 'Grasshopper' and 'Sedge' were mounted to clear this area and drive the terrorists northwards.[56] Towards the end of 1951 12 terrorists were killed in the Bentong area of South West Pahang during Operation 'Mahakal' and a further seven members of the 24th and 30th Companies, No 6 Regiment MRLA, were eliminated during Operation 'Pursuit', which was mounted after the murder of the High Commissioner Sir Henry Gurney near Raub on 6 October.[57] While a concentrated effort was being made against the CTO in South West Pahang, Negri Sembilan and North West Johore, the remaining military operations of 1951 were mainly directed against elements of No 5 Regiment MRLA in the Tapah and Ipoh areas of Southern and Central Perak. Following Operation 'Gallows' in January a series of operations was launched in this area throughout the year, 'Rumble', 'Rainbow', 'Redskin', 'Raven', 'Rover', 'Mermaid' and 'Marker' being followed between August and December by 'Sludge', 'Rebel' and 'Springtide', during all of which 14 terrorists were killed, 33 were captured, 4 surrendered, 38 of their camps were destroyed and the supply organization of the local CTO was seriously disrupted.[58]

The first eight months of 1951 witnessed the zenith of the Emergency in Malaya, with the peak of terrorist violence and the widespread expectation of the wholesale occupation of South East Asia by the Communists. Credit is due to the civil and military administration and to the local populace who bore the brunt of the terrorist attack, for preventing the situation from getting out of hand while at the same time creating the conditions which enabled ultimate victory to be achieved. Nevertheless, although the terrorists lost nearly 30 per cent of their total casualties to date between January and August 1951,[59] most of these were made good by further recruitment and, with the backing of a widely supported 'Min Yuen', they looked capable of continuing their insurrection indefinitely. The third phase of the Emergency, which opened in August 1951, began, therefore, with a call for renewed vigour in the prosecution of the campaign against the terrorists. With the appointment of General Sir Gerald Templer as High Commissioner and Director of Operations in February 1952 the civil and military administration was unified for the first time and, under his forceful direction, such complacency as remained in Government departments was swept away and priority was given to reorganizing and training the Police and to improving the intelligence and information services. By this time the main aspects of the Briggs Plan had begun to mature, nearly half a million squatters had been resettled into New Villages, the policy of deportation of undesirables was being implemented and Security Force operations were being effectively co-ordinated with food denial measures. These developments, combined with the fact that the Communists were being held in Korea and Indo-China, led to an upsurge in public confidence in the outcome of the campaign which was reflected in an increase in the flow of information from them about terrorist locations, with a resultant rise in the contact rate achieved by the Security Forces to a peak for the whole Emergency.

As the initiative passed to the Security Forces the terrorists, realizing their increasing isolation from the main body of the populace on whom they relied for recruits and supplies, became markedly less aggressive and their efforts were turned increasingly towards subversion and ensuring the survival of their remaining forces. Following instructions published in the Cominform Journal, to the effect that Communist parties in Colonial territories should follow the Chinese revolutionary model and confine their attacks to military or para-military targets while increasing their efforts to infiltrate and subvert labour and other organizations,[60] the Central Politburo of the MCP issued a directive in October 1951 which decried aggressive incidents that were likely to alienate the public, such as attacks on railways or damage to the people's means of livelihood.[61] In addition a significant proportion of the MRLA was withdrawn to build up its strength in deep jungle bases, where cultivation plots were to be laid out in an attempt to lessen their dependence on the local population. The effects of this directive were evident by the end of 1952 and the incident rate, which had averaged 507 a month during 1951, fell to 194 a month from July to December 1952. Attacks on estates and mines fell from 138 in February 1952 to 10 in December of that year, while the number of rubber trees that were slashed by the terrorists decreased from 70,000 to 600 a month during the same period.[62] As the terrorists withdrew into the deep jungle the number of civilian and military casualties which they inflicted fell from 200 a month in mid-1951 to 30 in December 1952. Even so, despite the increasing difficulty of making contact with them, the Security Forces managed to eliminate slightly more of the terrorists during

1952 than they had in 1951 and the final figure for the year of 1,094 killed included a significant number with the rank of Branch Committee Member of the MCP or above.

The 'framework' deployment of the military forces was continued throughout 1952 but combined 'search and destroy' and food denial operations in specific areas were stepped up, especially in the most densely populated states of West Central Malaya. Operation 'Broderick' was launched against the 39th Independent Platoon of No 5 Regiment MRLA in the Kroh Chikus Forest Reserve area of South Perak in January, followed by Operations 'Puma' and 'League' in the Cameron Highlands area of North West Pahang in February and April, 'Techchi' and 'Noah' in the Triang and Bentong areas of South West Pahang in January and February and 'Hive' and 'Hammer' in the Seremban and Kuala Langat areas of North West Negri Sembilan and South West Selangor in August and October 1952. At least 30 terrorists were eliminated during these operations, the CTO in South Selangor was seriously disrupted and several hundred aborigines were rescued from terrorist domination. Outside this area notable operations in 1952 included Operation 'Helsby' against the Headquarters of No 12 Regiment MRLA in the Belum Valley area of Northern Perak in February, during which paratroops were used for the first time during the campaign,[63] Operation 'Pancake' in January, against the 5th Platoon, No 8 Regiment MRLA in Kedah, and Operation 'Habitual' between May and August 1952, which seriously weakened the supply organization of No 7 Regiment MRLA in the Kuantan area of East Pahang.[64] Largely as a result of the elimination of ranking terrorists during these operations the higher command of the MCP passed to two 'Bureaux' in the north and south of Malaya in place of the three previously maintained.

The marked improvement in the Emergency situation that was evident in 1952 continued throughout 1953, which was a year of steady progress against the background of increasing security and the improved morale of the civilian population. The growing feeling that the forces of law and order had the situation under control was fostered by public relations operations, such as Operations 'Question', 'Service' and 'Ginger', which were designed to improve the public's attitude towards the Police and the Emergency measures that were still considered necessary and to encourage them to give information of terrorist movements. The rate of terrorist inspired incidents fell from a monthly average of 310 in 1952 to 99 in 1953, while the number of casualties sustained by the Security Forces fell from an average of 22 a month to eight a month. The number of terrorists that were killed also fell, from 104 to 81 a month, as the contact rate declined but there was a steady increase in the number who surrendered, with an average of 31 a month during the year.[65]

The reduction in the terrorist threat during 1953 enabled the Army to hand over its 'framework' responsibilities in many areas to the increasingly efficient Police force and to concentrate for offensive operations against the terrorists in specific localities. The original plan to clear the Federation from the south northwards was proving impracticable, however, and it was decided to attack the terrorists where they were weakest, in the central states of Malacca, Pahang, Negri Sembilan and Selangor.[66] Thus a wedge could be driven between the main terrorist forces in the north and the south of the country and the Police and Home Guard could be left to maintain security in these areas while the bulk of the Army was freed to deal with the most recalcitrant targets in Johore and Perak. To this end several large scale combined operations were launched in Pahang and the neighbouring states during 1953, including Operations 'Cato', 'Matador', and 'Sword' against No 6 Regiment

MRLA in the Raub, Mentakab and Bentong areas of South West Pahang between March and July, Operations 'Wellington II' and 'Maze' against No 1 Regiment MRLA in the Port Swettenham and Kuala Lumpur districts of Selangor between April and December, Operation 'Valiant' against No 5 Regiment MRLA in the Cameron Highlands area of North West Pahang in October,[67] Operation 'Screw' in the Tapah area of Perak, Operations 'Commodore' and 'Cornwall' against Nos 3 and 4 Regiments MRLA in the Kluang and Segamat areas of Northern Johore in January and June and Operation 'Ibex' against No 7 Regiment MRLA in the Kuantan area of East Pahang in August 1953. At least 75 terrorists were killed during these operations, 12 during Operation 'Commodore' and 36 during Operation 'Sword' alone, during the last of which 106 terrorist camps were also found in what was one of the most successful combined operations to date.[68] These operations seriously weakened the CTO in the central states of Malaya and by the end of the year it was possible to lift Emergency restrictions from a large part of Malacca, which became the first 'White' area. Apart from these major operations greater attention was turned towards depriving the terrorists of the support of the local aboriginal population during 1953 and the number of forts in the deep jungles of Perak, Pahang and Kelantan was increased to seven during the year.[69]

By the middle of 1954 the average number of civilian and military personnel killed each month was 35, in contrast to 188 during 1951, over 7,500 terrorists had been eliminated and only 3,500 still remained at large in the jungle. These survivors, however, represented the core of the MRLA and the nature of the terrain in the jungle-clad spinal range to which they had retreated ensured that they were becoming increasingly difficult to locate and that they could not be entirely prevented from attacking targets close to the jungle, particularly where Security Force pressure had been temporarily relaxed. The monthly rate of terrorist inspired incidents was only reduced by 10, from 99 to 89, during 1954, while the number of terrorist eliminations achieved by the Security Forces fell from an average of 81 to 77 a month and the number of terrorists who surrendered during the year was only 210—162 less than in 1953. Consequently, the final phase of the Emergency, the protracted attrition of the remnants of the CTO opened in July 1954, soon after Lieutenant-General Sir Geoffrey Bourne had replaced General Templer as Director of Operations, with the pronouncement of a new tactical plan that was designed to overcome the dangers of a stalemate in the campaign.[70] Greater responsibility for local security was given to the Police and Home Guard while the Army was employed more offensively by occupying and dominating jungle areas for considerable periods until the local CTO was either eliminated or driven from the area. Such protracted operations relied heavily on air support, especially that of the troop-carrying helicopter force that had recently arrived in the theatre, and reflected the degree of confidence that the Army had developed in the air forces by this time.

As in the previous year, most of the combined operations that were mounted during 1954 were concentrated in the central states of Malaya in order to isolate the main bodies of terrorists in Southern Johore and Northern Perak. The most important operations of the year were 'Galway', 'Inland' and 'Termite'[71] against No 5 Regiment MRLA in the Ipoh and Sungei Siput areas of Southern Perak, 'Hawk' and 'Apollo' against No 6 Regiment MRLA in the Raub and Kuala Lipis areas of Pahang, 'Jekyll' against No 2 Regiment MRLA in the Bahau area of Negri Sembilan and 'Kitchener' and 'Ajax' against No 4 Regiment in the Rangam and Kulai areas of Johore. Two hundred and forty-three terrorists were eliminated during these operations and the high proportion of surrenders included in this number was evidence of the declining morale of the insurgents in the face of this offensive against their rest and and training areas in deep jungle. During April 1954, however, it became clear that the terrorist leaders were inflicting strict disciplinary action and security measures on the rank and file of the CTO in order to discourage them from defecting and were also undertaking more aggressive action against selected targets in order to raise their morale. Coupled with Communist successes in Indo-China and at the Geneva Peace Conference, these measures led to a temporary improvement in terrorist resistance and at the end of 1954 over 3,000 seasoned terrorists were still at large in the jungle.

Nevertheless, by the beginning of 1955, nearly one-third of the population of Malaya lived in 'White' areas that were free from Emergency restrictions[72] and the terrorist threat had been reduced to little more than an annoyance to the well-being of the country. Civilian and Security Force casualties during 1955 were reduced to 12 and 15 a month respectively, in contrast to 86 and 102 during the peak months of the Emergency in 1951, and the terrorist inspired incident rate of 65 a month was only 13 per cent of the 1951 rate. Throughout the year the terrorists maintained their policy of avoiding contact with the Security Forces and only 665 eliminations were made in 564 contacts, compared with 926 eliminations in 993 contacts during 1954.[73] During 1955 the Security Forces' policy of concentrating against the weakest terrorist targets by 'area domination' operations was intensified and their efforts were rewarded by a conspicuous success in Pahang, where a series of intensive food denial operations, Operations 'Rooster' in the Kuala Lipis area, 'Huntsman' in the Raub area and 'Latimer North', 'Latimer South' and 'Asp' in the Temerloh and Triang areas, resulted in the decimation of No 6 Regiment MRLA and the disintegration of the local CTO and its supporting 'Min Yuen' cell.[74] Over 130 terrorists were eliminated, one of the three deep jungle bases which the terrorists had been trying to establish was disrupted and the whole state was cleared of terrorists by the end of the year, except for the Temerloh and Cameron Highlands area. A second more localized victory was achieved by Operation 'Nassau' in South Selangor with the destruction of a gang of 50 terrorists in the Kuala Langat area[75] and the net result of these successes was the creation of a large 'White' area in Central Malaya which contained nearly half the total population of the country.[76] A wedge had been driven between the main terrorist concentrations and the severance of the main courier routes between the Northern Bureau of the MCP, by now relatively safe in their base in the Betong salient of Southern Thailand, and the Southern Bureau ensured that the latter operated autonomously from now on. These successes in Central Malaya enabled the Security Forces to concentrate on extending the breach in the terrorists' ranks to the south and west against the South Malaya Bureau and to this end priority was given to operations in South West Pahang and North East Negri Sembilan towards the end of 1955, although Operation 'Shark', which had been launched against the 26th Independent Platoon MRLA in the Sungei Siput area of Perak in September 1954, continued throughout 1955 and had achieved 35 terrorist eliminations by the end of the year.

Meanwhile, however, the setbacks suffered by the terrorists and the holding of the first Federal elections as the first stage in the transition from Colonial rule to Independence, which deprived them of their strongest propaganda line, had persuaded the MCP leaders to attempt to negotiate a peace settlement. The newly elected Alliance Party refused to negotiate but, in recognition of the changed situation, they declared an amnesty on 9 September 1955 and agreed to meet Chin Peng, the Secretary General of the MCP to clarify the surrender terms which they now offered.[77] Restrictions on Security Force actions were imposed in view of this amnesty but were lifted again on 21 November as the terrorists were taking advantage of them to prove that they were still a force to be reckoned with before the Peace Talks were held at Baling in Northern Kedah on 28 and 29 December 1955. At these talks Chin Peng demanded recognition of the MCP and the release of all those terrorists who surrendered without detention or further investigation. The Chief Minister of the Federation, Tunku Abdul Rahman, rejected these demands, which amounted to a licence for the MCP to continue their subversive aims unopposed, and Chin Peng retired to the jungle declaring that the terrorists would fight on to the last man rather than accept the amnesty surrender terms. Terrorist activity, lulled during the 'wait and see' period that had overshadowed the abortive peace talks, broke out again, especially in Johore where the remaining terrorists in that state proved increasingly intransigent in the absence of any higher direction.

It was clear by now that the MCP had lost the shooting war and, with Independence guaranteed, they could no longer play on the nationalist sympathies of the populace. The party's only hope lay, therefore, in leaving the jungle under some form of guarantee that it would be allowed to remain in existence and to this end they launched a 'peace offensive' early in 1956 in an attempt to lay the blame for the continuing Emergency on the Federal Government. This appeal met with some sympathy, especially amongst the Chinese element of the populace, and the Government was compelled to step up their counter-propaganda offensive in order to bolster civilian interest in maintaining that pressure against the terrorists which was essential if they were to be prevented from reorganizing and rebuilding their strength and remaining as a malignant cancer in the body of the country. For, by 1956, most of the waverers amongst the terrorists had been eliminated and those that remained were well disciplined and virtually immune to propaganda appeals. Inspired by Mao Tse-tung's 20 year wait for power in China they were determined to avoid contact with the Security Forces and sit it out in the jungle until external Communist aid or a further opportunity for leading a popular revolution presented itself. Their morale, which had been severely shaken by their leaders failure at the Baling talks, was now stiffened by intensive indoctrination based on the claim that Chin Peng had in fact achieved a moral victory at the talks and that the eyes of the world had been focused on their plight.

As a result of this propaganda a 'wait and see' attitude was engendered amongst the terrorists and the surrender rate fell from an average of 21 a month during 1955 to 12 a month during 1956, while the incident rate showed a similar decline from 63 to 39 a month. However, despite their continuing evasive tactics and the law of diminishing returns which made the remaining terrorists increasingly difficult to contact, a total of 473 were eliminated during 1956, 20 per cent of their remaining strength, and only 2,063 remained at the end of the year. A major success was achieved in April 1956 with the elimination of Ycong Kwo, the Deputy Secretary General of the MCP and the principal architect of the party's political offensive, by a patrol of the Rifle Brigade near Semeniyeh in Selangor,[78] while virtually the whole of the 7th Independent Platoon MRLA was wiped out by an air strike during Operation 'Kingly Pile' in February.[79] Other major operations that were mounted during the year followed the usual pattern of a protracted period, during which intelligence material was garnered, followed by a period of strict food control from which additional information became available for exploitation by Security Force patrols and ambushes. Each operation, supported when necessary by offensive and air transport support, lasted for six to nine months or more and most were mounted in adjoining areas and continued into 1957. The most important were Operations 'Shark North' and 'Shark South' in the Ipoh, Sungei Siput and Cameron Highlands area of Perak, 'Gabes North' and 'Gabes South' in the Perak and Kelantan border area, 'Bonanza' in Southern Selangor, 'Latimer South' and 'Enter' against the South Malayan Bureau of the MCP in the Bahau and Rompin area of North and North East Negri Sembilan and 'Huckster' and 'Tartan Rock' in the Kluang and Kulai areas of Johore.[80] Over 200 of the remaining 2,500 terrorists were eliminated during these operations.

In accordance with the general plan to project the successes gained in Central Malaya northwards through Selangor and into Southern Perak and southwards into North Johore, priority for military operations had been switched to Selangor and Negri Sembilan in July 1956 and although neither state was completely clear of terrorists by the end of the year a further eight areas, containing a quarter of a million people, were declared 'White' and Emergency restrictions had been relaxed in areas covering over half the Federation and containing over half its population.[81] In certain selected areas that did not yet justify the designation 'White' a new policy of handing over to the people the responsibility of denying support to the terrorists was introduced in April 1956 and bore fruit in October of that year when the inhabitants of two Malay villages took the law into their own hands and turned over seven terrorists to the authorities.[82] Good Citizens Committees were also encouraged in the New Villages to rally public support to the Government's anti-terrorist campaign for it was becoming increasingly important to counteract the tendency towards complacency in the conduct of the Emergency if the surviving terrorists were not to come out of the jungle when Independence was declared in 1957 under the banner of a victory against imperialism. The ranks of the MRLA may have been decimated but the real strength of the MCP lay in the fact that 170 of its leaders still remained in the jungle and the CTO in Johore, Perak and Kedah was still relatively intact and well supported by the local Chinese.

On 1 January 1957, therefore, military priorities were switched from the unrewarding targets offered by the few remaining terrorists in Negri Sembilan and Selangor to the larger concentrations in Southern Perak and Northern Johore. Operation 'Latimer South' in the Bahau and Rompin area of Negri Sembilan was continued throughout 1957 largely by the Police while the Army concentrated on Operations 'Shark North', 'Shark South' and 'Chieftan' in the Ipoh, Cameron Highlands and Tapah area of Perak and Operations 'Cobble', 'Shoe' and 'Huckster' in the Gemas, Segamat and Kluang areas of Johore with the aim of creating a 'White' area from Tapah in the north to Kluang in the south before Independence Day on 31 August 1957.[83] This target was largely achieved as, by the date set, the last platoon of the MRLA in Selangor and Negri Sembilan had been destroyed, Central Selangor had been declared 'White', to complete a 'White' belt from coast to coast across the Federation, and in July 1957, for the first time in any month of the Emergency, not one person, military or civilian, was killed by the terrorists and no major incident occurred. On Independence Day some 1,830 terrorists remained at large, of whom 550 were located in the Thailand border area, including 450 actually in Thailand and to all intents and purposes out of reach of the Security Forces, 500 in Central Perak and 500 in Southern Johore.[84]

As 'Merdeka' Day approached the Federal Government came under some pressure to come to terms with the remaining terrorists but recognized the dangers of forsaking the position so painstakingly gained and declared that the Emergency would continue in the hope that it could be terminated by the first anniversary of

Independence Day. For political reasons, however, it was thought desirable to gradually diminish the number of Commonwealth troops that were engaged on anti-terrorist operations, to restrict their use as far as possible to operations in Southern Johore and Northern Perak and to avoid bringing them into direct contact with populace.[85] Coupled with the 'Malayanization' of the civil administration and the diversion of the Police effort to internal security duties, these developments were reflected in an inevitable reduction in the tempo of the campaign and in the efficiency with which it was managed. Terrorist eliminations fell to 15 during September 1957, the lowest monthly total of the Emergency to date, and the total for the whole of 1957 was only 394.

By this time one-third of the remaining terrorists were located in Southern Thailand, where they were determined to lie dormant until the Malayan Government was deluded into thinking that they were no longer a threat to the internal security of the country and would negotiate peace on the MCP's terms. As the threat which they represented could not be ended solely by a shooting war the psychological warfare effort was stepped up in order to persuade them to surrender. New surrender terms were offered in connection with Independence and several terrorists took advantage of them, but their effect was nullified to some extent by a new peace overture from Chin Peng which encouraged a resurgence of the terrorists 'wait and see' policy. However, as the loss of public support after Independence and the effect of continuing Security Force Pressure was brought home to them, a feeling of frustration was engendered amongst the terrorists and the number of surrenders increased. The extension of the 'Merdeka' offer to 30 April 1958, and subsequently to 31 July 1958, paid dividends and the surrender rate rose to the highest level since the Emergency began. Altogether 478 of the 650 terrorists who were eliminated during 1958 gave themselves up.[86] Satisfaction was tempered, however, by evidence that many of these had surrendered in order to further Communist aims through subversion, by obtaining voting rights in preparation for overt political action, and the Federal Police had to proscribe several societies that were clearly Communist front organizations. Nevertheless, the majority of those that surrendered had been genuinely persuaded that their cause was no longer worthwhile through intensive combined operations and associated propaganda offensives.

Priority for military operations during 1958 was given to Central Perak and Southern and Eastern Johore, while mopping up operations in Negri Sembilan, Southern Pahang, Selangor and Southern Perak were to be completed as a secondary task. In the Tapah area of Southern Perak Operation 'Chieftain', launched in 1957, ended in November 1958 with only 10 terrorists still at large there to be dealt with by the Police Field Force and the area was declared 'White' soon afterwards. In the central part of Perak all known terrorists, 61 in number, were eliminated during Operation 'Bintang', leaving those that had fled to the north east, between Ipoh and Grik, to be dealt with by Operation 'Ginger'. In Selangor, food denial operations, allied to systematic shelling and bombing by the Army and the RAF, encouraged the surrender of 27 terrorists in one month in the Sekinchang Swamp area and the remaining terrorists were flushed out of the Rasa area and either surrendered or fled northwards.[87] In Negri Sembilan the area of Operation 'Latimer South' was frozen for most of the year for Police Special Branch operations, which eliminated all but two of the terrorists in the state by the end of the year. The greatest success of 1958, however, was achieved in Johore where 130 terrorists were persuaded to surrender in the northern part of the state, largely through appeals by the former State Committee Member Hor Lung, and the area was declared 'White' in September.[88] All semblance of political or operational control of the terrorists in the southern half of the Federation ceased with the destruction of the South Malaya Bureau and, after the South Johore Regional Committee had disintegrated in the Operation 'Tiger' area of Southern Johore and the 9th Independent Platoon MRLA had been eliminated during Operation 'Badak' in the eastern part of the state, Johore was finally declared 'White' on New Year's Eve 1958.[89] These large scale defections in Johore also persuaded the Malacca/Johore Border Committee of the MCP to give up the struggle and Malacca was also declared 'White' before the end of 1958.

The charted strength of the CTO stood at 868 at the end of 1958, including 485 in Southern Thailand, 300 in Kedah and North Perak and a number of small but determined bands in Pahang.[90] It was clear that, despite the Chief Minister's aim to end the Emergency by the first anniversary of Independence, military operations to eliminate these remnants would have to continue into 1959. As the Emergency moved towards the end of its tenth year, therefore, intensive efforts were made to break the morale of the remaining terrorists through psychological warfare techniques in order to avoid the prospect of the stalemate which the dwindling rate of contacts and eliminations presaged. Whenever minimal intelligence material became available Security Force operations were mounted but few successes were forthcoming. In April 1959, however, the Operation 'Ginger' area of Central Perak was turned over to the Police Special Branch and in August 1959 priority was given to mopping up operations in the Operation 'Seladang' area of Central Pahang.[91] These were successfully completed and the final phase of the military campaign was directed against the remaining terrorists in Operations 'Brooklyn' and 'Bamboo' which were mounted near the borders of Kedah and Perak with Thailand.[92]

By the middle of 1960 it was clear that, in view of the equivocal attitude of the Thai Government, there was little that could be done about the 500 terrorists who had withdrawn to the relative sanctuary of the Betong salient, strategically situated just outside Malay territory between Kedah and Northern Perak. Here, under their leader Chin Peng, the remnants of the fighting arm of the MCP were to be kept in being as a continuing threat to the security of Malaya, awaiting the day when political and racial difficulties, fostered by subversion, would create conditions under which the armed conflict could be renewed. Federal troops and police would have to maintain patrols along the northern borders of Malaya for an indefinite period in order to prevent armed infiltration from Southern Thailand. This residual threat could not be overcome solely by military means, however, but only by a reformed public opinion and growing prosperity, reinforced by effective and enlightened administration, and this could best be assured by dispensing with the outstanding burden of Emergency regulations. On 31 July 1960, therefore, the Emergency in Malaya was finally declared over.

Results of the Emergency[93]

The Communist insurrection in Malaya was mounted by a relatively small number of armed terrorists which the combined forces of the military and civil administration took twelve years to finally defeat. The disproportionate effort required to combat guerilla forces in a jungle theatre is shown by the fact that the MRLA contained a military force (excluding the police and Home Guard on normal watch and ward duties) whose numerical strength varied between five and twelve times their own. Some impression of the achievement of the terrorists is given by the fact that the incident rate was not reduced below 100 a month for over five years and that, in the nine years that preceded Independence in Malaya, they killed 2,461 civilians and wounded 1,383 others—seven out of every ten thousand people in the country.[94] During this period the total cost of the Emergency exceeded £700 million, of which the United Kingdom provided £520 million, and much of the revenue of the Federation was diverted into providing the balance.[95] The vital rubber and tin industries of Malaya suffered both from physical damage to their plant and from the virtual cessation of new development and for the first three years of the Emergency the CTO was a very real threat to the security and economic recovery of the Federation from the depredations of the Second World War. If the Communists in China had not been pre-occupied with their own revolution and the conflict in Korea and Indo-China the prospects of the MCP would have been good, but the failure to elicit any external aid for their cause ensured that its tenuous position in the Federation became increasingly precarious and ultimately untenable.

The reduction in the terrorist threat to life and property in Malaya was the first measure of the success of the Security Forces during the Emergency. In 1951 nearly 100 military and civilian lives were lost every month, but this figure had been reduced to three by Independence Day on 31 August 1957, by which time the Security Forces had killed and captured 7,643 terrorists and persuaded a further 1,938 to surrender at a cost to themselves of 1,851 killed and 2,526 wounded.[96] These results were achieved in some of the most difficult terrain in the world in which to hunt down an enemy, whose primary aim after 1952 was to avoid contact with the Security Forces, and they were the reward of countless hours of jungle patrolling or lying in ambush. By 1955 it was estimated that any member of the Security Forces could expect to complete 1,000 hours of patrolling or 300 hours lying in ambush before he encountered one terrorist.[97]

The most significant achievement of the Security Forces, however, was not the actual number of terrorists whom they eliminated but the halt which they called to the advance of World Communism, which seemed to be rapidly engulfing South East Asia between 1948 and 1951. Amidst a population that was over half Chinese sufficient confidence was generated in the central government throughout these years to contain the terrorist threat and to enable it to be decisively defeated once the tide had begun to turn against Communism in Asia. Besides encouraging resistance to the Communists throughout South East Asia, the defeat of the terrorists in Malaya also prevented them from dominating a strategic area that lies across the main routes between Europe and Australasia and which contains the largest single source of rubber and tin in the world.

During the course of twelve years many lessons were learnt about the conduct of the campaign against the terrorists in Malaya, several of which, if applied earlier, would have had a decisive effect upon its course and duration and which are equally applicable to future insurrections of a similar nature. In retrospect it is clear that the seriousness of the terrorist threat to the internal security of Malaya was not appreciated early enough and that there was an unfortunate delay in implementing measures to counteract it. There was an obvious failure to create and maintain an adequate Police intelligence system before the outbreak of violence, which must have recognized the signs of incipient revolt and provided information on which to base counter-measures. Greater attention should have been applied to the Police Special Branch from the start of the Emergency as it was through this department that information which led to the great majority of contacts with the terrorists was ultimately derived.

Guerilla forces depend on the support of certain sections of the population and a major lesson of the Malayan Emergency was the necessity of grouping these elements so that they could be effectively controlled and protected and their co-operation won by effective government and intensive propaganda. Once the security and loyalty of the people on whom the terrorists depended had been guaranteed, Security Force operations could be directed towards eliminating the insurgents. The Malayan Campaign proved, however, that operations by large numbers of troops met with little success in jungle areas and that most successes were achieved by companies or platoons that were familiar with the terrain and were acting on specific information provided by the Police Special Branch. It is some indication of the importance of acclimatizing military forces to the exigencies of jungle warfare in this type of campaign that the most successful of all the units of the Commonwealth Forces that were employed during the Emergency were the Fijians and the East Africans (with an average of 1·13 kills per contact between 1953 and 1955), followed by the Gurkhas and then the British and Malays together (with averages of 1·00 and ·68 kills per contact during the same period).[98]

The interdependence of both the military and the civilian arms of the Security Forces during the Malayan Campaign underlined the fact that responsibility for counter-insurgence measures was indivisible. The Emergency was essentially the responsibility of the civil administration, who called upon the military to assist them in restoring law and order, but it is clear in retrospect that it was only directed with maximum efficiency between 1952 and 1954 when the posts of High Commissioner and Director of Operations were combined and there was no dichotomy of interest between civil and military measures and appointments which could have led to a reduction in the impetus behind the prosecution of the campaign.

CHAPTER 2

THE ORGANIZATION AND OPERATION OF THE
AIR FORCES IN MALAYA

Commitments of the Air Forces

Throughout the twelve years of the Malayan campaign the RAF and associated units of the Commonwealth air forces were entrusted with rendering such assistance as they could to the Security Forces in the fight against the Communist terrorists. This support proved invaluable and took many different forms. Offensive air support, although problematical in the prevailing conditions, was provided when required and was occasionally used with decisive effect and great economy of force. The most important contribution of the air forces to the successful prosecution of the campaign, however, was the provision of transport support, which incorporated trooplifting, supply dropping, casualty evacuation and liaison missions, and which considerably increased the mobility and flexibility of the ground forces and effected a great saving in infantry manpower. In addition, such unusual tasks as crop spraying, leaflet dropping and loud-hailing were carried out by the transport forces and contributed largely to the success of the food denial and psychological warfare campaigns. Finally, but by no means of least importance, the visual and photographic reconnaissance that was carried out by the air forces made an important contribution to the basic intelligence material upon which the elimination of the terrorists relied. As well as the air effort, the RAF also took an active part in the campaign on the ground and the efforts of the RAF Regiment (Malaya) were greatly appreciated by the ground forces with whom they served.

Throughout the Emergency the activities of the air forces were necessarily concentrated against the Communist terrorists but it should be remembered that this was not their only commitment. The primary function of the offensive support force remained the air defence of the Federation of Malaya, the Colony of Singapore, North Borneo and Sarawak and even its maritime role in co-operation with the Royal Navy took precedence over the campaign against the terrorists. Similarly, the transport squadrons in Malaya were primarily responsible for maintaining scheduled air services within the area of the Far East Command, which involved regular flights between Singapore, Hong Kong, Saigon, Negombo, Labuan and Iwakuni besides the provision of staging and maintenance facilities for the trunk routes flown by Transport Command, while photographic reconnaissance aircraft had a permanent commitment on behalf of the Survey Department of the Colonial Office. Group Headquarters was responsible for the direction of the air effort against the terrorists but also had its normal peace time tasks to fulfil, which included operational, general service and professional training, the preparation of a long-term defence schemes in accordance with Overseas Defence Committee instructions, the establishment of a raid reporting and control system and the administration of the Malayan Auxiliary Air Force (MAAF) and the Malayan Air Training Corps (MATC). These commitments occupied a considerable amount of time at AHQ Malaya and ensured that the aircraft under its command were withdrawn from

'Firedog' operations to carry out training in their primary role as often as was commensurate with providing the support required by the ground forces and that only a proportion of the total air forces in Malaya was engaged on anti-terrorist operations at any time.[1]

Strength of the Air Forces

Details of the air forces that were employed in the campaign against the terrorists in Malaya from 1948 to 1960 are given in Annex L,[2] while the size and deployment of individual units are discussed under the roles which they performed.

Throughout the campaign there were never more than 15 full squadrons in Malaya to carry out the peacetime roles of the command as well as the heavy commitment of Operation 'Firedog'. In general the campaign was fought on a shoestring from the air point of view, with an increase in strength during the early 1950's and a decrease after 1955, and at no time were the air forces in Malaya adequate to meet all the demands that were made on them satisfactorily.

In the offensive support role, the two fighter squadrons, one light bomber squadron and, if misemployed, one flying boat squadron that were available at the beginning of the Emergency were increased to a maximum force of two medium bomber, two light bomber, two fighter and two flying boat squadrons during 1950. By 1953 two medium bomber, three fighter and two flying boat squadrons were available; by 1956 there were one medium bomber, one light bomber and three fighter squadrons and during the last eighteen months of the campaign there were three light bomber squadrons and three fighter squadrons in Malaya, most of which, however, belonged to the Commonwealth Strategic Reserve and were not employed on Emergency operations.

The commitment for medium range transport aircraft during the campaign was borne almost entirely by four RAF squadrons, including the Far East Communication Squadron, which were reinforced by elements of a RAAF squadron and a RNZAF squadron between 1950 and 1952 and between 1955 and 1960. For most of the campaign only one of these squadrons at a time was employed in the important task of air supply while the remainder were engaged in maintaining scheduled communication flights and special flights which arose from the Emergency. Invaluable work in the air transport role was also provided by one short range transport squadron of the RAF from 1954 onwards while a squadron of Austers operated under RAF and Army auspices throughout the campaign. Helicopters proved to be the most important innovation that was made in the air transport role during the campaign but there were never enough to meet all the demands that were made on them. In 1950 there was only one flight of helicopters in Malaya and although reinforcements brought the strength up to two squadrons by 1953, one of which belonged to the Royal Navy, and to three squadrons by 1955, one of these was disestablished at the end of 1957 and another in 1959.

Finally, one squadron operated in the photographic reconnaissance role throughout the campaign, while the few remaining aircraft in the theatre, that were attached to station flights, the Armament Practice Camp and the MAAF, were occasionally used on Emergency operations although they generally were maintained solely for training purposes.

The main characteristic of the air forces in Malaya during the Emergency was the variety of its component parts. The air forces of the United Kingdom, Australia and New Zealand were represented by an average of over a dozen different types of aircraft at any one time, few of which were present throughout the Emergency as obsolete types were gradually replaced under re-equipment programmes. During the first two years of the campaign, Lincolns, Sunderlands, Beaufighters, Brigands, Spitfires, Tempests, Mosquitos, Yorks, Dakotas, Ansons, Devons, Austers, Harvards and Tiger Moths were flown in support of Operation 'Firedog' while the flypast at Kuala Lumpur on 1 August 1960 that marked its ending included Canberras, Sabres, Meteors, Seahawks, Valettas, Bristol Freighters, Beverleys, Pioneers, Austers and Sycamores.[3] To this list can be added Hornets, Venoms, Vampires, Shackletons, Hastings, Pembrokes, Chipmunks, Whirlwinds and Dragonflies which were also flown during the interim period on anti-terrorist operations.

Despite the number of aircraft types that were flown on Emergency operations the squadrons that operated them showed a notable continuity. The Far East Communication Squadron and two of the three other medium range transport squadrons served throughout the Emergency and the remaining one was only withdrawn at the end of 1957 after more than ten years of operations in Malaya. An Australian medium bomber squadron bore the brunt of offensive operations from 1950 to 1958, while two RAF fighter squadrons served in Malaya virtually throughout the campaign, as did the photographic reconnaissance squadron and the Auster squadron.

Aircraft Serviceability

The variety of aircraft types that were flown by these squadrons, many of which were obsolete, created servicing problems that were exacerbated by the extreme climate and primitive conditions under which most of them were forced to operate on the Malayan mainland, and also by the logistical difficulty of reinforcing, re-equipping and providing an adequate spares backing for a command 6,000 miles from its source of supply. In this last respect, medium bomber detachments from the United Kingdom had to return home for second line servicing after 150 hours flying time, over half of which was expended in transit, while convoy escorts and spares backing at staging posts *en route* had to be provided for fighter reinforcements.[4]

The operation of new types for the first time in the Far East was usually reflected in a decline in the serviceability rate—a trend that was especially noticeable after the introduction of jet aircraft in 1951. On the other hand the aircraft which they replaced were obsolete and could not have been maintained at an acceptable rate of serviceability for much longer. The average serviceability rate for Beaufighters and Spitfires had fallen to about 35 per cent and 50 per cent respectively in the year before their withdrawal. Their replacements, Brigands, Tempests, Hornets and Vampires, achieved an average serviceability rate of 50–60 per cent but this could not be maintained when they were replaced in turn by Venoms. Lincoln medium bombers were notably reliable, with a monthly serviceability rate nearly always in excess of 70 per cent—considerably higher than that of their Canberra replacements. Similarly, an average of over 75 per cent of the ageing Dakotas were serviceable at any time right up to their replacement in 1951 and 1952 by Valettas, which could not manage a serviceability rate of more than 55 per cent for some time afterwards. Austers and Sunderlands proved fairly reliable, with average serviceability rates of 60–65 per cent, while light helicopters picked up from about 50 per cent for Dragonflies during their experimental stage from 1950 to 1952 to 60–65 per cent for Sycamores during the peak of their operations from 1955 to 1957. Naval S 55 medium helicopters were also fairly reliable, until four years of continuous operation in Malayan conditions took their toll, but reasonable maintenance of their RAF counterpart, the Whirlwind, was only achieved by a quite disproportionate effort and, even so, averaged only 41 per cent in 1956.[5]

Flying Conditions and Aircraft Accidents

Average serviceability rates of about 50 per cent may not appear remarkable but they were comparatively high for aircraft that were operated for much of the time at their maximum capabilities under extreme climatic conditions. Uncertain weather, especially the rapid build up of cumulus cloud and sudden, violent tropical storms, was a constant hazard to flying in Malaya, while the broken terrain and paucity of navigational aids and alternative landing fields considerably increased the dangers that faced aircrews in this theatre. Several fatalities were caused by collision with the ground on low-flying airstrike or supply dropping missions as it was difficult to judge the deceptively steep rise and fall of the broken terrain once the horizon had been lost by descending below the level of the surrounding hills. This danger was accentuated by the need to concentrate on the search for target areas in the monotonous jungle cover, when only fleeting attention could be given to the attitude of the aircraft. To combat this danger instructions were given to aircrews to refer to their instruments and re-orientate themselves from a datum such as the horizon whenever possible.[6]

Accidents that were caused by pilot error became fewer as the campaign progressed and aircrews became more experienced but even in 1956 four fatal accidents on supply dropping missions could still be attributed in some measure to this cause. The accident rate attributable to structural failures in aircraft was also reduced as time went by and obsolete types were replaced. In the first nine months of 1951 ten of the twelve fatalities amongst RAF aircrews in Malaya were caused by defects in Brigands or their armament, but during the next 18 months only four fatal accidents could be attributed to similar causes and during 1957 only one accident was caused by a technical failure.[7] Between 1955 and 1958 there were just over 30 major accidents each year in Malaya, of which an average of three each year proved fatal. Aircraft in the Malayan command, however, flew 60,000 or more hours in every year during this period and the accident rate fell from 6·4 per 10,000 flying hours in 1955 to 4·7 in 1958—a rate which compared favourably with other commands and was reasonably good for a group that was operating a wide variety of aircraft under far from ideal conditions.[8]

Deployment of the Air Forces

At the outbreak of the Emergency the RAF was unprepared for any commitment on the mainland of Malaya. During the period of retrenchment after the Second World War experiments had proved that Malaya could be reinforced by detachments from units in the United Kingdom* and, as economy measures, the garrison force had been reduced and the last wartime RAF station on the mainland, at Kuala Lumpur, had been closed down at the beginning of May 1949,[9] leaving the airfield at Butterworth near Penang as the last RAF foothold in the Federation. When the Emergency was declared in June 1948 all the RAF squadrons that were available for assisting the Army and Police in restoring law and order were deployed

---

* Six Lincolns of No 97 (Straits Settlements) Squadron had flown to RAF Tengah in April 1948 (Operation 'Red Lion II') to gain experience in dealing with the problems of reinforcing the ACFE from the United Kingdom in times of emergency.

entirely on Singapore Island at the three RAF stations of Changi, Tengah and Sembawang and the Maintenance Base at Seletar.

From 12 April to 9 May 1948 a small RAF task force operated from the airstrip at Taiping in support of Operation 'Haystack' in Northern Perak.[10] It soon became apparent, however, that in order to implement the full plan for restoring law and order the RAF would be required to play a significant role in the campaign and, if this was to be effective, a forward base would have to be formed in the Federation of Malaya. Following a meeting between the AOC Malaya and the Officer Administering the Government an RAF task force was established at the civil airport at Kuala Lumpur by the end of the first week in July 1948 and was renamed RAF Kuala Lumpur on 20 September 1948.[11] The choice of Kuala Lumpur was inspired by the tactical advantage of operating from a base centrally situated in Malaya and by the proximity of the seat of Government of the Federation and of the Army and Police headquarters, with which close co-operation was expected.

Kuala Lumpur was the main centre of flying operations against the terrorists throughout the Emergency but, as ground force operations moved further north, it became necessary to transfer part of the offensive support force to Butterworth in 1950 and RAF and RAAF aircraft flew from this base in support of the Army and Police in Northern Malaya for the remainder of the campaign.

Meanwhile, on 16 January 1950, Sembawang had been handed back to the Royal Navy on the expiration of its two year lease[12] and in the same year the decision was taken to concentrate all offensive support aircraft at Tengah and all the transport forces at Changi.[13] Tengah, with a runway length of 6,000 feet and capable of taking aircraft with an all up weight of 105,000 lb,[14] was the only station able to accommodate the medium bomber forces that arrived in the theatre in 1950 and armament dumps were accordingly developed there while stores and servicing facilities for the transport support force were developed at Changi. It was from these two main RAF stations on Singapore Island that temporary or permanent detachments of both offensive and transport support aircraft were maintained at Kuala Lumpur or Butterworth on the mainland throughout the Emergency. The Maintenance Base at Seletar was the base of the Far East flying boat force throughout this period.

Besides Kuala Lumpar and Butterworth there were a number of less important airfields in the Federation of Malaya, such as Taiping and Ipoh, and it is conceivable that in the type of campaign that prevailed, with a number of local actions being mounted simultaneously, there could have been some tactical advantage in deploying small detachments of aircraft to operate from these at Brigade level. In fact, Taiping was used by a small task force for one month prior to the outbreak of the Emergency in 1948 but the airfield was waterlogged for two hours every day and was quite unsuitable for offensive aircraft.[15] Towards the end of the campaign steps were taken to improve the airfields at Alor Star, Gong Kedah, Payar Lebar and Kuantan to meet future strategic requirements,[16] but the expense of improving airfields such as these and the difficulties that would have arisen from decentralizing administrative and servicing facilities ensured that the air forces involved in the Malayan campaign were concentrated as much as possible on the two RAF stations in the Federation and the three on Singapore Island. By 1955, however, there were 11 airfields located throughout the Federation on which medium range transport aircraft could land if the occasion demanded[17] and these played a vital role in the air transportation of troops and stores that was necessary in a country where surface communications, especially from East to West and down the eastern coast, were quite inadequate.

Even more important in establishing communication links with operational areas was the network of grass airstrips, suitable for light aircraft only, that covered the whole of the Federation. By 1955 there were 72 of these strips,[18] most of which were located west of the central spinal ridge of Malaya in the states of Perak, Selangor, Pahang, Negri Sembilan and Johore where the main operational areas lay. Six of these were rough strips adjacent to the police forts that had been established in deep jungle areas to protect the aboriginal populations from exploitation by the terrorists, and could be used by Pioneer aircraft only. A further 28 could take Austers in addition to Pioneers and the remainder could also be used by Beavers.

In addition to these light aircraft strips numerous temporary helicopter 'pads' were cleared in the jungle by the ground forces, especially after 1952 when troop-lifting into jungle areas became one of the major commitments of the air transport force. By the end of the Emergency hundreds of natural or artificial helicopter landing zones throughout the Federation were recorded at the AHQ in Kuala Lumpur.

Command and Control of the Air Forces

Overall control of RAF units in the Far East during the campaign was exercised by the CinC, Air Command Far East (ACFE) (redesignated Far East Air Force on 1 June 1949),[19] while operational and administrative control was carried out by the AOsC of the three territorial regions of Malaya, Hong Kong and Ceylon. The Cs inC of the three services in the Far East were collectively responsible to the Chiefs of Staff and their committee was responsible for all matters affecting the employment of British armed forces in the region. Together with the Governor General of the Malayan Union they formed the British Defence Co-ordination Committee (Far East) which was concerned with strategic issues and the co-ordination of all civil and military matters that had any bearing on the defence of South-East Asia.[20]

Below the Cs inC, the AOC Malaya, the Rear-Admiral Malaya and the GOsC of Malaya and of Singapore sat with the High Commissioner of the Federation of Malaya and the Governor of Singapore on a local defence committee and, without them, on a local inter-service committee that was concerned with military matters relating to the defence of Malaya and Singapore. In addition to these duties the AOC Malaya also acted as adviser on air matters to the Governors of Borneo and Sarawak.[21]

At the start of the campaign against the terrorists the command organization of the RAF in Malaya was not properly organized to meet the demands that were immediately made on it. The suggestion put forward in 1948 that AHQ Malaya should be disbanded and its duties taken over by HQ, ACFE had been forestalled as it was felt that Britain should show some proof of its intention to defend Malaya, especially as the RAF was now regarded as the first line of defence in the area.[22] RAF Kuala Lumpur had been closed down, however, and the limited forces that were available were concentrated entirely on Singapore Island. Such detachments as had been undertaken since the end of the war to such places as Car Nicobar and Kuching had been limited in size and mounted with plenty of warning. The problem of setting up a task force on the Malayan mainland at short notice, therefore, revealed serious deficiencies in the preparations made by AHQ Malaya for a mobile campaign and strained its resources to the utmost.[23]

With the establishment of a task force at Kuala Lumpur it was appreciated that control of the rear and forward elements of the RAF in Malaya and Singapore could not be effectively exercised by the Main AHQ at Changi. Consequently, an Advanced AHQ was established at Kuala Lumpur on 6 July 1948, not as part of the task force on the airfield but alongside the Army HQ, Malaya District, in the town itself.[24] A joint operations and intelligence centre was also set up at Army HQ, which included staff from all three services, the police and some civilian liaison officers.

In view of the importance of close and continuous contact with Government officials and service commanders at this early stage of the campaign, the AOC Malaya, Air Vice-Marshal A. C. Sanderson, made the Advanced AHQ at Kuala Lumpur his base for the remainder of his tour, visiting the Rear AHQ at Changi when occasion demanded.[25] His successor, Air Vice-Marshal F. J. Mellersh, continued this arrangement for some time but returned to Changi in the middle of 1949 as the situation in the Federation had become more stabilized by then and a great deal of work was accumulating at the Rear AHQ in connection with the basic administration of the RAF in the area and its organization for its primary role of air defence. In response to his request a group captain was established as his representative at the Advanced AHQ Kuala Lumpur and took over control of the aircraft based there in October 1949.[26]

Until November 1949 the air forces operating in support of Operation 'Firedog' were under the direction of two AHQs. Squadrons based on Singapore Island were controlled by the Rear AHQ in support of the Army in Johore Sub-District but, since only two of the offensive support squadrons located there (Nos 28 and 60 (Spitfire) Squadrons) played any part in anti-terrorist operations at that stage in the campaign, their control was delegated to the officer commanding their base at Sembawang. In the Federation aircraft based at Kuala Lumpur operated under the control of the Advanced AHQ on behalf of the Army in Northern and Central Malaya. Since the commitments of the RAF extended beyond Emergency operations Rear AHQ were notified of all operational orders that were issued by Advanced AHQ so that they could allocate their resources accordingly. All air support at this time was provided by personal arrangement between the GOC of the Malaya and Singapore Districts and the AOC Malaya or his representative at Kuala Lumpur and the officer commanding RAF Sembawang. There was little co-ordination between the two areas of operation except on the few occasions when a greater air effort was required for operations in Southern Johore than could be provided by Sembawang, when requests for reinforcements were relayed to Kuala Lumpur by the Operations Control Room at Rear AHQ, Changi—an arrangement that on occasions worked in the opposite direction.

On 1 May 1949 the division which had hitherto existed in the system of Army command in Malaya was rectified when Johore Sub-District passed from the control of the GOC Singapore District to that of the GOC Malaya District.[27] All military operations in connection with the Emergency were now directed from Kuala Lumpur and the logical parallel on the air side was for the Advanced AHQ to be given operational control of all aircraft operating against the terrorists under the general direction of Rear AHQ. This step was duly taken on 1 November 1949.[28]

On 1 April 1952 No 230 Group (redesignated AHQ Singapore on 16 February 1953) was formed to take over the administration of all RAF units in Singapore Island except Tengah, including Changi, and its satellites at Car Nicobar and Labuan, and Seletar.[29] AHQ Malaya retained full operational and administrative control of Tengah on Singapore Island and Kuala Lumpur and Butterworth on the mainland as well as operational control of those parts of the Far East Flying Boat

Wing at Seletar and the Far East Transport Wing at Changi that were allocated to Operation 'Firedog' tasks. The main purpose of this division of responsibilities was to relieve the AOC Malaya of all extraneous duties so that he could transfer his head-quarters to Kuala Lumpur and concentrate solely on Emergency matters. The proliferation of the links in the chain of command back to HQ, FEAF, however, only exacerbated existing difficulties and meant that, in effect, the Director of Opera-tions responsible for all Emergency matters had now to deal with two AOsC. The AOC Malaya was directly concerned with the operational efficiency of the Far East Flying Boat and Transport Wings yet their station requirements were now the responsibility of No 230 Group, their unit establishment and the allocation of their tasks was decided by HQ, FEAF and Transport Command retained some control over their training programme through their Examining Teams. Similarly, the AOC Malaya was responsible for air supply operations in support of the ground forces in Malaya and also for the air defence of Borneo yet in the one case the packing of parachutes at Changi and in the other the RAF station at Labuan were both under the control of No 230 Group.[30]

At least one of these difficulties was sorted out when the Far East Flying Boat Wing was placed under the administrative control of the AOC Malaya on 27 April 1953[31] but the fact remained that the transference of long-term planning duties to HQ, FEAF and of much of the administrative work on Singapore Island to HQ No 230 Group did not leave enough work to justify the maintenance of the Rear AHQ Malaya. Its amalgamation with HQ, FEAF was considered too unwieldy and impolitic but, on the other hand, the relatively minor role of the RAF in the cam-paign against the terrorists hardly justified the establishment of a complete AHQ alongside the Army HQ at Kuala Lumpur, especially as the latter only issued general directives whose application was worked out by co-operation between the Army and the Police at State level. Such planning as was necessary between the Army and the RAF for Emergency operations was carried out quite adequately by the Land/Air Operations Room at the Advanced AHQ in Kuala Lumpur.

Nevertheless, following the decision to concentrate operations against the terror-ists at their weakest point in Central Malaya, the proposal to move the Rear AHQ from Changi to Kuala Lumpur was revived and, after some delay owing to accommodation difficulties, this move was carried out on 15 February 1954,[32] thus completing a cycle as AHQ Malaya had left Kuala Lumpur for Changi in 1946. However, whilst the Air Control Centre, which controlled all aircraft while they were airborne over the Federation of Malaya, and the Administrative, Technical and Signals Staffs were located at the Rear AHQ on the airfield at Kuala Lumpur, the Air Staff was located at the Advanced AHQ, which now became the Main AHQ Malaya and continued to operate from the Army HQ in the town itself. Here a Joint Operations Centre was set up which represented the final evolution in the joint system of command and control exercised by the ground and air forces during the Emergency and which was the keystone of the inter-service co-operation on which the campaign was fought and won. For the first time in the Emergency centralized control and joint planning of all operations was exercised by a small, efficient unit that co-ordinated all bids for air support from police, army or civilian authorities. Since the AOC Malaya was a member of the Director of Operations Committee as well as in control of the Joint Operations Centre, he could make a close appraisal of the tactical requirements for the daily conduct of air operations against the terrorists and could allocate his small forces most effectively between them and the other commitments of the RAF in the theatre. Simple operational orders were issued by the Joint Operations Centre to the officers commanding the stations concerned, whether on Singapore Island or in the Federation, who then allocated specific aircraft and briefed aircrews for each operation. The final execution of these orders in this type of campaign, however, placed a high degree of responsibility on the initiative of individual aircraft captains, which was unusual in a period of inflationary command systems.

As long as planning for joint operations required some form of Joint Operations Centre at HQ Malaya Command, it was not possible to achieve complete unification of the two AHQs at Kuala Lumpur but this dichotomy became more apparent as the offensive support role of the RAF in the campaign decreased and increasing emphasis was placed on the development of an efficient air defence organization and the completion of planning for wartime operations. All branches except the Operations and Intelligence Staff were moved from HQ Malaya Command to the AHQ at RAF Kuala Lumpur on 5 April 1957 and the Joint Operations Centre followed when the Army HQ moved to Seremban on 1 July 1957.[33] By now the RAF contribution to Operation 'Firedog' was increasingly dominated by air supply operations and, in January 1957, the post of Officer Commanding the Air Supply Force had been established at Kuala Lumpur to ensure the supervision of operational procedures and training in this role.[34]

When Malaya became independent on 31 August 1957 the conduct of Emergency operations and the maintenance of law and order became the exclusive responsibility of the Governments of Malaya and Singapore but, at their request, the Governments of the United Kingdom, Australia and New Zealand agreed to give such assistance as was practicable in the light of their total commitments.[35] The AOC Malaya, as commander of the Commonwealth air forces, was responsible to their governments through the CinC, FEAF but he now took his operational directions relating to the Emergency from the Federation's own Director of Emergency Operations. The campaign was controlled by the Emergency Operations Council through the Operations Sub-Committee and the AOC Malaya was a member of both, although he usually delegated his membership of the latter to the officer commanding RAF Kuala Lumpur. In principle the Overseas Commonwealth Forces in Malaya were employed after Independence only when suitable Federation forces were not available. In effect, this meant that the Commonwealth air forces continued to provide all the air support that was needed.[36]

With the achievement of Independence by the Federation of Malaya, however, it became politically embarrassing for the AOC Malaya to retain his title—a title that became even more inappropriate when it was finally decided to rectify the unequal division of responsibility in the area by disbanding AHQ Singapore and transferring all its flying units to the command of AHQ Malaya.[37] On Independence Day, 31 August 1957, therefore, AHQ Malaya became HQ No 224 Group,[38] an appropriate title since No 224 Group had been formed originally at Singapore in 1941 and, after the Burma campaign, had taken part in the liberation of Malaya and Singapore and had received the surrender of the Japanese at Kuala Lumpur (under its commanding officer the Earl of Bandon who was the current CinC, FEAF in 1957) before becoming AHQ Malaya in October 1945.

No 224 Group continued to control the RAF Stations at Tengah, Kuala Lumpur and Butterworth and took over control of Changi from AHQ Singapore on 11 November 1957.[39] On 1 January 1958 AHQ Singapore was dissolved and its last remaining responsibility, the RAF Maintenance Base at Seletar, was transferred to the control of HQ, FEAF[40] No 224 Group continued to control RAF Butterworth but, on 1 July 1958, it was transferred to the RAAF[41] and became the headquarters of the RAAF command that had been established at Changi a month earlier to administer a fighter and a bomber wing as part of the Commonwealth Strategic Reserve.[42] This command replaced No 90 (Composite) Wing RAAF that had administered Australian air forces in Malaya since June 1950.

RAF Kuala Lumpur continued as the last RAF station in Malaya but its transfer to the embryonic Royal Malayan Air Force (RMAF) was heralded on 1 April 1959 when HQ No 224 Group moved back to Singapore Island after five years in the Federation to concentrate on the primary task of training the Strategic Reserve.[43] The RAF Maintenance Base at Seletar became the new group headquarters on 3 April 1959 and was renamed RAF Station Seletar on 1 August 1959 since units were now deployed there that were not associated with maintenance duties.[44] It was not until 1 November 1960, however, that the administrative control of this base was transferred from HQ, FEAF to HQ No 224 Group in exchange for that of Changi.[45]

Coincident with the move of HQ No 224 Group from Kuala Lumpur, No 224 Group 'Firedog' Transport Support Force had been formed there on 1 April 1959 to carry out the remaining transport duties in the campaign under the direction of the commanding officer of the station until the RMAF was able to take over this commitment.[46] The Joint Operations Centre continued to operate at Kuala Lumpur but, on 30 June 1960, it was handed over to the RMAF who assumed operational control of all Commonwealth transport aircraft flying in support of Operation 'Firedog' on 1 July 1960.[47] At the same time the Air Control Centre at Kuala Lumpur closed down and some of its signals facilities were transferred to RAAF Butterworth as the 'Firedog' Air Reporting Section to carry out surveillance of all Commonwealth aircraft still participating in the campaign on behalf of HQ, FEAF. Finally, on 1 October 1960, two months after the Emergency had been declared over, RAF Kuala Lumpur, the nexus of air operations against the terrorists throughout the twelve years of the campaign, was handed over to the RMAF.[48]

CHAPTER 3

OFFENSIVE AIR SUPPORT IN THE MALAYAN CAMPAIGN

Limitations of Offensive Air Support

The mounting of air strikes against the enemy and his supply routes is one of the major roles of air forces in support of ground forces in a conventional war. The Malayan campaign, however, was not a conventional war and local conditions prevented the air forces from adopting their traditional role in policing a semi-civilized country, those of regional interdiction and the inverted blockade.[1] Instead they were called upon to fight a campaign in a theatre in which they had little experience of offensive air support and in which all the advantages appeared to lie with the enemy—all that is except the absence of ground or air opposition which prevailed throughout the campaign.

Successful air strikes normally depend on a number of factors, including high grade intelligence information giving the exact location of an identifiable target, an accurate method of pinpointing this target and an attacking force capable of accurate navigation to the target and carrying a weapon suitable for its destruction. In Malaya all these conditions were problematical. In the dense jungle that covers 80 per cent of a country the size of England and Wales less than 10,000 terrorists operated in gangs normally less than 100 strong and afforded, at least in the later stages of the campaign, a highly mobile fleeting target that was effectively screened from the air.[2] These terrorists were the only legitimate target, but they were difficult to discriminate from innocent inhabitants of jungle areas, they retained the initiative in the timing and location of their attacks and were not necessarily dependent on permanent and vulnerable bases, while their intelligence and warning systems often appeared more effective than those of the ground forces that opposed them. By 1951 they had become increasingly sensitive to all forms of air attack and were taking the necessary precautions to protect themselves, including the screening of temporary camps from the air, the posting of air-raid sentries and, less commonly, the digging of deep shelters and slit trenches in areas where they hoped to remain undisturbed for long periods. In any case, the cover of the jungle trees and undergrowth, especially in secondary jungle, provided a natural air-raid protection. Direct casualties from aerial bombardment were, therefore, at the best fortuitous and the destruction of their temporary 'bashas' was hardly more than an inconvenience to the terrorists.

Besides the absence of clearly defined targets the inevitable delays that occurred, while the necessary preliminaries to all air-strike action in the campaign were carried out, prejudiced the element of surprise on which most successful attacks depend and also prevented an attack from being made at the optimum psychological moment. Over all lay the hazard of local weather conditions that could, and did, frustrate many air-strike missions and which ensured that, before the advent of radar target marking techniques in 1955, offensive air support could only be guaranteed in the mid-morning period after the dispersal of the early morning ground fog or thin stratus and before the rapid build up of cumulus around mid-day which generally developed into storms that frequently lasted well into the night. This limitation in the time factor severely restricted the scope of associated ground operations on which the offensive air support force was normally entirely dependent for employment.[3]

Under these conditions the characteristics of most air-strike aircraft, speed of action, surprise, accurate hitting power and mobility could not be exploited to the full and, since there was a general lack of information about the results of their action, their obvious limitations in this type of campaign ensured that offensive air support was only provided amidst conflicting views of its purpose and value and that constant thought was given to the evolution of tactics designed to improve the effectiveness of the air weapon.

Aims of Offensive Air Support: 'Pinpoint' and Harassing Attacks

The basic intention of all air strikes in the Malayan campaign was to kill as many terrorists as possible and to this end two main types of offensive air action were employed; those that were mounted against pinpoint targets, such as a terrorist camp, and those against an area of jungle that was reliably reported to contain a number of terrorists. The emphasis on these two main types of attack changed as the campaign progressed. In 1948, before the terrorists fully appreciated their danger from air attack, camps for 200–300 were commonly to be found in clearings in the jungle and provided excellent pinpoint targets.[4] It was unfortunate that at this time the potential of the offensive air support force was not fully appreciated by military commanders. By early 1949 the terrorists had become sensitive to the dangers of air attack and adopted elaborate camouflage techniques which rendered the detection of their camps from the air extremely difficult. Attacks were therefore carried out on the basis of area targets that averaged 1,000 yards square, or line targets up to 6,000 yards in length, with the intention of achieving the indirect elimination of the terrorists by 'flushing' them out of the target area into prepared ground ambushes, by 'softening up' an area before the ground forces entered it, by upsetting the sentry organization of the terrorists and splitting them into smaller, more vulnerable groups and by creating 'stop-lines' or offensively patrolled corridors 100 yards wide that were strategically deployed to direct the terrorists' line of retreat.[5] Because progress through the jungle was slow it was possible to contain the terrorists within a limited area by sustained harassing operations from the air until the ground forces arrived. In this type of attack direct kills by air-strike action were considered in the nature of a bonus. The main drawback to 'flushing' attacks, however, was that they demanded close co-operation with the ground forces and the placing of ambushes even as far away as six miles from a terrorist camp invariably excited their suspicion and was enough to make them disperse from the target area. The RAF did not always appreciate the need for these ground 'stops' and considered that unsupported air strikes would be more effective provided they were given a clearly defined area of jungle as a target.[6]

During the latter part of 1952 and early 1953 the bombing of large areas of jungle with small numbers of aircraft was considered wasteful and uneconomic and a change in policy occurred. An improvement in intelligence reports, derived from information given by surrendered terrorists, as the initiative in the campaign swung towards the security forces, offered an increasing number of pinpoint targets and the main offensive effort by all available aircraft was directed against these.[7] The implementation of this policy, however, coincided with, and therefore clearly influenced, a marked decline in the number of terrorist surrenders and the general policy governing offensive air support was changed yet again. While still not accepting the validity of indiscriminate area bombardment, air strikes were no longer directed solely against pinpoint targets and large-scale harassing operations were again undertaken in conjunction with food denial operations in jungle areas that were known to contain terrorists.[8]

By 1954 the impending introduction of new aircraft into the theatre and the necessity of concentrating on their primary task of training for air defence, coupled with the lack of evidence about the effectiveness of air-strike action, ensured that air strikes were limited solely to a harassing role except when first rate target intelligence relating to pinpoint or small area targets was available.[9] The depletion of war-time bomb stocks and the resultant economies in weapon expenditure, however, made it necessary to abandon large scale harassing operations in favour of concentrated attacks that were mounted only on reliable information.[10] The greater accuracy of bombing which this policy required was achieved by improved target location and marking techniques and it was possible to revive, during 1955 and 1956, the principle that air strikes were designed primarily to kill rather than to harass the enemy. However, the paucity of target intelligence at this stage in the campaign, as the size of the terrorist forces was gradually whittled down, made the acquisition of an accurate aiming point increasingly rare and from 1956 to the end of the Emergency the air forces had to resign themselves once more to a harassing role. This decision was unwelcome in some quarters since this type of attack was considered of doubtful value and a misuse of offensive air power[11] and, during 1958, a further decline in target information and the replacement of the last piston-engined aircraft in the air-strike force by jets made it necessary to economize still further in expensive harassing operations and offensive air support to the ground forces ceased altogether in August 1959.

Immediate Air Support

While the merits of pinpoint or harassing air strikes provided scope for debate throughout the campaign, the air forces were reluctantly forced to accept, although not until 1952, that one of their major roles in conventional warfare, that of immediate close support action, was impracticable in the conditions that prevailed in the Malayan campaign.[12] This form of air support is only of value against an enemy whose position is accurately known and who is anxious to retain the ground he occupies and neither of these conditions applied to the terrorists in Malaya. Their strength lay in concealment and mobility and every one of their operations was planned with the intention of avoiding contact with the security forces. When contacts did occur the ensuing engagement was a brief, fleeting affair and the time factor seldom, if ever, permitted strike aircraft to be brought over the target before it ceased to exist. Information that was received about possible terrorist locations was usually inaccurate and had to be checked on the ground, which resulted either in an immediate engagement or the dispersal of the enemy. If contact was not made with the terrorists the information remained too inaccurate to be justifiably offered as a basis for air-strike action. Even if aircraft had been in the air on immediate call, after the 'cab-rank' principle developed in the Second World War, the necessary task of ascertaining the position of any security forces or civilians in the area extended the reaction time to a request for air support until it was ineffective.[13] Besides, ground to air communications were reduced to 25 per cent of their normal efficiency in jungle conditions and the current Army 62 wireless set weighed 150 lb (a ten man load for jungle patrols) and needed a tree aerial which took time to erect.[14] The alternative use of a control car to call up air support was generally impracticable as it could not get right into the contact area. Moreover, as several ground operations were undertaken simultaneously throughout the Federation, the number of patrols that might contact a terrorist gang at any one time ran into hundreds and it was as impracticable for the air forces to provide continuous standby patrols for all of them as it was for them to delay an engagement. The number of potential contacts in the period 1 to 20 May 1952, for example, came to over 2,000 and in the 145 actual contacts that were made direct air assistance was of possible value on only one occasion.[15] In any case, the dangers of disseminating the responsibility for calling up offensive air support to the company or platoon level on which the ground campaign was fought hardly need stressing in view of their fluid tactical deployment.

Thus, although ground-attack aircraft were maintained in a good state of readiness* and could be airborne within 30 minutes of the receipt of a call for air-strike action,[16] the normal chain of communication from platoon or company through battalion and brigade to the Joint Operations Centre at Kuala Lumpur ensured that the quickest response to a bid for an air strike was about $3\frac{1}{2}$ to 4 hours and that most offensive air support was provided as part of pre-planned operations. One form of immediate air support action that was practised effectively, however, was in the defensive role of providing air cover for road convoys, which was a regular commitment and undoubtedly forestalled many attempted ambushes.

Offensive Air Support Aircraft

The number, strength and deployment of the squadrons that were available for offensive support operations against the terrorists in Malaya are summarized in Annex M. In general these forces proved adequate to meet the demands that were made on them but they were only made available amidst considerable controversy about the efficacy and the necessary scale of offensive air support in this type of campaign.

At the start of the Emergency only the equivalent of three and a half squadrons, with 29 aircraft, were available for offensive operations in the Malayan theatre but reinforcements brought this number up to a maximum of seven squadrons by mid-1950 and six or seven squadrons, with an average total strength of just under 70 aircraft, continued to carry out the air-strike commitment for most of the remainder of the Emergency. This force consisted of fighters, light bombers and flying boats for the first two years of the campaign, with the addition of medium bombers between 1950 and 1958. Fighters comprised just under two-thirds of this force with the remainder divided almost equally between light bombers, medium bombers and flying boats.[17]

When the Emergency was declared in June 1948 the only available offensive aircraft in the area were the sixteen Spitfires of Nos 28 and 60 Squadrons at Sembawang, the eight Beaufighters of No 84 Squadron at Tengah and four Sunderlands of No 209 Squadron at Seletar. Three Spitfires of No 60 Squadron helped to form the task force at Kuala Lumpur on 3 July 1948 and they were soon joined by the rest of the squadron and one Spitfire of No 28 Squadron.[18] It soon

---

* At the start of the campaign air-strike aircraft were kept at a readiness state of four hours, which had been reduced to one hour by 1950 (largely owing to the introduction of standing orders for the relief of Police posts under attack). At the height of the campaign in 1951 and 1952 four fighters and two light bombers were on immediate call, as was one medium bomber in 1954 and 1955—after which readiness states were generally relaxed to four hours or more.

became apparent, however, that a more powerful striking force would be required and three Beaufighters of No 45 Squadron were detached from Negombo in Ceylon to Kuala Lumpur in August 1948.[19] So useful did they prove, each Beaufighter having the equivalent hitting power of two Spitfires, that part of No 84 Squadron was sent to Kuala Lumpur from Tengah in September for a few days prior to the transfer of the whole squadron to the Middle East Air Force.[20] The strength of the air-striking force in Malaya was maintained, however, by the arrival of the remainder of No 45 (Beaufighter) Squadron at Kuala Lumpur on 16 May 1949, while the loss of No 28 (Spitfire) Squadron, which had been transferred to Hong Kong five days earlier, was offset by the arrival of No 33 (Tempest) Squadron on board HMS *Ocean* at Seletar on 8 August 1949 and the increase of the Spitfire strength of No 60 Squadron from eight to seventeen aircraft on 15 August.[21] No 205 (Sunderland) Squadron was transferred from Ceylon to Seletar on 3 September 1949,[22] bringing the total air-strike force that was available after 15 months of the Emergency to ten Sunderlands, seventeen Spitfires, sixteen Tempests and eight Beaufighters. The Beaufighters were withdrawn from service at the end of 1949, No 45 Squadron being re-equipped with eight Brigands on 6 December,[23] while a further eight Brigands of No 84 Squadron arrived at Tengah on indefinite detachment from MEAF on 9 April 1950 (Operation 'Tireless').[24]

On 20 March 1950 a new phase in offensive air operations against the terrorists in Malaya opened with the arrival of eight Lincolns of No 57 Squadron at Tengah (Operation 'Musgrave').[25] By this time a virtual stalemate had been reached in combined operations against the terrorists and the qualified optimism, based on the mistaken belief that the type of air attack being provided was sufficient to achieve its aim, had evaporated. It was clear to the AOC Malaya that the current air effort was not enough to achieve positive results and that there was a clear necessity for a greater striking force in order to attain the necessary density of bomb pattern over the increased target areas that were resulting from less accurate target information. Since the terrorists rapidly dispersed under air attack a heavy initial blow was essential and this could best be achieved by a formation of medium bombers. It was stressed that many of the sceptical opinions that had been propounded on the value of air-strike action were based on the light attacks so far carried out by small numbers of fighters and light bombers. By 1950 there was some evidence that the physical results of air strikes were better than could be assessed and that they were having a considerable effect in harassing the enemy and increasing the chances of driving them into contact with the security forces. The advent of improved navigational aids and target marking techniques opened the possibility of mounting sustained attacks round the clock and, as it was considered vital not only to maintain the existing pressure on the terrorists but to take exceptional measures to prevent the situation from worsening, a request was made for at least twelve or sixteen medium bombers.[26]

In Whitehall this request was met by opposing counsels. The former CinC, FEAF, Air Marshal H. P. Lloyd, considered that heavy saturation bombing was not the answer to the problem of attacking the terrorists in the jungle owing to the lack of positive aiming points and the absence of any sort of bomb-line for the protection of the security forces in the vicinity of an air strike. He considered that the existing resources of strike aircraft and weapons in the theatre were adequate to deal with the available fleeting targets that were far more vulnerable to quick precision attacks than to heavy blast bombing.[27] Bomber Command stressed the prejudicial effects on their training programme that any reinforcement of the air forces in Malaya with medium bombers would have, quite apart from the considerable logistical problems that would have to be faced in the supply and maintenance of such a force in a theatre where there were no spare parts and servicing facilities were quite inadequate.[28] Faced with these opposing viewpoints the Air Ministry agreed that eight Lincolns should be detached to Malaya from Bomber Command for a period of two months, which was later extended to four and then to six months (Operation 'Musgrave').[29] At the request of both the Colonial and the Foreign Offices an attempt was made to play down their arrival for fear of the adverse propaganda their use would provoke, especially if they should prove ineffective.[30]

No 57 Squadron arrived at Tengah on 20 March 1950 and was succeeded by detachments of eight Lincolns from No 100 Squadron on 10 July and from No 61 Squadron on 1 December.[31] Meanwhile, representations had been made to the Australian government that the campaign in Malaya was not merely a matter of the internal security of a British colony but an active front in the cold war against Communism.[32] This appeal elicited a welcome response in the form of a further six Lincolns of No 1 (RAAF) Squadron which arrived at Tengah in June 1950 and were to be the mainstay of the offensive air support operations for the next eight years. All the medium bombers that arrived in 1950 were operated from Tengah as this was the only station with adequate facilities for them.[33] The inconvenience of this deployment for air-strike operations against the terrorists in Northern Malaya was offset to some extent by the fact that these bombers were always flown in support of pre-planned operations when a quick reaction time was not essential. Tengah had become the main base for all the air-strike forces in the theatre after the return of Sembawang to the Royal Navy on 16 January 1950[34] and it was from here that detachments of light bombers and fighters were maintained at Kuala Lumpur, between 1948 and 1952, and at Butterworth, from May 1950 until the end of the Emergency, to provide immediate air support in Northern Malaya if required. Any further deployment of small air-strike forces to minor airfields was ruled out by the difficulties of providing servicing and administrative facilities and would in any case, have offered little advantage since all parts of Malaya were within an hour's flying time from either Tengah, Kuala Lumpur or Butterworth and the necessity of quick reaction to provide immediate air support became progressively less as the campaign developed.

After two years of the Emergency the air-strike force reached its maximum strength of sixteen Spitfires, sixteen Tempests, sixteen Brigands, fourteen Lincolns and ten Sunderlands. The situation in the second half of 1950 became less satisfactory, however, as the war in Korea necessitated the departure of No 209 (Sunderland) Squadron to Iwakuni in Japan on 9 October and the five Sunderlands of No 205 Squadron was left to maintain the flying-boat commitment in the Malayan campaign for the next two years.[35] The loss of No 209 Squadron was potential rather than actual, however, as the type of action for which they were best suited was rare at this stage of the campaign. More serious was the departure of No 61 (Lincoln) Squadron without relief when its tour ended on 29 March 1951.[36] Towards the end of 1950 the Air Ministry had been subjected to further pressure from Bomber Command to end the detachment of part of their force to the Far East since they had been reduced to six Lincoln Squadrons in the United Kingdom and were concerned about maintaining their commitment to NATO during the coming period of conversion to Washingtons and then to Canberras.[37] Moreover, air strikes against indeterminate and undefended targets in Malaya were no training for a bomber force, especially with regard to night and blind bombing techniques. Concern was also expressed over the heavy expenditure on air weapons that was occasioned by the Lincoln force in Malaya.[38]

Between March 1950 and February 1951 £1,357,500 had been spent on 1,000 lb and 500 lb bombs alone in the theatre and the estimated future cost of £2 million per annum on air weapons was equivalent to the cost of 100 fully equipped Vampire fighters.[39] There was also a serious shortage of 1,000 lb bombs in the theatre and a surplus of 500 lb bombs that were suitable for arming lighter aircraft. Under these circumstances some definite proof was required that the results achieved by the medium bomber force in Malaya was commensurate with the effort involved and, since none was forthcoming, the Lincolns of Bomber Command were withdrawn as an unnecessary luxury, much to the regret of the AOC Malaya.[40]

The conflicting views that were put forward over the efficacy of the Lincolns that were detached from Bomber Command to Malaya was a prime example of prosecuting a cold war while at the same time preparing for a hot war with inadequate resources to carry out both satisfactorily. There is no doubt that, as the Air Ministry and Bomber Command feared, heavy air strikes against the terrorists in Malaya during 1951 were being used largely through lack of any alternative method of harassing and killing the enemy and to this extent they justified themselves to the local commanders who were concerned with maintaining the offensive until the local administration was capable of carrying out the necessary civil measures. To observers in Whitehall, however, concerned as they were with wider issues and imbued with an increasing belief in an ultimate political and economic solution to the Emergency, the temptation was to reduce air-strike action to the minimum commensurate with maintaining the *status quo*, especially as any exaggeration of its efficacy against the terrorists might have created a demand for its increase at the expense of further ground force action.[41]

Part of the reduction in the air-strike potential caused by the termination of the Lincoln detachment from Bomber Command was offset by increasing the establishments of No 1 (RAAF) Squadron from six to eight Lincolns and of No 45 and No 84 Squadrons from eight to ten Brigands each.[42] However, as two of the fighter squadrons in the command underwent re-equipment at about this time there was a marked reduction in the availability of strike aircraft for anti-terrorist operations. The last fourteen Spitfires in service with the RAF were withdrawn from No 60 Squadron in December 1950 and January 1951, having carried out over 1,800 operational sorties against the terrorists and were replaced by Vampire 5s.[43] The whole squadron was out of line from 2 January to 26 April 1951 for training in its primary role of air defence, after which it helped to maintain the fighter detachment at Butterworth but was otherwise available for 'Firedog' operations only to a limited extent for the remainder of the campaign. The Tempests of No 33 Squadron, the last in service with the RAF, had also become a wasting asset by 1950 due to low serviceability and they were replaced by Hornets early in 1951.[44] Conversion of this squadron was undertaken gradually so that while the last flight did not finish operations with Tempests until June 1951 the first flight was flying Hornets by July and the whole squadron was operational at Butterworth by August, although only at three-quarter strength. Despite this re-equipment programme the serviceability rate of the air-strike force was maintained at 60·7 per cent throughout the period January to August 1951 but its potential was considerably reduced when the use of guns on Brigands was prohibited after the aircraft had been grounded for a spell for examination.[45] Soon afterwards Vampires experienced trouble with their ammunition chute doors and the guns of the Hornets were restricted when it was found that ejected links were damaging the tailplanes. Finally the bomb carriers of both Vampires and Hornets developed faults that required modification in their design.[46]

The reduction in the air-strike potential became so acute that for short periods in December 1949 and in January and November 1950, Harvard communication aircraft of Station Flights and the training element of fighter squadrons were fitted with bomb carriers and pressed into service as dive bombers.[47] Further relief was provided from the end of July to mid-September 1950 by twelve Seafires of No 800 (RN) Squadron and eighteen Fireflies of No 827 (RN) Squadron from HMS *Triumph*, which were made available for operations against the terrorists in Malaya.[48] The assistance of these aircraft proved welcome to both services and naval-strike aircraft from carrier groups that were cruising in Malayan waters were used subsequently in the campaign when the opportunity arose, including those from HMS *Glory* in October 1952 and those from HMS *Warrior* in September 1954.

By the end of 1951 the air-strike force that was available for 'Firedog' operations consisted of eight Lincolns, twenty Brigands, sixteen Hornets, sixteen Vampires and ten Sunderlands (No 88 (Sunderland) Squadron having returned temporarily from Hong Kong).[49] The re-equipment programme started in 1951 continued throughout 1952, however, with a deleterious effect on the availability of operational strike aircraft. No 45 Squadron was withdrawn from operations on 31 January 1952 for conversion from Brigands to Hornets, returning in June at half strength, while No 60 Squadron exchanged their Vampire 5s for Vampire 9s on 24 March.[50] At the end of December 1952 the Brigands of No 84 Squadron had to be grounded because of structural failure and the squadron was reduced to a cadre basis on 1 February 1953. Its number plate was transferred to MEAF on 20 February 1953.[51] Eight Lincolns, thirty-two Hornets, sixteen Vampires and nine Sunderlands were left to carry out offensive support operations against the terrorists.

Throughout 1952 the Air Staff in London had continued to be concerned with economizing in the air-strike effort that was being expended in Malaya and the AOC Malaya was exhorted to consider all reductions that could be achieved without altering the course of the campaign so that squadrons could concentrate on training for their primary theatre role and on other commitments such as 'showing the flag' in other parts of the Far East. During 1953, however, full scale combined operations were planned in the hope of terminating the campaign and, in order to increase the available offensive air support, additional medium bomber reinforcements were requested to supplement No 1 (RAAF) Squadron.[52] The Air Ministry readily agreed and plans were mooted to send the Lincoln squadron that was normally sent on a training cycle to the Middle East during the winter months (Operation 'Sunray') or even the complete wing of twenty-four aircraft that were available to reinforce the Middle East in an emergency (Operation 'Alacrity').[53] However, for administrative reasons and because of the unpredictability of future operations against the terrorists, it was important to have one squadron standing by in Malaya at all times and on 1 September 1953 No 83 Squadron arrived at Tengah from Hemswell to reintroduce the Bomber Command detachment of medium bombers that were to form part of the air-strike force in Malaya for the next three years.[54] Between September 1953 and March 1955 detachments of eight Lincolns (Operation 'Bold') from Nos 83, 7 and 148 Squadrons were deployed at Tengah for tours of three to five months, after which this commitment was taken over until August 1956 by detachments of six or eight Canberras from Nos 101, 617, 12 and 9 Squadrons (Operation 'Mileage') that operated from Butterworth.[55]

The two medium bomber, three fighter and two Sunderland squadrons that constituted the offensive air support force at the end of 1953 continued to operate throughout 1954 and 1955, although with some change in their constituent aircraft in the latter year. At the beginning of 1955 Nos 205 and 209 Squadrons were amalgamated at Seletar with the eight remaining Sunderlands[56] and soon afterwards the Vampires of No 60 Squadron at Tengah were exchanged for Venoms.[57] On 31 March 1955 Nos 33 and 45 Squadrons were amalgamated with a total strength of twenty Hornets and the combined squadron began retraining with sixteen Vampires soon afterwards, prior to its re-equipment with sixteen Venoms in October 1955 when it was renumbered No 45 Squadron and operated from Butterworth.[58] The total number of fighter squadrons was brought up to three again with the arrival at Tengah from Cyprus of the sixteen Venoms of No 14 (RNZAF) Squadron in April and May 1955[59] and the year ended with the replacement of Lincolns by Canberras in the Bomber Command detachment and its transfer from Tengah to Butterworth. This detachment ended in September 1956 since its maintenance was prejudicing Bomber Command's commitments to SACEUR[60] but smaller detachments were sent to Malaya in its place for periods of two weeks every three months that were timed to coincide with any major operations against the terrorists.[61]

The air-strike force of one Lincoln, three Venom and one Sunderland squadron that was available for Operation 'Firedog' at the end of 1956 was retained throughout most of 1957, although No 45 (Venom) Squadron returned from Butterworth to Tengah on 15 November to re-equip with Canberras.[62] During 1958, however, the reduced commitment in the offensive air support role in the campaign against the terrorists was reflected in a run-down in the available forces. During 1954 and 1955 the value of air-strike action in carrying the war to the diminishing number of hardcore terrorists had achieved wide recognition which culminated in the directive that it was to be employed whenever ground force action could not be mounted quickly or easily.[63] From 1956 onwards, however, the continuing lack of evidence of the results achieved for a high expenditure on air weapons and the need to concentrate on primary training roles ensured that offensive air support was reduced to the minimum. Strict selection and careful categorization of targets submitted by the ground forces was exercised and full support was provided only if there was a reasonable chance of furthering their aims and only if there was a high probability that terrorists were present.[64]

As part of the gradual reduction in air-strike forces Sunderlands were employed for the last time on 'Firedog' operations in March 1958, prior to the re-equipment of the combined No 205/209 Squadron with Shackletons that concentrated solely on their maritime rescue and reconnaissance roles,[65] while on 1 September 1958 the medium bomber commitment ceased with the departure of No 1 (RAAF) Squadron to Australia.[66] The potential air-strike force received considerable reinforcements in the second half of 1958 with the build up of the Commonwealth Strategic Reserve in Malaya but only a small part of this force was actually required for the remaining offensive air support commitments in Operation 'Firedog'. The Venoms of No 14 (RNZAF) Squadron were replaced at Tengah by the Canberras of No 75 (RNZAF) Squadron on 1 July 1958, while Nos 2(B) and 3(F) Squadrons of the RAAF, equipped with Canberras and Sabres respectively, arrived at Butterworth on 11 November, where a small detachment of Bomber Command Valiants was also deployed for short periods of two weeks at three monthly intervals (Operation 'Profiteer').[67] The arrival of these forces at Butterworth restored the ability of the air forces to respond quickly to bids for strike action in Northern Malaya, that had been affected by the withdrawal of No 45 Squadron to Tengah in November 1957, but such action was hardly ever required at this stage in the campaign. By the end of 1958 three light bomber and two fighter squadrons were deployed in the Malayan theatre but demands for air-strike action of any kind had declined so much that No 45 Squadron was released from all operational commitments on 29 September 1958, shortly after celebrating the tenth anniversary of its first sortie against the terrorists, and only one of the remaining Canberra squadrons was kept in operational readiness at any one time.[68] A further Sabre squadron, No 77(F) RAAF, arrived at Butterworth on 1 February 1959 and the Venoms of No 60 Squadron at Tengah were replaced by Meteor night fighters on 1 October 1959.[69] By then, however, the offensive support role of the air forces in the campaign against the terrorists in Malaya had ended.

Most of the strike squadrons that participated in the twelve year campaign in Malaya achieved long records of service in the theatre, even though most underwent re-equipment during this period. The brunt of the offensive air support from June 1950 to September 1958 was borne by the Lincolns of No 1 (RAAF) Squadron while, in the light bomber role, the Beaufighters and Brigands of No 84 Squadron served until 1 February 1953. Similarly, aircraft of No 45 Squadron arrived in Malaya in August 1948 and were still there when the Emergency ended in July 1960 although the squadron had exchanged their Beaufighters in turn for Brigands, Hornets, Venoms and finally Canberras in the intervening period. The most notable record, however, was achieved by No 60 Squadron, whose Spitfires opened the campaign in June 1948 and were replaced in turn by Vampires and then by Venoms which operated against the terrorists until they were replaced by Meteor night fighters in the final few months of the Emergency. Even the Sunderlands of Nos 205 and 209 Squadrons, despite the commitments of the Far East Flying Boat Wing in Hong Kong and Korea, were available when required for all except the final two years of the campaign.

While the potential offensive air support force was provided by six or seven squadrons throughout most of the Emergency, not all of their aircraft were available for operations against the terrorists at any one time. Medium bombers on detachment from Bomber Command had only between 75 and 120 flying hours left in the theatre on arrival[70] and had to be employed sparingly, while fighter and light bomber squadrons were temporarily withdrawn from 'Firedog' operations at intervals for training in their primary role, notably at the Armament Practice Camp that operated at Butterworth between the beginning of 1949 and 1956.[71] Except for Lincolns, poor serviceability amongst strike aircraft was common in Malayan conditions and Nos 33 and 60 Squadrons, with only 10 of their 33 aircraft available in June 1951, were not untypical of the general state of affairs at that time.[72] The introduction of jet aircraft into the theatre tended to exacerbate the difficulties of maintaining an adequate rate of serviceability and they generally proved to be less suitable for their required tasks than were the obsolete types which they replaced.

The range, endurance and bomb load capacity of the Lincoln for example, proved well suited to fulfilling commitments in the medium bomber role. With full tanks (2,850 gallons) they had an endurance of eleven hours at 180 knots and, armed with fourteen 1,000 lb bombs and able to fly in a close 'vic' formation of five aircraft in most weather conditions, they could deliver a high concentration of bombs anywhere in the Federation of Malaya at any time of the day or night.[73] Throughout the whole of 1950 the serviceability rate of the Bomber Command Lincoln detachment only twice fell below 75 per cent.[74] In contrast, Canberras, which took over the bombing offensive in 1955, were too elaborate for the task they were required to carry out. They carried half the bomb load of Lincolns and their cruising speed of 250 knots at the optimum bombing height required more elaborate navigational aids and made map-reading impracticable and visual bomb-aiming difficult.

The pilot had a poorer visibility than in a Lincoln and the Canberra could not be flown at night or in close formation and could not be employed in a strafing role. They suffered, in common with all jet aircraft in the tropics, from a serious limitation in their endurance at low level, which precluded the possibility of postponing or delaying an air strike once they were airborne. This was a serious disadvantage in the uncertain weather conditions of Malaya, especially in 1958 when Canberras were operating in the northern part of the country far from their parent base at Tengah near Singapore, and was reflected in an increase in the rate of abortive air strikes when they replaced Lincolns. When flown at their normal speed at low altitudes the swirl vanes of Canberra engines suffered badly from metal fatigue in the hot, turbulent air which also made flying conditions difficult for their pilots. For those Canberras that were not fitted with Godfrey air coolers, sun canopies, cooling trollies and external compressed air supplies had to be employed to combat the danger of loss of bodyweight through sweating which could amount to as much as 3 lb per sortie.[75]

Both from the point of view of maintenance and flying conditions Lincolns were preferable to Canberras in the type of campaign that prevailed in Malaya and the advantages of the older, piston-engined types of aircraft were underlined by the Sunderland flying boats, whose great endurance, low speed, concentrated fire-power and ability to carry three hundred and sixty 20 lb fragmentation bombs proved of great value during sustained harassing operations when accuracy was not of paramount importance.[76] Similar advantages of older types were apparent in comparing the performances of the fighter and fighter bomber aircraft that were employed during the Malayan campaign. The Spitfires that were used during the early months had a relatively low fire-power and range, between 290 and 360 miles at 200 knots according to their armament, and, since they were virtually obsolete at that time, they afforded serious problems of maintenance.[77] Their Tempest and Hornet replacements, however, were well suited to their task, providing a stable firing platform for a reasonable weight of rocket and cannon fire, and, with ranges of up to 500 miles, they were capable of loitering at low level for some time until they could attack small, pinpoint targets with the minimum of compromise in relatively poor weather conditions.[78] Brigands, with a bomb load of 2,000 lb, had similar capabilities although the lack of a bomb-sight attachment made low-level attacks essential for the sake of accuracy but exposed them to a slight risk of being hit by fragments from the explosion of their own bombs.[79] Eventually, however, Tempests, Hornets and Brigands became obsolete and difficult to maintain and were replaced by Vampires and Venoms which suffered from similar disadvantages to Canberras in the Malayan theatre. Their speed was not essential in view of the lack of opposition and only made low-level attacks over broken terrain more difficult. At low altitudes the range over which they could operate was considerably restricted and their limited endurance ensured that they had little freedom of action in a country where there were few diversionary airfields and virtually no fighter navigational or control systems. The accuracy and the weight of the bomb pattern which they were capable of delivering were inadequate for the demands of the Malayan campaign while the effect of the humid conditions on their refined electronics systems created serious problems of serviceability. Thus, although Venoms had a fixed life of 750 hours, only one in three attained this figure while their average serviceability throughout 1957 was only 58 per cent.[80] Finally, the stress of flying jet aircraft in Malayan conditions ensured that Sabre pilots could only fly one sortie a day in contrast to the two or three that were frequently flown by the pilots of Tempests or Hornets.

Air Weapons

The debatable question of the overall strength of the offensive air support force used in the Malayan campaign and of its component types of aircraft affected, and was affected by, the type and number of weapons they were capable of delivering. Exigencies of expense, availability and effectiveness were constant factors in the debate over aircraft armament which continued throughout the campaign and many of the answers to the problem of devising the most suitable weapons were provided by the armoury tests that were held at the Song Song Island bombing range in May 1951 under the auspices of the Scientific Adviser to the Air Ministry.[81] These tests evaluated the 'mean area of effectiveness' of each weapon—a calculation based on the chances of hitting a small target in an arbitrary area of 1,000 square feet of jungle. Thus if one weapon gave a 20 per cent chance of achieving a 'kill' it contributed 200 square feet to the 'mean area of effectiveness' of the total weapon load. In order to equate various weapon loads the number of sorties by different types of aircraft that were needed to achieve a 'mean area of effectiveness' of one million square feet was calculated.

The largest weapon that was employed during the Malayan campaign was the 4,000 lb HE bomb but its blast effect in jungle terrain was not proportional to its size and it achieved an unfortunate political connotation when it was introduced in 1950 that hindered its employment.[82] It could not be dropped without express permission of the High Commissioner for the Federation of Malaya and was, in fact, not used until May 1953 during Operation 'Commodore' in Johore. Very few of these bombs were dropped during the remainder of the campaign. The 1,000 lb HE nose-fused bomb, with a 'mean area of effectiveness' of 75,000 square feet, proved to be the most effective weapon that was employed during the campaign because of its efficiency and also because of the great total weight that could be delivered by one medium bomber against a pinpoint target. 1,000 lb bombs were first used when medium bombers were introduced into the campaign in 1950 and their expenditure ceased with the withdrawal of these aircraft in 1958. The 500 lb HE nose-fused bomb, with a 'mean area of effectiveness' of 15,000 square feet, that was introduced into the campaign in August 1948 was the air weapon most commonly used after the 1,000 lb bomb, its reduced effectiveness being offset to some extent by the greater number of explosions that was achieved for each bomb load, which was of value during harassing operations against area targets. Even more effective in the harassing role was the 20 lb fragmentation bomb, with a 'mean area of effectiveness' of 1,000 square feet that was introduced into the campaign early in 1949. The noise of its detonation was not appreciably less than that of a 500 lb bomb and as the recipient got sixteen instead of one its effect on morale, if not its lethal power, was greater— although it could also be claimed that a large number of small bombs gave a greater chance of killing the enemy in ill-defined jungle targets than did one large bomb. The 20 lb bomb was, therefore, a weapon of great potential value but as the Sunderland alone was capable of carrying sufficient quantities to justify its employment, it was not used in great quantities and none were dropped after these aircraft were withdrawn in 1958. Similarly, 350 lb clusters of 19 lb fragmentation bombs, with a 'mean area of effectiveness' of 27,500 square feet, were more effective than 500 lb bombs but they were only introduced into the campaign in 1951 and were in such short supply that they were rarely used thereafter.[83]

The question of whether bombs were fused at the nose or tail was of great importance in the Malayan campaign since it determined whether they exploded at ground level or at 150 feet or more at tree top height. Nose fused bombs that burst at an average height of 50–75 feet were found to be potentially the most effective, achieving the greatest spread of fragmentation and blast, while tail fused bombs penetrated the ground before exploding and dissipated much of their energy in forming a six feet deep crater which directed most of their blast effect upwards. The 'mean area of effectiveness' of nose and tail fused 1,000 lb bombs was 75,000 and 6,000 square feet respectively and that of 500 lb bombs was 15,000 and 3,000 square feet. It was clear that tail fused bombs should not have been used when the main object was to kill the enemy but were permissible if it was decided that the noise of explosions at ground level would have a greater psychological effect on them. Up until October 1950 the No 44 nose pistol was in general use on bombs used in the Malayan campaign but it was then proscribed by both the RAF and the RAAF for lack of a positive safety device and bombs were armed with the No 65 tail pistol instead. An immediate and marked fall in the number of casualties attributable to air-strike action underlined the superiority of nose fusing and the situation did not improve until this practice was re-introduced. Most bombs were then fused at both nose and tail to ensure that they did explode* but tail fuses were dispensed with in 1953 because of expense.[84] In addition to the usual nose and tail fuses, VT Fuse No 906 Mk I was developed in 1954 to function at certain pre-set heights above the ground irrespective of the height or the speed at which the bomb was released.[85] Short delayed action fuses were developed in 1950 as instantaneous explosions had caused serious damage to low-flying Brigand aircraft and bombs whose ignition was delayed for six, twelve or even thirty-six hours were used successfully thereafter, especially during prolonged harassing operations.[86]

Besides bombs, rocket projectiles, with a 'mean area of effectiveness' of 1,500 square feet, were used during the Malayan campaign, mainly by ground-attack aircraft, but they had little lethal effect since the semi-armour piercing capability of their 60 lb head combined with soft-skinned target buildings to carry them into the ground before exploding and dissipated much of their effect. When there was a definite aiming point, however, they were more accurate than bombing from a medium height and, according to surrendered terrorists, strafing with rockets and 20 mm cannon shells was greatly feared and had a marked effect. ·5-inch and ·303-inch ammunition on the other hand were relatively useless in jungle terrain, with 'mean areas of effectiveness' of four square feet or less, and their expenditure decreased significantly in the later stages of the campaign and virtually ceased after 1956.[87]

Apart from the conventional explosive weapons that were used during the Malayan campaign the Operational Research Section of AHQ Malaya experimented with various other devices to find the most effective weapons against jungle targets. During 1950 napalm, or jellified petroleum, in 200 lb canisters exploded by a static line, was tried out but its fire raising effect proved extremely localized in green jungle and its expense outweighed any transitory effect that it might have had on enemy morale—an effect that was quickly lost as the limitations of the weapon was realized by the recipients.[88] Similar trials employing depth charges as a weapon in jungle

---

* The number of unexploded bombs amounted to 2 per cent of the total number dropped by 1958 and ground force patrols were locating them at a rate of approximately one each week. In March 1957 a joint Army and RAF bomb disposal unit was formed at Kuala Lumpur, under the control of AHQ No 224 Group. Teams consisted of an RAF NCO with one or two engineers from 50th Gurkha Field Engineer Regiment. During 1957 they demolished fourteen HE bombs, fourteen HE bomb clusters, thirteen rocket projectiles and eight Army missiles.

warfare came to nothing[89] but smoke bombs were used successfully on a few occasions when limited force was required, as for example when recalcitrant Sakai aborigines needed persuading to move into new resettlement areas in the Sungei Yum and Sungei Plus areas of Perak in September 1950.[90] Nothing came of a proposal that was put forward in March 1950 to use a non-lethal gas or spray that would penetrate the jungle ceiling and cause unconsciousness for 48 hours, thus immobilizing the terrorists for long enough to enable security force patrols to eliminate them without causing permanent damage to innocent inhabitants.[91] A toxic spray* was, however, used with great effect against the jungle cultivation upon which the terrorists largely relied for sustenance after their withdrawal into deep jungle areas in 1954.[92]Finally, when the cost of weapon expenditure began to cause concern in 1954, 'screamers' such as empty beer bottles were occasionally employed during continuous harassing operations and, when interspersed with lethal bombardments, the alarming noise which they made proved quite effective in inducing surrenders while achieving a considerable saving in cost.[93]

The total number of air weapons that was expended during the Malayan campaign showed a sharp increase in 1950 and 1951 with the arrival of medium bombers in the theatre, followed by a gradual decline in 1952 and 1953, a slight recovery in the expenditure of the heavier weapons in 1954 and 1955 with the re-introduction of medium bombers and then a rapid decline as offensive air support became increasingly redundant in the overall campaign. In the peak year of 1951 over five thousand 1,000 lb bombs were dropped as well as over fourteen thousand 500 lb bombs, thirty-four thousand 20 lb bombs, twenty thousand rocket projectiles, sixty thousand rounds of 20 mm cannon shell, five hundred and fifty thousand rounds of ·5-inch ammunition and seven hundred thousand rounds of ·303-inch ammunition.[94]

Since 1,000 lb bombs cost £125 each in 1951 and 500 lb bombs, 20 lb bombs and 60 lb rocket projectiles cost £56, £4 10s and £18 10s respectively, the cost of arming the offensive air support force for operations against the terrorists was considerable while, in addition to their armament, the cost of each Lincoln and Brigand sortie was £750 and £200.[95] In 1952 alone £7,247,236 was expended on flying operations in support of Operation 'Firedog' of which £1,842,387 represented the cost of air weapons.[96] It was important, therefore, that the cost of air weapons as well as their efficiency should be taken into account when arming aircraft for air strikes against the terrorists and in this respect the Lincoln armed with 1,000 lb nose fused bombs proved most economical. In order to achieve a 'mean area of effectiveness' of one million square feet it required only one Lincoln, armed with fourteen 1,000 lb nose fused bombs, at a total cost of £2,500, while eighteen sorties were required by Lincolns armed with tail fused 1,000 lb bombs at a total cost of £32,000. To achieve the same effect sixteen Brigands armed with four 500 lb nose fused bombs were required, at a total cost of £7,000, or thirty-three Hornets each armed with two 500 lb nose fused bombs. If tail fused bombs were used by Brigands or Hornets 80 and 160 sorties respectively were required to achieve the same effect at the exorbitant cost of £35,000 or more.[97] It is not surprising, therefore, that Lincoln bombers armed with 1,000 lb nose fused bombs bore the brunt of the aerial offensive against the terrorists.

Planning and Initiation of Air Strikes

Preceding all air strikes against the terrorists in Malaya was a considerable

---

* *See* under 'Crop Spraying' in Chapter 4.

amount of planning and preparation which inevitably wasted a good deal of time between the receipt of a request for air-strike action and the final delivery of the attack. Time, however, was not normally of the essence in this campaign and these preparations were inevitable since the air forces were acting entirely in support of the civil power in a subordinate role to the ground forces, upon whom they relied entirely for employment.

The prerequisite of all successful air-strike action was reliable intelligence information, without which neither ground nor aerial reconnaissance was likely to locate possible targets without detection. Reports from all branches of the security forces about possible terrorist locations were carefully graded but actual knowledge of enemy camps and concentrations came invariably from informers, usually captured or surrendered terrorists. Unfortunately, owing to the low mentality of the majority of these informers and their inability to read maps or assess distances accurately, much of this target information was unreliable and aircraft were often despatched on abortive missions as a result. In general there was a tendency to overgrade the reliability of information received from informers but, since they were the main source of target intelligence, there was little alternative.[98] When attempts were made to verify such information by investigation on the ground the terrorists were frequently forewarned of an impending air attack and rapidly dispersed from the target area. Since the air forces were largely reliant on the ground forces for target intelligence it is not surprising that, especially during the early years of the campaign, they considered that they were given neither enough of this information nor sufficient time to act decisively upon it.[99] To remedy this situation, and to make ground force commanders more aware of the potential of air strike action, RAF intelligence officers were attached to State Police Headquarters and were also sent on ground force patrols to encourage a greater exploitation of the available offensive air support. As the campaign developed it was recognized that opportunities for immediate air support were extremely rare, but a greater degree of understanding was achieved between the ground and air forces in the planning of large scale combined operations. At first air strikes had been arranged on an *ad hoc* basis by personal agreement between the Army and Air Force commanders but, after November 1949, they were ordered through the combined Land/Air Operations Room at GHQ Malaya District, Kuala Lumpur, which became the nucleus of the Joint Operations Centre that evolved in its final form in 1954.[100]

The overall offensive campaign against the terrorists was planned by the Director of Operations Committee after 1950 and was executed at State and Settlement level by the local War Executive Committees. The Police and Army commanders on these committees channelled all requests for air support into the Joint Operations Centre or its predecessor, where the AOC Malaya allocated his resources according to the priorities decided by the Director of Operations Committee of which he was a member. This channelling of a request for air support, from Company or Police Circle through District or Battalion and Brigade or State Police Headquarters, to a central controlling organization at Kuala Lumpur was not the quickest method of laying on air strikes and when there was a possibility that immediate air support might be required Air Support Signals Units were detached to operational areas to pass requests from ground patrols or reconnaissance aircraft directly to the airfield concerned so that briefing could be carried out while permission for the strike was obtained from the Joint Operations Centre.[101] Apart from these instances, experience had proved by 1955 that, in certain circumstances and subject to certain provisos, air strikes were often mounted more quickly and more effectively when requests were passed direct to the RAF stations, where all the necessary planning was carried out. Where the ground forces were unable to mount operations against the terrorists and the air forces alone were able to maintain pressure against them the procedures of Operation 'Thermos' were adopted whereby the officers commanding RAF Tengah and Butterworth were given the responsibility of planning and conducting air-strike operations in clearly defined areas for a limited period of time.[102] Similarly, under the dictates of Operation 'Smash Hit', certain Army units on specified operations were authorized to request offensive air support direct from the RAF stations concerned without prior permission from the Joint Operations Centre for limited periods of up to four days.[103] These refinements in procedure, however, did not invalidate the principle that the command and control of all air-strike operations was carried out by the Joint Operations Centre, since the duty officer there had to be notified before any air strike mounted under these contingencies could be carried out.

Target Clearance

The overriding control of air-strike action by a single, central authority was exercised mainly because of the necessity of obtaining clearance to attack a specified target area. This was an indispensable preliminary in operations against a militant Communist element whose strength represented only a small fraction of the total population and were just as liable to be present in populated areas as were innocent civilians. Even when air-strike operations were mounted in the densely forested, inaccessible and sparsely populated regions of Kelantan and Northern Pahang, care had to be taken, for political reasons, not to inflict casualties on the aboriginal Sakais, even if they were known to be actively aiding and abetting the terrorists— albeit under duress. Furthermore, the constant activity of ground force patrols and their lack of direct signals links with attacking aircraft required some safeguards to ensure their safety from air-strike action. As a general rule no troops, civilians or habitations were allowed within 3,000 yards of the target along the undershoot and overshoot lines of attack or within 2,000 yards of the flanks, although when more refined target location devices were introduced in 1956 the area of this arbitrary safety zone was reduced to a minimum of 2,000 by 1,000 yards for bomb attacks and 500 yards square for strafing attacks by fighters.[104]

The necessity of these stringent safety precautions was underlined by the harmful propaganda that followed the few unfortunate incidents that did occur, which far outweighed the value of eliminating a few terrorists. On 7 February 1950 faulty clearance procedures resulted in a Beaufighter attack being made close to a settlement at Kulai in Johore and a school was damaged and five civilians were wounded.[105] In November of the same year a combination of bad weather and faulty bomb loading techniques caused a Lincoln on a sortie against a terrorist position near Rawang in Central Selangor to unload its bombs 600 yards short of the edge of the target, killing 12 civilians and injuring 26 others.[106] The dangers faced by ground forces in the vicinity of an air strike, even when safety precautions were observed, was exemplified in August 1953 when the premature release of a six bomb stick from a Canberra, due to an electrical failure in the release mechanism, caused the deaths of one British officer and seven other ranks in the Tasak Bera area of Pahang.[107]

It was clearly necessary to obtain clearance of a target area before taking air-strike action but there is no doubt that the element of surprise that is inherent in all successful air attacks was seriously prejudiced as a result. The inevitable delay that occurred while the position of innocent civilians was ascertained and those that were in the danger area were physically removed was often enough to alarm the terrorists and give them the opportunity of dispersing. Clearance to attack had also to be obtained from the police in case the target area was reserved for a Special Branch operation and even when strike aircraft arrived over the target they were not allowed to attack unless the aiming point could be clearly identified, while any targets of opportunity that presented themselves outside the briefed area had to be ignored. In addition to the precautions taken against inflicting unnecessary casualties, great concern was taken to avoid damaging civilian property because of the liability of paying heavy compensation. An absolute embargo was placed on all air strikes against inhabited or cultivated areas, except identified terrorist plots, while rubber estates, reputed to be worth £10 per tree, carried the threat of court martial if hit and other areas of jungle were protected in case bomb splinters damaged local sawmills when the timber was cut.[108]

Not unnaturally the air forces chafed at these restrictions which often resulted in complete negation of their efforts and prevented the most effective use of the air weapon. It was even suggested that, apart from a general warning, police clearance of an area should be dispensed with since the population should learn that to be in the same area as Communist terrorists was to risk air attack without any prospect of compensation.[109] This suggestion was put forward in 1951 when the air forces in Malaya were growing impatient with the impediments to successful air-strike action which they faced and was coupled with demands for increased participation in the collation of intelligence material in order to determine potential air-strike targets and for experiments to improve ground to air communications in order to enhance the prospects of providing immediate air support. In retrospect it is fortunate that these recommendations were not acted upon for the restrictions on air-strike action, although irksome, were essential in a campaign in which the battle for the minds and loyalties of the civilian population was of equal, if not greater, importance than the infliction of a few casualties on the enemy.

Target Briefing and Navigation

After clearance to attack had been received by the Joint Operations Centre briefing for air strikes was carried out, almost invariably from aerial photographs since maps of Malaya were insufficient and inaccurate. In order to facilitate briefing, areas where terrorist activity was common were given code-names (such as 'Hawk', 'Dagger', 'Kuda' for the Selangor, Segamat and Southern Kelantan/Northern Pahang areas) and these were further subdivided into target designations relating to specific map references or recognizable points. Operation 'Vulture' for example referred to the area in Johore and Negri Sembilan bounded by the Kuala Langat Forest Reserve, Gemas, Triang, Seremban and Semeniyeh and contained targets designated by the names of flowers—Violet, Phlox, Sunflower, Daisy, Pansy, Lily, Iris and Rose.[110] Code names such as 'Blowpipe' and 'Bluetit' referred to prearranged briefs for air strikes mounted to relieve police posts at Kampongs Aur and Bala while further standing orders under the comprehensive code-name of Operation 'Medal' were prepared for operations mounted in support of various jungle forts in case of attack by terrorists.[111]

Navigation to the target area was mainly achieved by dead reckoning with the aid of aerial photographs as target folders. Throughout an attack air-strike aircraft were in communication with the Air Control Centre Malaya either directly or through a series of forward relay stations at Fraser's Hill, Brinchang and Kedah Peak.[112] A VHF direction finding network service employing Eureka Mk 7 beacons was inaugurated at Kuala Lumpur in 1954 and a second station was opened at Kuantan in June 1957 to facilitate the control of fighter aircraft in Northern Malaya.[113] A plan to extend this network by erecting a further station at Gunong Batu Brinchang was abandoned in November 1957 when it became clear that future requirements for its use would not justify the cost.[114]

Arriving in the target area, local control of air-strike action was often provided at the start of the campaign through ground to air communications from an Army Contact Car ('Rover Joe'), a technique which had been used successfully in conjunction with fighter aircraft during the closing stages of the Second World War. In order to co-ordinate large scale attacks that were carried out under 'Rover' control a Dakota was generally used as an airborne control point to receive target information from the ground, call up the attacking forces, assess the weather conditions, brief the aircrews and mark the target.[115] This technique was frequently employed in 1948 and 1949 but, since the terrain nearly always prevented the contact car from reaching the position of a clash with the terrorists and immediate air support proved impracticable, it was used on less than 20 per cent of all air strikes by 1951 and nearly all attacks from then onwards were carried out by aircraft with no direct communications links with the ground forces.[116]

Target Identification and Marking Techniques

The second prerequisite of a successful air strike, after accurate intelligence information, was an accurate method of pinpointing the target in a country where map-reading by the ground forces was difficult and where an error of 100 yards in the aiming point could nullify any effect an air strike might have. At the start of the campaign targets were identified visually in relation to a salient topographical feature or a lighter patch on an aerial photograph. As pilots became experienced in flying over Malaya they acquired a remarkable knowledge of the jungle terrain and could navigate by the light patches in the jungle cover that were associated with the dead vegetation caused by previous bomb explosions. Detailed landmarks in the jungle were rare, however, and as it was possible to lose sight of salient features such as a river bend several times during a bombing run it was frequently necessary to circle the target area to make even the most provisional identification of the aiming point. This practice compromised the element of surprise in the attack and enabled the terrorists to disperse while cumulative errors in accuracy were inevitable since only the strike leader identified the target and the remaining aircraft bombed or strafed on the bomb bursts of their predecessor.

The solution to this problem lay in the development of target marking techniques and in the practice of carrying out bombing runs from an established datum point some distance from the target on the basis of a fixed bearing and flying time to the bomb release point. Pilots of Auster aircraft, normally familiar with the target area and flying at low level, were able to mark the most inconspicuous targets with a high degree of accuracy. The recognized drill was for the pilot of the marker plane to contact the attacking force at a rendezvous some twenty miles from the target and then proceed to the 'gate' position close to the target but still far enough away to avoid any loss of security. The strike leader then counted out the minutes to release time and the Auster left its position to be over the target 1½ minutes before the appointed moment. Marking was carried out by phosphorous grenades or reconnaissance flares and as soon as the Auster had left the target area the strike force bombed visually on this aiming point. This technique was occasionally used at night and was the general practice for all air strikes between the end of 1951 and 1955. Its disadvantages lay mainly in the time-lag between marking and bombing which, although seldom more than 1½ minutes, often allowed the terrorists to take cover or to escape from the target area.[117]

The second technique employed on air strikes required an identifiable datum point from which to calculate the bearing and distance of the target. At the start of the campaign natural features were chosen as identification points but as these were rare in the featureless jungle artificial methods such as smoke signals, balloons and ground marker flares were increasingly employed from 1950 onwards. During daylight raids, however, the blanketing effect of the jungle canopy meant that an Auster target marking plane often had to be used as well to identify the ground flares and mark the target for the strike force. For night strikes two searchlights were set up, one pointing at 45° towards the target to provide the correct bearing and the other pointing vertically to act as the datum from which to commence a timed bombing run. Searchlights were more visible than flares in broken country or jungle and were used with success on a number of occasions, but their employment was dependent on clear weather conditions and reasonable access routes to the target area for the requisite 3-ton trucks.[118]

The great advantage of ground datum markers placed within 400–700 yards of the target was the elimination of the errors of location that were inherent in ground force patrols' assessment of their true position in featureless, ill-mapped jungle terrain. Most, however, suffered from the disadvantages of weight and bulkiness of the equipment involved and exposed the manning party to the risk of ambush by the terrorists. To overcome these difficulties delayed action ground marker flares were developed in 1956 to enable ground patrols to retire to a safe distance from the target and also to time their ignition to coincide with an air strike mounted at night when there was a greater chance of the terrorists being present.[119] Even more ingenious was 'Lodestone', a small radio transmitter developed by the Operational Research Staff in 1957 which emitted a continuous signal at a pre-set frequency for 24 hours.[120] An Auster could fix the position of this signal within 100 yards at a distance of 5,000 yards, beyond audibility range on the ground, and could then receive target directions from the ground patrol which had retired from the target area. However, since static terrorist camps were rare and well guarded by this time, the placing of 'Lodestone' within the optimum distance of 300 yards from the target demanded a coincidence of luck and skill that rarely occurred—only once during 1958 in fact. In any case, from the middle of 1956 onwards air strikes were mounted employing the most successful target location device that was developed during the campaign—the Target Director Post. This was a self-supporting mobile radar unit which provided a narrow beam passing over the target down which attacking aircraft flew until they received a signal to bomb at a distance from the transmitter calculated on the basis of airspeed, bomb ballistics, height, stick length and slant ranges.[121] The advantages of this technique over target or datum marking methods was that sustained air strikes could be mounted with a high degree of accuracy by day or by night under all conditions of weather and surface visibility while still preserving the element of complete surprise. Satisfactory control was afforded between 6,000 and 25,000 yards but, used in conjunction with a timed run from the limit of the radar beam, an average radial error of 175 yards could be achieved at a range of 40,000 yards.[122] The only disadvantage in using radar control rather than ground datums was its greater reliance on the accuracy of the initial target location. Only two Target Director Posts, however, were needed in Malaya to put any target within one hundred miles of the equipment and although they were normally deployed for several weeks at a time in areas where major operations were planned they could be readily moved to within twenty miles of the target area for special operations.

The first Target Director Post was established at Kluang in Johore for operational trials on 9 June 1956, equipped with an Army AA GL Radar No 3 Mk 7 and staffed largely with RAF personnel.[123] No 2 (Army) Target Director Post, staffed with Army personnel, was formed on 18 March 1957 and by June of that year both units were deployed at their administrative bases in Ipoh and Simpang Rengam to provide coverage for Northern and Southern Malaya.[124] By then thirty-one suitable sites had been surveyed in the main operational areas and both units were ready to deploy at short notice.[125] The No 1 (RAF) Unit moved from Ipoh to Butterworth in October 1958, partly to take advantage of the facilities offered by the Song Song Island bombing range, while the No 2 (Army) Unit was deployed on Singapore Island.[126] Both units, however, were idle for long periods throughout 1958 owing to the lack of suitable targets and with the cessation of hostilities in the Southern part of the Federation of Malaya only one unit was required to cover the remaining operations. This commitment was accepted entirely by the Army until October 1959, when the Target Director Post ceased to exist as an operational unit.[127] The fact was that such a refined method of target location was developed too late to have any marked effect on the course of the campaign. By 1957 the increasing alertness of the remaining terrorists ensured that only the most stealthy and unobtrusive methods had any chance of enabling a surprise attack to be made and the appearance of a radar unit or a ground datum party was sufficient to alarm them. By the time of their disestablishment in 1957 the Operational Research Section of the Director of Operations Staff were already turning to the field of applied science, including the use of autolycus and infra-red apparatus to detect camp fires, in an attempt to outwit the remaining terrorists and to provide suitable target information.[128] There is no doubt, however, that had the target marking techniques that were available in 1957 been available at the start of the campaign when pinpoint targets were more frequent, air-strike action at that time would have been far more effective than it was.

Air-Strike Techniques

Even after the introduction of refined target location devices the tactics of weapon delivery by air-strike aircraft in the Malayan campaign were conditioned by the unavoidable inaccuracy of the aiming point as well as the need to preserve the element of surprise. Except when a visible pinpoint, such as an enemy camp, was available it was the general practice to lay down the largest possible bomb pattern in order to cover anticipated errors in target location. As the terrorists rapidly dispersed at the sound of approaching aircraft it was also important to concentrate the maximum effort into the initial blow, since aircraft arriving after the first wave were unlikely to achieve any significant results, while the inevitable loss of accuracy coincident with medium or high level bombing had to be accepted in order to preserve the element of surprise for as long as possible.[129] The timing of air attacks was also important since they were likely to be most effective at night when the terrorists were in camp. If air strikes were made close to dawn the ground forces were able to enter the area of the bomb pattern before survivors could remove their wounded comrades and important documents or equipment.[130] This plan of attack was most favoured by Army commanders but it had to be balanced against the fact that the maximum air-strike forces could not be employed during the hours of darkness and the Army were persuaded to accept the principle that the timing of each air strike should be decided according to the importance of the target.[131] Clearly it was more important to concentrate the maximum available force against the possible location of a terrorist leader than it was for harassing an area target that might or might not contain a number of less important terrorists.

Finally, techniques of weapon delivery were necessarily determined by the aircraft employed. In the absence of any opposition the conventional roles of fighters, fighter bombers and medium bombers, whether it was air defence, tactical or strategic bombing, did not apply and all were employed in either a close support or tactical bombing role and differed only in the weight of weapons they were capable of carrying and in the methods of their delivery. A formation of Lincolns armed with 1,000 lb bombs could bring down the greatest weight of weapons in the shortest possible time against a pinpoint or small area target but since these were not supposed to exceed 500 yards square by 1954, they could be hit effectively without using the maximum available effort.[132]

At the start of the campaign air strikes were mounted by individual fighter and fighter bomber aircraft using rockets and small anti-personnel bombs of doubtful killing power. After the introduction of medium bombers in 1950, however, a heavier weight of attack could be brought to bear and tactics could be varied. For daylight attacks when the maximum effort was required it was usual for a formation of six to ten Lincolns, flying in 'vics' of three or five at about 6,000 feet, to open the attack with high explosive bombs.[133] Initially Lincolns were flown with a 75-yard separation but, as errors in range proved to be rare, the stick length was reduced to 50 yards to obtain greater lethality in a normal target area of 600 by 400 yards.[134] When Canberras replaced Lincolns, however, additional safety precautions meant that the average length of bomb patterns had to be reduced from 650 yards with a 50-yard spacing to 375 yards with a 75-yard spacing.[135] During 1950 and 1951 medium bombers were usually followed over the target by fighter bombers attacking from a low-level with bombs and rockets while fighters strafed possible escape routes from the target area with rocket and cannon fire. Protracted and haphazard blasting of the area by Sunderlands armed with small anti-personnel bombs was then carried out during the 24 or 48 hours following a major air strike in order to harass the survivors and create the greatest feeling of anxiety and uncertainty.[136]

Apart from concentrated daylight attacks various elements of the air-strike force were also used independently. As a result of extensive training No 1 (RAAF) Squadron were able to fly five Lincolns in 'vic' formation on bright moonlit nights, although on dark nights their formations were reduced to three aircraft, while their Canberra replacements were normally flown in line astern with intervals of two or three minutes during night strikes.[137] Apart from medium and light bombers, Sunderlands were also used independently at night, although almost exclusively in a harassing role. Fighter attacks were also mounted independently at dawn or dusk to catch the terrorists leaving or returning to camp and to leave the day free for operational training, but they were only really effective when a visual aiming point was available, which rarely happened after 1954.

Summary of Offensive Air Support Operations

In the following paragraphs a summary is given of the development of offensive air support during the Malayan campaign, including accounts of some of the major air strikes that were carried out. Statistical details of the number of strikes and sorties that were flown in each month of the campaign are collated in Annex T.

At the start of the campaign air strikes were carried out on an opportunity basis whenever suitable information became available. This was rare, however, and the ground force commanders were generally unaware of the potentialities of air-strike action or were reluctant to call for it, even though it frequently offered the best chance of bringing pressure to bear on the terrorists. The idea of inter-related close support in the campaign was still in its infancy and most strikes were mounted mainly as a declaration of intention to restore civilian morale and to show the terrorists that they were not inviolable. The first strike of the campaign took place on 6 July 1948 when two Spitfires of No 60 Squadron attacked and virtually destroyed a terrorist camp near Ayer Karah in Perak but nine days elapsed before the next strike was mounted, by three Spitfires of the same squadron, against a group of huts located in mountainous country near Bentong in Pahang.[138] On the following day, 16 July 1948, a strike was mounted against a hut near Telok Anson in Central Perak which was surrounded by swamp and was not readily accessible from the ground. Ten terrorists were killed and a clear demonstration was given of the correct use of the air weapon. On 22 July 1948 a strike was mounted in support of a road convoy of The Malay Regiment at Sungei Yu which was on its way to relieve a police post at Gua Musang that had been captured by the terrorists. This action illustrated the value of immediate air support by fighter aircraft and, owing largely to the advocacy of the AOC Malaya and the salesmanship of itinerant RAF liaison officers, demands for air-strike action increased and offensive support operations rose to a peak in August 1948. Most strikes during July and August were flown in support of 'Shawforce' which was operating in the Pulai valley of Northern Perak and the speed with which they were mounted from the advanced base at Kuala Lumpur was greatly appreciated by the ground forces. Towards the end of these operations, however, the accidental release of a rocket on the ground, due to faulty wiring in the ageing Spitfires, caused the death of a civilian in the village of Salak South and a complete embargo was placed on the carriage of bombs and rockets in these aircraft. The offensive potential of the air forces was maintained, however, by the dispatch of two Beaufighters of No 84 Squadron from Tengah. Their armament was equivalent to four Spitfires and one low-grade, unconfirmed report of their first attack, on a camp north of Batu Melintang on the border between Kelantan and Thailand on 12 August 1948, credited them with killing 30 terrorists. This strike was one of a series that were mounted near the frontier with Thailand to intimidate two bodies of 600 terrorists that were reported to be massing the other side of the border.[139] With the arrival of three more aircraft of No 45 Squadron from Ceylon on 12 August, five Beaufighters were located at Kuala Lumpur for one week, before those of No 84 Squadron left for the Middle East. During this period four strikes were mounted, that on 17 August near Bentong in Pahang, which involved five Beaufighters and five Spitfires, being the heaviest to date in the campaign although it eliminated only one terrorist.

By now the terrorists were beginning to realize the effectiveness of air-strike action and pinpoint attacks against visible targets were gradually replaced by attacks on area targets covering the approximate location of camouflaged terrorist camps or concentrations. The arrival of Beaufighters at Kuala Lumpur, however, meant that it was possible to harass the terrorists still further by attacking them at night. The first planned night strike of the campaign, against a target near Kuala Krai in Kelantan, was aborted on 19 August owing to weather conditions but a successful strike was carried out on the night of the 22/23 August on a target north of Parit in Perak. No further night strikes were to be carried out until June 1950 but the feasibility of such operations, at least under moonlit conditions, had been proved and further experiments showed that flares could be successfully employed to illuminate the target area on darker nights.

After the peak in August 1948 the tempo of offensive air support operations declined towards the end of November 1948, in which month only five strikes were mounted. This decline was considered at the time to be due to the loss of contact with the terrorist forces as they split into smaller groups for operations in populated areas, but was in fact due to their withdrawal into the jungle for a period of recuperation after their failure to establish a 'liberated' area in Southern Kelantan. With the decline in air-strike activity the Spitfires at Kuala Lumpur returned to Sembawang but the introduction of drastic Government measures, including plans for resettlement and deportation, resulted in an increased flow of information concerning terrorist locations and a corresponding increase in air-strike activity. No 60 (Spitfire) Squadron returned to Kuala Lumpur, leaving No 28 Squadron to support ground force operations in Southern Johore. Twenty strikes were carried out in December 1948, bringing the total since the campaign began to 84, with an average of fourteen per month.

The year 1948 closed with the revival of an earlier demand by the Advanced AHQ Malaya at Kuala Lumpur to be allowed to mount an air attack without the preliminary siting of ground force ambushes which might prejudice the element of surprise. A compromise was arranged whereby troop movements preceding the strike were disguised and the first attack along these lines was carried out by four Spitfires and three Beaufighters on 21 December on a target near Bruas in Perak, albeit with no significant results. On 28 February 1949, however, a similar air strike, the largest in the campaign so far, was carried out by four Beaufighters and eight Spitfires (the latter carrying 20 lb fragmentation bombs for the first time) on a target near Mengkuang in South Pahang. Ground forces were impeded from following up the strike by the extensive fires which it started but subsequent intelligence revealed that at least 15 terrorists had been killed during this combined operation, at least nine of which had died as a direct result of the air strike. This was one of the most successful air strikes of the entire campaign and there is no doubt that one of the main reasons for its success was the complete surprise occasioned by the absence of troop movements in the area before the attack.

However, the tempo of air-strike activity during the first few months of 1949 showed little increase over the monthly average for 1948 as the ground forces still preferred to tackle potential targets themselves, thus denying the air forces many eminently suitable targets. A change in this so-called 'flat-foot and kukri' complex became apparent however, after Beaufighters of No 45 Squadron and Spitfires of No 60 Squadron mounted six strikes in twelve days during April 1949 against a target in the Kuala Langat Forest Reserve area of Southern Selangor. The cumulative effect of these attacks was responsible for 37 out of the 45 eliminations that were achieved and the ability of the air forces to play a major offensive role in the campaign, with no support from the ground forces other than the provision of intelligence, could no longer be ignored.[140] Demands for air co-operation steadily increased and 84 strikes were flown in the period from May to July 1949 compared with the 42 that were flown in the first four months of the same year. In May 1949 four terrorists were killed as a direct result of two strikes mounted in support of Operation 'Pussycat' in the Kaki-Bukit area near the border of Perlis with Thailand.

Although demands for air-strike action slackened off in August and September 1949 they revived, as a result of an increased flow of information from surrendered terrorists, to such an extent that they exceeded the potential of the air forces in Malaya for the first time in the campaign, despite the arrival of No 33 (Tempest) Squadron in August, and selection of the most suitable targets had to be made. On 21 October the largest strike to date, involving 62 sorties by Spitfires, Beaufighters, Tempests and Sunderlands of the RAF and Fireflies and Seafires of the RN, was carried out against a target south-east of Gemas in Negri Sembilan and during the last two months of 1949, 62 strikes, involving 388 sorties, were flown against targets throughout western and central Malaya, especially in Northern Selangor and adjoining parts of Pahang.[141] By the end of 1949 over 300 air strikes had been mounted against the terrorists with a monthly average of seventeen.

The increase of air-strike activity at the end of 1949 continued into 1950 and 58 strikes, involving over 300 sorties, were carried out in January—the highest monthly total of the Emergency so far. Forty-one sorties by aircraft of the RAF and RN were flown against targets in Negri Sembilan on 1 and 2 January alone.[142] On 7 February, however, a setback occurred when a strike was mounted too near a squatter settlement near Kulai in Johore and the exaggerated Communist propaganda that followed the resultant wounding of five civilians caused the Federal Police to issue orders to avoid the repetition of such an incident which resulted in the virtual cessation of police requests for offensive air support. The overall air-strike effort for March 1950 was reduced by over 50 per cent in comparison with the previous month and it was only after representations were made by the Advanced AHQ Malaya that these orders were clarified and the upward trend in air-strike activity was resumed. Despite this setback, however, nearly as many strikes were flown in the first four months of 1950 as in the whole of the first year of the campaign.

The offensive potential of the air forces in Malaya was considerably enhanced by the arrival of Lincolns and Brigands at the end of March and the beginning of April 1950 which enabled a greater weight of weapons to be concentrated against the more extensive targets that resulted from increasingly unreliable information. Despite the concern of Advanced AHQ Malaya to improve the technique for attacking opportunity targets by extending the practice of maintaining aircraft on an immediate call basis, the majority of air strikes continued to be mounted against pre-planned area or pinpoint targets as part of combined operations with the ground forces. Operation 'Jackpot' mounted between 15 March and early May 1950 was a typical example of one of these operations. The objective was No 2 Regiment MRLA that was located in South-Eastern Selangor and Northern Negri Sembilan and contained about 260 terrorists under the notorious Lieu Kon Kim. During the initial harassing operations, that were designed to drive the terrorists into two killing areas, three heavy air strikes were carried out on the 14, 15, and 16 April, which involved 98 sorties by Lincolns, Brigands, Spitfires, a Sunderland and a Dakota acting as an airborne tactical headquarters. Between 27 April and 30 May five more air strikes, involving 108 sorties, were mounted during the closing stages of an operation that achieved a final tally of 44 terrorist eliminations.

The arrival of medium bombers in Malaya led to a revival of night attacks, first held in August 1948, when six Lincolns attacked a jungle area near the Sungkai-Tapah road in the Trolok area of Perak on the night of 23/24 July, using twin searchlights to provide a datum.[143] On their return from this and subsequent night strikes reconnaissance flares were dropped on selected targets, which had a considerable effect on the incident rate by discouraging terrorists from attacking estates and mines and from ambushing railways, especially in the neighbourhood of Kluang, Segamat and Gemas in Johore and Negri Sembilan. Lincolns of No 57 Squadron had carried out their first operation on 26 March against a target in the 'Three Thousand Acre' jungle in Negri Sembilan[144] and on 26 July No 1 (RAAF) Squadron went into action for the first time in the campaign against a target in the Kulai-Kota Tinggi area of Southern Johore.[145] These reinforcements to the offensive air support force enabled the number of air strikes to be stepped up to a record monthly total of 106 in September 1950, involving 504 sorties, which was nearly one third more than the previous record month. By the end of December 1950 687 strikes had been flown during the year with an average of 69 a month—more than four times the monthly average for 1949.

Heavy rainstorms and floods curtailed security force action in January 1951 and there was a corresponding decline in air-strike action, but terrorist reaction to the Briggs Plan in the following month led to a recrudescence of violence in Johore, Negri Sembilan and Malacca and a series of combined operations was mounted to counteract this threat. During Operation 'Letter', in the Penggerang Peninsular of Southern Johore, spasmodic bombing and strafing over a long period caused the terrorist organization located there to split up and disperse. During the subsequent Operation 'Rumble', mounted from 10–24 February 1951 in the Kroh-Chikus and Bikam Forest Reserves of Southern Perak, 117 sorties were flown in the offensive air support role, the largest effort yet put into this area, and contributed significantly to the final tally achieved by the security forces of three terrorists killed and 23 surrendered. As a result of the success of Operation 'Rumble' a series of minor operations, 'Rainbow', 'Raven' and 'Rover', were mounted in Southern Perak up to the end of July 1951 with the limited aim of stirring up the terrorists and forcing them to keep on the move. Demands for offensive air support were continuous throughout these operations and resulted either in an increase in the rate of terrorist eliminations or a decrease in the incident rate, while the boost it gave to civilian morale was reflected in an increased flow of information from this source.

In March 1951 the Lincolns of No 61 Squadron left Malaya without relief after a four months tour during which they had participated in 97 air strikes and flown 282 sorties on which their aircraft had dropped over two thousand 1,000 lb and 500 lb bombs. An immediate drop in the tonnage of bombs dropped was apparent, only one hundred and eighteen 1,000 lb bombs being dropped in May and June 1951 compared with 996 in March and April, and a high strike and sortie rate was necessary to compensate for the loss of the Lincolns with aircraft carrying lighter weapons. Towards the end of March 1951 bombing and strafing attacks in the dense and hilly jungle terrain between Karak and Temerloh in Pahang during Operation 'Sabai' caused the complete migration of a terrorist unit and enabled Gurkha ground patrols to kill six of them. On 16 June as part of the Briggs Plan to clear Malaya of terrorists from the south northwards the largest combined operation of the Emergency so far, Operation 'Warbler', was mounted in Johore and the air forces were employed to harass the terrorists by denying them river crossings, escape routes and assembly areas and by attacking clearings and camps beyond the immediate reach of the ground forces. During the first week of this operation 242 sorties were flown by strike aircraft and the air effort was maintained at a varying intensity over a period of two months during which 145 air strikes, involving 610 sorties, were carried out. The temporary grounding of Brigands following an accident and the limitation in the range of the Vampires with which No 60 Squadron had recently been re-equipped, threw a severe strain on the air forces and when Operation 'Grasshopper' was launched on 27 June to deny the borders of Northern Johore to terrorists who had escaped from the area of Operation 'Warbler', numerous requests for immediate air-strike action could not be met, especially as three other operations, 'Raven', 'Marker' and 'Langkap', were in progress at the same time in other parts of the Federation. However, all requests that were supported by good information were accepted and carried out. Eighty-one sorties were flown in support of Operation 'Grasshopper', with no tangible results, and when Operation 'Sedge', the third and final stage of operations in the three southern states of Malaya, was launched in the Bahau area of Negri Sembilan on 12 July 1951, a further 61 sorties were flown against pre-selected targets by strike aircraft. Altogether 118 air strikes were mounted in June 1951 and 153 in July, the latter being easily the highest number mounted in any one month of the campaign as September 1950, with 106 air strikes, was the only other month when more than 100 strikes were achieved. Many of these strikes were night attacks which had become a regular commitment since their re-introduction in June 1950 with the aim of dispelling any illusions the terrorists might have that they were immune from attack after dark. Between January and August 1951, 47 strikes, involving 88 Lincoln sorties mainly by No 1 (RAAF) Squadron, were carried out at night, over half of them against targets in Perak.

On 14 August 1951 a notable air strike was carried out by Hornets, Brigands and Vampires near Sitiawan in South-Western Perak which succeeded in flushing out a strong element of No 8 Regiment Malayan Races Liberation Army (MRLA) that ground forces engaged in Operation 'Sludge' had been prevented from approaching in secrecy because of the nature of the terrain. The following month, on 12 September, a similar strike was launched by three Brigands against a terrorist camp located in the Ulu Bernam swamp area of Kuala Selangor that was inaccessible except across open water and on 8 November a further strike was mounted against this camp on receipt of information that it was still occupied. Fourteen Brigands, eight Hornets, four Lincolns and one Sunderland succeeded in almost obliterating the camp and although floods prevented troops from following up this strike to assess the damage a further convincing demonstration had been given of the ability of air-strike action to carry the offensive to the terrorists in places where ground forces could not reach.

Following the murder of the High Commissioner for the Federation of Malaya, Sir Henry Gurney, on 6 October 1951 on the Kuala Kubu Bahru to the Gap road, Operation 'Pursuit' was mounted to catch the terrorists responsible and the air forces were used to cut off their retreat and drive them into contact with the ground patrols. Extensive use was made of Lincolns and Sunderlands to maintain an air blockade along a line 5,000 yards long and three miles to the east of the scene of the ambush and offensive air support continued throughout the operation, which closed on 21 November with a disappointing tally of only seven terrorist eliminations. Similarly, few definite results were achieved by the offensive air support given to Operation 'Substitution' that was mounted near Muar in Johore from 4 to 13 December 1951, although it did enable the army unit that was operating in the area to be relieved without interruption from terrorist activity.

Little tangible result accrued from air-strike effort throughout the final months of 1951 and its effect continued to be prejudiced, as it had since the beginning of the campaign, by the necessity for target clearance and identification. Demands, however, continued at a high level and on 30 December 1951, the 1,000th air strike of the year was flown, making this year the most active in the campaign from the point of view of offensive air support. Over 4,500 sorties were flown on 1,002 air strikes during 1951—an average of 84 a month or nearly three a day that was nearly half as many again as the next most active years of 1950 and 1952.

The tempo of air-strike activity remained fairly high throughout 1952, with an average of 56 strikes flown every month, but some change was apparent in their objectives. At the beginning of the year harassing attacks against area targets over 2,000 yards square were general but the steady improvement in the quantity and quality of intelligence material as terrorist cultivation plots were spotted by photographic and visual reconnaissance planes and further information was elicited from surrendered terrorists, resulted in an increase in the number of pinpoint targets. The air forces as a result were required to provide more accurate bombing methods and the development of target marking techniques by Auster aircraft was an important step in this direction, although inaccuracies of target maps and the distortions inherent in aerial photographs frequently caused targets to be missed by the vital 200 or 300 yards. This concentration on fewer but more accurately located targets was reflected in the trend of offensive air support operations towards days of little or no activity interspersed with an occasional maximum effort.

One of the biggest efforts made during 1952 by the air-strike forces was during Operation 'Puma' in mid-February when an attack was initiated solely by the air forces, with no ground forces involved at all, for the first time during the campaign. The target area lay in Western Pahang around the rivers Enchek, Jelai-Kechil and Lenjang—a mountainous area of thick, primary jungle, fast-flowing streams and peaks over 6,000 feet in height. Up to 400 terrorists were estimated to be hiding in the area behind a protective screen of 300 aboriginal Sakai that ruled out any chance of a surprise attack on foot. It was decided, therefore, that the attack should be mounted solely by the air forces and between 13 and 15 February, eighteen Lincoln sorties were flown, followed by thirty-five Brigand sorties during the following three days. One hundred and thirty-two 1,000 lb bombs, two hundred and sixteen 500 lb bombs and 6,800 rounds of 20 mm cannon ammunition were expended on these sorties and considerable damage was caused but, as it was impossible for ground forces to follow up these strikes, no further information of its results became available.

In the latter half of February and the beginning of March 1952 several air strikes were flown in support of Operation 'Helsby' in the remote upper reaches of the Sungei Perak/Belum area of Northern Perak, six miles south of the border with Thailand. Although no positive results were achieved terrorist activity in the area was suppressed for some time and subsequent periodic strikes helped to deter its recrudescence. In the second half of 1952 strikes were flown in support of Operation 'Habitual' in the Kuantan area of East Pahang and South Trengganu, Operation 'Hive' in the Seremban area of Negri Sembilan and Operation 'Hammer' in the Kuala Langat area of Selangor. By the end of 1952 nearly 700 targets had been attacked during the year on just over 4,000 offensive sorties and over 4,000 tons of bombs, 10,000 rockets and 2 million rounds of ammunition had been expended.

During the first six months of 1953, however, offensive air support was reduced to a new low level and only 114 strikes, involving 852 sorties, were mounted, in contrast to the 364 strikes, involving 1,551 sorties, that had been mounted during the corresponding period of 1952. This reduction was entirely due to the policy of directing the main offensive air support against a few pinpoint targets and avoiding the bombing of large areas of jungle with small numbers of aircraft that was now considered to be uneconomical.[146] Some harassing strikes in support of long-term food denial operations were still carried out, however, and very occasionally the opportunity arose for mounting Hornet and Vampire attacks in close support of troops in contact with the enemy. One of the operations that was supported during the first half of 1953 was Operation 'Commodore' that was mounted at the end of May against a possible venue of a Johore State Committee meeting North-East of Kluang.[147] Nearly all the Lincolns, Vampires and Hornets that were available bombed and strafed the target area on 24 and 26 May during an operation that lasted for sixteen days and resulted in the elimination of nine terrorists and twelve of their camps.

In June 1953 offensive air support reached its nadir for the year when only five air strikes were mounted, the lowest monthly total since the first month of the campaign. In July 1953, however, the policy of restricting air strikes to heavy attacks against pinpoint targets was revised when the decline in the terrorist surrender rate over the preceding months proved that it was affected by prolonged harassing attacks from the air over wide areas. Although indiscriminate area bombardment was not accepted large scale harassing operations were re-introduced in areas where terrorists were known to be located.[148] As a result of this change in policy there was an immediate increase in the scale of offensive air support and in the last six months of 1953 one hundred and eighty-four air strikes were mounted and the number of sorties flown during the first half of the year was almost doubled. By the end of the year 298 air strikes had been mounted but the monthly average of twenty-five was less than half that of 1952.

The arrival of No 83 (Lincoln) Squadron in September 1953, in response to the Director of Operations call for a new offensive to end the Emergency, doubled the medium bomber force that was available and up to fourteen Lincolns could be provided on the few occasions when a maximum effort was required. The tonnage of bombs dropped showed a marked increase with the arrival of these reinforcements and the intensification of air-strike effort—five hundred and eighty-two 1,000 lb bombs and twelve hundred and forty-two 500 lb bombs being dropped in November 1953 in contrast to the twelve 1,000 lb bombs and one hundred and four 500 lb bombs that were dropped in March of the same year.[149] On one of these intensive air strikes in November 1953, seven Lincolns of No 1 (RAAF) Squadron succeeded in killing three of Chin Peng's bodyguard and wounding three others although the Secretary-General of the Malayan Communist Party (MCP) himself escaped injury.[150] On another occasion an example of the results that could be obtained by these relatively massive attacks that were carried out in the second half of 1953 was provided by the 145 aborigines who appealed for Government protection after one such strike, providing the security forces with valuable information while depriving the terrorists of an intelligence screen and a supply and maintenance organization by their defection.[151]

The latter part of 1953 also saw the introduction of a new phase of protracted combined operations that were carried out over a period of a year or more, instead of the one or two months of previous operations, in order to extract the maximum results and clear the country systematically state by state of the terrorist threat. The first of these operations was Operation 'Sword', mounted in an area of 100 square miles in the Bongsu Forest Reserve area of Southern Kedah from July 1953 to March 1954.[152] A series of fairly large jungle areas, including all known terrorist camps, were chosen as targets and throughout the first week of the operation Lincolns, Sunderlands and Hornets bombed and strafed them during the hours of daylight while intermittent field artillery and mortar fire maintained the offensive at night. During this week 37 Lincoln, 237 Hornet and seven Sunderland sorties were flown and since Butterworth was only 30 miles away No 33 Squadron was able to maintain its Hornets over the target area constantly during the hours of daylight. This display of concentrated air power had an excellent effect on the morale of the ground troops and during the following fortnight eleven terrorists were killed and four surrendered. Harassing air strikes were provided when required for the remainder of the operation and made a notable contribution to the disintegration of the discipline and morale of the terrorist organization. By the end of Operation 'Sword' 36 terrorists had been killed, 19 had been captured or had surrendered and 106 of their camps had been destroyed, which made it one of the most effective operations of the whole campaign.

At the beginning of 1954 the tempo of air-strike activity showed a slight increase, the 61 strikes that were mounted in March alone being the largest monthly total since August 1952. Most of these were harassing attacks except in the few cases of pinpoint or small area targets that were known to contain a reasonable concentration of terrorists. Towards the end of the year, however, improvements in target marking techniques by day and by night made it possible to achieve greater success in operations designed primarily to kill the terrorists and some increase in the number of pinpoint attacks that were carried out occurred which, together with attempts to economize in air-strike action, reduced the average monthly total of air strikes to about 25. Lincolns bombing in patterns or individually provided the main effort with Hornets acting in a supporting role. The success of this technique was evident during the offensive air operations that were mounted in July 1954 in support of Operation 'Eclipse' in the deep jungle of Kedah, when Lincolns attacked the main targets while Austers marked pinpoint targets close by which were immediately attacked by Hornets.[153] Support was also given to Operations 'Kitchener', 'Hawk' and 'Jekyll' in Johore, Pahang and Negri Sembilan during the first half of 1954[154] and, in July, Operation 'Termite' was launched. This was the most comprehensive combined operation to date in the campaign and involved a maximum effort by Lincoln and Hornet aircraft against terrorist base areas in the Kinta and Raia valleys east of Ipoh.[155] Two suspected main camps were bombed simultaneously by two formations of five Lincolns and secondary targets were bombed and strafed by Lincolns and Hornets for a period of three days. By the end of the operation in November 1954, thirteen terrorists had been killed, one had surrendered and 181 camps had been found and destroyed. In September 1954 the first attempt was made to bomb a pinpoint target by night, in this case a camp in the Jelai Gemas Forest Reserve in Kedah.[156] Ground flares were used to provide a sighting datum and all bombs fell within 100 yards of the camp, killing at least one terrorist. The State Committee member in the Kedah area was said to be so impressed with the accuracy of air strikes at this time that he was convinced that there was a traitor in his party. Another night attack in the Kuala Pilah area of Negri Sembilan, however, achieved no result as the ground liaison officer had placed datum flares on the basis of an inaccurate 1-inch map—an incident which underlined the necessity of using aerial photographs when planning air strikes in the Malayan campaign.[157]

In addition to the operations already mentioned, offensive air support during 1954 was also provided for a series of protracted operations such as Operation 'Sword', which finished in March 1954. Operation 'Ajax' in the Kulai area of Johore began in August 1954 and continued into 1955 while in September and December 1954 Operations 'Shark' and 'Latimer North' and 'Latimer South' were started in the Sungei Siput area of Perak and the Temerloh and Triang areas of North-Eastern Negri Sembilan and South Pahang, which were to last throughout 1955 and into 1956.[158] By the end of 1954 four hundred and twenty-six air strikes had been mounted during the year, with a monthly average of 36—nearly half as many again as in 1953 and a figure that was not to be exceeded during the remaining five and a half years of the Emergency.

The year 1955 began with a marked increase in air-strike activity, the 458 sorties that were flown on 65 strikes in January being the greatest number flown in any one month for over two years. However, the replacement of Lincolns by Canberras, using production bombs as stockpiles in the theatre had been depleted, meant that economies were made as far as possible in target selection. When Venoms replaced Hornets in April and October 1955 more time had to be spent on training in their primary role of air defence and further efforts were made to reduce the amount of offensive air support that was given to the ground forces. The monthly average of air strikes flown against the terrorists was reduced to less than 30 by the middle of 1955—none of which achieved any significant results. In April 1955, for example, 200 terrorists were reported to be in the Bukit-Resam Ambat area on the borders of Negri Sembilan and Selangor and since the nature of the terrain and the presence of an aboriginal security screen prevented ground forces from approaching them in secrecy, Operation 'Beehive' comprising an air attack mounted in conjunction with an airborne follow-up was launched.[159] Eleven Lincolns, four Canberras and twelve Hornets bombed and strafed the target area on 4 April 1955 but paratroops found no trace of any terrorists and the operation merely underlined the dangers of mounting a large scale operation on the uncorroborated report of one aborigine.

On 9 September 1955 an amnesty was declared in the campaign against the terrorists and an embargo was placed on all offensive air operations which was maintained for the rest of the month, all of October and most of November.[160] The terrorists, however, took advantage of this respite and, following an attack on Kea Farm New Village in the Cameron Highlands area of Northern Pahang on 20 November, restrictions on the use of offensive air support were relaxed, although ground force action was still curtailed.[161] On 25 November Canberras of No 12 Squadron based at Butterworth attacked camps in the Taiping area of Perak and three days later Operation 'Saturation' was launched following reports that Yang Kwo, the Vice Secretary-General of the MCP and Ah Ho, State Committee Secretary of the Johore Secretariat, were encamped on a hill south-west of Simpang Pertang New Village in Negri Sembilan.[162] While five battalions of troops attempted to seal off the area, Lincolns and Canberras began a systematic and intensive bombardment of the target, during which seven hundred and fifty-two 1,000 lb. bombs were dropped in the course of ten days, but with no significant results. Despite the amnesty, 300 air strikes were flown during 1955—the monthly average of 25 equalling the corresponding figure for 1953 but representing a reduction of one third over that for 1954.

Air-strike action at the beginning of 1956 continued to show the gradual decline that had been apparent at the end of the previous year but, on 6 February the Director of Operations, concerned at the paucity of kills achieved by the ground forces against the remaining hard-core terrorists, issued a directive that air attacks should have priority against all identified camps where conditions were suitable for an experimental period of two months.[163] Shortly afterwards, on 21 February, the air forces achieved their first major success in their offensive campaign when Goh Peng Tuan, the notorious commander of the 7th Independant Platoon MRLA, and thirteen other terrorists were eliminated during the course of an air strike against a camp near Kluang in Central Johore. This operation, 'Kingly Pile', took months to prepare and the target was the only camp that was attacked during the whole campaign that was definitely known to be occupied at the time. The attack was carried out by seven Lincolns of No 1 (RAAF) Squadron bombing on a time and distance to run basis from a ground marker, followed by four Canberras of No 12 Squadron bombing on a smoke marker dropped by an Auster. Two 1,000 lb bombs straddled the camp with an interval of 80 yards that was designed to produce sufficient concussion to kill all life between them—which it did. In fact, although only fourteen bodies were identifiable and were allowed as kills, up to eight others had been completely disintegrated by the force of the explosions.[164]

The elemination of this gang was a severe blow to the terrorist organization in Johore and exemplified the dividends that could accrue from offensive air support when the target location was accurately identified. Largely as a result of this operation the Director of Operations permanently enforced, on 23 April 1956, the directive giving the air-strike forces priority of action against those camps which had been located with sufficient accuracy to make them acceptable for air attack and which were known to be probably occupied at the time. However, apart from June 1956, the busiest month of the year with a total of 22 air strikes, offensive air support showed a persistent, if fluctuating, decline throughout 1956. In terms of weapon expenditure the offensive air support that was provided in 1956 was less than one quarter of that provided in 1951. This decline was attributed to the fact that army commanders were using the loopholes provided by their directive to retain potential air-strike targets for ground force action, but in fact high-grade intelligence on which air attacks could have been mounted was becoming extremely rare by this time. Most strikes continued to be mounted against Grade Four targets, that is areas of 1,000–2,000 yards square which were believed to contain some terrorists. Even when pinpoint targets were available the intelligence was not reliable and no kills were confirmed as a direct result of bombing action, despite the development of delayed action ground marker flares and radar target location devices.[165]

Apart from Operation 'Kingly Pile', most air-strike missions in 1956 were flown in support of protracted combined operations such as 'Shark', North and South, in the Sungei Siput and Cameron Highlands area of Perak and North Pahang, 'Latimer', North and South, and 'Enter' in North and North-East Negri Sembilan and South Pahang—all of which series of operations had begun at the end of 1954 and continued into 1957.[166] During December 1956 only three air strikes were mounted, bringing the total for the year to 129—the average of twelve a month being less than half that of the previous year.

During 1957 the trend towards a reduction in offensive air support action was confirmed. As the strength of the terrorists gradually declined and they turned increasingly to the defensive by avoiding all contact with the security forces, information leading to worthwhile targets became rarer. Most contacts with the terrorists were achieved by patrolling or prepared ambushes and necessitated immediate action by the ground forces. It was anticipated that the dwindling flow of precise target information that was being given to the air forces might dry up altogether and they had to accept that their remaining task lay mainly in the harassing role, which accounted for 55 per cent of the air-strike activity in 1957 in comparison with $28\frac{1}{2}$ per cent in 1956. In some quarters this was considered a misuse of air power but, since the activity of the ground forces had become largely ineffective in many parts of the Federation, harassing air attacks alone could exert the additional pressure required to increase their chances of making contact with the terrorists. Moreover, in view of the Prime Minister of the Federation's determination to use all available methods to end the Emergency by August 1958, the first anniversary of Independence, it was generally accepted that the high cost of mounting harassing air strikes for no material result was justified.

The most important target that became available in January 1957 was a pinpoint thought to be a camp of Chan Tai Chee, a District Committee Member of the Southern District of Selangor, and seven of his attendant terrorists.[167] Four Lincolns of No 1 (RAAF) Squadron dropped fourteen 1,000 lb bombs on 19 January under the control of a Target Director Post but most of them fell 600 yards from the aiming point owing to poor formation flying which caused the radar operator to lock on to a straggler and misdirect the main force. During February 1957 no air strikes at all were mounted, the first time in the Emergency, except during the amnesty in October 1955, that the air forces had not contributed offensively to the campaign in any one month. Air-strike activity continued at a low ebb during March and April 1957, those missions that were flown being mainly in support of Operations 'Shark' and 'Latimer' but with no appreciable results. In May 1957, however, the receipt of the one accurate pinpoint target in the whole year resulted in a successful air strike which, in conjunction with ground force operations, virtually destroyed the 3rd Independent Platoon MRLA under its notorious commander Teng Fook Loong in a camp seven miles North-West of Klawang in Negri Sembilan. Some 545,000 lb of bombs had already been dropped on the supposed camping site of this platoon at the end of 1956 and the beginning of 1957 but lack of accurate pinpoints had nullified their effect. At the beginning of May 1957 five Lincolns of No 1 (RAAF) Squadron and twelve Venoms of No 60 (RAF) Squadron and No 14 (RNZAF) Squadron dropped a further 94,000 lb of bombs but, although information leading to this attack was good, it was not accurate enough as the aiming point proved to be 250 yards from the terrorist camp. On 15 May, however, further information was received about this terrorist gang and 70,000 lb of bombs were dropped by five Lincolns of No 1 (RAAF) Squadron during a night strike in the Jelebu district of Negri Sembilan. Four terrorists were killed, including Teng Fook Loong and his wife, and continuous harassing by the air forces from May to October was partly responsible for the surrender of the remaining members of the 3rd Independent Platoon MRLA in the neighbourhood of Seremban in Negri Sembilan.

After this successful operation the offensive support provided by the air forces was limited to occasional harassing attacks which achieved little except keeping the terrorists on the move and further lowering their morale. Between 12 and 14 November 1957 Lincolns dropped fifty-six 1,000 lb bombs during the hours of daylight and a Sunderland dropped one hundred and ninety 20 lb bombs at night as part of a combined operation against a terrorist concentration in the Kroh-Chikus Forest Reserve in Perak and ten days later one hundred and thirty 500 lb bombs were dropped by Lincolns and Sunderlands in the Tanjong Tualang area of Perak to exploit information gleaned from two terrorists who had surrendered as a result of an air strike on 18 August 1957. Terrorist morale was known to be low in this area and it was hoped that these attacks would finally persuade them to surrender, but there is no evidence that they had any effect. By the end of 1957 only 48 air strikes had been mounted during the entire year, involving 383 sorties which was little more than one third of the offensive air support provided in 1956 and less than half the monthly totals achieved at the height of the campaign in 1950 and 1951.

During 1958 demands for offensive air support continued to decline as the few remaining terrorists became even more elusive. Static camps were practically unknown by now except along the border of Malaya with Thailand and, even when good target intelligence became available, it was often best exploited by Police Special Branch and military operations, while the shrinkage of 'black' areas where Emergency regulations still prevailed made it increasingly difficult to obtain clearance for air-strike action. Moreover, during March 1958 Sunderlands were withdrawn from 'Firedog' operations and when the last Lincolns were replaced by Canberras in September the expense of mounting harassing operations with jet aircraft for at the best debatable results became a more weighty consideration. It was generally agreed that such operations could now only be relied upon to induce terrorist movement and rarely caused them to surrender, although they continued to be useful when terrorists were located beyond the reach of the ground forces. Therefore, although sufficient aircraft were maintained throughout 1958 to meet all likely demands, the majority underwent training in their primary theatre role and economies were made in such harassing operations as were undertaken by limiting the target areas to 800–900 yards square and by putting a minimum of six 500 lb bombs into each area of 1,000 yards square in the shortest possible time.

Altogether 47 air strikes were mounted during 1958, the same number as in the previous year, but the departure of the last medium bomber squadron was reflected in a marked increase in the number of sorties that were flown by aircraft with a lighter armament. Fifteen attacks were made on accurately known targets during the year but no results were achieved as the camps were probably unoccupied at the time. Thirty-one harassing attacks were made, including a series mounted in the Ipoh/Chemor area of Perak in March and in the Parit Forest Reserve in the same state during Operation 'Bintang', which ended in September 1958 with a tally of 61 terrorist eliminations, at least five of which had surrendered as a result of a near miss during a bombing attack. This was an unusual occurrence since the terrorists had become rather disdainful of air strikes by now, believing that their chances of being hit were remote. In fact, by the end of 1958 it was clear that if offensive air support were completely denied to the ground forces for the remaining duration of Operation 'Firedog' its progress would not be greatly affected.

Despite the insignificant rate of kills achieved by air strikes, however, there was no disposition on the part of the ground forces to dispense with this form of support. Nevertheless, as the terrorist forces shrank to proportions where they constituted little more than a harassing element in the community and the hard core remnant retreated to comparative immunity beyond the Thailand border, it became necessary to review the policy of providing offensive air support solely in order to carry the offensive to the enemy when ground force patrols proved ineffective. By the beginning of 1959 the returns were no longer worth the effort and air-strike action was drastically reduced. No strikes at all took place during the first seven months of the year but, in August, several terrorist camps east of Bentong in Northern Pahang were spotted by Auster reconnaissance aircraft and, as there were no troops available in this area, two targets were bombed on 13 August by Canberras of Nos 2 (RAAF), 45 (RAF) and 75 (RNZAF) Squadrons, under the control of a Target Director Post, while a formation of Sabres from Nos 3 and 77 (RAAF) Squadrons at Butterworth strafed pinpoints that had been marked by an Auster. Four days later, on 17 August 1959, a target on the northern slopes of Bukit Tapah in Perak was attacked by Canberras and the offensive air support provided during the Malayan campaign came to an end, even though the Emergency continued for a further eleven months.[168]

Results of Offensive Air Support

The contribution made by offensive air support to the elimination of the Communist terrorists in the Malayan campaign cannot be evaluated solely in terms of the material results for any estimate of the number of casualties inflicted and the physical damage caused by the immense expenditure of bombs, ammunition and flying effort would suggest that air-strike action in this type of campaign was simply not worthwhile. For example, the eight Lincolns of No 1 (RAAF) Squadron dropped 17,500 short tons of bombs between 1950 and 1958, over half the total tonnage of bombs that was dropped during the entire campaign, and were credited with killing only sixteen terrorists and destroying twenty to thirty of their camps.[169] *In toto* some 35,000 short tons of bombs were dropped during the course of 4,067 air strikes in the campaign and expenditure on armament alone exceeded £1½ million a year at the height of the Emergency.[170]

In return for this effort several factors conspired to prevent an accurate assessment of the results it achieved. At the beginning of the campaign it was felt that the ground forces attached too little importance to the value of ascertaining the effects of individual air strikes but exigencies of time and terrain frequently prevented them from following up an attack. In any case, assessment of the casualties inflicted by air-strike action was impeded by the terrorists' practice of removing their dead and wounded from the scene of attack. For the sake of morale the rank and file of the terrorists were forbidden to discuss their own casualties amongst themselves and, since most of them were of low intelligence anyway, little information about the results of air strikes could be gleaned from those that surrendered or were captured. Few reports were ever received of terrorists who died as a result of wounds sustained during air attacks even though there must have been a number of these in view of the rigorous conditions under which they existed in the jungle and the shortage of drugs and medical supplies. Lack of information, therefore, renders any figures of casualties inflicted by air-strike action during the Malayan campaign of dubious value but some idea of the scale of achievement is given by the few statistics that are available.

During the first fifteen months of the campaign high-grade intelligence reports credited air-strike action with the deaths of 98 terrorists and the wounding of 22 others, while a further 51 had been killed and 38 wounded according to less reliable information.[171] During this period the security forces as a whole killed nearly 1,000 terrorists. One year later 126 deaths by air-strike action had been confirmed, with a further 141 unconfirmed, out of the total number of 1,641 terrorists that had been killed by the end of 1950.[172] Air-strike action was, therefore, credited with less than 10 per cent of terrorist deaths and even this estimate was almost certainly too high and was considerably reduced as the campaign progressed.

It is not surprising that few kills were achieved by air-strike action since it was inevitable that much of the air effort was wasted against an enemy who could not be seen from the air and whose exact location was rarely known even by the ground forces. Accuracy in target location and bomb aiming was essential since bomb damage was slight in jungle terrain and the effect of blast was rapidly dissipated by the trees. If a bomb missed the target by 100 yards its effect was largely nullified and in the majority of cases the inaccuracies of initial intelligence and available maps and the distortion inherent in aerial photographs ensured that this is what happened.

Air-strike action, however, was only one aspect of the offensive that was maintained against the terrorists and formed an integral part of the combined operations carried out by the security forces. Its effects, therefore, cannot be studied in isolation and the contribution it made to the successful outcome of the Emergency was not limited solely to the physical results which it achieved. By delaying the withdrawal of terrorists along certain escape routes and driving them towards prepared ambushes air strikes considerably increased the ground forces' chances of making contact with the enemy. By harassing the terrorists into moving into fresh base areas where they were not at first known or feared, a useful increase in information was frequently elicited from the local populace, while the disruption of the terrorists' camp and command organization and their need to establish new sources of food, information and money considerably weakened their offensive potential. Aerial bombardment also contributed significantly to the elimination of the terrorists by inducing surrenders. The average terrorist was of low intelligence, which was further dulled by the monotony and hardships of his existence in the jungle and, at least during the first half of the campaign, he was frequently demoralized by an attack to which he had no answer but to hide. The effect of air strikes on terrorist morale was cumulative and many captured or surrendered enemy personnel testified to their efficacy in causing panic and abandonment of camps, leaving behind valuable intelligence material. Air strikes also had a decisive effect on the morale of the native populace by encouraging them to resist terrorist exploitation and to co-operate with the security forces.

It is impossible to assess accurately the indirect effect that offensive air support had on the terrorist elimination rate but it was by no means inconsiderable. By the end of 1950 police interrogation had revealed that thirty-two terrorists had surrendered and twelve had been captured as a direct result of air-strike action[173] while the efficacy of combined ground and air operations was exemplified on 19 June 1952 when a group of terrorists were attacked by Hornets near Ipoh in Perak and all were killed by a patrol of The Malay Regiment while endeavouring to escape from the target area.[174] In 1952, the AOC Malaya decided that the success of air-strike operations could only be properly evaluated in terms of the successes achieved by the security forces being supported at the time. On an arbitrary basis all air strikes that had occurred within ten miles of the elimination of a terrorist in the preceding 28 days were considered and the results suggested that air strikes assisted the ground forces in achieving as much as 30 per cent of their eliminations.[175]

Such evidence provides sufficient justification for providing offensive air support to the ground forces in the Malayan campaign but a more telling argument in its favour is provided by those who criticised it most. At various times throughout the campaign it was claimed that air-strike action was being used to maintain the offensive against the terrorists for want of a better alternative.[176] Certainly by 1957 ground force patrols were proving largely ineffective and the terrorists would have been able to evade them indefinitely if they had not been subjected to the additional pressure of air-strike action which, by making some areas untenable, reduced the size of the area that remained to be searched. Therefore, although it was expensive and misemployed to some extent, air power frequently performed tasks which the ground forces were unable to carry out for themselves and thus played an important part in bringing the Emergency to a successful conclusion. Moreover, if further justification were needed, the effectiveness of the air effort was even more apparent when the number of men required to maintain and operate the offensive air forces is set against the number of security force personnel that were deployed on the ground. The provision of liberal offensive air support may have achieved few spectacular results but, viewed against the vast effort expended on deploying the security forces in the field, it is clear that any action that was likely to shorten the Emergency by one day was worthwhile as it achieved savings in every sphere of operations against the terrorists.

The value of offensive air support in the Malayan campaign can be readily substantiated but whether the most effective use was made of the limited resources that were available is more debatable. At the start of the campaign large terrorist groups were located close to villages in the jungle fringes and provided far better targets than occurred later on, but inaccurate maps and poor intelligence prevented them from being exploited to the full. If a greater effort had been put into improving these drawbacks at this stage, and if the target location and marking devices that were developed in the later stages of the campaign had been available at this time, offensive air support would have been more successful than it was in eliminating the terrorist threat. As more effective target marking techniques were evolved offensive air support became more effective and even with a reduced effort the casualties inflicted by aerial attack increased. Between 1956 and 1958 about thirty terrorists were killed during air strikes and on two occasions when an accurate target location was obtained and aircraft were guided on to it, fourteen out of sixteen and eight out of twelve of the terrorists present were killed.[177] Target information, however, was rarely so good and for the greater part of the campaign offensive air support was provided in a harassing role over area targets. In retrospect the systematic bombing of map squares 1,000 yards square did not achieve much and a reaction against this technique had set in by 1955. At the beginning of the campaign, however, when information was scarce, it was the only method of attempting some offensive air action. Nevertheless, continuous pressure by small numbers of aircraft tended to build up a disregard for the threat which they constituted and towards the end of the campaign spasmodic but concentrated attacks were favoured to keep the terrorists in a constant state of apprehension. It was the harassing role of the air forces that received most criticism from those concerned with economizing in offensive air support but the testimonies of captured or surrendered terrorists bore witness to the effect it had and the fall in the surrender rate after the cessation of area bombardments in 1953 substantiated their claims. Throughout the campaign it was essential to maintain pressure on the terrorists and in many cases this could be achieved with decisive effect and economy of force by offensive air-strike action. Definite limitations were imposed on such action in this type of campaign, however, and in the final analysis it had to be accepted that the cost of air operations and the effort expended bore little relation to the primitive character and the numerical weakness of the forces attacked in what was, after all, essentially a police operation.

CHAPTER 4

AIR TRANSPORT SUPPORT IN THE MALAYAN CAMPAIGN

Aims of Air Transport Support: Medium and Short Range Transport Commitments

The most important role played by the RAF in the campaign against the terrorists in Malaya was the provision of air transport support, which had the three-fold aim of enhancing the mobility and flexibility of the ground forces, by enabling them to concentrate rapidly against targets anywhere in the Federation, of sustaining operations in deep jungle for long periods, by supplying patrols and evacuating casualties, and of providing communications facilities for commanders and their staffs in the field. The poor surface communications of Malaya made it certain that, without the support of the air transport forces, the ground campaign would have been substantially prolonged and its outcome seriously prejudiced.

The various commitments of the air transport forces in Malaya ranged from flying over scheduled trunk routes to vertical take-off operations in deep jungle and required a wide variety of aircraft. These fell into two categories, medium range and short range transport aircraft, although their roles overlapped to some extent. The carriage of freight and personnel on supply dropping and paratrooping operations and on communication flights between major airfields was the primary task of medium range transport aircraft while the carriage of troops and freight into and out of jungle landing zones and commitments in the light liaison role were carried out mainly by short range transport aircraft.

The air transport support force was the largest element of the air forces that were employed in the campaign against the terrorists, with up to eight squadrons incorporating fifteen different types of aircraft operating throughout most of the Emergency.[1] Most of these aircraft were operated from their main base at Changi, from where they were detached at intervals to supplement the small force at Kuala Lumpur which bore the brunt of transport operations in support of the ground forces that were directly involved with the terrorists. In order to increase the efficiency of the administration of these transport aircraft the Far East Transport Wing was formed at Changi on 1 January 1952[2] and continued to operate until 1 April 1959, when No 224 Group Firedog Transport Support Force at Kuala Lumpur took over control of the remaining transport commitment of the campaign.[3] This deployment of transport forces and their centralized control permitted a degree of flexibility in their use which could not have been obtained if they had been detached in small units to various operational areas, although for liaison purposes one squadron of light aircraft was attached by flights to certain Army formations.

MEDIUM RANGE TRANSPORT ROLES

MEDIUM RANGE TRANSPORT AIRCRAFT

The entire commitment in the medium range transport role was carried out by a small force of four RAF squadrons, Nos 48, 52, 110 and the Far East Communications Squadron, which was supplemented at intervals by elements of No 38

(RAAF) Squadron and No 41 (RNZAF) Squadron. Only one of these squadrons was needed at any time to meet the transport support commitments at Kuala Lumpur and when the campaign began the first tour of duty there was undertaken by the Dakotas of No 110 Squadron,[4] which were relieved at intervals of six months by Dakotas of Nos 52 and 48 Squadrons.[5] In September 1949 the air transport support force was augmented by the arrival of a Dakota flight of No 41 (RNZAF) Squadron, one of whose aircraft was detached to support No 52 Squadron at Kuala Lumpur on 2 December 1949.[6] In June 1950 a flight of No 38 (RAAF) Squadron, also equipped with Dakotas, arrived in the Malayan theatre and undertook their first transport support commitments from their base at Changi soon afterwards.[7]

The first medium range transport squadron to convert from Dakotas to Valettas was No 48 Squadron, employing the first two Valettas that were received in the Far East for tropical trials, and the re-equipment of this squadron was completed by 1 April 1951.[8] No 52 Squadron completed its conversion to Valettas by September of that year, at the cost of withdrawing completely from operational commitments, while conversion of the Dakota elements of the Far East Communications Squadron, and No 110 Squadron was completed during November 1951.[9] On 30 November 1951, however, the air transport support force was depleted with the withdrawal of the Dakota flight of No 41 (RNZAF) Squadron for re-equipment in New Zealand,[10] but the four Dakotas of No 38 (RAAF) Squadron remained in Malaya and helped to compensate for the reduced serviceability which the other transport squadrons were experiencing with the Valettas.[11] They took over from No 110 Squadron for their first tour of duty at Kuala Lumpur in November 1951 but were withdrawn from operations a year later pending their return to Australia.[12]

At the beginning of 1953 one of the four Valettas of the Far East Communications Squadron was replaced by a Hastings to enhance the provision of long range transport services both within and outside the Far East theatre and in June 1955 a further element was introduced into the transport forces in Malaya with the arrival of four Bristol Freighters of No 41 (RNZAF) Squadron.[13] These aircraft were incorporated into the Far East Transport Wing and were employed on transport support operations until the end of the campaign, forming part of the detachment at Kuala Lumpur from November 1957 onwards.[14]

During 1957 the contribution of the medium range transport force to the improvement in the Emergency situation precluded any reduction in its strength but a greater concentration on its normal theatre role was heralded by the addition of a further Hastings to the Far East Communications Squadron and by the replacement of the eight Valettas of No 48 Squadron by eight Hastings on 1 May 1957.[15] On 31 December 1957, however, No 110 Squadron was disbanded, having served continuously in Malaya for over ten years, and two of its remaining Valettas were added to the complement of No 52 Squadron.[16] Throughout 1958 the medium range transport commitments were met by the Bristol Freighters of No 41 (RNZAF) Squadron and the Hastings and Valettas of Nos 48, 52 and the Far East Communications Squadrons. During 1959 four Beverleys were added to the establishment of eight Hastings in No 48 Squadron and two of the Valettas of No 52 Squadron were replaced by Dakotas.[17] By this time, however, the remaining transport commitment in direct support of the campaign against the terrorists was met by the three Valettas of No 52 Squadron and the Bristol Freighter of No 41 (RNZAF) Squadron which comprised the Air Support Force at Kuala Lumpur.[18]

Of the medium range transport aircraft that were employed during the campaign in Malaya, the Dakota and the Valetta were ideally suited for operations in the local environment. Both were capable of being manoeuvred in confined spaces, which was essential on operations over mountainous jungle terrain. Even in bad weather they demonstrated their ability to drop supplies on almost any dropping zone and remarkably few missions were aborted during the entire campaign. Of the two aircraft the Valetta was the most suitable as the Dakota had a low angle of climb, which made escape from narrow valleys hazardous, and the disadvantage of a poor forward and downward visibility which impeded the accuracy of supply drops. The serviceability rate of the Dakota, however, compared favourably with that of the Valetta. Between September 1951 and February 1952 84 per cent of the Dakota force was serviceable at any one time, compared with only 55 per cent of the Valetta force.[19]

There was little to choose between Dakotas and Valettas and Bristol Freighters, which also had a high serviceability rate, but the four-engined Beverleys that were tried out in Malaya during the later stages of the campaign proved unsuitable for operations in the prevailing conditions as they could not descend into small valleys, unload their cargoes and escape by turning in a tight circle. Contrary to expectations, however, Hastings aircraft proved successful in a tactical air supply role in Malaya. The position of the navigator in the nose of the aircraft enabled supply drops into small jungle dropping zones to be carried out extremely accurately, while the double doors in the Mark I version enabled four packs to be ejected simultaneously. With a maximum payload of 9,000 lb, compared with the 4,000 lb of the Dakota, the Hastings had considerable advantages as an air supply aircraft but, unfortunately, its wide turning circle made it unsuitable for operations over mountainous terrain and it was not used much during the later stages of the campaign when this capability became essential.[20]

SUPPLY DROPPING

Of the three major roles played by medium range transport aircraft during the Malayan campaign, supply dropping was the most important in carrying the offensive to the enemy and ensuring his ultimate defeat. Without air supply the depth of penetration of security force patrols into the jungle would have been limited by the amount of supplies which they could carry and beyond a range of five or ten miles from the jungle fringes the terrorists would have been free from molestation. Under such circumstances the security forces would have been reduced to holding a series of more or less isolated defended areas, leaving the terrorists free to operate at will over the rest of the Federation. As it happened security force patrols were able to penetrate the jungle as deeply as they wished and to remain there for periods of up to three months if necessary, instead of the four days to which they would have been limited without air supply.

Planning and Initiation of Supply Drops

Requests for air supply were radioed from jungle patrols to Army or Police District Headquarters who passed them on to the Joint Operations Centre at Kuala Lumpur for confirmation and the allocation of tasks. At the same time details of requirements were passed to the depot of No 55 Air Despatch Company RASC at Kuala Lumpur, who were responsible for packing the supplies, attaching their parachutes and also for providing personnel to act as air despatchers.[21] Supplies were normally prepared in 200 lb packs and generally consisted of the rations, clothing, ammunition and medical equipment that were necessary to maintain patrols in the field, as well as demands from individual patrol members for NAAFI supplies, including beer, cigarettes and hairdressings.[22] Care was taken however, to impress on the ground forces the necessity of limiting their requests to those that could be transported by no other means, or only at the cost of considerable time and effort, for it was easy in a country like Malaya to fall into the habit of calling on air transport aircraft for every individual requirement when these could have been made available by other methods with good planning and administration.

Air supply, however, was usually the only available method of supplying jungle patrols with heavy items such as assault boats, marine engines, wireless sets and batteries and demands for heavy and awkward loads increased when permanent forts were erected in deep jungle from 1953 onwards. Amongst items that were successfully dropped on the sites of these forts were barbed wire, screw pickets, water pumps, battery charging engines and earth augurs, as well as grass seeds for sowing the forts' airstrips and roofing felt, nails, hammers and other building materials and tools to supplement local supplies. On various occasions a tractor, equipped with disc harrows, rooters, earth scoops and grader blades, a caterpillar angle bulldozer and a railway system complete with lines and tipper trucks were successfully dropped in parts for assembly on the ground. In March 1957 55,530 lb of equipment were dropped into Fort Chabai to repair the fort's airstrip and it was not unusual for over 70,000 lb of supplies to be dropped during the first month of a fort's establishment. Thereafter, stores for the fort's shop, including gifts for the local aboriginal populace, ammunition, rations and clothing kept the average monthly weight of supplies that were dropped to each fort at not less than 20,000 lb until eventually some of this commitment was taken over by short range transport aircraft using the adjacent airstrip. To improve the amenities of these isolated forts armchairs and other furniture were dropped while chickens, ducks and goats were parachuted in to vary the diets of the garrison and several rat infested forts requested and received cats by the same method.[23]

The parachutes that were attached to supply packs were an expensive item of equipment since less than half were recovered and less than half of these were fit for renovation and re-issue. The average operational load of each parachute was 270 lb which approached the maximum weight and bulk of the load that could be handled by the RASC despatchers in the air. Since the operational load of the 'Irvin' parachute, costing £15 each, was limited to 180 lb, the more expensive 'R' type parachute, costing £32 each, was generally used, although at little more than half its maximum capacity of 450 lb. Only towards the end of the campaign, in August 1958, was the 'Utility' type of parachute developed which provided adequate support at a cost of £21 to £26 each, which, with an annual consumption of 18,000 parachutes in Malaya, represented a considerable financial saving in comparison with the 'R' type parachute.[24]

Techniques of Supply Drops

The main problem faced by aircrews on supply drop missions in Malaya was the location and identification of dropping zones in featureless primary jungle, a task which required accurate navigation and visual reconnaissance, often in bad weather, from inadequate maps or aerial photographs and one that had to be learned from scratch by pilots who had been employed almost entirely on route flying before the campaign against the terrorists began. The selection of dropping zones was the responsibility of the ground patrol commander and although an attempt was made to find some clearing or a patch of clearable secondary jungle, they seldom afforded the minimum desirable qualifications of size and visibility from the air. Most were mere holes in the jungle canopy ten yards in radius and on several occasions supply drops were made with no visual contact between the air supply aircraft and the ground. Pilots of these aircraft were briefed with the estimated map reference of the dropping zone before take off but the limited horizons of ground patrols ensured that they had only an approximate idea of their true location. As soon as the approaching aircraft was heard, therefore, a smoke grenade was fired to identify the dropping zone and coloured smoke signals and panels were used to provide an aiming point during the run-up. Radio communication between the air and the ground was normally good and the pilot awaited confirmation that the packs were recoverable before leaving the area.[25] Once over the dropping zone, however, there was little margin for error and as most were located amidst trees 200 feet high, often on the lee side of a hill, or were surrounded by swamp, it was generally extremely difficult, if not impossible, to recover supplies that missed the aiming point by as little as fifty yards. Since the flight path over the target areas was invariably at a height of under 300 feet and over dangerous terrain in uncertain weather conditions that were subject to rapid fluctuations in wind speed and direction, the fact that less than $1\frac{1}{2}$ per cent of all the supplies that were dropped during the entire campaign were lost is sufficient tribute to the high degree of skill that was acquired by the aircrews and despatchers that were employed on these operations.[26] Four or five separate supply drops were usually carried out during the course of one $2\frac{1}{2}$ hour sortie and these missions placed a severe strain on aircrews in the Malayan environment. Over 3 lb in bodyweight was commonly lost through perspiration on each sortie and fatigue was a serious problem. The casualty rate amongst supply dropping crews was four times as high as that of the infantry whom they maintained and could only be justified by the necessity of their work.[27]

While weather conditions usually prevented supply drops before mid-morning or early afternoon and frequently caused the last part of a ground patrol's day to be wasted in waiting to receive them, the main disadvantage of air supply was in compromising the security on which ground force operations depended. It was impossible to carry out supply drops surreptitiously as the position of the terrorists was unknown and they were able, therefore, to deduce the line of advance of a security force patrol from the noise made by an aircraft on a regular series of re-supply missions and take appropriate evasive action. As early as January 1949 an occupied terrorist camp was located during Operation 'Gargoyle' in Perak but was evacuated before contact could be made with the terrorists solely because the presence of the security force patrol was given away by a supply drop.[28] After this incident deceptive techniques, involving flying a regular sortie pattern over an area for some time before a supply drop, were evolved in order to convince the terrorists that this was a scheduled transport route, but the effort was never available to make much use of this practice.[29] The threat to the element of concealment and surprise which supply drops afforded is shown by those units, especially the Gurkhas, which received larger amounts of supplies than normal at longer intervals, using porters to carry them, which achieved a higher rate of terrorist eliminations as a result.[30]

Summary of Supply Drop Operations

Details of the number of supply drops and the weight of supplies delivered in this manner during the campaign are given in Annex U.[31] Unlike air-strike action the peak of air supply activity was reached in 1955 which coincided, not with the maximum terrorist offensive, but with the commitment of the maximum number of troops to deep jungle patrolling in an effort to eliminate the remaining hard-core units. Some idea of the development and the scale of air supply operations during the campaign is shown by the fact that just over 60,000 lb of supplies were dropped during the first six months of the Emergency while twelve times that amount were dropped in a single month in 1954.

The first supply drops of the campaign were carried out before the Emergency was declared, in support of Operation 'Haystack' in Northern Perak. One Dakota of No 110 Squadron was positioned as part of the RAF task force at Taiping on 12 April 1948 and carried out its first supply drop on 25 April.[32] Thereafter supply drops were made every three days until the task force was withdrawn on 27 May, after the Emergency had been declared, and a new task force established at Kuala Lumpur.[33] Altogether 222 containers were dropped on fifteen supply drops during Operation 'Haystack'. Throughout June and July 1948 occasional small supply drops to security force patrols were carried out by Dakotas of No 110 Squadron from Kuala Lumpur[34] but it was not until the withdrawal of the terrorists into the jungle after their initial offensive and the advent of trained jungle troops that the real value of air supply was appreciated by the Army. The police, however, were quick to realize that air supply provided the best method of maintaining remote posts in such states as Kelantan and Kedah and during July and early August 1948 two such posts at Batu Melintang and Gua Musang in North Kelantan were supplied almost entirely from the air.[35] With the start of operations by 'Shawforce' in Pahang and Kelantan in August 1948 and the simultaneous redeployment of troops throughout the Federation, air supply operations rose to a peak that was not reached again until January 1949. Fourteen supply drops to 'Shawforce' were carried out in 26 days by Dakotas of No 110 Squadron and by the end of August 1948 they had dropped 30,080 lb of supplies since starting their tour of duty at Kuala Lumpur.[36] During September 1948, however, there was a marked decline in the number of supply drop operations, the total weight of supplies dropped during the month being only 6,000 lb, most of which went to outlying police posts and the long range 'Ferret' groups that were operating in remote parts of Perak.

On 12 November 1948 No 110 Squadron lost their commanding officer near Serendah in Selangor in the second crash that had occurred so far on supply drop missions and soon afterwards they were relieved at Kuala Lumpur by No 52 Squadron.[37] This Squadron dropped nearly 20,000 lb of supplies before the end of the year, by which time 62,000 lb had been dropped on 41 missions since the outbreak of the Emergency. During the single month of January 1949, however, 35,920 lb of supplies were dropped on fifteen missions during a single week from the 22nd to the 29th, as a result of the expansion of the police forces which enabled larger military forces to be deployed on jungle operations. Operation 'Gargoyle' was mounted by the 2nd Gurkha Rifles on the borders of Perak, Pahang and Kelantan in January 1949 and in February Operation 'Holiday' was mounted in conjunction with the Thai police on the northern borders of Kedah and Perlis to bring the total weight of supplies that were dropped during the first two months of 1949 to 110,020 lb. The increased demand for air supply continued with Operation 'Nawab' in central Kedah in March and a total of 156,000 lb was delivered on 80 supply drops during the first three months of the year—more than twice as much as during the previous six months. These operations were carried out with a negligible loss of supplies and confirmed that air supply enabled troops, in whatever numbers, to operate in the jungle as an integral force.

From April to July 1949 68 Dakota sorties were flown in support of Operations 'Ramillies', 'Blenheim', 'Spitfire' and 'Sarong', which were mounted against more than 300 terrorists of No 5 Regiment MRLA in North Pahang and Kelantan[38] and a monthly record to date of 223,653 lb of supplies dropped was achieved during June 1949. Further operations, 'Snow White' and 'Daniel' in Pahang and Negri Sembilan, 'Pintail' and 'Widgeon' in Perak, 'Pathfinder' and 'Overall' in Kedah, 'Lemon' and 'Plunder' in Selangor and 'Leo' in Johore[39] continued the demand for air supply during the remainder of 1949. During October 1949 the eight Dakotas of No. 48 Squadron, who had taken over from No 52 Squadron at Kuala Lumpur, dropped over 400,000 lb of supplies during 200 sorties over 206 dropping zones— figures which were seven times the monthly average since the Emergency began and which were not surpassed until the height of the campaign in January 1951.

The pattern of air supply operations continued throughout 1950 with permanent commitments to police posts and larger supply drops to ground forces operating in jungle areas on pre-planned operations. April provided the peak activity of the year, with 70 sorties flown in support of Operation 'Carp' in the area east of Ipoh in Perak and 52 sorties in support of Operation 'Jackpot' in Negri Sembilan and South Selangor against No 2 Regiment MRLA.[40] During the second half of 1950 between 300,000 and 400,000 lb of supplies were dropped each month and the total for the whole year of nearly $3\frac{1}{2}$ million lb was nearly twice as high as that for 1949 and thirty times the monthly average for the first few months of the campaign. This tempo continued throughout the first few months of 1951 and the weekly record figure was broken in the last week of January when 132,000 lb were dropped over 78 separate dropping zones. Over 400,000 lb of supplies were dropped during each of the first five months of 1951, with a record monthly total to date of 479,780 lb in February. Such totals were not attained again until the end of 1953.

On 19 July 1951 the Dakotas of No 41 (RNZAF) Squadron and No 38 (RAAF) Squadron completed their first tour of duty at Kuala Lumpur, having dropped 916,632 lb of supplies in three months of intensive activity, and were relieved by No 110 Squadron who were starting their third operational tour.[41] With this change-over, however, the monthly supply drop commitment fell to under 150,000 lb, partly as a result of the progressive reduction and final termination of supplies provided on behalf of the Social Welfare Department, as it was feared that some of these were finding their way into terrorist hands, but mainly because of the re-deployment of troops in accordance with the Director of Operations Directive No 15, dated 7 August 1951.[42] This order limited 'Battle Zones' to the 'Outer Circle' of isolated mines and estates, which could be readily supplied by road, and reduced the scope of jungle patrols, although not ruling them out entirely. As a result, with the exception of the monthly commitment of about 3,000 lb to permanent police posts in Johore that was undertaken by transport aircraft based at Changi, the weight of supplies dropped to operational units declined steadily from 136,000 lb in September 1951 to 64,000 lb in December of that year. Nevertheless, the total weight of supplies that were dropped during 1951 amounted to nearly $3\frac{1}{2}$ million lb and was only slightly less than the total achieved in the previous year.

In January 1952 the severance of land communications, owing to extensive flooding throughout the Federation, resulted in an increase in the weight of supplies that were dropped in that month to 219,830 lb while the mounting of Operation 'Helsby' in February close to the borders of Perak with Thailand, caused a further increase in demand and a monthly figure of 306,511 lb.[43] During this operation Valettas were used for the first time on supply drop missions in Malaya and through-out the remainder of 1951 they shared a monthly supply dropping commitment of nearly 250,000 lb with the remaining Dakotas of the transport support force. Over 70 per cent of these supplies went into jungle clearings while the remainder went to the thirteen police posts whose supply by road was either impossible or entailed too great a diversion of troops for escort duties.[44]

During the first half of 1953 the volume of supplies dropped by air showed a considerable increase to an average of 12,000 lb a day in May and June owing to the construction of a number of permanent police forts in deep jungle areas whose only means of supply was by air and which required certain items of heavy equip-ment during the construction phase. This increased demand continued throughout the second half of the year with the advent of protracted ground force operations that were designed to clear the Federation systematically of the terrorist threat. From July 1953 to March 1954 two battalions of infantry were almost continuously deployed on Operation 'Sword' in the Bongsu Forest Reserve of Southern Kedah, while a further four battalions were deployed in the deep jungle of North West Pahang on Operation 'Valiant' from October to December 1953.[45] These forces were entirely dependent on air supply and in the latter case the appallingly difficult terrain of the operational area posed severe problems for the aircrews of the transport planes involved. Most of the dropping zones were at heights of 4,000 to 5,000 feet and were surrounded by cloud-enveloped peaks rising to 7,000 feet. Under such conditions several sorties were often required to deliver one load of supplies but, despite these difficulties the ground forces were kept supplied through-out the entire operation.

The mounting of several other operations in different parts of the Federation at the same time as Operation 'Valiant' meant that the Valettas of the Far East Transport Wing had to deal with more than double their normal supply drop com-mitment during November 1953 and extra aircraft had to be deployed from Changi to Kuala Lumpur while No 55 Air Despatch Company was reinforced from other RASC companies in Malaya.[46] In this one month 728,647 lb of supplies were dropped, a total that was not surpassed until March 1955 and the second highest monthly total of the entire campaign. By the end of 1953 nearly 4½ million pounds of supplies had been dropped during the course of the year—30 per cent more than in 1952.

During 1954 the air supply commitment continued to increase as the terrorists completed their withdrawal into deep jungle areas and security force patrols were sent after them. The construction of jungle forts progressed and necessitated dropping further heavy equipment as well as the normal monthly commitment of 20,000 lb of supplies to the seven that were already operational. From an average of 290,000 lb a month during the first quarter of 1953 the air supply commitment rose to 450,000 lb a month during the first quarter of 1954. To meet this demand No 55 Air Despatch Company RASC was re-established with two complete air supply platoons and plans were laid for deploying up to fourteen Valettas at Kuala Lumpur during special operations.[47] In July 1954 Operation 'Termite', the largest combined operation of the campaign, was launched in Northern Perak and the air supply force of six Valettas from Kuala Lumpur dropped 27,000 lb of supplies on the first two days of the operation into three dropping zones that had been prepared by paratroops of the 22nd Special Air Service Regiment.[48] During the first week of this operation 58,787 lb of supplies were dropped in difficult mountainous country and helped to raise the monthly total for July 1954 to 653,413 lb. The second half of 1954 showed no slackening of the demand for air supply and Operations 'Hawk' and 'Apollo' in the Raub and Kuala Lipis areas of Pahang and 'Ajax' in the Kulai area of Johore[49] helped to raise the monthly average weight of supplies dropped from July to December 1954 to over 650,000 lb, with a maximum of 724,230 lb in November. The total of supplies dropped during 1954 amounted to nearly 6·8 million lb—over 40 per cent more than in 1953 and the second highest annual total of the campaign.

The policy of deploying troops on protracted operations in deep jungle continued throughout 1955 and the numbers thus engaged reached a peak for the entire Emergency. The resulting air supply commitment placed a heavy burden on the resources of the Valetta force at Kuala Lumpur and the advent of four Bristol Freighters of No 41 (RNZAF) Squadron into the Far East Transport Wing provided welcome reinforcements.[50] Apart from Operations 'Apollo' and 'Shark' in Pahang and Perak, which had begun during the second half of 1954, a further series of large scale operations, 'Latimer North' and 'Latimer South' and 'Nassau', were mounted in South Pahang, North East Negri Sembilan and the Kuala Langat area of Selangor during 1955[51] and helped to raise the monthly average weight of supplies dropped to 650,000 lb on over 170 sorties. The final total for the whole year, nearly 7·8 million lb, was a record for the whole Emergency and represented an increase of 16 per cent over the amount dropped in the previous year. The record weight of supplies dropped in any single month of the Emergency was achieved in March 1955 when 808,035 lb were dropped during 218 sorties—a greater volume than had been dropped during the entire first year of the campaign.

Throughout 1956 the security forces remained fully extended on anti-terrorist operations, carrying out major sweeps during Operations 'Shark' in the Sungei Siput area of Perak, 'Gabes' in the deep jungle of the Perak and Kelantan border area and 'Bonanza' in South Selangor,[52] as well as routine patrolling and food-denial operations in all areas where Emergency restrictions still prevailed. In addition the paratrooping operations of the 22nd Special Air Service Regiment, designed to prevent the establishment of terrorist camps in deep jungle, were extended during 1956 and they required continuous re-supply from the air. Just over 6 million lb of supplies were dropped during the year, with a monthly average of 500,000 lb on 130 sorties—a decrease of over 20 per cent on the effort expended in the previous year.

Several of the ground force operations that were started during 1956 continued into 1957, including Operations 'Huckster' in the Kluang area of Johore, 'Latimer North', 'Latimer South' and 'Enter' in North and North East Negri Sembilan and 'Gabes' in Perak and Kelantan,[53] while the air supply of certain jungle forts remained a regular commitment. The monthly weight of supplies dropped continued at a fairly high level, averaging nearly 400,000 lb, but the final figure for the year of 4·8 million lb represented a decrease of 20 per cent over the amount dropped during 1956 and was 40 per cent less than the total achieved in the peak year of 1955. Nevertheless, although by the beginning of 1958 offensive air support could have been dispensed with without affecting the remaining course of the campaign, the successful prosecution of ground force operations against the remaining terrorists demanded a continuing effort from the air supply force of three Valettas and one Bristol Freighter at Kuala Lumpur and the addition of a further Bristol Freighter to this force during the bad weather of the final months of 1957 was of great value in meeting this commitment.[54]

During 1958 the dispersal of the main bodies of troops to the North and South of the Federation for operations in Perak and Johore resulted in the comparative isolation of the main air transport base at Kuala Lumpur from operational areas, but the endurance of the Valettas and Bristol Freighters proved equal to the increased length of sortie that was required of them. However, as the ground battle moved further away from lines of communication and deeper into the jungle demands for air supply increased, while the the re-arming of certain artillery units with 4·2 inch mortars in place of 25-pounder field guns added a new requirement for occasional heavy air drops of mortar ammunition.[55] Furthermore, throughout the second half of 1958, Pioneers were withdrawn from fort supply work, owing to their poor serviceability, and this commitment was added to the burden already carried by the Valettas of the air supply force.[56] Thus, although the planned task for the force during 1958 had been to drop 400,000 lb of supplies each month during the course of 100 sorties of $3\frac{1}{2}$ to 4 hours duration,[57] these figures were exceeded in all but two months of the year and the final total of over 5·3 million lb represented an increase of 17 per cent on the effort expended in 1957. Late in August 1958 a large scale offensive, Operation 'Tiger', was launched against the South Johore Regional Committee of the MCP[58] and helped to increase the weight of supplies dropped in that and the following month to over 500,000 lb—the highest monthly totals for eighteen months and amounts that were not to be exceeded during the remainder of the campaign.

By the beginning of 1959 anti-terrorist operations were concentrated almost entirely in Northern Malaya and fewer ground patrols were deployed on jungle patrols, but their deeper penetration into remote and difficult terrain ensured that there was little reduction in the air supply commitment during the early months of the year. Some slackening in demand was apparent towards the middle of 1959, however, when the monthly task fell to under 250,000 lb, largely because Operation 'Seladang' was mounted in an area of Pahang where good ground communications obviated the necessity for extensive air supply.[59] In October 1959, however, Operation 'Bamboo' was launched in a less accessible part of Perak and the air supply effort increased accordingly.[60] However, some relief was granted to the strained resources of the air supply force at Kuala Lumpur at this time by the advent of the RMAF to full operational strength and as their Pioneers gradually took over the re-supply of jungle forts it was possible to consider some reduction in this force since the Valettas were showing the effect of continuous operation and were affording serious maintenance problems.[61] In fact, by the end of December 1959 it became clear that the normal air supply commitment of about 225,000 lb a month could no longer be met and, although this form of support had been taken for granted by the ground forces for several years and no limit had been placed on it, Brigade Headquarters were warned that a temporary reduction in effort was inevitable and that they should prune their bids accordingly.[62] During January and February 1960 the 28th Commonwealth Infantry Brigade, operating in the Operation 'Bamboo' area of Perak, showed considerable ingenuity in re-supplying its troops without overtaxing the resources of the air supply force and the total amount of supplies dropped fell to 217,000 lb a month. This temporary respite enabled the Valetta force to regain its normal effectiveness and restrictions on their support were lifted. During March and April 1960 nearly 500,000 lb of supplies were dropped, mainly in the Operation 'Bamboo' area, but the withdrawal of the 1st Battalion The Royal Australian Regiment for redeployment in May was reflected in a reduction in the demand for air supply. In June 1960, however, the 3rd East Anglian Regiment was redeployed in inaccessible country in Perak[63] and the air supply commitment rose again to over 200,000 lb a month. In July 1960 No 52 Squadron was transferred from Kuala Lumpur to RAAF Butterworth near Penang and the saving in flying time to the main operational areas in Perak which this move effected resulted in an increase in their supply dropping capacity. During July, the last official month of the Emergency, 251,728 lb of supplies were dropped, including 30,485 lb by Pioneers of the RMAF, but the campaign continued for several months afterwards and the deployment of security forces in the border areas of Northern Perak necessitated an average supply drop commitment of over 200,000 lb a month for the remainder of 1960.

For twelve years air transport supply was the major contribution of the air forces in Malaya to the successful prosecution of the campaign against the Communist terrorists. Without its assistance in maintaining troops in the jungle and re-supplying remote police posts, much of the effort made by the security forces would have been nullified and it would have been impossible to maintain that pressure on the terrorists which led to their virtual elimination. It is not possible to assess the contribution made by air supply to the successes achieved by the ground forces in definitive terms, although some attempt to do so was made towards the end of 1952 when a calculation was made using the arbitrary parameter of any supply drop that had occurred within ten miles and the preceding 28 days of the elimination of any terrorist.[64] This analysis suggested that, during the last six months of 1952, air supply directly assisted security forces in achieving between 15 per cent and 18 per cent of their eliminations. The extended patrolling time of the ground forces in jungle terrain, which depended largely on air supply, clearly had a direct bearing on the terrorist elimination rate, therefore, but it also had an important indirect influence in harrying the terrorists and forcing them to retire to comparatively inaccessible areas in order to survive, thereby reducing their offensive potential to the stage where it constituted little more than a nuisance to the welfare and security of the country.

PARATROOPING

Besides increasing the mobility of the ground forces in Malaya by air supply, medium range transport aircraft also helped to increase the flexibility of their operations by carrying paratroops. With the partial withdrawal of the terrorists into deep jungle late in 1951 and early in 1952 some means of introducing troops swiftly into these areas, without betraying their presence to the effective aboriginal intelligence screen that invariably surrounded terrorist concentrations, was clearly required. The solution to this problem was provided by the air transport support forces which, using medium range aircraft in a paratrooping role and troop-carrying helicopters, not only preserved some of that element of surprise on which successful attacks on the terrorists depended, but also obviated the need for prolonged and exhausting jungle treks which so reduced the offensive potential of the security forces.

Techniques of Paratrooping

The problems of mounting paratroop operations in Malaya were greater than in most theatres of war. The rugged central spine of the country, to the foothills of which the terrorists had largely withdrawn by the end of 1952, was almost completely covered by primary jungle comprising trees that rose to heights of 200 feet or more and which formed an almost impenetrable canopy. Besides exposing paratroops to an unwarranted risk of injury the success of any operation was seriously prejudiced so long as the majority of each stick of paratroops was caught up in the tree tops. From August 1952 onwards, therefore, techniques designed to overcome this basic problem were evolved by the RAF Parachute Training School at RAF Changi and were tested on operations by the 22nd Special Air Service Regiment.[65] Initial experiments using a knotted rope for paratroops to descend from tree tops to ground level proved a failure because of the fatigue which they experienced so, during 1953, a special abseil gear was developed which consisted of 200 feet of webbing carried in a bag attached to a special harness. Over 300 operational descents were carried out using this gear without any major casualty during the early months of 1953 but three fatal accidents suffered during a drop of 50 paratroops in the Bongsu Forest Reserve of South Kedah during Operation 'Sword', which was mounted in July of that year,[66] indicated that the method of attaching the abseil harness was not entirely satisfactory. After exhaustive research at the Parachute Training School an improved lowering device was perfected which was used successfully by 40 paratroops during Operation 'Termite' in July 1954 with only seven minor injuries resulting[67]—a casualty rate that compared favourably with paratrooping operations over open country. Further research into improving the equipment and techniques employed on paratrooping operations in Malaya was not neglected, however, and in 1957 a reduction in the dead weight of the containers that were fastened to the paratroops before they jumped helped to decrease the risk of personal injury and to increase their fighting efficiency.[68] Unfortunately, experiments in the use of a lightweight abseil device proved disappointing under the arduous conditions imposed by jumping into tree top dropping zones and the heavy and awkward standard gear that was employed until the end of the campaign was a considerable handicap to the mobility of the paratroops.

Summary of Paratrooping Operations

Paratroops were employed for the first time in the Malayan campaign during Operation 'Helsby' in February 1952 when 54 members of B Squadron 22nd Special Air Service Regiment were dropped in the remote upper reaches of the Sungei Perak, some six miles from the Thailand border.[69] The dropping zone consisted of easily located 'padi' between two jungle covered massifs which rose to 4,000 feet, but high ground to the north meant that the four Dakotas employed on this operation had to make a tight circuit with a sharp descent to the dropping height and then an immediate sharp climbing turn to port to pull out of the valley. There was a rapidly increasing east wind over the dropping zone, which was accentuated by the funnel-like configuration of the valley, and this, combined with a natural reluctance to undershoot near a fast flowing river, ensured that all but four of the paratroops overshot the dropping zone. Forty-four troops landed in trees up to 150 feet in height but sustained only light casualties and, as they were each equipped with 100 feet of rope, they rapidly concentrated for the attack on the terrorist target. This operation provided the first proof that parachuting into primary jungle was feasible under operational conditions in the Malayan campaign. Considerable thought and training was therefore devoted to developing and improving paratrooping techniques, which culminated in November 1952 with a completely successful operational drop of ten men into deep jungle near Pasir Puteh in the Kuala Krai district of Kelantan during Operation 'Copley'.[70] The success of this operation led to an increased demand for paratrooping operations and, under the arrangements made for Operation 'Firebrigade' in February 1953, fifteen paratroops of the 22nd Special

Air Service Regiment, elements of No 55 Air Despatch Company RASC and one Valetta and its crew of the Far East Transport Wing were held in readiness at Kuala Lumpur to provide an immediate striking force.[71]

After Operation 'Sword' in South Kedah in July 1953[72] no more large scale paratroop drops were carried out until July 1954, during which period improvements were made to the abseil gear then in use. On 8 July 1954, however, 180 paratroops of A, B and D Squadrons of the 22nd Special Air Service Regiment were dropped from Valettas of the Far East Transport Wing into the Kinta and Raia valleys east of Ipoh in Perak during Operation 'Termite'.[73] Having landed on targets previously marked with smoke candles by an Auster of No 1907 Flight, No 656 Squadron, the paratroops cut dropping zones into which heavy supplies were dropped by re-supply aircraft. These included mechanical saws and explosives for the preparation of helicopter 'pads', into which non-paratrooping forces were flown. Although a disappointing total of only fifteen terrorist eliminations resulted from this operation it underlined the role that paratroops could play in combined operations in jungle territory. Since helicopters were scarce, their use was precluded at certain altitudes and as it was not always possible to provide landing zones for them, it was felt that there was a need for additional paratrooping forces to ensure flexibility in the overall conduct of the campaign. Plans were accordingly laid for establishing a fourth squadron of the 22nd Special Air Service Regiment and for training four more paratroop companies, one Malay and three Gurkha, while standing orders were prepared for reinforcing jungle forts by paratroops in case of emergency (Operation 'Medal') and for the provision of a Valetta and a jungle rescue team to stand by at one hour's notice at Changi in case an aircraft ditched in the jungle.[74]

However, few opportunities occurred for major paratrooping operations against the terrorists after 1954 as the helicopter force in Malaya was expanded and proved capable of introducing a greater number of less specialized troops into the jungle more quickly and with less risk of personal injury. When paratroops were employed on combined operations, they were usually the precursors of trooplifting helicopters. In fact, helicopters were also used for paratrooping operations, besides medium range transport aircraft, when it was necessary to achieve an accurate drop into a small target area—operations for which their ability to hover at about 750 feet above ground level, the absence of slipstream and their double exits made them especially suitable.

During 1956 the techniques of paratrooping into tree top dropping zones was not used once and there were only a few occasions when paratroop drops were called for over open ground. In June 1957 33 troops of the 22nd Special Air Service Regiment were dropped into an area of primary jungle in Perak[75] and a few other practice drops were successfully carried out. During 1958, however, there were only two calls for paratroop operations. In January a visiting RAF Beverley was used to drop troops into difficult jungle swamp in Perak and in June a routine training drop was diverted onto an open dropping zone on Penang Island as part of a show of force against the local terrorists.[76] There were no further operational paratroop operations during the campaign but the medium range transport aircraft of the air forces in Malaya continued to provide aircraft whenever needed for training purposes.

COMMUNICATIONS

In addition to their air supply commitment and the provision of aircraft for paratrooping operations, the medium range transport aircraft force in Malaya played an important part in the redeployment of ground forces against the terrorists by transporting personnel and freight between the main airfields of mainland Malaya and Singapore Island. At the start of the campaign there were not enough troops or police to combat the terrorist threat at all potential danger points and, in a country so poor in surface communications as Malaya, the transport services that were provided by the air forces were of vital importance in reinforcing threatened areas with the minimum of delay. Lateral communications from east to west of the country were particularly poor and airlifts from Ipoh or Taiping to Kota Bharu or from Kuala Lumpur to Kuantan were of particular value in reinforcing the remoter parts of Kelantan, Trengganu and Pahang. Furthermore, although transport between many areas in the Federation was possible overland it often entailed delay and the provision of heavy escorts and air transport proved quicker and more economical. As the campaign progressed, air transport support in a medium range communications role became a regular commitment and airfields that were capable of accommodating the Dakotas and Valettas of the Far East Transport Wing were developed throughout the Federation. By 1955 there were seventeen of these airfields (*see* Annex Q), five of them on Singapore Island, three in Perak, two in Kelantan and one each in Kedah, Province Wellesley, Johore, Selangor, Trengganu, Pahang and Negri Sembilan.[77] All of these airfields were within $2\frac{1}{2}$ hours' flying time by medium range transport aircraft from Kuala Lumpur.

In addition to special flights between airfields within the Federation of Malaya, the medium range transport aircraft that were based at Changi were also responsible for maintaining scheduled courier services and flying special missions on demand throughout the command area of the Far East Air Force, to places as far apart as Ceylon, Hong Kong, Saigon, Iwakuni in Japan, Rangoon, Clark Field in the Philippines, Kuching in Borneo and Australia.[78] Regular scheduled services were also provided within the Malayan theatre and by September 1950 weekly return flights were made from Changi to Butterworth and on to Car Nicobar in the Indian Ocean from Changi to Labuan in North Borneo, while twice-weekly flights were made from Changi to Kuala Lumpur and thrice-weekly flights from Changi to Saigon and Hong Kong.[79] Besides these scheduled passenger flights, weekly return ambulance flights between Changi and Kuala Lumpur, Ipoh and Taiping and between Changi and Labuan were inaugurated late in 1950 to transfer casualties from local British Military Hospitals to Singapore for evacuation to the United Kingdom along the trunk route services provided by the Hastings aircraft of the Far East Casualty Evacuation Service.[80] The internal casualty evacuation service within Malaya catered for both stretcher and sitting cases and its aircraft, initially Dakotas and subsequently Valettas, were fully equipped and staffed for their air ambulance role and considerably facilitated the repatriation of casualties sustained in operational areas. In addition to this regular commitment in support of the Malayan campaign, several ambulance flights were flown by the Far East Transport Wing during 1950 and 1951 between Changi, Hong Kong and Iwakuni in Japan as one stage in the repatriation of those wounded in the Korean War.[81]

Scheduled and unscheduled communications flights constituted the main commitment of those medium range transport aircraft of the Far East Air Force that were not on detachment at Changi for air supply and other duties, but even the latter aircraft were called upon to carry out numerous sorties in this role when the occasion demanded.

Summary of Communications Operations by Medium Range Transport Aircraft

Between 1951 and 1954 the Air Movements Section, FEAF handled about 2,000 tons of freight and 20–30,000 passengers a year, figures which rose to over 6,000 tons of freight and an average of nearly 70,000 passengers a year between 1956 and 1960.[82] Over half of this effort was expended in direct support of the campaign against the terrorists in Malaya.

At the start of the campaign before the expansion of the security forces eased the shortage of manpower, the rapid reinforcement of threatened areas was of particular importance and the services of medium range transport aircraft were in constant demand for the carriage of passengers and freight. During Operation 'Haystack' in Northern Perak in May 1948 Dakotas transported one squadron of the RAF Regiment to Taiping and soon afterwards two platoons of the Malay Regiment were flown from Changi to Kuantan.[83] Valuable experience was gained in moving large numbers of troops by Dakota aircraft and when the operations of 'Shawforce' in Perak in August 1948 required the large scale redeployment of troops to the north of the Federation,[84] these aircraft were equal to the demands that were made on their services. By the end of August 1948 Dakotas of No 110 Squadron at Kuala Lumpur, besides dropping over 30,000 lb of supplies, had airlifted 421 passengers and nearly 47,000 lb of freight since their tour of duty had begun in June. A notable example of the economy of effort combined with maximum achievement that could be obtained by the judicious use of the limited medium range transport force that was available occurred on 11 August 1948. Two companies of the Malay Regiment were airlifted across the Federation from Butterworth to Kota Bharu, from where 85 Police recruits were transported to Kuala Lumpur. In addition two large contingents of naval personnel were airlifted from Singapore to Penang to provide a total of 365 passengers carried on one day by four Dakotas, two of them from the task force at Kuala Lumpur and two from the main transport force at Changi. Out of a total of 38 flying hours by these aircraft only nine were unproductive and the overall task represented a saving of 6,150 man hours of travelling by surface communications.[85] This operation was typical of the communication tasks that were undertaken by medium range transport aircraft throughout the campaign in Malaya.

By September 1948 most of the available trained forces had been deployed and only 220 passengers and 19,000 lb of freight were transported by No 110 Squadron at Kuala Lumpur. However, the arrival of further troop reinforcements after November 1948 and the deployment of military units on jungle operations was reflected in a marked increase in airlift operations. Operations 'Gargoyle' and 'Holiday', which were mounted early in 1949 against the terrorist organization in Perak, Kelantan and Pahang,[86] caused an increase in the number of passengers that were carried by No 52 Squadron at Kuala Lumpur from 200 in January to just under 1,000 in February, while the amount of freight transported by this squadron during the same period increased from 20,000 lb to 60,000 lb. Meanwhile, aircraft based at Changi had been carrying out special communications flights and courier services both within and outside the Federation and the total number of passengers carried by medium range transport aircraft in the Malayan theatre during February 1949 had increased to 1,770—twice as many as the average number that were airlifted in each of the previous seven months of the campaign. For the remainder of 1949 the average number of passengers carried by these aircraft remained at over 800 a month, while freight was transported at an average rate of 60,000 lb a month. By July 1950 two of the medium range transport squadrons in Malaya had each achieved 60,000 ton miles in one month, although not all were in direct support of the campaign against the terrorists.[87]

On 6 September 1950 the first airlift by Dakota of casualties sustained in the Malayan theatre took place, when 36 soldiers were flown from Kuala Lumpur to Changi.[88] Altogether 166 casualties were airlifted on internal services within Malaya during September 1950 and, although as many as 214 were flown on these flights during March 1951, the average number remained at about 130 a month for the next four years. Meanwhile, on 13 September 1950 the first casualty evacuation flight by Hastings from Changi to the United Kingdom took place and the aero-medical services of the medium range transport aircraft of the Far East Air Force were further extended in the same month with occasional flights to Hong Kong and Japan.[89] In addition to the inauguration of these aeromedical flights, scheduled courier and special flights within the Far East theatre had increased to nearly 150 a month by the end of 1950. On those flights that were made to or from Seletar, Tengah, Changi, Butterworth and Kuala Lumpur, most of which were directly concerned with Emergency tasks, an average of 800 passengers, 60,000 lb of freight and 4,000 lb of mail were flown during each month of 1950.[90]

During 1951 and 1952 the Dakotas of the medium range transport force underwent progressive replacement by Valettas but, despite this conversion programme and continuous demands for air supply operations, scheduled communications and special flights in support of the campaign against the terrorists were maintained. The monthly average of passengers carried increased to over 1,000 while the amount of freight that was transported within the Federation showed a marked increase to over 400,000 lb a month. Notable operations during the year included the carriage of over 200 personnel of the 3rd Battalion, The Malay Regiment, together with 70 policemen and their equipment, between Kluang, Kota Bharu and Kuala Lumpur in December, and of 120 officers and troopers of the 22nd Special Air Service Regiment from Kuala Lumpur to Kota Bharu in support of Operation 'Helsby' in February.[91] Regular flights were made throughout the year to Kuching in North Borneo to ferry Dyak trackers to Malaya for use in jungle operations and, during the whole year, over 16,000 passengers and 4 million lb of freight were transported by medium range transport aircraft in support of the campaign.

During 1953 the withdrawal of the terrorists to deep jungle and the increasing efficiency of the Federal Police enabled troops to be concentrated for offensive action in Malacca, Pahang, Negri Sembilan and Selangor, with the intention that civilian security forces should subsequently take over responsibility for these states, thereby freeing the bulk of the Army for operations in Perak and Johore. This operational plan required a large scale redeployment of forces and the number of passengers carried by medium range transport aircraft within the Federation averaged over 2,000 a month throughout the year, while the amount of freight transported continued at the rate of over 400,000 lb a month. 1954 witnessed a further improvement in the general Emergency situation and the partial withdrawal of troops from Kelantan, Eastern Pahang and Western Perak ensured that there was no reduction in the communications commitment of the Valetta force in Malaya. In fact, the positioning of troops for a series of operations in Perak and Johore, in addition to their regular commitments, resulted in an increase of over 50 per cent in the number of passengers that were carried by this force during 1954 in comparison with the previous year.

During 1955 large parts of Kelantan, Trengganu and Pahang were declared 'white' and over half the remaining military forces that were deployed in these areas at the beginning of the year were concentrated in other areas where they were most needed before its end. A typical trooplifting operation was carried out in September when four rifle companies of one battalion were flown by Valettas from Kuala Lumpur to Kluang for further redeployment by helicopter.[92] Throughout 1955 the monthly trooplifting task achieved by the medium range transport force was consistently higher than in the previous year and the annual total represented an increase of over 100 per cent. 1955 proved to be the year in which this force achieved its maximum effort in a communication role but, even so, the number of sorties that were flown in meeting this task amounted to less than 25 per cent of those that were flown on air supply missions.

During 1956 and 1957 the amount of freight that was carried by the medium range transport force in Malaya increased to nearly three times the amount that was transported during 1953 and 1954 but the number of passengers that was carried declined as the areas free from Emergency restrictions expanded and troops were concentrated in the North and the South of the Federation for operations against the remaining terrorists. The total effort in the medium range communications role was halved during this period, which was fortunate as, by the beginning of 1958, the serviceability of the Valettas was giving cause for concern and it was only with difficulty that the air supply force at Kuala Lumpur was maintained at three aircraft.[93] Priority was given to supply drop operations and some communications commitments of those Valettas that were based at Changi were postponed or cancelled. Even so, the number of troops that were carried by these aircraft during 1958 showed a slight increase over the number carried during 1957 and a similar increase was apparent during the following year. Even during the last few months of the Emergency in 1960 medium range transport aircraft continued to provide scheduled services within the Federation while the gradual withdrawal of troops from operational areas as the campaign drew to its close necessitated a number of special trooping flights. The final totals of the number of passengers and the amount of freight that were transported during the year were nearly twice as high as the corresponding figures for 1954.

SHORT RANGE TRANSPORT ROLES

COMMUNICATIONS BY LIGHT AIRCRAFT

Throughout the campaign medium range transport aircraft played an important role in the carriage of freight and the deployment of troops throughout the Federation. There were, however, only seventeen airfields that were capable of operating these aircraft and most of those were located in the populous coastal regions, especially on the western littoral, and were some distance from the deep jungle areas of the spinal ridge where the main offensive against the terrorists was mounted after the initial defensive stage of the campaign. There was an obvious need, therefore, for aircraft that could establish communications within those areas where medium range aircraft could not operate and this fact, combined with the necessity of aerial reconnaissance as a remedy for the lacuna in intelligence of the terrorists' locations, ensured that a build up in the strength of the light aircraft force in Malaya came high on a list of priorities.

Airstrips Suitable for Light Aircraft

The main problem in establishing light aircraft communications in remote parts of Malaya before the introduction of helicopters, was the shortage of suitable airstrips. A number of temporary grass airstrips had been constructed during the Second World War and these were developed and augmented during the course of the campaign until they formed a fairly extensive network throughout the Federation (*see* Annex Q). In August 1951 there were 50 airstrips in Malaya that were suitable for light aircraft only, and by May 1955 there were 68, of which 33 could accommodate Auster, Pioneer and Beaver aircraft, 28 could accommodate only Austers and Pioneers and the remaining seven were attached to jungle forts and were suitable only for Pioneer aircraft.[94] Of these 68 light aircraft strips, eight of which were suitable for use only in an emergency, there were eighteen in Pahang, eleven in Johore, ten in Perak, nine in Selangor, six in Negri Sembilan, five in Trengganu, three in Kelantan, three in Kedah, two in Malacca and one on Singapore Island.

No 656 Squadron, Austers: Deployment and Summary of Operations

Throughout the campaign the main commitment in a short range communications and light liaison role was undertaken by the Austers of No 656 AOP/LL Squadron operating under the joint aegis of the RAF and the Army. In June 1948 there was only one Auster flight in the Far East, No 1914 Flight at Sembawang which was equipped with five aircraft.[95] On the outbreak of the Emergency it became evident that communications would play a vital role in the campaign and an immediate request was made by the Army for the support of a squadron of five flights of Austers to be deployed at strategic points throughout the Federation. No 1914 Flight was, therefore, transformed into No 656 Squadron, consisting of three reconnaissance flights and one communications flight which were equipped with the 28 Austers that had been lying crated at Seletar when the Emergency began and which were rapidly assembled by the RAF.[96] Personnel for the existing RAF flight and the new communications flight were provided by the RAF while the remaining flights were manned by the Army. The total complement of No 656 Squadron on its formation on 1 July 1948, with an Army major as the commanding officer and an RAF flight lieutenant as the adjutant, was 25 Army officers, four RAF officers, one RAF NCO pilot, 68 Army other ranks and 36 RAF other ranks.[97] Operational control of the constituent flights of the squadron was delegated to the Army units to which they were affiliated and their functional control to the squadron commanding officer, but the AOC Malaya retained overall control of their flying activities through the joint Army/RAF Operations Room, later the Joint Operations Centre, at Kuala Lumpur and also provided the normal administrative services given to other lodger units.[98]

On 7 July 1948 the RAF communications flight of No 656 Squadron moved to Kuala Lumpur in support of the task force there while the three Army flights were deployed in the north, centre and south of the Federation—No 1902 Flight at Taiping in Perak, in the command area of North Malaya District, No 1903 Flight at Seremban in Negri Sembilan in the Central Malaya District and No 1914 Flight at Kluang in Johore in the Johore Sub-District.[99] On 28 August 1948 a further flight, No 1907, was detached to Headquarters Malaya District at Kuala Lumpur to join the RAF Communications Flight which was disbanded on 1 September 1948,[100] leaving No 656 Squadron with four operational flights, Nos 1902, 1903,

1907 and 1914. Early in 1949 the Headquarters of No 656 Squadron was moved to Changi and No 1903 Flight was detached to RAF Kai Tak in Hong Kong,[101] leaving only three operational flights in Malaya. In July 1950, however, seven more Austers were added to the complement of No 656 Squadron and a further flight No 1911, was formed at Changi. The four flights of the squadron then in Malaya, Nos 1902, 1907, 1914 and 1911, were each equipped with five Austers and were detached to Brigade Area Headquarters at Taiping, Seremban, and Temerloh, with one flight at Sembawang and two aircraft at the Advanced Squadron Headquarters at Noble Field, Kuala Lumpur.[102] This deployment was maintained for most of the Emergency but individual flights were moved around between brigade areas, largely in order that over-familiarity with a particular region should not blunt the visual reconnaissance ability of their pilots. On 2 May 1951 No 1907 Flight at Seremban and No 1911 Flight at Sembawang exchanged locations, while No 1914 Flight moved from Temerloh to new Brigade Headquarters at Benta near Kuala Lipis.[103] Six weeks later No 1914 Flight at Benta and No 1911 Flight at Seremban exchanged locations and on 14 March 1952 there was a further redeployment with No 1914 Flight moving to Taiping, No 1902 Flight to Benta, No 1911 Flight to Seremban and No 1907 Flight to Sembawang.[104]

In May 1952 the functional designation of No 656 Squadron was altered from its Air Observation Post role as the communications commitments of its aircraft attained equality of importance with visual reconnaissance. Nos 1902 and 1914 Flights retained their Air Observation Post functions but Nos 1907 and 1911 Flights became Light Liaison units.[105] At the end of 1952 the four flights of No 656 Squadron in Malaya were redeployed yet again, No 1911 Flight to Taiping, No 1907 Flight to Benta, No 1914 Flight to Seremban and No 1902 Flight to Sembawang.[106] Early in 1953 No 1902 Flight moved to Taiping, No 1907 Flight to Sembawang and No 1911 Flight to Benta, while No 1914 Flight remained at Sembawang.[107] In October of that year a further Auster was added to each flight, bringing the squadron's complement to 26 Auster 6s and 7s, and a further exchange of locations took place—No 1914 Flight moving to Taiping, No 1907 Flight to Benta, No 1911 Flight to Seremban and No 1902 Flight to Sembawang.[108] Early in 1954 a further Auster 7 was added to each flight, bringing the squadron's establishment up to 31 aircraft and Nos 1914 and 1907 Flights at Taiping and Benta exchanged locations.[109] In August 1955 Nos 1914 and 1911 Flights at Benta and Seremban exchanged locations and in the following year No 1911 Flight moved to Sembawang, while Nos 1902 and 1914 Flights were transferred to two new locations at Ipoh and Port Dickson respectively as ground forces were redeployed for operations against the remaining terrorists.[110] During 1957 the complement of No 656 Squadron was reduced to 26 aircraft with the deletion of one Auster from each flight and the Headquarters' Unit at Kuala Lumpur and No 1914 Flight returned to Seremban from Port Dickson.[111]

On 1 September 1957 a major change in the status of No 656 Squadron occurred when the RAF surrendered all interest in its organization and control to the newly formed Army Air Corps.[112] Up until this time the RAF had provided the adjutant and all the servicing personnel of the squadron while the Army had provided the commanding officer, the pilots, signallers, transport drivers and general duties personnel. Now No 656 (Air Observation Post/Light Liaison) Squadron became No 656 (Light Aircraft) Squadron, Army Air Corps, and the responsibility for all first and second line servicing was handed over to the Army. However, as the squadron continued to rely on the RAF for technical advice and experienced supervisors,[113] this transfer of responsibility was effected without any loss of operational efficiency and did not cause any inconvenience to the ground forces engaged in the campaign against the terrorists. Coincident with this change in its status a fifth flight, No 16 Reconnaissance Flight was added to the squadron and stationed at its Kuala Lumpur headquarters, while the existing four flights, now redesignated Nos 2 and 14 Reconnaissance Flights and Nos 7 and 11 Liaison Flights, Army Air Corps, continued to be deployed at Ipoh, Seremban, Taiping and Sembawang (with a small detachment at Kluang), under the operational command of the 1st and 2nd Federal Infantry Brigades, the Commonwealth Infantry Brigade and the 63rd, 99th and 26th Brigades.[114] In June 1958 No 2 Reconnaissance Flight took over responsibility for operations on the Thai border from No 7 Flight at Taiping, which necessitated maintaining a small detachment at Alor Star, but the deployment of the other flights of No 656 Squadron remained constant until the end of the campaign.[115]

No 656 was the first squadron to contribute operationally to the campaign against the terrorists and the only unit to operate continuously throughout the twelve years of the Emergency. For the whole of this time they flew only Auster aircraft, whose characteristics of a short take-off, slow flying speed and economy of operation made it an admirable aircraft for the reconnaissance and light liaison duties which were its main commitments in Malaya. At the start of the campaign the provision of spares for these aircraft was a problem and each flight was only allowed 150 flying hours a month until the situation improved.[116] After this restriction had been lifted the Auster 5s and 6s, with which the squadron was equipped for most of the campaign, maintained a high rate of serviceability, with an average of over 75 per cent.[117] The operational and technical performance of the Auster 9s that were introduced into Malaya in 1956 were most disappointing, however, and an abnormal number of defects in these aircraft imposed a heavy burden on their maintenance personnel.[118]

The Austers of No 656 Squadron were the most versatile of all the aircraft that were deployed in the Malayan campaign for, in addition to their main commitment of providing liaison flights for Army commanders and their staffs and other miscellaneous flights in a communications role, they carried out visual reconnaissance of terrorist concentrations and numerous other tasks, including small tactical supply drops when the use of medium range transport aircraft was uneconomical, leaflet drops, casualty evacuation flights and target marking for air strikes. Statistical evidence of the variety of these tasks and their relative importance is given in Annex V.[119] Sorties made in a communications and transport role by No 656 Squadron accounted for nearly half its total commitment and the number of such sorties increased from just over 200 a month at the beginning of 1949 to nearly 1,000 a month at the height of the campaign in 1953 and 1954. Each one of these flights lasted for approximately one hour. Towards the end of 1955 the total commitment of No 656 Squadron was reduced as other short range transport aircraft became available and for the remainder of the campaign Austers flew an average of 1,200 sorties a month, of which half were in a communications role.

No 267 Squadron, Pioneers and Pembrokes: Deployment and Summary of Operations

Although Austers proved their worth in a light liaison role throughout the campaign against the terrorists they suffered from the severe limitation of an inability to carry more than one passenger, in addition to the pilot, with reasonable

safety over the type of terrain that was encountered in Malaya. If military commanders wished to be accompanied by one or more of their staff officers on visits to
operational areas a separate Auster had to be provided for each member of the
party. Such demands were uneconomical and placed a severe strain on the resources
of No 656 Squadron since its constituent flights were located at widely dispersed
points in the Federation, which made reinforcement impracticable. Since it was
either uneconomical or impossible to divert helicopters or Valettas for communications tasks between light aircraft strips there was an obvious need for an inter-
mediate type of aircraft to bridge the gap between the Auster and medium range
transport aircraft. Enquiries were made about the Canadian De Havilland Beaver,
which had been introduced by the Federal Government for operation by Malayan
Airways, but these proved abortive as the necessary dollar funds were not available
and the requirement did not merit the services of the United States Aid Scheme.[120]
The final choice, therefore, fell on the single-engined Prestwick Pioneer, which could
carry four passengers or 600 to 800 lb of freight in addition to the pilot and yet was
capable of operating from nearly all the improvised light aircraft strips in Malaya.[121]
In fact, the take-off and landing characteristics of the Pioneer were better than those
of the Auster and this aircraft effected considerable economies not only in maintaining communications between light aircraft strips but also by serving as an alternative
to medium range transport aircraft when they were operated below their maximum
capacity between the main airfields of Malaya and Singapore.

Pioneers carried out a variety of useful tasks during the Malayan campaign
including the carriage of staff officers, the replacement of a limited number of personnel at forward airstrips and the evacuation from them of stretcher-borne or sitting
casualties, the transportation of freight and the dropping of limited quantities of
supplies to jungle patrols. Their most important task, however, was the supply
and maintenance of the garrisons of those police forts that were established in the
deep jungle and swamp of Central Malaya, mainly in South Pahang and North
Johore, from 1953 onwards. These forts served as strategic centres from which the
indigenous aboriginal inhabitants of these areas, on whom the terrorists relied for
support and security, could be controlled and protected and from where offensive
patrols could be mounted. By 1953 nine of these forts were in operation[122] and, as
few were accessible by ground communications, their survival depended on air
supply. At first they were maintained by supply dropping aircraft but experiments
showed that landing light aircraft provided the most economic method of fulfilling
this commitment as well as utilizing the available force of Pioneers to its optimum.
One of the first tasks that was carried out at the site of a proposed fort, therefore,
was the construction of an airstrip that was suitable for operating Pioneers. Three
such airstrips had been completed by November 1954 and by the end of 1956 seven
jungle forts were similarly equipped. These airstrips had to be at least 150 yards in
length and 20 yards wide, with maximum longitudinal and lateral slope of 1 in 50
and 1 in 100 and a normal approach angle of not more than 5 degrees in jungle
terrain.[123] Even so, despite the 25 knot landing speed of the Pioneer, flights into and
out of these strips were often hazardous as they were commonly located in valleys
surrounded by primary jungle and the climate and the altitude caused a reduction
in engine performance which ensured that these aircraft were operated close to the
limits of their performance and that their operational load had to be reduced from
four passengers to two on some flights.

The first Pioneer arrived for service in Malaya at the beginning of 1953 and
by October of that year there were three in service with No 1311 Transport Flight

of No 303 Helicopter Wing at Seletar, which became the Support Flight of No 267 Squadron on 15 February 1954.[124] Two more single-engined Pioneers arrived at the end of 1954 but production was slow and the full force of ten Pioneers, providing a flight of eight aircraft with two in reserve, did not become operational until the middle of 1957.[125] Twin-engined Pioneers were introduced in 1959 and by the end of that year five twin-engined and nine single-engined Pioneers were in service in Malaya.[126] All of these aircraft were stationed at Kuala Lumpur as part of the air transport force there as it proved impracticable to deploy detachments at forward bases away from their main supply base and the location of police reinforcements.

While four or six of the Pioneers were reserved for fort supply work the remainder were available for alternative operations in a communications role. Details of the operational effort of this force are given in Annex W.[127] By the end of 1954, after a full year of operations with the three Pioneers then available, over 1,000 passengers and 100,000 lb of freight had been transported on over 1,200 sorties and this small force had proved its value as an integral part of the air transport support forces in Malaya. In July 1954 these three Pioneers carried out 223 sorties, during which they transported 286 passengers, 26,530 lb of freight and six casualties— figures that were not exceeded until April 1955. By the middle of 1955 the Support Flight of No 267 Squadron was regularly carrying over 500 passengers, 30,000 lb of freight and ten casualties into and out of jungle airstrips every month on an average of 400 sorties, each of which lasted about 40 minutes. During the whole of 1955 Pioneers completed 2,763 hours of flying on 4,691 sorties and carried 5,393 passengers, 358,648 lb of freight and 113 casualties—nearly four times the totals achieved in the previous year. The commitment of the Pioneer force continued to increase during 1956 and 700 passengers, half of whom were troops, and 100,000 lb of freight were regularly transported on over 600 sorties every month. By the end of 1956 nearly 8,000 passengers and over one million lb of freight had been carried on 7,527 sorties during the year—an increase in operational effort of 60 per cent over that of 1955. This proved to be the peak effort of the Pioneer force during the Malayan campaign but its commitment was only slightly reduced during 1957, in which year two more forts were added to their routine food supply schedules which now included weekly visits to eight out of the ten jungle forts that were in existence at that time.[128]

Although the serviceability record of No 267 Squadron's Pioneers was generally good, they began to show signs of wear towards the end of 1957 as it had never been envisaged in calculating the life of these aircraft that the intensity of their operations would demand over 1,000 landings in arduous conditions by each aircraft every year. Nevertheless, although the availability of single-engined Pioneers dropped for a few days on a number of occasions towards the end of 1957 they maintained an average serviceability rate of 63 per cent during the whole year.[129] Throughout 1958, however, airframe weaknesses were reflected in a low rate of serviceability and all but two of the remaining Pioneers were withdrawn from service during the first quarter of the year for an extensive modification programme which unfortunately shifted the centre of gravity of these aircraft towards the nose and necessitated a reduction in the maximum permissible loading weight.[130] The number of sorties flown by Pioneers of No 267 Squadron fell from 532 in January 1958 to 16 in April 1958 and during the second half of the year averaged only 275 a month, which was less than half the average monthly effort of the previous year. However, by practising strict economy measures, all essential Pioneer commitments were met during 1958 and a total of 3,609 passengers, 509,948 lb of freight and 43 casualties were carried during the course of 3,271 sorties. In December 1958, however, two of the remaining single-engined Pioneers were withdrawn from commitments in support of the campaign against the terrorists and were allotted solely to pilot training operations which were falling seriously behind schedule.[131] A considerable strain was thrown on the remaining single-engined Pioneers of the short-range transport squadron (which had been renumbered from No 267 to No 209 Squadron on 1 November 1958),[132] but these had been restored to a serviceability rate of 80 per cent by the beginning of 1959[133] after the structural alterations of the previous year, and were able to transport a monthly average of over 50,000 lb of freight and nearly 200 passengers.

Welcome relief was provided, however, with the build-up of the RMAF contribution to air transport operations in support of the campaign against the terrorists. By May 1959 one RMAF single-engined Pioneer had been committed to scheduled fort supply tasks and one RMAF twin-engined Pioneer was occasionally used for the carriage of staff officers.[134] During July 1959 Pioneers of the RMAF transported 15,372 lb of freight and 122 passengers in comparison with the task of 27,031 lb of freight and 201 passengers that was completed by the Pioneers of No 209 Squadron. The primary task of the RMAF Pioneers was the supply of jungle forts and this commitment was slightly reduced when Forts Brook and Dixon were re-supplied by foot as part of the plan to make these forts independent of air supply.[135] In August 1959 the RMAF received a further three aircraft, one twin-engined and two single-engined Pioneers[136] and, although their contribution to the campaign in this and the following month was relatively small as their pilots were undergoing training, their commitment was increased in October and November 1959, during which months they transported 46,395 lb of freight and 308 passengers compared with the 46,781 lb of freight and 310 passengers that were carried by Pioneers of No 209 Squadron. On 1 October 1959 No 209 Squadron had been transferred to Seletar to concentrate on flying training and although three single-engined Pioneers were left at Kuala Lumpur to help the RMAF with the reduced task of providing transport support for the ground forces operating in Perak, this detachment was also redeployed to the new squadron base on 1 April 1960.[137] Nevertheless, although the RMAF had taken over responsibility for the supply of the jungle forts, the Pioneers of No 209 Squadron continued to give some assistance when this task proved beyond the resources of the embryo national air force. The task of the Pioneers increased with the build-up of the 28th Commonwealth Brigade in Perak during February and March 1960 and the commitment of nearly 80,000 lb of freight and over 400 passengers was shared almost equally between the RMAF and No 209 Squadron. In April and May 1960 RMAF Pioneers carried 45,617 lb of freight and 408 passengers in comparison with the 2,897 lb of freight and two passengers that were transported by No 209 Squadron but in the final two months of the campaign the RAF Pioneers were still required to carry out 20 per cent of the total Pioneer commitment. In October and November 1960, four months after the Emergency had been declared over, Pioneers of No 209 Squadron transported 18,944 lb of freight and 342 passengers in comparison with the 13,968 lb of freight and 137 passengers that were carried by the Pioneers of the RMAF, and they continued to provide assistance for several months afterwards.

From their introduction in 1953 until the end of the Emergency Pioneers gave valuable support in the short range transport role, carrying over two million lb of freight and 20,000 passengers in the three peak years of their operation from 1955 to 1957. Their main commitment was the resupply of jungle forts and it was only when the requirements of these garrisons had been met that they could be spared for operations in a communications role between the main airfields and the light aircraft strips of the Federation. There was, therefore, an additional requirement for at least one six or eight seater aircraft at any particular time for the carriage of staff officers and other officials. In 1954 this requirement was met by chartering Beaver aircraft from the Federation's air services or by using the two Devon aircraft that were attached to the Far East Communications Squadron at Changi.[138] On the formation of No 267 Squadron at Kuala Lumpur, however, a Communications Flight of two Pembrokes and two Austers was added to the Support Flight of Pioneers.[139] Pembrokes formed the basis of this flight for the next five years, assisted by two or three Harvards in 1955 and 1956 and by two Pioneers in 1957.[140] A third Pembroke was attached to this flight in 1956 and two more were added in the following year.[141] The flight was finally disbanded on 1 October 1959 when its aircraft were attached to the Station Flight at Kuala Lumpur and to the Group Practice Flight at Seletar.[142]

The Pembroke was a good aircraft for operations in a communications role in Malaya but the reduction of its maximum seating capacity from eight to six, which arose from the need to reposition the dinghy and safety equipment for air/sea rescue operations at the rear bulkhead,[143] was a serious disadvantage and on occasions necessitated the use of two aircraft where one would normally have sufficed. Moreover, during 1958 the Pembrokes in Malaya experienced a low serviceability rate which was aggravated by the supply of engines that could not be fitted to these aircraft without extensive modifications to the airframe.[144] However, by restricting their operational use, all priority commitments were carried out and 571 passengers and 2,730 lb of freight were transported on 355 sorties during the year. Throughout their period of operation in Malaya the Pembrokes of the Communications Flight of No 267 Squadron carried an average of 20 passengers on as many sorties each month, which was less than 5 per cent of the task carried out by Pioneers of the Support Flight of this squadron but was nevertheless a significant contribution in the short range transport support role.

COMMUNICATIONS BY HELICOPTER

Both the Austers of No 656 Squadron and the Pioneers and Pembrokes of No 267 (later 209) Squadron provided valuable communication links between the main airfields of Malaya and the network of grass airstrips in outlying districts but their task was limited mainly to the carriage of staff officers and a small amount of freight, together with regular police reinforcements of jungle forts. Moreover, the terrain ensured that the airstrips that were capable of handling these light aircraft were limited in number and too widely dispersed to assist in the rapid tactical deployment of troops that was necessary to counteract the terrorist threat in a campaign where operational areas could not be foretold with accuracy. The problem of moving troops into areas that were inaccessible or difficult to reach by surface communications was solved partly by the use of paratrooping techniques but mainly by the advent of helicopters, which was certainly the most significant contribution that was made by the short range air transport forces in Malaya to the successful outcome of the campaign and also the major development in the techniques of combined operations between ground and air forces that occurred during the 1950's.

Fig 1   Large cone centred jungle leaves in which rain and dew accumulate to provide drinking water

Fig 2   A temporary shelter made from a waterproof cape in a jungle clearing

[See p 10

Fig 3   Three Brigands pass by jungle clad hills on their way to attack a target in South Malaya

Fig 4   Men of RAF Regiment (Malaya) go into action

[See p 30

Fig 5   Servicing a Beaufighter

Fig 6   Feeding belted ammunition in the ammunition tanks of a Vampire

[See p 48

Fig 7   The strike leader of a Hornet squadron briefing his pilots before taking off on an air strike

Fig 8   Pilots being briefed by the Army Liaison Officer at Butterworth, North Malaya. The aircrew tent is an attap (dried palm leaf) roofed hut

[See p 54

Fig 9   Heavily equipped paratroops on the way to a dropping zone in a Dakota

Fig 10   Stowing supplies in a Dakota to be dropped by parachute to a remote police outpost in North Johore

[See p 86

Fig 11   A WRAF operations clerk helps a navigator in the Flight Planning Section
at RAF Changi

[See p 88

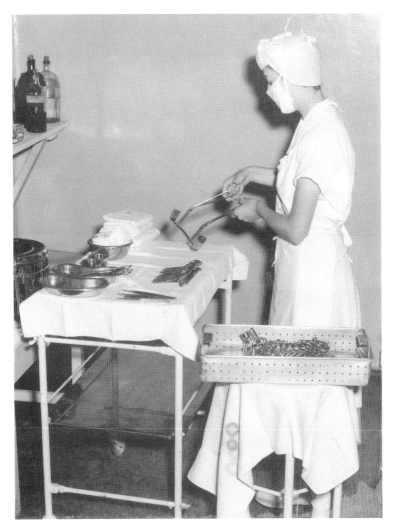

Fig 12   A WRAF operating theatre technician prepares for an operation at the
RAF Hospital Changi

[*See p 89*

Fig 13   A Sycamore alights near a military hospital while ambulance and crew wait to receive a wounded
passenger

Fig 14   A casualty being evacuated by Dragonfly to Ipoh hospital

[See p 106

Fig 15   A Sycamore of No 194 Squadron alighting in the 'well' of a jungle clearing to pick up a casualty

Fig 16   A Dragonfly on a jungle casualty evacuation sortie

[See p 107

Fig 17   Two Spitfires (Mk PR 19) of No 81 Squadron on one of their last operational photographic
reconnaissance sorties in Malaya

Fig 18   Mosquito RG 314 of No 81 Squadron made the last operational flight by a Mosquito on
21 December 1955

[See p 128

Fig 19   RAF Regiment (Malaya) patrol searching the shallow waters of a mangrove swamp which may conceal native boats used for carrying food to terrorists

Fig 20   Signallers of the RAF Regiment (Malaya) with mobile sets being briefed before an exercise

[See p 138

Fig 21   A Sunderland of No 205 Squadron flying over Singapore harbour on 15 May 1959

Fig 22   Lincolns of No 1 (RAAF) Squadron taxying into dispersal after air strike on bandit escape routes

[See p 150

The Role of the Helicopter and the Principles Governing its Employment

The introduction of helicopters into Malaya came at a crucial point in the campaign against the terrorists and marked a turning point in the fortunes of the Security Forces. Previously it had been difficult for these forces, operating from static defensive positions, to achieve a rapid concentration of troops before the terrorists had time to disperse, or to mount a surprise attack on them by avoiding ambushes and the screen of aborigines or Min Yuen supporters which were usually interposed between the terrorists and the probable line of any attack. Outlying estates were difficult to reinforce at short notice and casualties, prisoners or vital intelligence material could not be evacuated from jungle areas without entailing arduous and uneconomic escort duties. When the decision was taken in 1953 to employ more troops on deep jungle operations in an attempt to carry the offensive to the terrorists and to eliminate their leaders, without whom the command structure of the MRLA would crumble, it became even more necessary to increase the mobility of the security forces so that they could penetrate jungle areas quickly and retain some element of surprise in order to nullify the advantages held by the terrorists in fighting over terrain that was ideally suited to their evasive tactics. If air supply gave the ground forces sustenance in inhospitable country, trooplifting and casualty evacuation by helicopter gave them mobility in tactical areas and allowed their commanders more flexibility in planning offensive operations against the terrorists. Together these two aspects of air transport support radically increased the effectiveness of security force operations and multiplied the number of personnel that were engaged on active jungle patrolling by a factor of not less than four.[145] With a rate of advance of 800 to 1,000 yards an hour in jungle terrain, even under the most favourable conditions, trooplifting by helicopter frequently converted ten days of unproductive marching into active patrolling and, by eliminating the inevitable delay and fatigue that were inherent in arduous jungle treks, they enabled troops to arrive fresh in their operational areas and considerably increased their fighting efficiency as a result. Air supply enabled troops to remain on patrol for two or three weeks at a time and the evacuation of the sick or wounded by helicopter from jungle landing zones obviated the necessity of abandoning a patrol or of seriously weakening its strength by providing escorts back to base camps.

Jungle operations usually developed into a series of fluid company or platoon actions and helicopters also provided a valuable liaison service for battalion commanders and their staff who wished to co-ordinate and control their troops and to reconnoitre the terrain over which they would have to operate. Among the variety of other tasks for which helicopters were well suited in the Malayan campaign were the dropping of limited quantities of supplies when accuracy was of paramount importance, target marking for air-strike aircraft and the destruction of jungle cultivations by aerial spraying.

It was virtually axiomatic, however, that there were never enough helicopters in Malaya to meet the demands that were made for their services and their commitments had to be limited according to a fairly rigid set of priorities, of which the tactical deployment of troops and the evacuation of casualties from the jungle were the most important tasks. The medium and the light helicopters that were employed during the Malayan campaign cost £73 and £53 an hour respectively to operate, compared with the £35 and £15 an hour which it cost to operate Pioneer and Auster light aircraft[146] and this economic fact ensured that helicopters were never used when alternative methods of transport were available unless there were clear and overriding operational advantages to be gained. Whenever possible the tactical deployment of troops was carried out by surface communications or by fixed-wing aircraft since a helicopter operation which involved $1\frac{1}{2}$ hours of unproductive flying time for a task lasting ten minutes was only justified when it saved several days of marching and not a journey of 40 minutes by road. Although it was tempting to use helicopters for liaison tasks, in most cases they would have achieved only a small saving at a disproportionately high cost and were used, therefore, only on operations of the highest priority such as the carriage of live or dead terrorists, guides, informers and other sources of intelligence material recovered during the course of operations, whose rapid assessment by intelligence officers was considered important. In addition the visits of staff officers and the regular visits to jungle forts by doctors and state officials were also carried out by helicopter before the advent of the Pioneer provided alternative means of transport. The ability of the helicopter to fly slowly over the ground also made them more effective than Austers for aerial reconnaissance and on a few occasions this consideration outweighed the high operating cost and shortage of numbers which usually precluded their use for such tasks.

To carry out trooplifting operations with a small number of helicopters it was essential to strike a balance between the principle of economy of force and the need to achieve a rapid build-up of troops in an operational area. Thus only a few helicopters were needed to lift a large body of troops provided that the sortie links were kept to a minimum. For example, 25 medium helicopters were required in the Malayan campaign to lift 100 men at one time but only eight were required if each helicopter made three trips. Although the operation would have taken five times as long it was more economical since the proportion of unproductive positioning time to trooplifting increased with the number of aircraft employed, while the fact that jungle landing zones could usually take only one helicopter at a time was a limiting factor on the speed of operations regardless of the number of aircraft that were employed. The use of eight medium helicopters at one time during Operation 'Commodore' in May 1953, the first large scale helicopter operation of the campaign proved unwieldy and it was considered that five helicopters using reserve pilots would have been more efficacious.[147] This operation showed that a radius of fifteen miles was the best compromise between the air forces' desire to shorten the flying distance and preserve the effort of their helicopters and the ground forces' natural inclination to mount operations some distance from the target area in order to minimize the risk of a security leakage. Flying twelve to fifteen round trips of 30 miles each a medium helicopter could move 60 to 70 troops each day and could keep up this effort for three or four days in succession. This operation also proved that troops who were totally unfamiliar with helicopters could operate with them after only ten minutes briefing and that emplaning and deplaning by jumping from a height of six feet, climbing down ropes or nets from a height of fifteen feet or being winched down from 100 feet, could be carried out without prior rehearsal.[148]

Helicopters Employed

The helicopters that were employed in transport support roles during the Malayan campaign were the Dragonfly (S51) and Sycamore light helicopters and the Whirlwind and the S55 medium helicopters. The former pair were used primarily for casualty evacuation and liaison flights and the latter for trooplifting, but neither were used exclusively in these roles. When these helicopters were first introduced into Malaya they were still in an experimental stage and the exigencies of high temperature and humidity, uncertain weather conditions, high altitudes, mountainous terrain and the steep angle of entry and exit into jungle clearings, irrespective of wind direction, which they encountered ensured that they were invariably flown close to their operational limits and that their performance was considerably less efficient than in the United Kingdom. It is sufficient tribute to the skill of their pilots that both medium and light helicopters had a comparatively low accident record throughout their period of operation in the campaign against the terrorists in Malaya.

The Dragonfly or S51 light helicopter had a cruising speed of 70 knots at 80 degrees Fahrenheit and 75 per cent humidity in still air and an endurance of three hours at this speed, which gave it a maximum operational range of 225 miles and a safety radius of 90 miles from its base.[149] It could carry 400 lb or two passengers or two sitting or one stretcher borne case in a casualty evacuation role and, with an all-up weight of 5,450 lb it had a ceiling of 12,000 feet. It was not, however, an ideal aircraft for use in Malayan conditions because, quite apart from its maintenance record (it had a serviceability rate of less than 40 per cent between July 1953 and March 1954,)[150] it was tiring to fly for long periods, the problems of control made navigation difficult and it frequently required a jump take-off to escape from jungle clearings, while the poor downward visibility from the pilot's seat made a vertical descent a manoeuvre of considerable delicacy in a confined space. Its replacement as a light helicopter in Malaya, the Bristol Sycamore which was introduced in 1955, carried one extra passenger or stretcher case or 200 lb of freight and had a much better rate of serviceability—an average of 63 per cent throughout 1957.[151] With an external net it could deal with awkward loads up to 500 lb in weight and, after 1957, it was proved capable of trooplifting operations and eventually replaced the Whirlwind medium helicopter in this role without much loss in operational efficiency. The droop of its main rotor at low revolutions, however, required more stringent conditions than for some other helicopters in the preparation of landing zones.

The medium helicopter which bore the brunt of trooping operations in the Malayan campaign was the American S55, which had a cruising speed of 60 knots in still air and a range of 100 miles with a payload of 1,000 lb into large landing zones, or of 70 miles with a payload of 500 lb into small jungle clearings.[152] With an ideal operational range of 20 miles in Malayan conditions an S55 could carry five fully equipped troops with five days rations, or a 3″ mortar and its crew of three and 24 mortar bombs, or three stretcher cases and two walking wounded, or ten 100 lb boxes of stores, or fifteen 65 lb free-drop ration bales or 800 lb in a large crate slung in an external net. Its serviceability rate was generally good—averaging 90 per cent of the unit establishment between July 1953 and March 1954.[153] Unfortunately the British version of the S55, the Whirlwind Mk 4 was a poor, over-heavy copy of the original and when it was first introduced into Malaya in 1955 it could carry only three troops and could not operate economically above 3,000 feet.[154] Removal of all unnecessary equipment reduced its overall weight by 350 lb and enabled an extra passenger to be carried, but these aircraft proved difficult to maintain and continually absorbed a disproportionately large part of the technical manpower that was available. During 1956 the average serviceability rate of the Whirlwinds operating in Malaya was only 41 per cent and since components of this aircraft were never in good supply there was rarely a time when one or more aircraft were not grounded for lack of some spare part and the whole

Whirlwind force was out of line four times during 1957 for technical reasons.[155] The poor standard of the Whirlwind's overhauled Pratt and Whitney engines caused concern and resulted in a reduction of its life from 400 to 200 hours between overhauls, which doubled the servicing costs on engine replacements.[156] It was largely because of this mechanical unreliability that the proportion of Sycamores in the helicopter force in Malaya was increased at the expense of Whirlwinds towards the end of the campaign.

Experience in the Malayan campaign showed that the salient features of the ideal helicopter for jungle operations were a single rotor configuration, a power plant of about 1,200 hp, stable landing gear comprising four wheels with brakes, good ground clearance underneath the fuselage and the main and tail rotors, a large centre of gravity range, the ability to hover up to heights of 6,000 feet and a range of 400 miles with full tanks and a normal load in still air.[157] The S55 came nearest to fulfilling these requirements but a more powerful helicopter, such as the Wessex S58, with a seating capacity of ten or twelve troops instead of five or six, would have greatly improved the speed and efficiency of trooplifting operations. These aircraft, however, were only just coming into service when the campaign ended.

The use of any helicopter larger than the Wessex S58 was impracticable in Malayan conditions as it would have necessitated unrealistically exacting requirements in the preparation of landing zones. As it was the preparation of helicopter 'pads' always constituted a major problem in the Malayan jungle and even with the aid of plastic explosive and power saws it was difficult to completely clear the requisite area and it was often necessary for troops to embark and disembark from a hovering aircraft by means of a knotted rope or net.[158] Even the S55 had a main rotor clearance of only $10\frac{1}{2}$ inches and the minimum requirements of any helicopter landing zone was a level and firm area 30 yards in diameter that was cleared to the ground, with a perimeter ten yards wide that was cut to two feet from the ground and an approach path not less than 40 yards wide or steeper than 30 degrees.[159] The maximum angle of approach was reduced to 20 degrees at 3,000 feet and 10 degrees at 4,000 feet, while a clear run in was required above 5,000 feet. All helicopter landing zones varied a little according to the number of aircraft they could accommodate at once, the altitude or their approach angle and a careful record was kept at the Joint Operations Centre at Kuala Lumpur of the characteristic features of all known natural or artificial helicopter landing zones in Malaya. By the end of the campaign this list included the location of several hundred sites scattered throughout the Federation.

Build-Up of the Helicopter Force and Its Deployment

The first helicopters to be introduced into Malaya were three S51 Dragonflies which formed the Far East Casualty Air Evacuation Flight that was established at Seletar on 1 April 1950 and which moved to Changi on 22 May 1950.[160] Such was the demand for the services of this unit that further Dragonflies were added to its establishment in March, May and June 1952 to bring its complement up to five aircraft.[161] The total loss of one S51, however, and the unserviceability of the others, virtually eliminated this unit as an effective force and the flight was disestablished on 2 February 1953.[162]

In October 1952 it was decided to form a Short Range Transport Squadron to be known as No 194 Squadron. Its role would be to carry out casualty evacuation, tactical movement of troops, tactical reconnaissance and search and rescue operations.[163] For these tasks the squadron was to be equipped with nine UE plus three IR Dragonfly 3/4 aircraft and was to absorb the Casualty Evacuation Flight.[164]

No 194 Squadron was eventually formed at Royal Naval Air Station (RNAS) Sembawang on 2 February 1953 coincidentally with the disbanding of the Casualty Evacuation Flight at Changi.[165] On 8 January 1953 No 848 Naval Air Squadron* arrived in Malaya and was located at RNAS Sembawang. It was equipped with ten S55 medium helicopters that had arrived in the ferry carrier HMS *Perseus* of which four were held in Reserve.[166] No 303 (Helicopter) Wing was formed at RNAS Sembawang on 2 February 1953 to co-ordinate and control the activities of No 194 Squadron and No 848 Naval Air Squadron.[167] A detachment of three S55s and two S51s was deployed at Kuala Lumpur to carry out tactical troop movements and casualty evacuation in North and Central Malaya while the remaining three operational S55s and two S51s remained at Sembawang. Control of the entire helicopter force was vested in the Advanced AHQ Malaya but was decentralized to Air Control Teams that were attached to Army formation headquarters during large scale operations.[168] On 1 May 1953 No 303 (Helicopter) Wing moved from Sembawang to Kuala Lumpur and on 15 February 1954 it was disbanded and its constituent squadrons, No 194 (RAF) and No 848 (Naval Air) became part of the flying wing at RAF Kuala Lumpur.[169]

By the beginning of 1954 the wastage rate of the Dragonfly helicopters of No 194 Squadron had become so acute that they were progressively replaced by Sycamore HAR 14 helicopters. Even so, it became increasingly apparent that the helicopter force in Malaya was insufficient to meet the legitimate demands that were made on it. Operation 'Valiant' in North West Pahang at the end of 1953[170] had shown the effects of sustained operations on the serviceability rate of a small helicopter force while its centralization at Kuala Lumpur for maintenance reasons meant that many hours were lost in positioning time and that the average delay between the receipt of a message for helicopter assistance and their arrival at the pick-up point was twelve hours.[171] By the beginning of 1954 a crucial point had been reached in the campaign and in the Director of Operations report for that year it was emphasized that pressure had to be maintained on the terrorists as their strength and morale declined and as security force intelligence improved if the current stalemate, which had arisen after the terrorists' withdrawal into deep jungle, was to be broken.[172] To do this it was estimated that enough medium helicopters were required to lift two infantry companies in different parts of the Federation on any one day and to lift periodically the Federal Reserve Battalion of four infantry companies.[173] By the beginning of 1955 medium helicopter support would be required to start one deep jungle operation every month and to finish another, to provide reliefs for two operations in progress, to carry out 21 area domination operations and to provide six airlifts of 90 men each against opportunity targets. In addition, up to five jungle forts required regular relief every six months and eight required monthly visits by teams of administrators. The task of the light helicopter force was estimated at two casualty evacuations, three communication and two tactical reconnaissance or crop spraying sorties every day.[174]

For these commitments a minimum of ten medium and ten light helicopters was required at any time, which necessitated an establishment of fourteen medium and fourteen light helicopters, with four of each in reserve.[175] In fact there were

---

* No 848 Naval Air Squadron was formed at RNAS Gosport on 29 October 1952.

nominally only ten S55s and twelve S51s in Malaya in mid-1954 and these were showing signs of nearly two years of continuous operation. The nadir of their serviceability came on the 28 August 1954 when only one S55 and one S51 were available for operations and the situation was further aggravated by the prospect of a hiatus between the planned withdrawal of No 848 Naval Air Squadron in August 1954 and the arrival of RAF replacements in December 1954 and January 1955.[176] Fortunately the tour of duty of No 848 Naval Air Squadron was extended to April 1955 and the arrival of two Sycamores, nine RAF Whirlwinds of No 155 Squadron and five Naval Whirlwinds in HMS *Glory* on 18 October 1954 ensured that there was a daily availability of fourteen light helicopters and nine medium helicopters by the end of the year.[177] The Pioneers that had recently arrived in the Malayan theatre complemented the task of the Dragonflies and Sycamores and helped to meet the estimated requirement for light helicopters but the poor performance of the RAF Whirlwinds meant that only the equivalent carrying capacity of six S55s was available to meet the daily requirement of ten S55 medium helicopters.[178] Negotiations with the US Government for fifteen more S55s to be provided during 1955, either on loan or under the mutual aid programme, proved abortive[179] but the situation was rectified by improving the capacity of the RAF Whirlwinds and by retaining the services of the S55s of No 848 Naval Air Squadron for the remainder of their useful lives—which proved to be until 10 December 1956, when a series of accidents impelled their withdrawal after an exacting tour of nearly four years in Malaya.[180]

By the end of 1955 the establishment of seventeen Whirlwinds, with three in reserve, and eleven Sycamores and Dragonflies, with three in reserve, was sufficient to meet all reasonable demands for helicopter support and the improvement in their availability had permitted a greater degree of decentralization in order to provide a reserve in brigade areas for mounting attacks against opportunity targets. Previously small detachments of helicopters had been confined to the support of pre-planned operations and were limited to specified periods. On 9 May 1955, however, three medium and one light helicopter were deployed at Kluang in Johore in support of the 17th Gurkha Infantry Division, one light helicopter was positioned at Ipoh in Perak in support of the 1st Federal Infantry Division and another light helicopter was located at Benta in Pahang in support of the 18th Independent Infantry Brigade, in order to cover operations in the south, north and centre of Malaya.[181] These detachments remained under the operational control of the Joint Operations Centre at Kuala Lumpur. In March 1956 the medium helicopter force was again redeployed to facilitate second line servicing and improve their availability. The Whirlwind detachment of No 155 Squadron was withdrawn from Kluang to Kuala Lumpur, while No 848 Naval Air Squadron was moved from Kuala Lumpur to its maintenance base at Sembawang, from where it maintained the Kluang detachment to meet requirements for medium helicopter support in South Malaya.[182]

With the disestablishment of No 848 Naval Air Squadron at the end of 1956 seventeen Whirlwinds of No 155 Squadron and fourteen Sycamores of No 194 Squadron were left to meet all demands for helicopter support in Malaya.[183] Fortunately these became less as the Emergency situation improved, which was provident as the Whirlwinds gave considerable technical trouble during 1957 that finally led to a recommendation that they should be progressively replaced by Sycamores.[184] The conversion programme began to take effect with the deletion of four Whirlwinds from the establishment of No 155 Squadron on 1 December

1957[185] but it was temporarily interrupted in November 1958 by a defect in the main rotor blade of the Sycamore helicopter which caused the grounding of these aircraft for some time.[186] Considerable strain was then thrown upon the limited resources of the remaining helicopter force when the positioning time from Kuala Lumpur was increased with the dispersal of the main troop concentrations to the north and south of the Federation after the central areas had been declared free of Emergency restrictions. Recourse was made, therefore, to detachments of three Sycamores at Ipoh in Perak and of three Whirlwinds at Seletar on Singapore Island.[187] The problems of maintenance and administration which this deployment caused were exacerbated, however, when the FEAF was downgraded in priority for helicopter spares in favour of the MEAF and the Joint Operations Centre was compelled to reject all bids for helicopter support which could be met by other means.[188]

By October 1958 the number of operational Sycamores was reduced to one or two a day and ground force operations were beginning to be restricted by the non-availability of helicopters, but the situation eased slightly with the withdrawal of the Whirlwind detachment from Seletar when Emergency operations were terminated in Johore.[189] The detachment at Ipoh was maintained and it was planned that one squadron of twelve Sycamores based at Kuala Lumpur would meet the remaining helicopter commitment of the campaign.[190] On 27 April 1959, however, all Sycamores were grounded after a crash and when Nos 194 and 155 Squadrons were combined to form No 110 Squadron on 3 June 1959, only five operational Whirlwinds were left to carry out the remaining helicopter tasks in the campaign against the terrorists.[191] On 1 September 1959 No 110 Squadron, with a unit establishment of eight Whirlwinds, moved to RAAF Butterworth in view of the imminent transfer of RAF Kuala Lumpur to the RMAF and the concentration of ground force activity in the Thailand border area of Northern Perak.[192] Although the permanent detachment of helicopters at Ipoh was cancelled one Whirlwind remained at Kuala Lumpur until 19 January 1960 in support of clearing up operations in Pahang.[193] By November 1959, however, it was clear that the availability of helicopters in Malaya had become marginal owing to the short supply of spare parts and the additional training required for replacement pilots. The Commonwealth Brigade in Northern Perak was instructed, therefore, to drastically prune their bids for helicopter support[194] and restrictions on the tasks of the surviving helicopter force remained in being until the end of the Emergency to underline the fact that never at any time during its ten year career in Malaya was it really adequate to meet all the legitimate demands that were made upon it.

Summary of Casualty Evacuation Operations by Helicopter

Statistical evidence of the various tasks carried out by helicopters during the Malayan campaign are given in Annex X.[195] The first contribution which the helicopter force in Malaya made to the support of ground forces operating against the terrorists was provided by the three Dragonflies which formed the Far East Casualty Air Evacuation Flight on 1 April 1950.[196] The increase in terrorist activity during the first part of 1950 had underlined the need for the expeditious evacuation of casualties from operational areas and, because of the mountainous terrain and poor surface communications that were subject to terrorist ambushes, this was only practicable by air in most cases. Casualties were lifted from jungle clearings and flown directly to the nearest British Military hospital at Singapore, Kuala Lumpur (Kinrara), Kluang or Taiping, or to medical receiving stations at Penang,

Sungei Patani, Ipoh, the Cameron Highlands and Seremban, or to the nearest airfield or road and rail communications centre for transport to the nearest surgical unit and from there to the main British Military Hospital at Singapore.[197]

Apart from battle injuries, the casualties that were evacuated by helicopter from the jungle during the Malayan campaign suffered from many and varied complaints, including snake bites, fever, dysentery, jaundice and appendicitis, and many of these would certainly have proved fatal if the sufferer had not received treatment quickly, while in other cases survival would have been problematical in view of the long and arduous journeys out of the jungle that would have had to be undertaken on foot if air evacuation had not been available.[198]

The first casualty to be evacuated by helicopter during the Malayan campaign was lifted on 6 June 1950 when a wounded policeman was flown from an isolated police station in Southern Johore and taken to Johore Hospital, where the saving of his life was attributed to his speedy admission.[199] On 15 June 1950 the first military casualty to be evacuated by helicopter was flown to RAF Changi from Segamat airstrip, which had been rendered unserviceable for conventional aircraft by heavy rain, and on 20 June a Gurkha soldier with toothache was evacuated from the jungle near Kluang in Johore.[200] By the end of 1950 26 casualties had been evacuated from the Malayan jungle by helicopter and, although the number of evacuations was not particularly high, the realization that they were never out of reach of timely medical aid afforded a great fillip to the morale of the security forces and removed their fear of becoming a casualty and thus a burden on the remainder of the patrol. A typical example of the work of the small Casualty Air Evacuation Flight occurred on 13 October 1950 when four members of a patrol of the 1st Battalion The Worcestershire Regiment, including two stretcher cases, were evacuated to Segamat airstrip from a clearing to the East North East in one hour and 45 minutes. After a 35 mile road journey to the British Military Hospital at Kluang one of the casualties was treated for gangrene and undoubtedly owed his life to his speedy evacuation by helicopter.[201]

Throughout 1951 casualty evacuations by helicopter continued at a rate of four or five a month, with a total of 55 for the whole year. On 25 October 1951 one Dragonfly was lost in attempting to fly out of a small clearing in deep primary jungle[202] but the addition of three more Dragonflies to the Casualty Air Evacuation Flight in the first half of 1952 made it possible to evacuate a greater number of casualties from the jungle and also to detach one helicopter to the vicinity of prolonged ground force operations while the remainder maintained one helicopter at permanent standby at Changi to answer calls from anywhere in the Federation.[203] In February and March 1952 alone, 44 casualties were lifted out of the jungle, mostly from the Belum valley of Northern Perak during Operation 'Helsby', to bring the total number of evacuations that had been carried out by the Casualty Evacuation Flight since its inauguration a year earlier to over 100. During the whole of 1952 168 casualties were evacuated by helicopter to bring the overall total to date to 257. Although the number of casualties which occurred among the ground forces declined during 1952, three times as many were evacuated by helicopter during that year as had been during 1951, which indicated their growing dependence on this form of air transport support. Most of these evacuations involved casualties due to sickness or accident as a result of prolonged periods spent in the jungle but battle casualties continued at a steady rate of four of five a month while, on one occasion, helicopters were used to convey the seriously injured survivors of a train crash in a remote part of Kelantan.[204]

The advent of No 194 Squadron's Dragonflies and No 848 Squadron's S55s at the beginning of 1953 considerably increased the capabilities of the helicopter force in Malaya and the number of casualties that were evacuated from the jungle rose accordingly. From four evacuations in January 1953 the number of evacuations rose steadily to 85 in November of that year, when both S55s and S51s were flying several sorties daily in support of Operation 'Valiant' in the deep jungle of North West Pahang.[205] As this operation progressed dysentery, scrub typhus and other jungle diseases proliferated and caused most of the casualties that required evacuation by helicopter. By the end of 1953 S55s had carried out 280 evacuations in 318 hours of flying during the year while S51s had flown 213 casualties in 199 hours of flying. Of these 493 casualties, 10·5 per cent were wounded, 9·5 per cent had suffered accidents, 10·5 per cent had foot diseases and 59 per cent were suffering from fever or other illnesses.[206]

During 1954 743 casualties were evacuated by helicopter in the Malayan theatre, nearly 50 per cent more than in 1953—30 per cent of which were flown in S55s of No 848 Squadron and the remainder in the S51s and Sycamores of No 194 Squadron. In the following year, 1955, a total of 793 helicopter evacuations were carried out in Malaya with never less than 40 in any one month, of which 334 were carried by medium helicopters of Nos 848 and 155 Squadrons and 459 by the light helicopters of No 194 Squadron. 1955 proved to be the peak year for casualty evacuation by helicopter during the Malayan campaign but over 600 casualties were flown out of jungle areas in each of the next three years. However, the proportion of casualties evacuated by medium helicopters fell from 40 per cent in 1955 to less than 30 per cent in 1956. During 1956 the light helicopters of No 194 Squadron carried nearly 500 casualties, including their 1,500th since their arrival in Malaya, while the S55s of No 848 Squadron were finally withdrawn at the end of the year after evacuating 764 casualties during their four year tour in the theatre. During 1957 the medium helicopters of No 155 Squadron carried out only 15 per cent of the total number of casualty evacuations but in 1958 their contribution rose to nearly 30 per cent of the 733 casualties that were evacuated by helicopter during the year and, after the Sycamores of No 194 Squadron had been grounded at the end of April 1959, they completed the remaining task in this role until the end of the campaign.

Despite the reduction in the number of helicopters that were available for casualty evacuation work towards the end of the Emergency they were able to meet this commitment as the number of casualties suffered by the security forces showed a marked decline and less than 300 wounded or sick personnel were carried by helicopter during 1959 and 1960—well under half the number that were evacuated during the peak years of 1954 to 1957. When the Emergency ended in July 1960 ten years had elapsed since the inauguration of the Casualty Air Evacuation Service in Malaya, during which period helicopters of the RAF and the Royal Navy had transported almost exactly 5,000 casualties and saved numerous lives in the process.

Summary of Communications Operations by Helicopter

With the formation of No 194 Squadron orders restricting the employment of the light helicopter force in Malaya were rescinded and they became available for tasks in a communications role provided that sufficient aircraft were retained for their primary commitment of casualty evacuation.[207] From the beginning of

1954 to their final withdrawal from operations in mid-1959 the Dragonflies, and later the Sycamores, of No 194 Squadron regularly transported between 150 and 300 passengers every month on communications flights. At the beginning of this period the S55s and Whirlwinds of Nos 848 and 155 Squadrons carried rather more than half this number of passengers each month, but the withdrawal of the former at the end of 1956 reduced the contribution of medium helicopters to the communications commitment to less than 15 per cent of the total task. However, after mechanical failures beset the remaining Sycamores at the end of 1958, RAF Whirlwinds carried out the remaining task of transporting about 50 passengers each month until the end of the Emergency. During the whole campaign about 12,500 passengers were carried by medium helicopters and a further 6,500 by light helicopters.

In addition to the transportation of passengers during the Malayan campaign, helicopters were also used to carry freight into jungle landing zones when supply drops were impracticable. Notable commitments in this role included the carriage of the heavy construction equipment that was flown into the sites of jungle forts for clearing the land and preparing light aircraft strips. For the carriage of freight the Whirlwind and S55 medium helicopters, with their greater capacity, were preferable to light helicopters and, with the withdrawal of No 848 Squadron at the end of 1956, they carried out 75 per cent of this commitment. During 1954 medium helicopters transported nearly 165,000 lb of freight and light helicopters a further 80,000 lb, while in 1955 their combined task more than doubled to nearly 600,000 lb. During 1956, however, the total freight carrying commitment of the helicopter force in Malaya fell by 25 per cent and a greater proportion of the task was carried out by light helicopters, especially after the withdrawal of No 848 Squadron at the end of the year. The Sycamores of No 194 Squadron carried over 75 per cent of the 415,000 lb of freight that was transported by helicopter during 1957 and well over half of the 630,000 lb that was carried during 1958, which proved to be the highest annual total for any single year of the campaign. After the withdrawal of the Sycamores from operational service in Malaya in 1959 the amount of freight that was transported by the remaining Whirlwinds fell to an average of 10,000 lb and the 200,000 lb that were carried during the last eighteen months of the campaign represented little more than the monthly totals of June and July 1958.

During the course of eight years of operations in a transport and communications role in Malaya helicopters carried about 19,000 passengers and $2\frac{1}{2}$ million lb of freight, which can be compared with the 16,000 passengers and nearly $3\frac{1}{2}$ million lb of freight that were carried by RAF and RMAF Pioneers and the 500,000 passengers and 80 million lb of freight that were carried by medium range transport aircraft in the Malayan theatre during the same period.

Summary of Trooplifting Operations by Helicopter

It was not, however, the carriage of passengers, freight or wounded personnel that represented the most important contribution of the helicopter force to the successful conclusion of the Malayan campaign, but the transportation of troops in operational areas, which was the most significant development in air transport support that occurred during the Emergency. During 1952, when there were only a few S51 helicopters of the Far East Casualty Air Evacuation Flight in Malaya, two events focused attention on the potentialities of helicopters for trooplifting operations. In February 1952 a patrol of fourteen men of the 1st Battalion The Cameronians was successfully evacuated from a swamp in the Ulu Bernam area of North West Selangor when rising water threatened to cut them off[208] and, in March 1952, several army commanders, civilian administrators, doctors and sick and aged evacuees were flown into and out of the Belum area of Northern Pahang during the course of Operation 'Helsby'.[209] Without helicopters these operations would have involved days of arduous travelling through difficult jungle terrain with heavy escorts and the obvious application of this lesson to the problem of the tactical deployment of troops was primarily responsible for the subsequent demand for helicopter reinforcements in Malaya. The advent of the S55s of No 848 Squadron at the beginning of 1953 had a pronounced effect on the conduct of air transport support in Malaya and trooplifting into and out of operational areas became the main preoccupation of the Air Operations room at Kuala Lumpur.

No 848 Squadron carried out its first operational trooplift on 16 February 1953 during Operation 'Wellington II', when three S55s lifted twelve men of the 1st Battalion The Worcestershire Regiment and a surrendered terrorist into a small peninsula south of Port Swettenham in Selangor in an attempt to capture a local District Committee member of the MCP.[210] Previous attempts to approach this terrorist hideout had failed because of the security screen which surrounded it and, although this particular operation also failed in its main objective, it did prove that troops could be lifted by helicopter at short notice without any previous experience of this form of air transport support. Over 300 trooplifting sorties were flown by helicopter during the next two months and the largest effort of this role that was made during 1953 occurred on 24 May when Operation 'Commodore' was mounted North East of Kluang in Johore in an attempt to capture the State Committee of the MCP.[211] Following an air strike and a paratroop drop into adjacent jungle, 564 troops were lifted over a distance of nine miles into a jungle landing zone by eight S55s of No 848 Squadron during the course of seven hours, in a move that would have taken at least two days on foot. At first no contact was made with the terrorists but on 25 May further information was received and another trooplift was carried out from the original landing zone into a new area where nine terrorists were killed and twelve of their camps were destroyed. During this fourteen day operation eight S55s lifted a total of 1,623 troops and 35,000 lb of stores on 415 sorties while two S51s carried out a further 94 sorties on reconnaissance and communications flights. Altogether 1,902 troops were airlifted by helicopter during May 1953—a monthly total that was not exceeded until March 1955.

In October 1953 the Central Politburo of the MCP and several terrorist camps were located in an area of deep jungle in North West Pahang and four battalions of troops were deployed on the offensive in Operation 'Valiant' in an attempt to destroy them.[212] Movement on foot was virtually impossible over any distance in this type of country and the operation relied heavily on helicopter support. The operation began with an airlift of one battalion of 500 troops over a distance of nineteen miles into two small jungle landing zones and thereafter companies of the remaining battalions engaged in the operation were deployed and redeployed almost entirely by S55 helicopters, while the poor wireless communications in the broken terrain of the operational area forced brigade and battalion commanders to rely heavily on S51 helicopters for liaison purposes. Over 2,700 troops were positioned by helicopter in Malaya during October and November 1953 to bring the total for the year to nearly 12,000 troops in 1,700 hours of flying by S55 helicopters, which represented over half the total operational effort of No 848 Squadron.

The strain of continuous operations made itself felt on the serviceability rate of both medium and light helicopters at the end of 1953 and their operational effort was accordingly reduced in the first few months of 1954. Nevertheless, when Operation 'Termite', the largest combined operation of the Emergency, was mounted in Perak in July 1954, most of the troops involved were flown by helicopter into landing zones that had been previously prepared by paratroops of the 22nd Special Air Service Regiment.[213] From May to September 1954 an average of over 1,000 troops a month were flown by the S55s of No 848 Squadron on 2,448 sorties, each of which averaged 40 minutes in duration. Towards the end of the year the problems of maintaining these helicopters again became acute as they had to bear the entire trooplifting commitment until the RAF Whirlwinds, which began arriving in Malaya in October 1954, were modified to enable them to carry out this role effectively. Nevertheless, during 1954 as a whole, the S55s of No 848 Squadron flew over 215,000 miles in transporting more than 10,000 troops in different parts of the Federation.[214]

During 1955 the unit establishment of No 155 Squadron was increased to seventeen Whirlwinds and this expansion in the helicopter force in Malaya doubled its trooplifting capacity. Monthly trooplifting totals rose from 1,285 troops in January 1955 (73 of whom were carried by light helicopters) to 3,461 in July 1955—the highest figure to date in the Emergency. The monthly average number of troops lifted into or out of the jungle by helicopter during the whole of 1955 was 2,250, compared with 735 in 1954, and the annual total came to nearly 28,000 troops—nearly three times the number that were lifted in the previous year. 43 per cent of all the troops that were positioned by helicopter during 1955 were transported by the S55s of No 848 Squadron during the course of 2,413 hours of flying, which represented a slight increase in their effort of the previous year. One notable trooplifting operation that was carried out during 1955 occurred three weeks after the amnesty was declared in September, when two infantry battalions were moved from central Malaya to Johore.[215] Having been assembled at Kluang by medium range transport aircraft and rail, one complete battalion and two companies of the other were deployed in their operational areas entirely by helicopter and in the course of two days nearly 600 troops were positioned by helicopter at a distance of over 150 miles from their former locations. This operation showed the advantages that could accrue from a combination of medium and short range air transport support.

During 1956 No 848 Squadron was redeployed to Sembawang and operated mainly in Johore,[216] a move which, combined with the reorganization of the technical wing at Kuala Lumpur, achieved a marked improvement in the daily availability of medium helicopters and enabled them to meet the continuing commitment of lifting an average of over 2,200 troops a month throughout the year. The final total of 25,700 troops lifted by helicopter during 1956 was the equivalent of positioning every soldier in Malaya by helicopter at least once during the year. Notable operations that were supported by trooplifting helicopters during the year were Operations 'Latimer South' and 'Enter' in North and North East Negri Sembilan, 'Huckster' in the Kluang area of Johore and 'Bonanza' in South Selangor.[217] These operations achieved the elimination of over 150 terrorists towards the end of the year and were continued into 1957, with medium helicopters providing a valuable service in deploying and relieving troops in operational areas. The trooplifting capacity of the medium helicopter force in Malaya was reduced, however, with the withdrawal of No 848 Squadron at the end of 1956 after it had transported over 45,000 troops and passengers during its four year tour of duty in Malaya.[218]

Sycamores of No 194 Squadron took over part of the trooplifting commitment during 1957 but the main effort was provided by the seventeen Whirlwinds of No 155 Squadron. The Whirlwinds proved technically unreliable, however, and were out of line four times during the year, including nearly the whole of February. During this month trooplifting operations were restricted to the most urgent requests and the monthly total of 454 troops transported by helicopter was the lowest for over two years. By May 1957, however, the trooplifting commitment had risen again to over 2,000 a month, of which 10 per cent were carried by light helicopters. Altogether 16,862 troops were carried by Whirlwind medium helicopters during 1957 and a further 2,867 by Sycamore light helicopters—a decrease of 20 per cent in comparison with the task completed in the previous year.

The reduction in the trooplifting commitment of the helicopter force in Malaya during 1957 was partly due to the lower intensity of security force operations, as the area free from Emergency restrictions expanded, and also to the concentration of troops in limited areas of the north and south of the Federation on protracted operations against the remaining terrorists, which required only routine reliefs rather than frequent tactical deployment by helicopter. Fortunately this trend continued throughout 1958 as both Whirlwind and Sycamore helicopters suffered severe operational limitations owing to poor serviceability during the year. In the second half of 1958 maximum productive utilization of the small number of helicopters that was available was achieved by small detachments of three Sycamores and three Whirlwinds at Ipoh and Seletar respectively[219] and, by exercising the strictest control over their use through the Joint Operations Centre, all the most important operational trooplifting requests were met with a minimum amount of disruption to the plans of ground force commanders. In fact the task achieved by this force during the year was remarkable and the final total of 26,867 troops that were carried by helicopter during 1958 was only just below the figure for the record year of 1955. A notable achievement in 1958 was recorded during Operation 'Tiger' in South Johore when an intensive drive was launched by the 63rd and 99th Brigades against the Regional Committee of the MCP and its supporting District Committees.[220] In support of this operation the detachment of Whirlwinds at Seletar flew over 600 troops into the area in late August 1958 and a further 1,600 troops were deployed there during October. During the latter month 4,133 fully equipped troops were ferried into and out of jungle landing zones in North and South Malaya, which constituted a record for any one month of the campaign. Of these troops, 60 per cent were transported by light helicopters as the policy of replacing the Whirlwinds with Sycamores had begun to take effect. This conversion programme was halted by the unserviceability of the Sycamores at the end of 1958 and ground force operations had to be restricted as the supply of light helicopters was reduced to only one or two a day. Nevertheless, by the end of the year Sycamores had carried nearly 8,000 troops in the preceding twelve months— nearly 30 per cent of the total number of troops that were transported by helicopter during 1958.

At the beginning of 1959 the rundown in the strength of the Whirlwind squadron, No 155, led to some curtailment of trooplifting operations but an average of nearly 2,000 troops was still transported each month and on one occasion in February 1959 two medium helicopters carried 230 troops over a distance of nine miles in under four hours.[221] After the Sycamores of No 194 Squadron had finally been grounded in April 1959 only five Whirlwinds of the newly formed No 110 Squadron remained to carry out the residual trooplifting commitment of the campaign and the monthly total of troops carried by helicopter fell to less than 200. In October 1959, however, Operation 'Bamboo' was mounted in Perak and demands for trooplifting operations increased fourfold.[222] No task of this size had been expected of the helicopter force in Malaya since Operation 'Tiger' in the previous year but, by practising rigid economies in the use of their aircraft and by enjoining the Commonwealth Brigade to prune its bids for helicopter support to the minimum, all the important operational tasks were carried out and over 1,600 troops were lifted during the months of October and November 1959. Fortunately, little troop-lifting support was required for Operation 'Seladang' that was in progress in Pahang at the same time as surface communications in the operational area were adequate.[223] By the end of 1959 nearly 5,400 troops had been transported by helicopter during the year, less than 30 per cent of the number carried during 1958 and the lowest annual total since this type of transport support began in 1953. Nevertheless, the task carried out by each individual aircraft was higher than it had ever been and the five remaining operational Whirlwinds in the theatre continued to carry over 500 troops a month throughout the first half of 1960. By July 1960, the last month of the Emergency, the redeployment of the 1st Battalion The Royal Australian Regiment and the 1st Battalion 3rd East Anglian Regiment in the Operation 'Bamboo' area of Perak had been completed[224] and the monthly average number of troops that were transported by helicopter fell to 350. It rose again to over 600 a month towards the end of 1960, however, as ground force operations were continued against the terrorists in the Thailand border area and regular reliefs were provided for troops patrolling this region.

By the end of 1960 over 6,000 troops had been transported by helicopter in Malaya during the year, more than in 1959, and the total number of troops lifted by helicopter during the entire campaign had exceeded 110,000, of which 90 per cent had been flown in Whirlwind and S55 medium helicopters. This effort may be compared with the 19,000 troops that were carried by one flight of Pioneers during the same period. It is not possible, however, to compare the relative merits of the helicopter and the Pioneer in the Malayan campaign as the former enabled operations to be carried out which the latter could not have assisted and this fact, despite the expense of operating helicopters, was a powerful military argument for their employment. Moreover, analysis of the operational effort of both Pioneers and helicopters during 1955 and 1956 showed that under a short term policy the use of the former produced little savings in operational costs. This was because Pioneers had to complete 1,320 hours of flying before the difference between their operating costs and those of helicopters equalled the cost of building an airstrip at the jungle forts whose supply was the Pioneers' main function.[225] Once these airstrips were completed, however, Pioneer aircraft proved their worth as they were cheap and relatively easy to operate and maintain and a small number were sufficient to maintain all the jungle forts that were constructed during the campaign. They were not capable, however, of meeting the requirements for the tactical deployment of troops on jungle operations. The success of these operations depended largely on the mobility that was given to the ground forces by the use of helicopters, which effected a great saving in infantry and represented a new era of combined operations in jungle terrain. Helicopters were still in an experimental stage when they were introduced into Malaya in 1950, being underpowered, difficult to maintain and operate away from their main base and having a small load capacity. Ten years later they had been largely responsible for carrying the offensive to the terrorists in their jungle hideouts, which was the major factor in their ultimate defeat. Experience in the Malayan campaign showed, however, the need in future warfare of a similar nature for a medium helicopter with a load capacity of ten or fifteen troops that was easy to maintain and which could operate away from its main base for extended periods. Nevertheless, despite the problems inherent in operating a barely adequate force of helicopters close to its operational limits in a difficult environment, it was a vital component of the air transport forces in Malaya and made a significant contribution to the successful outcome of the campaign against the terrorists.

Summary of Crop Spraying Operations by Helicopter

Nearly all the tasks that were performed by helicopters during the Malayan campaign were in a transport role, whether carrying troops, passengers, casualties, freight or army commanders on reconnaissance and liaison flights, and there is only one recorded instance of an armed helicopter being used in an offensive role during the entire campaign.[226] There was, however, one unique role that was played by helicopters during the campaign which, although strictly part of their transport support functions, was introduced as one aspect of the offensive that was mounted against the terrorists after their withdrawal into deep jungle areas from late 1952 onwards. This role was the spraying of terrorist cultivation plots with toxic liquid. The success of the Briggs Plan and the disruption of the terrorists' established methods of food supply ensured that food production became the most important factor affecting their ability to survive. They were compelled, therefore, to deploy a large proportion of their forces in remote jungle areas in order to cultivate the food that was necessary for their survival, with the aim of stockpiling the produce and building up dumps of complementary and essential foodstuffs. Jungle cultivations as established by the terrorists were small in size and screened by jungle vegetation, except from the air, while the aborigines who were frequently pressed into service as an additional labour force on these plots also provided an intelligence screen which made it almost impossible to approach them on foot undetected. Occasionally ground forces were employed to destroy terrorist cultivations in secondary jungle, during the course of either routine or special operations, but this method was an uneconomic use of manpower and the troops involved generally showed signs of physical and mental deterioration on arduous patrols which offered little or no chance of contacting the enemy. It was realized, therefore, that aerial attack offered the best means of destroying these cultivation plots and, since high explosive and fire bombs proved ineffective in this role, a scheme for the use of chemical sprays was propounded.[227] At first sodium arsenite was used with effect but it was poisonous and the danger which it afforded to the lives of the indigenous population of the jungle was politically unacceptable.[228] Imperial Chemical Industries suggested the use of Fernoxone but the toxic spray that eventually proved the most efficacious was a mixture of trioxene and diesolene, which formed a non-poisonous herbicide that killed all types of vegetation and rendered the ground unusable for a period.[229]

The spotting and location of jungle cultivations was carried out by Austers of No 656 Squadron and became an increasing commitment of these aircraft when the terrorists' cultivation programme got under way in 1952. When a number of these cultivations had been plotted a spraying operation was mounted, using both light and medium helicopters. The first of these operations was Operation 'Cyclone

I', which was mounted on 31 August 1953 in the Kluang and Labis area of Johore.[230] Ten cultivations, all fairly close together, had been located in the Mar Okil Forest Reserve and, after they had been marked by Austers, they were strafed by pairs of Hornets to eliminate any ground resistance. Two S55s and one S51 helicopter were then flown into the area from Kluang and, although they operated in pairs for safety's sake, they managed to deal with twenty cultivations on the first day of the operation. As the remaining cultivations were more scattered the daily achievement of this small helicopter force was reduced but, after the two S55s had carried out spraying operations for one and a half days and the S51 for a further two days, some thirty cultivations had been dealt with and one terrorist had been killed during associated ground force operations. One of the lessons learnt from this operation was that Auster reconnaissance aircraft were an essential part of the crop spraying force as it was difficult to spot a series of terrorist cultivations from a helicopter once it had descended to a low level to carry out its task.

The second crop spraying operation, Operation 'Cyclone II',[231] was carried out soon after the first and, by the end of 1953, 88 terrorist cultivations had been effectively destroyed from the air during the course of 48 hours of flying by S51 helicopters and 15 hours of flying by S55s.[232] By February 1954 a total of five crop spraying operations had been carried out[233] but a temporary reduction in the available helicopter force put an end to these operations for some months. They had commenced again, however, before the end of 1954, using Whirlwind helicopters, but thereafter they remained in abeyance for most of the remainder of the campaign through lack of sufficient aircraft both for spraying and for the tactical reconnaissance of terrorist cultivations.

As part of the general food-denial campaign that was carried out against the terrorists, crop spraying operations helped to render terrorist camps in deep jungle zones untenable, thereby forcing their inhabitants to contact their supporters amongst the civil population in order to obtain essential supplies and thus increasing the security forces' chances of contacting them. However, even more effective than aerial spraying of cultivation plots in persuading the terrorists to leave their jungle hideouts were the arts of psychological warfare, which provided a further example of the employment of the air transport support forces, both medium and short range aircraft, in a quasi-offensive role.

AIR TRANSPORT SUPPORT FORCES AND THE PSYCHOLOGICAL WARFARE CAMPAIGN

The Role of the Air Forces

Under the direction of the Psychological Warfare Department of the Director of Operations Staff and the Emergency Information Services, the main aims of the 'war of words' that was inaugurated during the Malayan campaign were to induce surrenders amongst the terrorists, by breaking their morale and causing disaffection within their ranks, and to win the battle for the minds and loyalties of the uncommitted populace in face of the propaganda offensive that was launched by the Communists. The main problem faced in this unconventional warfare was that of communication with an elusive enemy whose primary tactic was to avoid contact with the security forces. The local populace was indoctrinated through the media of the press, radio, films and itinerant information teams and the local

'Min Yuen' and other Communist sympathizers could be relied upon to relay some of the information thus disseminated to the terrorists in the jungle. A more direct method of contacting the terrorists was required, however, and the problem was largely solved by the use of printed leaflets and broadcast recordings. The air forces were merely one of the agencies for the delivery of both tactical and strategic messages that were devised by the Psychological Warfare Department but, especially when the terrorists withdrew into deep jungle areas, the dropping of leaflets and the broadcast of messages from the air was often the only means of making contact with them and without these means of disseminating propaganda much of the effect of the psychological warfare campaign would have been nullified.

Techniques of Leaflet Drops and Loudhailing Operations

At the start of the Emergency the technique of loudhailing from the air had not been developed and the role of the air forces in the psychological warfare campaign was limited to dropping leaflets. These were usually despatched from supply-dropping aircraft of the medium range transport force and occasionally by bombers of the offensive support force as the conclusion to an air strike. As on supply drops, No 55 Air Despatch Company of the RASC provided the despatching personnel on leaflet dropping sorties and, with loads of up to 800,000 leaflets in Dakota or Valetta aircraft, it was found that a good distribution was achieved over an area 1,000 yards square by despatching 5,000 leaflets at a time at the end of a static line.[234] If accurate drops of a limited quantity of leaflets into small pinpoint targets were required, usually when the need to exploit a success achieved by the security forces necessitated a quick reaction, then Austers of No 656 Squadron and occasionally Harvards of the MAAF were employed on leaflet dropping missions.[235]

The technique of broadcasting recorded messages from aircraft was not introduced into the Malayan campaign until October 1952 when General Templer, the Director of Operations, borrowed a US Army Dakota for experimental purposes.[236] As a result of these experiments, two Valettas of Headquarters, FEAF were fitted with broadcasting equipment and began operations early in 1953.[237] However, since an excessive amount of engine noise was transmitted over the broadcasting system of these Valettas, they were replaced by Dakotas in December 1953 and March 1954.[238] The Dakota, although obsolete in the RAF by that time, was more suited for a loudhailing role than the Valetta as its engine noise was less, thus improving the tone and clarity of the broadcasts, and also because its lower cruising speed enabled the broadcasting time on each sortie to be increased. In January 1954 an Auster was equipped with a broadcasting unit for loudhailing missions over small targets on the fringes of the jungle or adjacent to roads, where accuracy was important and where the employment of the Dakota or the Valetta was uneconomical.[239] In the following month a further loudhailing Auster was added to C Flight, No 267 Squadron but the remaining Valetta crashed on the slopes of Mt Ophir in North West Johore on 23 February 1954 and the flight was left with one Dakota and two Austers to carry out its broadcasting task.[240] In March 1954 a second Dakota was acquired and with the arrival of a third Dakota in January 1955 the Voice Flight of No 267 Squadron attained its maximum complement of three Dakotas and two Austers.[241] For most of the campaign this flight operated from Kuala Lumpur but in November 1958 No 267 Squadron was renumbered No 209 Squadron[242] and the Voice Flight, consisting of three Dakotas, was detached to the civil airfield at Bayan Lepas, Penang on 19 January 1959 to carry out the residual loudhailing commitment in support of ground force operations in Northern Perak and Kedah.[243] The cessation of anti-terrorist operations in Johore at the end of 1958 and the concentration of ground force activity in the mountainous regions of Northern Malaya resulted in the disestablishment of the Auster element of this flight[244] as the extra load of loudhailing equipment that was carried by these aircraft rendered them suitable for broadcasting operations only over relatively flat terrain at low altitudes while, for reasons of safety, they could not venture too far from lines of communication. The Voice Flight continued to operate from Penang until the end of the Emergency, although its two remaining Dakotas were transferred from No 209 to No 52 Squadron on 2 November 1959.[245]

The broadcasting component that was fitted to the loudhailing Dakotas consisted of a diesel generator which powered four modified Tannoy loudspeakers that were mounted under the aircraft and offset to the port side.[246] Loudhailing Dakotas normally operated at heights of 2,500 to 3,000 feet over the target area and in good weather conditions a broadcast message could be heard up to 2,500 yards below and to the port of the aircraft. Normally a straight course was followed over the target area with 2,000 yards between flight paths in order to ensure full coverage but a pinpoint target could be circled to give continuous ground reception. Auster loudhailing aircraft were fitted with a smaller power unit and one loudspeaker was fitted under each wing, which gave clear audibility up to 1,000 or 1,500 yards below and to the port of the aircraft.[247] Flying at 40 to 45 knots a message broadcast from an Auster could be heard for considerable periods and was usually repeated three or four times in normal weather conditions. In April 1954 a modification consisting of an endless loop tape, was introduced into the recording equipment that was installed in the 'Voice' Auster which dispensed with the need to carry a 'voice' operator,[248] thus effecting a considerable saving in weight and improving the aircraft's flying time.

Planning and Initiation of Leaflet Drops and Loudhailing Operations

Requests for loudhailing or leaflet dropping sorties emanated through police channels, such as the 'Voice Area Committees' at State headquarters, and were passed on to the Joint Operations Centre at Kuala Lumpur where decisions were taken on the missions to be flown in accordance with the dictates of target priority and aircraft availability. The duty operations officer at the Joint Operations Centre checked that the mission did not conflict with an air strike and that flying conditions were suitable if an aerial broadcast was to be made and then the duty controller issued the operational orders and passed details of the flight to the Air Control Centre, Malaya.[249] The average interval between the receipt of a bid for a broadcasting operation and the take off time was about four hours between 1954 and 1957, but after that date the Director of Operations staff solved the technical problem of producing tapes of a satisfactory quality in operational areas and the average delay was cut to one or two hours, with a consequent improvement in the psychological impact of tactical 'voice' missions.[250] Requests for loudhailing flights were co-ordinated so that as many bids as possible were fulfilled on one sortie but requests were invariably made for a series of broadcasts over a particular area for a period of three or four days in order to achieve the maximum psychological effect.

Summary of Leaflet Drops and Loudhailing Operations

Details of the effort made by the air forces in assisting the psychological warfare campaign in Malaya are collated in Annex Y.[251] Throughout the campaign leaflets remained the chief medium for disseminating information and propaganda to the terrorists in the jungle and, in common with the general trend of transport support operations, the maximum effort in terms of the number of leaflets dropped increased to a peak in 1955 and thereafter decreased as the residual terrorist threat was eliminated, although the maximum number of leaflet dropping sorties was actually flown in 1951.

Few leaflets were dropped during the first few months of the campaign as the psychological offensive was still in its infancy. During July and August 1948 several sorties were flown over Perak, Southern Selangor and Southern Johore, but a total of less than 100 leaflet dropping sorties were flown during the first nine months of the campaign. Most of the leaflets that were dropped at this time were of a strategic nature to inform the local populace of the state of the Emergency. The monthly average of ten leaflet dropping sorties was maintained from April 1949 to December 1950, during which period 12,520,000 leaflets were dropped on 229 sorties. Notable amongst the tasks that were carried out in this period was the dropping of over one million leaflets over known terrorist concentrations to announce the first surrender terms of the Emergency that were issued on 6 September 1949.[252]

During the second half of 1950 tactical leaflets were developed with the employment of surrendered terrorists to make direct appeals to their former comrades, in order to encourage their defection, and numerous leaflet dropping sorties were carried out in support of ground force operations as a result. As the Briggs Plan got under way in 1951 a greater effort was directed at advertising rewards for informers and propaganda efforts were stepped up against youths who had fled into the jungle to escape the Manpower Regulations of the Government.[253] Both of these developments increased the demands made on the air forces for leaflet dropping missions and during the first nine months of 1951, which coincided with the peak of terrorist activity, 261 missions were flown and the average sortie rate and number of leaflets dropped trebled in comparison with the previous two years. A notable achievement was recorded in June 1951, during the course of which month $2\frac{1}{4}$ million leaflets were dropped on 106 sorties, mostly in support of Operation 'Warbler' in Johore[254]—the maximum number of leaflet dropping sorties that were flown in any one month of the campaign.

From September 1951 to February 1952 a further 1,633,000 leaflets were dropped on 237 sorties by Dakotas and offensive support aircraft over Johore, Perak, Selangor, Negri Sembilan, Kelantan and Pahang, most of which contained safe conduct passes and details of the rewards that were offered for information concerning terrorist locations.[255] In the second half of 1952 the average number of leaflet dropping sorties fell to less than ten a month, most of which were carried out by Valettas of No 52 Squadron, although the monthly totals of leaflets dropped remained at over one million. A notable effort was made in August 1952 when 3,276,000 leaflets were dropped by No 52 Squadron, mostly in the Operation 'Habitual' area near Kuantan in Eastern Pahang.[256]

During 1953, as a result of further evidence from surrendered enemy personnel that the terrorists were susceptible to propaganda, the leaflet dropping commitment of the air forces gradually rose from an average of eleven sorties a month in the first half of the year to 23 in the second half. During the whole of 1953 over sixty million leaflets were dropped, more than five times as many as in the previous year, with a maximum monthly effort in October when 19,536,000 leaflets were dropped on 51 sorties. Included in the total for this month were fifteen million leaflets bearing a message from a surrendered ranking terrorist which were distributed by Lincolns of No 1 (RAAF) and No 83 (RAF) Squadrons during Operation 'Bison 1'.[257] This operation was supported by the two loudhailing Valettas that had begun operations earlier in the year and which flew an average of fifty sorties a month during the second half of 1953 as surrendered terrorists confirmed that it was the advice of broadcast messages, allied to one of the millions of leaflets that now festooned the jungle, which finally convinced them that their cause was no longer worth the sacrifices involved.

During 1954 the commitment of the air forces in the psychological warfare campaign continued at a high level. Valettas of the Far East Transport Wing from their base at Kuala Lumpur and Austers of No 656 Squadron flew 146 strategic and 182 tactical leaflet dropping missions during the year,[258] during which they dropped over sixty million leaflets. Half of these leaflets were distributed by light aircraft on pinpoint targets and terrorist cultivation plots in deep jungle areas. The highest monthly total of the year was achieved in November when 7,220,000 leaflets were dropped during thirty supply drop sorties over operational areas throughout the Federation. Throughout 1954 the loudhailing unit of one or two Dakotas and two Austers also carried the psychological offensive to the terrorists during tactical missions that were designed to exploit the elimination of any terrorist as soon as possible after the event. Over 600 loudhailing sorties were flown during the year, nearly two thirds of them by Dakotas and the remainder by Austers. Dakota loudhailing missions involved sorties which averaged just over one hour in duration while those flown by Austers lasted for an average of just over forty minutes.[259] The maximum loudhailing effort of 1954 occurred in August when 89 sorties were carried out in thirteen days over 400 targets throughout the Federation in a special operation which proclaimed the peace agreement in Indo China.[260]

The year 1955 witnessed the peak of activity in the psychological warfare campaign and the contribution made by the air forces doubled in comparison with the previous year with the delivery of 141 million leaflets on 365 leaflet dropping sorties and of 906 hours of broadcasting from the air during the course of the 922 sorties that were flown to meet 2,111 requests for loudhailing support. The declaration of the amnesty on 9 September 1955 heralded the largest leaflet dropping operations of the Emergency and within the following seven days, 21 million leaflets were dropped by Valettas over jungle areas to inform the terrorists of the surrender terms, while a further six million tactical leaflets were dropped to inform them of the location of 'safe areas' and surrender points.[261] Voice aircraft were committed to the initial publicity of the amnesty terms over special areas but their major contribution to the operation was made when requests from District War Executive Committees began to arrive at the Joint Operations Centre for special messages to be broadcast over specific areas where terrorist groups were known to be hiding.[262] Between 9 and 21 September the three Dakotas and two Austers of the Voice Flight of No 267 Squadron carried out 106 sorties in answering these requests as promptly as possible and in one case a message was broadcast over the Raub area of Johore within three hours and fifty minutes of the surrender of the District Committee member of the MCP, Miew Pak.[263]

When the prospect of peace talks became a reality all forms of anti-terrorist propaganda were curtailed and the number of leaflets that were dropped from the air fell from over 29 million in September 1955 to under five million in each of the last three months of the year, although nearly 100 tactical loudhailing sorties were still required during this period. However, the failure of the Baling talks in December 1955 and the announcement of the end of the amnesty on 8 February 1956 were given wide publicity and 20,685,000 leaflets were dropped between 2 and 12 January during Operation 'Hebrides'.[264] From 18 to 20 January a further 9,720,000 leaflets were dropped during Operation 'Tasmania'[265] to stress the end of the amnesty and to draw the attention of the terrorists to the approaching Chinese New Year, with its associated thoughts of family reunion and anticipation of the future. The psychological warfare campaign, however, suffered to some extent from the aftermath of the abortive peace talks and the leaflet dropping commitment of the air forces fell to four or five million a month between February and October 1955 and less than 50 'voice' sorties were carried out each month during this period. In November 1956, however, Government efforts to counteract the terrorists' 'wait and see' policy by emphasizing the determination to fight on after Independence until militant and subversive Communism in Malaya was completely destroyed, resulted in 9,500,000 leaflets being distributed from the air during Operation 'Iceland',[266] which brought the monthly total to over fifteen million leaflets and the total for the whole of 1956 to just over 100 million—the second highest total of the Emergency. Thirteen million of these leaflets had been delivered by Austers of No 656 Squadron and the remainder were dropped during the 333 leaflet dropping sorties that were flown by the Valettas of Nos 48, 52 and 110 Squadrons and the Bristol Freighters of No 41 (RNZAF) Squadron.

'Voice' operations also increased to an average of over 75 sorties a month towards the end of 1956 and the 2,246 requests for loudhailing missions that were met during the year, as well as the 309 hours of flying achieved by the Voice Flight of No 267 Squadron in this role during August 1956, represented the maximum annual and monthly effort of the whole Emergency, although the 766 hours of broadcasting that were carried out during the year were less than the 906 hours achieved in 1955. 1,761 of the 2,295 hours of flying that was expended on 'voice' operations during 1956 were accredited to the three loudhailing Dakotas and the remainder to the two Austers of the Voice Flight of No 267 Squadron.[267] Much of this loudhailing was concerned with the tactical exploitation of specific terrorist eliminations, such as the killing of Ah Ho, the South Malayan Bureau Representative and State Committee Secretary of the MCP in Negri Sembilan, on 11 October.[268] Meanwhile the strategic policy of underlining the high terrorist elimination rate and the disintegration of their organization continued unabated.

The main aspects of the psychological warfare campaign continued throughout 1957 but the reduction in the number of terrorists that remained in the jungle meant that there were fewer eliminations to exploit and both the number of leaflets dropped and the number of 'voice' broadcasts that were made showed a marked decrease over the totals that were achieved in 1956. Altogether just under 87½ million leaflets were dropped during 1957, including 20 million during Operation 'Greenland I'[269] which was mounted a few days after Independence was declared on 31 August to give details of the new 'Merdeka' offer of surrender terms that were to apply until the end of the year. During this operation 8,320,000 leaflets were dropped by Valettas of the air transport support force at Kuala Lumpur between 7 and 9 September, while Austers of No 656 Squadron delivered a further 3,600,000 leaflets during the same period. Towards the end of 1957 it was decided to extend the closing date of the 'Merdeka' peace offer until 30 April 1958 and a further leaflet dropping operation, 'Greenland II',[270] was mounted, during which Valettas and Austers dropped 12,950,000 leaflets between 17 and 21 December 1957.

'Voice' broadcasts during 1957 occupied 707 hours in meeting 1,801 requests, which represented a slight reduction in effort compared with the previous year and was over 20 per cent less than the task carried out during 1955. This reduction was partly due to aircraft unserviceability, which was becoming an increasing problem and was responsible for the abortion of 105 sorties during the year,[271] but was mainly a result of the lack of exploitable incidents, of which there were only sixteen during February 1957[272]—less than half the monthly average of 1955. A slight intensification of 'voice' broadcasting occurred in May 1957 when the elimination of Teng Fook Loong was followed by 35 sorties over Negri Sembilan in order to induce the remainder of the 3rd Independent Platoon MRLA to surrender,[273] while the elimination of Ah Futt, the State Committee Secretary of the MCP for Selangor, and the withdrawal of the Armed Work Force from South Kedah and Province Wellesley shortly afterwards, were followed by similar intensive propaganda activity.[274] During Operation 'Duffle' in July 1957[275] 'voice' aircraft were used for the first time during the Emergency in conjunction with offensive air support when a broadcast was made immediately after the bombs had been released in order to persuade the recipients to surrender before worse befell them.

As the number of terrorists decreased and contact between those that remained and the ground forces became increasingly rare, it was envisaged that psychological warfare, by means of air-dropped leaflets and aerial broadcasts, would play a greater part in combined operations than hitherto and no reduction in effort on the part of the air forces acting in this role was expected during 1958.[276] In the event slightly more than 86 million leaflets were dropped during 1958, almost as many as in 1957, of which 43 million were used to exploit specific successes achieved by the security forces and the remainder were strategic leaflets used to announce general developments in the campaign and to prosecute the long-term anti-communist offensive.[277] The increase in the number of terrorist eliminations had a cumulative effect, however, which combined with the fact that a high proportion were achieved by the Police Special Branch in Northern Johore and Southern Perak, and were not immediately publicized for fear of prejudicing the outcome of their operations,[278] to ensure that the tactical loudhailing task was considerably reduced during 1958. Furthermore, in order to conserve the limited flying time that was left to the ageing 'voice' Dakotas, the average number of broadcasts that were made over each target area was reduced from five to three[279] and the broadcasting time on each sortie was reduced even further as ground force operations were mounted further away from Kuala Lumpur and involved additional positioning time. Altogether 503 hours of aerial broadcasting were completed in 1958, 30 per cent less than in 1957, while the proportion of broadcasting time to total flying time fell to less than 25 per cent by the end of the year.

In a strategic role the success of the 'Merdeka' peace offer resulted in its extension to 31 July 1958 and details of this development were disseminated by Operation 'Greenland III',[280] during which 8,500,000 leaflets were dropped and numerous aerial broadcasts were made over areas where the remaining terrorists were located. In addition some $2\frac{1}{2}$ million leaflets were dropped regularly each month as part of the general anti-communist propaganda offensive.[281] Tactical leaflet operations that were mounted during 1958 included Operation 'Elba' and Operation 'St. Helena',[282] during which $15\frac{1}{2}$ million leaflets were dropped to announce the collapse of the MCP in Southern Perak and Northern Johore and the surrender of State Committee Member Hor Lung, while the leaflet dropping and loudhailing support that was given to Operations 'Ginger', 'Bintang' and 'Chieftain' in Perak and to Operations 'Leo' and 'Tiger' in Selangor and Johore[283] materially assisted their successful conclusion. In particular, a large number of terrorists surrendered as a direct result of hearing aerial broadcasts in the Operation 'Bintang' area of Central Perak, while a further 33 terrorists were eliminated in the Operation 'Leo' area of Selangor primarily as a result of similar efforts.[284]

By the beginning of 1959 ground force operations were largely concentrated in Central Kedah and particularly in Northern Perak and opportunities for the tactical exploitation of individual successes had become rare. With the closure of operations in Johore Austers were considered unsuitable for loudhailing missions in the mountainous regions of Northern Perak and the remaining commitment in this role was carried out by a detachment of two Dakotas of No 209 Squadron from their base at Bayan Lepas on Penang Island.[285] By ensuring that the acceptance of bids for aerial broadcasting was governed by factors of operational justification rather than aircraft availability, all important commitments were met despite the low serviceability of these obsolete and ageing aircraft and their temperamental loudhailing equipment. A total of 200 hours of aerial broadcasting were carried out during 1959, less than 50 per cent of the task completed in 1958, while the 40 million leaflets that were dropped during the year represented a similar decrease in effort. By the end of 1959 opportunities for the tactical exploitation of terrorist eliminations had dwindled almost to nothing and the situation was exacerbated by the delays that were involved in obtaining clearance to operate 'voice' or leaflet dropping aircraft over Thai territory.[286] This difficulty destroyed the utility of any tactical message, which depended primarily on a quick reaction to information received for any success it might achieve, while the relative sanctuary that was offered by crossing the border nullified the pressure maintained on the terrorists by the Security Forces which was necessary for obtaining any significant results from a psychological offensive. Consequently, apart from inducing the last remaining terrorists in Selangor to surrender after the elimination of State Committee Member Hoong Poh,[287] almost all leaflet dropping and loudhailing operations during the last few months of the Emergency were concerned with the delivery of strategic messages to isolated groups of terrorists in Northern Perak exhorting them to avail themselves of existing surrender terms. This commitment continued even after the Emergency had been officially declared over and five to ten hours of aerial broadcasting and nearly $1\frac{1}{2}$ million leaflets were still being delivered from the air each month at the end of 1960.

During the entire Malayan campaign nearly 500 million leaflets were dropped on more than 2,500 sorties and nearly 4,000 hours of aerial broadcasting were completed on a further 4,500 sorties by aircraft of the air transport support forces.

Results of the Air Forces' Contribution to the Psychological Warfare Campaign

The main aims of the psychological warfare campaign in Malaya were to persuade the terrorists to surrender and, by so doing, to disrupt their organization and to spread disaffection amongst their former comrades, and to encourage the civil population to oppose them. The chief instruments of this campaign were the printed leaflet and the broadcast message and it is sufficient to note that without the assistance of the air forces in the delivery of these media of communication much of the effort that was put into the psychological warfare campaign would have proved abortive.

The success of the secondary aim of this campaign, although less spectacular, was made apparent in Penang in 1951 when air dropped leaflets advertising rewards for information about terrorist locations resulted in a fivefold increase in the amount of intelligence material that was volunteered to the police.[288] With regard to the offensive that was mounted against the morale and loyalties of the terrorists, the sole yardstick for measuring its success lay in the number of terrorists whose decision to surrender was influenced in some measure by this subversive campaign. Although the exact number who were thus persuaded will never be known, it undoubtedly represented a large percentage of those who surrendered while the doubt and suspicion and the dislocation of plans which this constant psychological harrying engendered amongst the remaining terrorists seriously weakened their offensive potential and played an important part in bringing the Emergency to a successful conclusion. In any battle for the minds and loyalties of men, however, it is not to be expected that quick or spectacular results will be forthcoming and it was not until the number of terrorist surrenders reached the proportions of a major defeat from 1955 onwards that the full effects of the long and patient psychological offensive could be appreciated. Thus in 1959 130 terrorists in Johore and Negri Sembilan were persuaded to give themselves up to the Police Special Branch by messages emanating from their erstwhile leader, Hor Lung, who had agreed to work for the Psychological Warfare Department.[289] Nevertheless, even as early as 1949 48 of the 207 terrorists who surrendered between September and December of that year in response to the Government's offer of surrender terms, did so after reading leaflets that had been dropped from the air[290] and by 1953 most of the terrorists who wished to surrender availed themselves of the safe conduct passes that were attached to these documents. Similarly, the statements of surrendered enemy personnel provide plentiful evidence of the persuasiveness of aerial broadcasts in influencing their decision to defect. During the first two months of regular 'voice' operations in May and June 1953, eight terrorists came out of the jungle as a result of hearing aerial broadcasts and others claimed to have been partly persuaded by them.[291] By 1955 70 per cent of all surrendered terrorists who had heard one of these aerial broadcasts stated that it had influenced their decision and in many cases it was the major factor involved.[292] The statement of just one surrendered terrorist serves to summarize the effectiveness of leaflet dropping and aerial broadcasting in encouraging defection from the Communist cause:[293]

> 'After the attack on our cultivation area we fled to another area where we saw many Government propaganda leaflets and safe conduct passes. I picked up some of the leaflets intending to use them when coming out to surrender. A few days later we heard voices coming from an aeroplane calling on us all to surrender and offering good treatment. We all agreed to this suggestion.'

CHAPTER 5

AIR RECONNAISSANCE IN THE MALAYAN CAMPAIGN

Intelligence and Air Reconnaissance

In the Malayan campaign the key to the success of combined operations against an elusive enemy operating in relatively featureless jungle terrain was the provision of reliable information about his location and movements. Sources of this basic intelligence were many and varied but one of the most important was aerial reconnaissance—the third major role played by the air forces in the campaign against the terrorists after the provision of offensive and transport support and one on which the other two were largely dependent.

After the Second World War intelligence establishments throughout the Far East Command had been scaled down and at the start of the Emergency there was a dearth of information about Malaya and its inhabitants which the development of aerial reconnaissance went a long way towards solving. In the absence of this information there was no such thing as the target intelligence which would be expected to exist in a normal campaign and operations against the terrorists had to be mounted on an *ad hoc* basis by sifting and screening numerous reports from all branches of the Security Forces, including those based on aerial reconnaissance. Not only was aerial reconnaissance a profitable source of basic intelligence but it also played an important part in confirming and pinpointing targets which had been reported, usually inaccurately, by police informers and other agents. Aerial reconnaissance was a constant commitment of the air forces throughout the campaign and comprised two well-defined roles—photographic and visual reconnaissance.

PHOTOGRAPHIC RECONNAISSANCE

Aircraft

Almost the entire photographic reconnaissance (PR) commitment of the campaign was undertaken by aircraft of No 81 Squadron, one of the few squadrons to serve throughout the Emergency without relief and the only unit of its kind in the Far East. In February 1948 No 81 Squadron, equipped with nine Mosquitos and two Spitfires, was transferred from Changi to Tengah and in May of that year one of the Spitfires was attached to the small RAF task force that was operating from Taiping in support of police operations in Northern Perak.[1] When the Emergency was declared in June 1948 it was planned to place a detachment of Mosquitos from No 81 Squadron with the RAF task force at Kuala Lumpur but, owing to the difficulties of maintaining these aircraft under field conditions in the tropics and the tactical nature of the photography required, it was decided to send a small detachment of two Spitfires instead.[2] In June 1949 a further Spitfire was converted to the photographic reconnaissance role and joined this detachment at Kuala Lumpur.[3] On 20 March 1950 this detachment of three Spitfires from No 81 Squadron was transferred as a separate flight to No 60 Squadron at Tengah and on the same day the nine Mosquitos and one Anson that remained in No 81 Squadron were transferred from Tengah to their new base at Seletar.[4] Normally the PR Spitfires of No 60 Squadron were limited to operations within 150 miles of Tengah and all other reconnaissance missions were flown by the Mosquitos of No 81 Squadron at Seletar, but urgent tasks that the aircraft of either squadron were unable to fulfil in their own operational areas were passed on to the other squadron. The Spitfires of No 60 Squadron were briefed at Tengah but landed at Seletar for de-briefing, except when they flew missions in Northern Malaya from the advanced base at Kuala Lumpur.[5]

On 21 November 1950, after only eight months in operation, the dichotomy in the photographic reconnaissance forces was remedied when the three PR Spitfires of No 60 Squadron were transferred to No 81 Squadron at Seletar, bringing its total strength to nine Mosquitos, five Spitfires and one Anson as two more Spitfires had just been delivered.[6] The aircraft of No 81 Squadron, however, were already beginning to show signs of their advancing age and it became clear that re-equipment was essential if the increased operational effort was to be maintained. It was not until the end of 1953, however, that the five PR Spitfires of No 81 Squadron were replaced by five PR Meteors and one training Meteor and the six surviving Mosquitos were not finally withdrawn from service until the end of 1955.[7] With their departure the total strength of No 81 Squadron fell from fifteen to six aircraft but a further PR Meteor and four PR Pembrokes were added to its establishment in 1956.[8] On 1 February 1958 three of these Pembrokes were withdrawn and two months later No 81 Squadron, armed with five PR Meteors and two training Meteors and one PR Pembroke, was transferred from Seletar back to Tengah, where it remained for the remainder of the campaign although temporary detachments were sent to Kuala Lumpur on various occasions.[9] By 1959 No 81 Squadron was reduced to only three PR Meteors and one training Meteor but the Squadron was brought up to strength again in October of that year with the arrival of three PR Canberras and one training Canberra.[10]

No 81 Squadron bore the brunt of the photographic reconnaissance commitment throughout the campaign but some assistance was provided towards the end by temporary detachments of PR Canberras from No 3 Group Bomber Command (Operation 'Planter's Punch'). Four Canberras of No 542 Squadron arrived at Changi in May 1955 and were replaced at three monthly intervals by similar detachments, reduced to two aircraft on 14 June 1956, of Nos 540, 82 and 58 Squadrons.[11] These detachments ceased as a regular commitment with the return of No 58 Squadron to the United Kingdom in October 1956 but Bomber Command continued to provide two PR Canberras in the Far East for periods of two months twice a year, usually from January to March and from July to September, for the remainder of the campaign.

Techniques of Photographic Reconnaissance, Strategic and Tactical Reconnaissance

Photographic reconnaissance from the air was undertaken during the Malayan campaign in both a strategic and tactical role, the object of the former being the revision of existing maps and the provision of new maps of areas that had not been previously surveyed while the latter involved direct support of the security forces through the medium of large scale aerial photographs both for initial intelligence and for briefing purposes.

In the strategic role the aerial survey of Malaya's 51,000 square miles was completed by the RAF in three stages.[12] The initial commitment was undertaken in 1945 on behalf of the Colonial Office Survey Department in order to revise the incomplete map coverage of the country but, owing to the small size of the force engaged on this task and other urgent commitments within the theatre, progress was slow and intermittent and by 1948 a total of only 16,460 square miles had been photographed and no revised maps had yet been produced. When the Emergency was declared in June of that year this revision programme had to be accelerated and a start made on the photography of areas for which no one inch to one mile maps existed. At that time the only available maps on which to plan operations against the terrorists were reprints of pre-war issues on a one inch to one mile scale which, although tolerably accurate, covered only the populated areas of Western Malaya. The only available maps of those areas in Northern and Central Malaya where operations against the terrorists were undertaken at that time were a few of pre-war vintage on a scale of $2\frac{1}{2}$ inches to one mile, on which the most important ground features were located with some degree of accuracy but others, including even rivers, were misplaced or omitted altogether and large areas were still marked 'unexplored'. These maps were virtually useless for the ground force operations that were mounted in difficult jungle country during the early stages of the campaign and it was essential that revised or completely new maps of the main operational areas at an adequate scale should be produced as quickly as possible. This second phase of the aerial survey of Malaya was completed by September 1950 with a coverage of 23,590 square miles of Malaya and about 7,000 square miles of Southern Thailand. The final stage of the overall programme was then undertaken by No 81 Squadron, which entailed photographing the remainder of Malaya at a scale of $2\frac{1}{2}$ inches to one mile and, by August 1952, a total of 13,740 square miles had been covered and the aerial survey of the entire country was virtually complete.

As a result of this photographic survey of Malaya No 2 Air Survey Liaison Section (the Army unit working in co-operation with No 81 Squadron) produced, by the beginning of 1953, 129 new air reconnaissance maps at a scale of one inch to one mile and fourteen new quarter inch to a mile maps which were of inestimable value in planning and mounting the offensive against the terrorists during the later stages of the campaign.[13]

The production of new or revised one inch to one mile maps of Malaya was a considerable help to jungle patrols but there was still a need for tactical air photographs on a larger scale to provide both initial intelligence of the location of terrorists hideouts and to assist in the briefing of ground and air forces in difficult jungle areas. For example, a survey photograph at a scale of $1\frac{1}{2}$-inches to one mile could reveal a clearing but not the presence of terrorists while a tactical photograph taken at a scale of 1 : 10,000 could reveal that the clearing contained newly cultivated vegetable plots and expert interpretation could determine whether or not these were of Chinese origin. Similarly, a survey photograph might show a ground patrol that a swamp area lay between them and their objective but was not detailed enough to indicate the easiest way through it. Intelligent use of tactical air photographs at a scale of 1 : 10,000 could save ground force patrols hours of marching and enable them to surround an area where an incident had occurred before the enemy had time to disperse.

Tactical air photography had been carried out since the start of the Emergency but only on a limited scale and as occasion demanded. By 1951, however, its value was fully appreciated as it was found that even recently revised one inch to one mile maps were no longer fully effective aids for ground force patrols. As the programme for the resettlement of squatters got under way the site of former villages reverted to swamp and secondary jungle within six months while, within the same period, new rubber estates could be developed and the terrorists could clear cultivation plots from virgin jungle and produce crops of tapioca from them. It was clear that systematic tactical photography of the whole country on a scale which gave adequate information of tracks, cultivation plots and temporary camps was the only effective method of recording the changing face of the jungle. This task, which entailed flying over 800 'mosaics' each measuring 10,000 by 20,000 yards at a scale of 1 : 10,000, was accepted by No 81 Squadron in October 1951 and was virtually completed during the course of the next two years. By this time, of course, earlier 'mosaics' were out of date and had to be revised while demands for the special coverage of particular operational areas, both before and after ground and air attacks helped to maintain the demand for tactical photographic reconnaissance throughout the remainder of the Emergency.

The co-ordination of tactical photographic 'mosaics' was not easy since it was difficult to pinpoint an aircraft's position accurately over areas of comparatively featureless jungle and aircrews also had to contend with the normal hazards of bad weather in Malaya which often rendered photographic reconnaissance virtually impossible. A further problem arose in consideration of the height from which these tactical air photographs were taken, and therefore their scale, which necessitated reconciling two conflicting requirements. On the one hand these photographs had to show a minimum amount of detail while, on the other hand, it was necessary to avoid arousing the terrorists' suspicions that they had been located. The Malayan People's Anti-Japanese Army (MPAJA) had learnt about the capabilities of aerial reconnaissance from British liaison officers during the Second World War and experiments at Kuala Lumpur in 1948 had shown that, under ideal conditions, aircraft could be heard, if not seen, up to a height of 15,000 feet. Unfortunately, photographs taken from 16,000 feet with a twenty foot focal length camera only achieved a scale of 1 : 10,000. Photographs produced at a scale of 1 : 5,000 or even 1 : 8,000 gave so much more detail that the problem of interpretation was both more accurate and more rapid.[14] During the early part of the campaign, therefore, it was a case of assessing on each particular sortie whether it was wise to risk compromising the security of a possible ground or air attack in order to have the advantages of a large scale photograph or to remain undetected and accept the limitations of a smaller scale. Fortunately, by the time that the RAF accepted tactical photographic reconnaissance as a regular commitment on a systematic basis in 1951, the standard of photographic interpretation had increased so much through the acquisition of local knowledge that a scale of 1 : 10,000 was acceptable in most cases. Vertical photographs on a scale of 1 : 5,000, as well as close-up obliques, were still produced, however, for special operations when conditions of terrain and weather permitted.

Photographic 'mosaics' at a scale of 1 : 10,000 and measuring three feet by two feet were annotated with datum points and, in the absence of target maps, became essential tools for the planning and briefing of operations mounted by both the ground and air forces. For the sake of convenience, smaller annotated 'mosaics', measuring twenty inches by fourteen inches, were produced for use in the field. These photographs served as basic operational maps and enabled patrol commanders to acquire an accurate knowledge of the type of terrain over which they had to operate. As they became more experienced they were able to memorize complete operations, in the various aspects of attacks and sweeps, and also recognize the best locations for the preparation of ambushes, by the security forces or the terrorists, entirely from these photographs. Similarly, the variations in light and shade that were apparent on air photographs proved invaluable to aircrews in fixing their exact location over featureless jungle terrain.[15]

One difficulty that arose when locating targets from large-scale photographs that had been taken from low-flying aircraft was the distortion caused by the deeply dissected terrain. To overcome this difficulty pinpoints were first located on small scale survey photographs, on which the distortion was less marked, and these were transferred to tactical photographs by cross reference with salient features of the landscape. This work was a small part of the task carried out by No 103 Army Photographic Interpretation Section (APIS) at HQ, Malaya District and Joint Air Photographic Intelligence Centre (JAPIC(FE)) at RAF Kuala Lumpur, Seletar, Tengah and Butterworth,[16] whose meticulous preparations and interpretation of the air photographs taken by No 81 Squadron was largely responsible for their successful operational application. When the Emergency was declared there was a dearth of trained intelligence officers in Air Command Far East (ACFE) and General Duties officers were transferred from Changi to carry out this task at Kuala Lumpur.[17] By September 1948, however, five trained intelligence officers had been attached to the Advanced AHQ and they became the nucleus of the joint Army and RAF photographic interpretation units that operated with considerable success throughout the remainder of the campaign. Since terrorists camps, at least after the opening stages of the campaign, were seldom identifiable from an air photograph alone unless a certain amount of local information was available, these units also sifted evidence from all branches of the security forces and cross-examined police informers and surrendered enemy personnel with the aid of air photographs. By this method it was often possible to pinpoint a concealed terrorist camp, of which there was no trace in the photograph, by reference to salient topographical features in the vicinity. This type of work required time and patience in dealing with illiterate informants through the medium of interpreters and the situation was exacerbated by the backlog of prints that tended to accumulate as the maximum use had to be made of the limited periods of weather that were fine enough for aerial photography. In some operations, however, time was of the essence and the work of photographic production and interpretation centres often had to be delivered to operational units within 48 hours. On one occasion, in 1954, a certain area was photographed and the prints delivered to a unit 350 miles from Changi on the same day,[18] but normally photographic reconnaissance tasks took from fourteen to thirty days from the receipt of a demand to the final delivery of the prints. Some idea of the amount of work undertaken by these units is given by the fact that in the six months from April to September 1954 No 103 APIS and the JAPIC(FE) detachment at Kuala Lumpur interpreted the results of 225 photographic sorties, carrying out the detailed examination of over 56,000 prints and issuing 537 'mosaics' as a result. In the same period 227 'mosaics' were laid by similar units at Tengah, of which 128 were used for the detailed briefing of air strikes and provided 100 pinpoints and 131 area targets, while a further 123 pinpoint targets were afforded by the 53 'mosaics' that were laid by a JAPIC(FE) detachment at Butterworth.[19]

Summary of Photographic Reconnaissance Operations

Details of the number of sorties that were flown by No 81 Squadron in the photographic reconnaissance role during the campaign against the terrorists in Malaya are given in Annex Z.

The first operational sortie carried out by this squadron in Malaya was flown on 21 April 1948 by a PR Spitfire of the small RAF task force that was operating from Taiping in support of the police operation, Operation 'Haystack', in the Sungei Perak valley.[20] The mission was aborted because of weather conditions, however, and because of the poor serviceability of the Spitfire such photographic reconnaissance as was required during the remainder of this operation was carried out by Austers of No 1914 Air Observation Post (AOP) Flight, No 656 Squadron. It was only when a detachment of two Spitfires of No 81 Squadron arrived at Kuala Lumpur in July 1948 that tactical photographic reconnaissance missions were flown with any degree of frequency and even then demands were satisfied as they occurred and the commitment lacked co-ordination and systematic planning.[21] In fact, for the first two or three months of the campaign, all photographic requirements in the tactical role were flown by one Spitfire and one pilot of No 81 Squadron who once flew for 56 days in succession and carried out over 60 sorties, of which about 40 were successful.[22] For the first eighteen months of the campaign an average of twenty to thirty tactical photographic reconnaissance sorties each month by the Spitfires of No 81 Squadron were sufficient to meet the demands of the Army and the Police and it was rarely necessary to divert the squadron's Mosquitos at Tengah from their primary task of the Malayan Survey, which required a similar monthly effort since half of their sorties were aborted by bad weather.

The tempo of photographic reconnaissance operations remained fairly constant until the end of 1950, although the monthly output of photographic prints increased from 22,000 in April 1949 to 83,000 in December 1950.[23] The acceptance of the 'Firedog Mosaic' commitment in October 1951, however, resulted in a marked increase in the operational effort of No 81 Squadron and, since over 75 per cent of its aircraft potential was occupied in this task, few Mosquitos could be spared for work on the Malayan Survey.[24] The average monthly effort rose to over 80 sorties and by the end of June 1952 over 700 sorties had been flown on the block cover of the Federation of Malaya, 415 of them, covering 280 tactical areas, in the five months between September 1951 and February 1952.[25] Demands had been flown on a priority basis so that all areas where incidents had occurred, or were likely to occur, had been photographed by the middle of 1952.

Despite difficulties in maintaining the ageing Spitfires in a serviceable condition, the sortie rate of No 81 Squadron increased to a maximum for the whole Emergency in 1953, with an average of over 100 a month, of which only one-third, however, produced satisfactory results.[26] During 1954 Mosquitos and Meteors of this squadron shared the average monthly task of about 70 sorties almost equally but Mosquitos carried out only 10 per cent of a similar commitment during 1955 and went out of service at the end of the year.[27] By this time the increasing use of elaborate camouflage techniques by the terrorists had reduced the amount of intelligence material that could be gleaned from tactical photographic reconnaissance and most of the effort of No 81 Squadron was directed towards obtaining the topographical cover, at a scale of 1 : 20,000, that was required for mounting and conducting ground force operations, and also the photographs at a scale of 1 : 10,000 that were taken of all target areas after air strikes that were carried out after September 1958.[28] Meteors of No 81 Squadron met this commitment with about 50 sorties each month from 1956 to the beginning of 1959, with a slight fall in effort towards the end of the campaign while occasional photographic reconnaissance flights were made by the Pembrokes that were attached to the squadron in 1956.[29]

VISUAL RECONNAISSANCE

Aircraft

Even more important than photographic reconnaissance in locating terrorist hideouts was the visual reconnaissance which was the main commitment of the twenty to thirty Austers that were operated by No 656 Squadron throughout the Emergency. The formation of this squadron, and the deployment of its component flights at brigade level throughout the Federation of Malaya, has been discussed under the section dealing with its communications role.[30] In addition to these Austers, which were jointly operated by the Army and the RAF, air-strike and medium range transport aircraft were sometimes employed on visual reconnaissance missions, especially at the beginning of the campaign, while Sunderland flying boats of Nos 88, 205 and 209 Squadrons based at Seletar undertook coastal patrols in co-operation with the Royal Navy as a regular commitment.

Techniques of Visual Reconnaissance

The visual reconnaissance that was undertaken by the Austers of No 656 Squadron took various forms, the most important of which was the routine and systematic searching for terrorist camps and other signs of their presence in order to remedy the general lack of information about their whereabouts that was the biggest single drawback to Security Force operations. Each brigade area, covering some 150 by 60 miles, was allotted one flight of five or six Austers and as the pilots gained experience they acquired an intimate knowledge of a particular area and were able to spot any variant in the current picture that was maintained on a master map at flight headquarters.[31] Care was taken, however, to exchange the locations of individual flights at intervals so that over-familiarity with one particular area should not lead to any oversight being made.[32] Even so, visual reconnaissance in the conditions that prevailed in Malaya required considerable luck as well as constant vigilance for hours on end, sometimes in cloud and torrential rain, over broken and precipitous terrain where no possible landing grounds existed. To achieve the best results most visual reconnaissance was carried out before 1400 hours if possible, after which the clouding over of the sun made it impossible to see objects on the jungle floor. The difficulties inherent in visual reconnaissance are shown by the fact that in 1955 it required an average of nine hours of systematic searching to produce one 'find'.[33]

Despite the Auster's low airspeed of only 80 knots it was virtually impossible to spot terrorist camps unless they were located in relatively open clearings. By 1950, however, most camps were located under the jungle canopy or, if they were in small clearings, they were effectively concealed from the air and became visible only when they had been vacated and their camouflage of fresh, green leaves had been dried and bleached.[34] Auster pilots were, therefore, advised not to waste their time looking for terrorist camps but to concentrate on other tell-tale signs of their activity such as tracks that had no apparently legitimate reason, circular water holes, smoke from cooking fires and clothes that were hung out to dry. Main terrorist camps were frequently located near prominent landmarks, such as unusual tree or rock formations, which therefore merited special attention, while staging camps that were used on the night before or after an incident were often to be found in the 'belukar' or zone of secondary, scrub jungle close to inhabited areas.[35]

At the beginning of the campaign there was a tendency for visual reconnaissance to be carried out from a height that was too low to cover a sufficiently large area on each sortie and, by 1951, Auster pilots were advised to use binoculars from a height of 3,000 feet in order to scan the ground and to descend for a closer look at any suspicious sign.[36] The height at which Auster pilots on reconnaissance missions flew was an important consideration since it was necessary to achieve the most effective coverage of an area without compromising the security of subsequent ground or air operations by their presence. By 1953 the terrorists had become extremely conscious of aerial surveillance and were liable to move away from an area if they thought that they had been spotted from an Auster aircraft on the assumption that it heralded the presence of ground forces or imminent air-strike action.[37] Care had to be taken, therefore, not to circle suspected enemy locations in order to obtain confirmation of their presence while deception tactics, designed to make it appear that reconnaissance Austers were engaged on regular communications tasks, had to be employed if necessary. By the time, however, the terrorists had begun their withdrawal into the deep jungle of the spinal ridge of Malaya and routine reconnaissance flights to locate the cultivation plots on which they depended for survival became an increasing commitment of No 656 Squadron. In order to have any chance of spotting the small, brown patches in the green jungle that denoted a terrorist cultivation plot it was usually necessary for Auster pilots to fly below 1,000 feet, which exposed them to a danger that was virtually unknown during the Malayan campaign. Aircraft were usually immune from attack from any quarter but so efficacious was the work of Austers in the food denial campaign that the MCP departed from its usual policy of evasion in 1954 and issued a directive that they were to be engaged with small arms and light automatic fire whenever possible. There is only one recorded occasion, however, when this directive was implemented and no damage was caused to either the aircraft or its pilot.[38]

Apart from the systematic searching for signs of terrorist activity, Austers of No 656 Squadron were employed in various other reconnaissance roles. Owing to the difficulty which ground force patrols had in fixing their location exactly and in maintaining ground communications in jungle terrain, Austers were frequently employed in a contact reconnaissance role to guide them to their objective. When they were contacted by wireless ground patrols put up smoke markers whose grid references and the bearings and distances to their objectives were then worked out and passed on to them by Auster pilots. As well as acting as an airborne signals link, Austers also carried out passenger reconnaissance to give company or platoon commanders a general appreciation of their operational areas while, on a few occasions, they were also able to operate in their primary role of providing an air observation post for directing artillery fire, both from field batteries and from naval guns.[39] Artillery observation was difficult in jungle conditions, however, as individual explosions were difficult to spot and the irregular format of the tree tops hindered the accurate adjustment of gunsights. Austers of No 656 Squadron also carried out a limited amount of photographic reconnaissance, usually of an urgent nature as when the ground forces required photographs of an ambush area so that they could position their troops with the minimum amount of ground reconnaissance and possible loss of security. As well as these reconnaissance tasks and their other major commitment in the light liaison role, Austers were also employed on a number of miscellaneous tasks that have already been mentioned under the sections dealing with the provision of offensive and transport support. These included escorting helicopters on casualty evacuation flights and providing their pilots with initial reconnaissance and an airborne signals link with the ground, a limited amount of free-fall supply dropping and target marking and raid reporting during air strikes.[40]

Maritime Reconnaissance

Apart from the task undertaken by the Austers of No 656 Squadron over the mainland of Malaya, the only other regular commitment that was flown by the air forces in the visual reconnaissance role during the Emergency was the patrolling of the coastal waters by aircraft of the Far East Flying Boat Wing. The islands off the East coast of Malaya had always been a medium through which seaborne illegal entries had been made and when the Emergency broke out it was felt that the dangers of this immigration and the smuggling of arms and equipment to the terrorists by sea had greatly increased.[41] Illegal immigrants started from anywhere on the China coast up to as far away as Hainan and crossed the Gulf of Siam in small craft, usually junks, especially during the period of the North-East Monsoon. Reaching the islands off the east coast of Malaya, such as Tioman, during the hours of daylight, they waited on the lee-shore until they could cross to the mainland under cover of darkness. It was quite impossible for the Royal Navy by themselves to keep watch on all the islands from Kota Bharu in the north to the southern tip of Johore in the south while, on the other hand, aircraft were of little use by themselves since there was nothing that they could do even if they did sight a suspicious vessel. Consequently combined patrols, using one sloop or destroyer and one aircraft, were carried out in selected areas according to a pre-arranged plan based on such intelligence as was available of the likely moves of illegal immigrants. The two types of patrol that were involved were the 'Blue Water' patrol, up to 80 miles out to sea and covering 100 miles of the coast in order to intercept any craft attempting to run direct for the shore, and the 'Coastal and Island' patrol to investigate inlets and anchorages in the Tioman group, the southern tip of the Johore coast and the islands off the north-east coast of Trengganu and Kelantan.[42] At the start of the campaign these patrols were carried out by Dakotas and Beaufighters as well as Sunderlands according to the availability of aircraft but, as the intensity of operations against the terrorists increased, this task was left entirely to the flying boats. By 1951 nine lettered air patrols had been established on the east coast of Malaya but, as the combined efforts of the air forces, the navy and the police kept the dangers of illegal immigration well under control and few attempts, if any, were being made to smuggle arms shipments to the terrorists, this commitment did not involve more than one or two sorties a week for the remainder of the campaign.[43]

Summary of Visual Reconnaissance Operations

Owing to the lacuna in information about terrorist movements that existed at the beginning of the campaign, visual reconnaissance was the first commitment of the air forces after the Emergency had been declared and involved a considerable proportion of their total flying time. At the end of April 1948 three Austers of No 1914 Flight were attached to the RAF task force at Taiping that was operating in support of Operation 'Haystack' in Northern Perak.[44] They remained there until 27 May 1948 but were only of limited value owing to their pilots' inexperience in flying too low and the poor quality of the maps which they used.[45] When the Emergency was declared in June 1948 it immediately became necessary to improve the intelligence situation and, for this purpose, two Dakotas of No 52 Squadron were sent from their parent base at Changi to Butterworth to cover the area north of a line from Port Weld to Kota Trengganu as far north as the border with Thailand, while two Dakotas of No 110 Squadron were sent to Kuala Lumpur to cover central Malaya between this line and another through Port Swettenham and Pekan, leaving the remainder of the Federation south of this line to be covered by Dakotas of No 48 Squadron operating from Changi.[46] The first visual reconnaissance patrols of these aircraft were carried out on 28 June 1948 and, on the same day, one Sunderland of No 209 Squadron was ordered to carry out a daily patrol throughout the hours of daylight along the east coast of Malaya to report any movement of shipping within the harbours and within forty miles of the coast.[47] Soon afterwards Spitfires of Nos 28 and 60 Squadrons were ordered to carry out daily patrols of the Pontian Pipeline and Gunong Pulai Reservoir, which were the main sources of the water supply of Singapore and were vulnerable to terrorist attack.[48]

These patrols were carried out throughout the first week of the Emergency and, when the RAF task force was set up at Kuala Lumpur on 3 July 1948 its first week of operations was devoted entirely to reconnaissance flights, with especial attention to the Thailand border area, the east coast between Kelantan and Trengganu and the islands off the coasts of Johore and Pahang.[49] Two aircrews of No 110 Squadron were employed solely on the reconnaissance of the Thailand border area and, by combining photographic with visual reconnaissance, they acquired a mass of information by late August and early September from which existing maps were annotated to help the police in preventing infiltration from across the border along the many paths and river valleys in the area.[50] Until the outbreak of the Emergency all the air forces in the Malayan theatre had been deployed on Singapore Island and such flights as had been undertaken to airfields on the mainland had been purely transit in nature and few aircrews had any substantial knowledge of the terrain, which poor maps did nothing to remedy. These early reconnaissance flights, therefore, gave aircrews experience in distinguishing the essential features of the Malayan landscape so that they could appreciate the correct significance of any unusual or suspect feature. In fact, during these early days many curious phenomena were reported by aircrews which turned out on investigation to be quite normal features of the environment. Even if few tangible results accrued from these long and tedious sorties, therefore, the visual reconnaissance that was a regular commitment of all types of aircraft in the task force at Kuala Lumpur during the first six months of the campaign provided an invaluable basis for their future operations.

By the end of 1948 most of the visual reconnaissance commitment had been taken over by the Austers of No 656 Squadron as its component flights became operational—even though they were limited to 150 flying hours a month, which was less than 10 per cent of the monthly effort they achieved in 1955.[51] Most of their work at this time was directed towards assisting ground force patrols in the contact reconnaissance role, although they did have some success in plotting terrorist camps. They also observed for one naval bombardment and on one occasion, on 22 September 1948, one Auster of No 1902 Flight, flying in support of the 1st Battalion 6th Gurkha Rifles in the Rambat area of Perak, actually opened fire with a Bren gun against a band of fleeing terrorists.[52]

Throughout 1949 and 1950 the visual reconnaissance commitment of No 656 Squadron continued to increase, although communications flights still occupied the majority of its time. With the introduction of other light aircraft into the theatre in 1951, however, the light liaison role of the squadron became less important and more of its time was devoted to the intensified search for terrorist camps, while the advent of a battery of field artillery in Malaya gave the squadron the opportunity to practise their primary role.[53] Between September 1951 and February 1952 just over 1,578 hours were flown by Austers of No 656 Squadron on visual reconnaissance tasks in comparison with the 2,122 hours that were flown on communications sorties and the 1,057 hours on other tasks.[54] During 1952, however, the visual reconnaissance effort of the squadron increased until it occupied over half its total task, particularly after the terrorists began their withdrawal into deep jungle and the spotting of their cultivation plots became of vital tactical importance to the ground forces. Squadron pilots developed a high standard of observation in spotting these plots and cross checks with air photographs showed that they could plot them within two or three hundred yards of their exact position and could also assess accurately the nature of the crops grown on them and the state of their growth.[55]

By the end of 1952 Austers of No 656 Squadron were regularly exceeding their allotted flying task by over 14 per cent in achieving a monthly average of 1,250 flying hours and a total for the year of 12,240 hours, which represented nearly 600 hours for each one of their aircraft and a flying effort far in excess of any other unit of the RAF in operation at that time.[56] The squadron's task continued to increase throughout 1953 and in October of that year its pilots flew a total of 1,708 hours to complete 50,000 flying hours and over four million miles since their arrival in Malaya in 1948.[57] Some indication of the size of their task can be seen in the fact that they achieved a total of 16,665 flying hours during 1953 out of the total of 37,000 flying hours that was expended on all types of air operations flown in connection with the Emergency.[58] 70 per cent of the squadron's work was now concerned with visual reconnaissance in deep jungle and many successful combined operations were mounted as a result of the numerous camps and cultivation plots which they located.[59]

As with other air operations flown during the Emergency, visual reconnaissance continued to increase throughout 1954 and No 656 Squadron, now equipped with 31 Austers, flew for 23,752 hours during the year, an average of over 1,800 hours a month, of which two-thirds were spent on routine reconnaissance over jungle areas.[60] During 1955, however, visual reconnaissance became progressively more difficult as the terrorists intensified their use of camouflage and partially abandoned their policy of growing food in jungle cultivation plots. The flying effort of No 656 Squadron, which averaged over 2,000 flying hours a month at the beginning of the year, had fallen to 1,500 hours a month by the end, with a final total of 21,970 hours for the whole year.[61] However, in December 1955, despite this slight decrease in effort compared with 1954 the squadron achieved its 100,000th flying hour since its arrival in Malaya.[62] As well as their normal reconnaissance tasks they had flown over 100 observation sorties in one month during 1955 in support of the guns of the 25th Field Regiment and the 1st Singapore Regiment, Royal Artillery and those of HMS *Concord*, HMS *Comus* and HMS *Newcastle*, which were supporting ground forces in the successful Operation 'Nassau' in the Kuala Langat area of Selangor.[63]

By the end of 1956 only 8,300 of the 19,000 hours that were flown by No 656 Squadron during the year were concerned with jungle reconnaissance and this task was further restricted during 1957 as the remaining hardcore terrorists became even more elusive and the danger that the presence of an Auster aircraft might compromise a potential target increased.[64] By now the only place where the terrorists could be expected to remain static after scrutiny from a reconnaissance aircraft was on the Thailand side of the Malayan border where they were immune from aerial attack. During 1958 No 656 Squadron, now part of the Army Air Corps and not a RAF squadron, still achieved over 15,000 flying hours, with a first line strength of 24 aircraft, of which 10,900 hours were flown in direct support of the ground forces.[65] By the end of the year, however, only two flights of No 656 Squadron were fully occupied on Operation 'Firedog' tasks. Central Malaya, covered by Nos 14 and 16 Reconnaissance Flights, was relatively quiet and required only an occasional operation of short duration, while in the south of the country the work of No 11 Liaison Flight came to an end after it had helped security forces to conclude their operations in this region by reporting several cooking fires during its dawn and dusk patrols, as a result of which information several successful air strikes were mounted. On one occasion an Auster of this flight actually saw a small terrorist party which was a rare occurrence at this stage of the campaign. On the Thailand border, however, No 7 Reconnaissance Flight continued to operate throughout 1958 and into 1959 and produced some valuable 'finds', including occupied terrorist camps, resting places and cultivations. This flight supported the 28th Commonwealth Brigade in Operation 'Ginger' and their report of ten terrorist camps in July 1958 provided the basic information for 22nd Special Air Service Regiment during Operation 'Boulder' that was mounted east of Grik in Northern Perak. In Southern Perak, operations by No 2 Reconnaissance Flight were restricted during the early part of 1958 while the Police Special Branch rounded up the remaining terrorists in the area and the flight then took over the Thailand border area from No 7 Reconnaissance Flight and flew several successful missions from Alor Star in support of the 1st and 2nd Federal Infantry Brigades.[66]

By the end of 1958 only half of No 656 Squadron was still committed to the support of security force operations while the remainder underwent training in their primary theatre role. However, although the overall tempo of visual reconnaissance continued to decline in accordance with the general trend of Emergency operations it remained fairly high right up until the end of the campaign.

Results of Aerial Reconnaissance

In providing much of the best, and sometimes the only intelligence of terrorist locations, as well as confirming information received from other sources, aerial reconnaissance made a significant contribution to the successful outcome of the campaign in Malaya. No accurate figures are available of the number of terrorists who were killed, captured or who surrendered during operations in which aerial reconnaissance had a direct bearing but they certainly represented the major proportion of the total number of terrorist eliminations that were achieved by the Security Forces. The products of photographic reconnaissance were used during nearly all ground and air operations as a matter of course and materially contributed to any success which they had. The part played by visual reconnaissance in these operations is less easy to define but some idea of its overall contribution can be assessed from the fact that, in the six months between March and August 1955, Austers of No 656 Squadron located 155 confirmed terrorists camps, 77 possible terrorist camps, 313 terrorist cultivations, 31 re-cultivations, 194 clearings that were probably made by terrorists and 21 aborigine farms that were under terrorist domination.[67] During 1956 a further 263 terrorist camps were plotted as a result of the efforts of this squadron, as well as 65 clearings and 112 cultivations of terrorist origin.[68] With regard to the number of eliminations that were achieved as an indirect result of the visual reconnaissance provided by No 656 Squadron, No 1907 Flight claimed that, during six months operations in Pahang in 1953, 44 terrorists were killed by ground forces acting on information which they had provided.[69]

CHAPTER 6

LOCALLY RECRUITED AIR FORCE UNITS IN THE MALAYAN CAMPAIGN

To the role played by the air forces of Great Britain, Australia and New Zealand in the campaign against the terrorists must be added the contribution that was made by those elements of the air forces in Malaya that were recruited locally, which included flying personnel and their ancillary tradesmen and technicians as well as gunners trained in an infantry role for ground defence duties. These belonged to the Malayan Auxiliary Air Force (MAAF) and its successor the Royal Malayan Air Force (RMAF), the RAF (Malaya) and the RAF Regiment (Malaya), all of which were developed during the course of the campaign and played supporting roles of varying importance in its successful conclusion.

The Malayan Auxiliary Air Force

At the beginning of 1949 only two regular fighter squadrons were available in the Far Eastern theatre to carry out commitments in the air defence role and these were primarily engaged on tasks connected with the Emergency in Malaya.[1] To augment this force plans were drawn up at a meeting of the Air Council in March 1949 for the formation of three auxiliary fighter squadrons in Malaya, Singapore and Hong Kong which would relieve regular squadrons of at least part of the internal security commitment in time of war and would ensure that some fighter squadrons were permanently in the Far East even if war compelled the withdrawal of regular squadrons.[2] In addition these auxiliary squadrons would act as an outlet for volunteer enthusiasm and would serve as a basis of the air forces which the Far Eastern colonies would need when they achieved independence.

The initial formation of these auxiliary air forces was the responsibility of the Colonial governments concerned and they retained overall administrative control of them. However, since the object of these squadrons was of equal interest to Great Britain their functional control was invested in the local Air Officer Commanding and the Air Ministry agreed to provide the aircraft and spares required on free loan if the local governments would meet the costs of work services, freight charges and the necessary personnel. Some difficulty was experienced in persuading the governments of the Federation of Malaya and the Colony of Singapore to pass the necessary legislation but, after the financial and legal difficulties had been solved and accommodation had been found, ordinances establishing the MAAF were finally promulgated in May and June 1950 and recruiting and training began in earnest.[3]

Under pressure from FEAF the original policy of the Air Ministry for a Malayan and a Singapore Auxiliary Fighter Squadron was amended and plans were made to create four operational fighter squadrons in the Malayan theatre, supported by three associated fighter control units, within four years of the formation of the MAAF.[4] With the deterioration of the internal situation in Malaya, however, this period was reduced to two years. Recruiting for the Penang and Singapore Fighter Squadrons began at Butterworth and Tengah in May and June 1950 and for their complementary fighter control units in January and October 1951.[5] A third fighter squadron was formed at Kuala Lumpur in December 1951 and plans were advanced for the formation of its associated fighter control unit and for a second fighter squadron on Singapore Island to complete the complement of the MAAF.[6]

The initial plan for the fighter squadrons of the MAAF was that they should gain experience in flying light aircraft, DH82As (Tiger Moths) and Austers, and then progress to flying Harvards and surplus Spitfires until they were eventually re-equipped with jet aircraft. On their formation the Penang, Singapore and Kuala Lumpur Squadrons were each equipped with four Tiger Moths, to which four Harvards were added during the course of 1951 and 1952, while the Singapore Squadron was also provided with three Spitfires towards the end of 1951.[7] The policy at this time was that all three squadrons should be equipped as soon as possible with eight Spitfires each, as well as two Harvards for training purposes, at an annual cost to the Air Votes of £40,000 and to the Federal Government of £25,000.[8] However, one year after its establishment the Singapore Squadron had only three pilots that were ready for conversion to flying Spitfires, four who were carrying out advanced training on Harvards and five who were in the *ab initio* stage of training on Tiger Moths. In the Penang Squadron three pilots were training on Harvards and eight on Tiger Moths and no progress had been made on converting them to flying Spitfires.[9] Experience had already shown that these squadrons were unlikely to be able to cope with anything more than the first line servicing of aircraft and demands were made for the assistance of the RAF for both first and second line servicing which they could ill afford to meet in view of the operational effort required of the regular fighter squadrons at that period of the Emergency.

In view of this disappointing progress efforts were made towards the end of 1951 and throughout 1952 and 1953 to clarify the future policy of the MAAF and to obviate a recurrence of the teething troubles which had followed its inception.[10] In March 1953 it was still optimistically hoped that the original aim for the MAAF would be achieved sometime in 1954 but, as it became clear that none of the pilots under training would be ready to fly Vampires by then, even if these aircraft had been available and the governments of Malaya and Singapore had been willing to finance their operation, the policy of providing auxiliary fighter squadrons for the air defence role was finally abandoned.[11] Apart from an agreement about its eventual replacement by a regular Malayan Air Force no firm policy about the future of the MAAF was formulated until 1957, but in the interim period the shortage of light aircraft in the theatre for short range transport and visual reconnaissance work encouraged the AOC Malaya to employ the MAAF in these roles on anti-terrorist operations.

With this change in policy plans for the formation of a fighter control unit at Kuala Lumpur and a second fighter squadron at Singapore fell into abeyance and the three Spitfires of the existing Singapore Squadron were withdrawn at the end of 1952 and the beginning of 1953, leaving all three squadrons of the MAAF equipped with four Tiger Moths and four Harvards each.[12] Two more Harvards were added to the complement of each squadron in 1954 but these were withdrawn from the Kuala Lumpur and Penang Squadrons in 1955.[13] In 1957 the ageing Harvards and Tiger Moths were finally withdrawn from service and were replaced by four Chipmunks in each squadron.[14] In April 1958 the base of the Singapore Squadron was moved from Tengah to Seletar.[15]

While the role of the MAAF was being finally clarified as the training of pilots to form the nucleus of the future national air force and the carrying out of light liaison and reconnaissance duties in connection with the Emergency, determined efforts were made to improve the standard of the pilots and to foster the expansion of an efficient force of ground tradesmen.[16] Between September 1951 and February 1952 the total strength of the MAAF rose to 290 and before the end of 1952 it had doubled again to 550.[17] Of these 49 were pilots, of whom 23 were training on Tiger Moths, 26 on Harvards and 12 were beyond 'wings' standard, while 119 airmen had undergone trade tests and had qualified for the rank of aircraftman 1st class or higher. By the end of 1953 only 16 pilots and 170 tradesmen were left in the MAAF.[18] The strength of the force remained fairly static from the beginning of 1954 to November 1958 when approval was finally given by the Federal Government that the Penang and Kuala Lumpur Wings of the MAAF should be disbanded and their aircraft and spares backing incorporated into the RMAF.[19]

While the Singapore Squadron carried out occasional reconnaissance sorties and dropped leaflets over cultivation plots in Southern Johore, the Kuala Lumpur and Penang Squadrons carried out similar missions in Kedah and Negri Sembilan. During 1952, the total number of hours that were flown by all three squadrons was 130 while, of the 20,000 reconnaissance sorties that were flown in support of Operation 'Firedog' between January 1955 and July 1958, mainly by Austers of No 656 Squadron, the Singapore, Kuala Lumpur and Penang Squadrons of the MAAF contributed 86, 102 and 15 sorties respectively.[20]

The Royal Malayan Air Force

The successor to the MAAF was the RMAF, the national air force that was established by a bill passed by the Federation of Malaya's Legislative Council in May 1958.[21] It was initially planned that this force should consist of four twin-engined Pioneers, one of them the civil version and the other three the military version, four single-engined Pioneers, four Chipmunks and 120 personnel, of which 50 per cent would be seconded from the RAF, 20 per cent would be transferred from the RAF (Malaya) and the remainder would be recruited locally.[22]

The first twin-engined Pioneer for the RMAF arrived in Malaya in April 1958 and the remaining Pioneers were delivered between January and June 1959.[23] All these aircraft were based at Kuala Lumpur, together with those units of the Commonwealth air forces that still remained in the Firedog Transport Support Force. On 1 July 1960 the Joint Operations Centre was handed over to the RMAF, who thus assumed overall direction of all flying in support of Operation 'Firedog', and on 1 October 1960 the RAF station at Kuala Lumpur was handed over to the RMAF.[24]

From its inception it had been planned that the RMAF should start operations in the short range transport role in support of Operation 'Firedog' as soon as possible. The RMAF was able to commence these operations by the beginning of March 1959 and by September of that year the force was working to its full potential.[25] The main commitment of this small force was to relieve the Commonwealth air forces of the air supply and maintenance of the jungle forts that were manned by units of the Federal Police. Throughout 1959 these forts were gradually reduced in number to their peacetime establishment and, when the responsibility for their supply was taken over by the RMAF in September of that year, the task was almost within their capacity. However, the limitation of the flying hours of this force to 90 a month, as well as the shortage of pilots for their single-engined Pioneers and servicing difficulties with their

Twin Pioneers, prevented them from fulfilling their entire commitment and for the first few months of 1960 RAF Pioneers of No 209 Squadron were called upon to assist them.[26] In February 1960 the RMAF carried out their first operational supply drop to a jungle fort from a Twin Pioneer and from then onwards to the end of the campaign in July of that year they were engaged in transporting troops to jungle forts and dropping supplies and leaflets over Northern Perak from their advanced base at Taiping.[27] In July 1960 Twin Pioneers of the RMAF dropped 30,485 lb of supplies but even this valuable contribution did not meet the entire requirement of the police garrisons of the remaining jungle forts and represented only a relatively small proportion of the 251,728 lb of supplies that were dropped by all units of the air forces in Malaya in this final month of the campaign against the terrorists.[28]

The RAF (Malaya)

Besides the development of local auxiliary air forces to help in the air defence of the Far East and to serve as a nucleus for future national air forces, the Air Council also decided, late in 1947, to recruit local forces into RAF units in the Far Eastern theatre in order to ease the shortage of manpower for ground duties.[29] At that time the Air Command Far East (ACFE) were already employing two to three hundred civilian technicians and, with the memory of the pre-war Singapore Special Training Corps and the government subsidies that were being paid to locally recruited forces of the RN (Malaya) and The Malay Regiment, as well as in the interests of security and discipline, it was decided to incorporate these men into a uniformed force known as the RAF (Malaya). Initial proposals envisaged a ceiling establishment of 1,000 tradesmen in 44 clerical and technical trades, excluding the 790 personnel of the RAF Police Auxiliaries (Malaya) who were also to be transferred to this force. The RAF (Malaya) was to be recruited over a period of four years and employed at the RAF Maintenance Base at Seletar and the RAF Stations at Changi, Tengah and Butterworth.[30] By 1951 the yearly intake of this force amounted to 250 recruits, divided into seven courses,[31] and for the remainder of the Emergency they provided valuable administrative and maintenance services for the air forces in Malaya while, on a few occasions, they even took part in jungle patrols which achieved a number of terrorist eliminations. The most active participation by locally recruited airmen in the campaign against the terrorists, however, was undertaken by the personnel of the RAF Regiment (Malaya).

The RAF Regiment (Malaya)

The ground defence of all RAF installations depends primarily on combatant personnel of the RAF Regiment, a specialist force who are trained for ground combat and are prepared to move by air at short notice. In overseas theatres it has long been the practice to employ local volunteers in this force whenever possible and the RAF Regiment (Malaya) was constituted by an Order in Council signed by King George VI in April 1947 to conform as closely as possible to the RAF Regiment in its structure and function.[32]

At the outbreak of the Emergency the RAF Regiment (Malaya) consisted of only two rifle squadrons, No 91, formed at Kuala Lumpur in January 1948, and No 92, formed at Kuala Lumpur on 1 April 1948.[33] Plans for further squadrons were accelerated and No 93 Squadron was formed on 1 May 1948, No 94 Squadron on 1 August 1948 and No 95 Squadron on 1 Janaury 1949.[34] By then the RAF Regiment

(Malaya) consisted of five rifle squadrons and a headquarters staff at its depot at Sembawang, to where it had moved from Kuala Lumpur on 11 May 1948 and from where it moved to Changi on 15 August 1949 when Sembawang was handed back to the Royal Navy.[35] At full strength each squadron contained 180 to 200 officers and men who were divided into five flights, which included four rifle flights, armed with Bren guns, light machine guns, Sten carbines, rifles, light 2-inch mortars, high explosives and smoke grenades, and a support flight, armed with four 3-inch mortars and additional Bren guns for its secondary role as an anti-aircraft flight. All members of the RAF Regiment (Malaya) were fully combatant, the primary trade of the drivers, cooks and storemen at squadron headquarters being that of a gunner. The transport establishment of each squadron contained 15- and 20-cwt and 3-ton trucks and motor cycles to give mobility, while wireless communications in the field were maintained by walkie-talkie sets with a two to five miles range and a more powerful link to squadron headquarters was provided from a wireless set mounted in the squadron commander's jeep.[36]

Recruitment of Malayan citizens for the RAF Regiment (Malaya) was carried out by itinerant teams throughout the Federation and the new recruit was sent to the Regimental Depot at Telok Paku, RAF Changi, for a medical examination and fifteen weeks basic training before posting to a squadron for secondary training or undergoing specialist courses for ancillary tradesmen. At squadron level the recruit was instructed in the uses of firearms under battle conditions at the Pasir Lebar firing range, which included the use of small arms against low-flying aircraft. Regiment gunners were trained not merely as static security guards but as members of a fully mobile fighting force capable of providing screens against an advancing enemy, of sending out fighting and reconnaissance patrols, of counter-attacking should infiltration occur and of delivering sustained mortar fire on enemy concentrations. Personnel of the RAF Regiment (Malaya) were liable to serve anywhere in the Federation in peacetime and anywhere in the world in times of Emergency.[37] Initially all officers and NCOs of the Regiment were drawn from the RAF Regiment but gradually these posts were 'Malayanized' and by 1954 all NCOs except warrant officers were Malayan, as were six officers of the Regiment.[38]

The standard of ground combat training achieved by the RAF Regiment (Malaya) proved of particular value in the campaign against the terrorists in Malaya. In June 1948 the demands that were made on the Army and the Police for action in patrolling and the provision of guards were legion and it was clearly beyond their capacity to meet all these requests before the strength of the security forces had been augmented. A request was made, therefore, by Headquarters Malaya District for the assistance of the RAF Regiment (Malaya) in an ordinary Army role. No 91 Squadron, then at Changi, was selected for the task and placed under the command of Headquarters Johore Sub-District at the end of June 1948.[39] This marked the beginning of the RAF Regiment (Malaya)'s active participation in the campaign against the terrorists which, broken only by periods of re-training, lasted for almost the whole of the Emergency. Of the five squadrons in the Regiment three were usually retained for static guard duties in their primary role at RAF airfields in Malaya and Singapore, one was stationed at RAF Kai Tak, Hong Kong and the remaining squadron was employed on anti-terrorist operations under the control of the Army. At a certain stage in the year each squadron in turn was withdrawn from airfield guard duties for training in jungle warfare techniques, including the rehearsal of patrols, ambushes, signals, action to be taken when attacking or being attacked and elementary jungle navigation.[40] Iban trackers from North Borneo were attached to each squadron for tracking purposes since the Malay airman, although he had a fine sense of direction, was only a mediocre tracker and the aboriginal Sakais of Malaya were unreliable. The culmination of this period of training came with a jungle tour of four months, which was extended to six months at the beginning of 1954. Personnel of the RAF Regiment (Malaya) showed great enthusiasm for jungle operations and contact with experienced troops provided a fillip to their training and morale. Squadrons of the Regiment, although under functional control of AHQ Malaya, operated under the administrative control and the command of local Army brigade and battalion headquarters and, from 1953 onwards, they were permanently represented on the staff of the Director of Operations, with members on the Combined Emergency Planning Staff, the Psychological Warfare Staff and the Combined Intelligence Staff.[41]

Just before the outbreak of the Emergency the two squadrons of the RAF Regiment (Malaya) that were in existence, Nos 91 and 92, were deployed at Changi and Seletar respectively. On 30 April 1948 No 92 Squadron was flown to Taiping as part of the RAF Task Force that was sent to assist ground forces in Operation 'Haystack' in Northern Perak.[42] The squadron was deployed at Lenggong to carry out general garrison duties and to relieve police units of the duty of occupying disused terrorist camps so that they could concentrate on further searches. For political reasons, however, as a state of Emergency had not yet been declared, No 92 Squadron was unable to participate in active operations where there was any chance of making contact with hostile forces. The squadron stayed at Taiping until 27 May 1948, when it was transferred to Seletar for airfield defence duties, but provided a flight at Kuala Lumpur on 5 July as part of the RAF Task Force that had been established there.[43] Meanwhile a state of Emergency had been declared and No 91 Squadron had taken up its field position in the Segamat area of Johore on 23 June, under the control of Johore Sub-District.[44] At the time its duty was defined as 'assisting the police to the limits of its power' and its task consisted mostly of patrolling local rubber estates and neighbouring areas. Within four days of its arrival in their operational area No 91 Squadron had apprehended a wanted Chinese and, towards the end of July, following an increase of terrorist activity in the area and reinforcement by two companies of the 1st Battalion The Seaforth Highlanders, patrols were extended deeper into the jungle and ten suspects were arrested and large quantities of subversive literature and incriminating documents were discovered.[45]

After three weeks in the Segamat area No 91 Squadron moved to the Kota Tinggi and Mersing areas of Southern Johore where, owing to the extensive river communications, many of their patrols necessitated long waterborne journeys to outlying rubber estates and suspected terrorist locations in the jungle.[46] It was on one of these patrols that the RAF Regiment (Malaya) suffered its first casualty when a British NCO collapsed from heat exhaustion and later died. Extensive patrolling of these areas resulted in the arrest of eight suspects in the first week, one of whom gave information which led to the destruction of a disused terrorist camp. During August 1948 terrorist activity flared up on the Telok Sengat estate bordering the Johore River and the two flights of No 91 Squadron that were despatched there detained a number of suspects including two of the raiding party. By 4 September 1948 No 91 Squadron had apprehended and handed over to the military authorities a total of 60 suspected terrorists.[47] On 26 September No 91 Squadron began the final operation of its operational tour which entailed five days continuous patrolling in deep jungle territory, relying entirely on air supply, during which a Malay corporal opened fire on a band of about thirty terrorists and hit at least three before they were carried off by the remainder. During these patrols the squadron was forcibly reminded of the problems of location that were faced by jungle patrols when they took a wrong track in the Kota Tinggi area and found that the jungle was too thick for signal fires to be visible while the surrounding hills were so full of iron that compasses were useless.[48] In October 1948, after five months of active patrolling, during which they had set the pattern for future operations by the RAF Regiment (Malaya) in the campaign against the terrorists, No 91 Squadron was withdrawn to Changi for airfield defence duties.[49]

For most of 1949 squadrons of the RAF Regiment (Malaya) were occupied with airfield defence, with No 91 Squadron at Changi, No 92 Squadron at Seletar, No 93 Squadron at Butterworth, No 94 Squadron at Kuala Lumpur and No 95 Squadron completing their training at Sembawang in May of that year.[50] In June 1949 No 91 Squadron was posted to Kai Tak in Hong Kong and was relieved at Changi by No 92 Squadron which was replaced at Seletar in August by No 93 Squadron from Butterworth.[51] On 16 August 1949 the Depot of the RAF Regiment (Malaya) moved from Sembawang to Changi and No 95 Squadron, on completion of its training, moved to Tengah.[52]

When the anti-terrorist drive was intensified at the beginning of 1950 the Federal Government asked whether two squadrons of the RAF Regiment (Malaya) could be spared from their normal duties to take part in security operations in connection with Anti-Bandit Month. No 94 Squadron was moved from Kuala Lumpur to Rawang in Selangor on 1 March 1950, coming under the operational control of Headquarters Malaya District and the command of the 2nd Battalion Scots Guards, and No 95 Squadron moved from Tengah to the Mersing area of North-Eastern Johore and came under the operational control of the South Malaya Sub-District and the command of the 1st Battalion The Seaforth Highlanders.[53] The performance of these two squadrons was such that both the Federal Government and the Army pressed for their continued employment in an operational role after the conclusion of the Anti-Bandit Month and, in the prevailing circumstances, this was agreed upon under the clear understanding that the Federal Government was responsible for the provision of a permanent Auxiliary Police Guard for Kuala Lumpur airfield. Difficulties in connection with this provision led to a consideration of the need to withdraw at least one of the squadrons on active operations but counter arguments from the Government and Army made it clear that both were now regarded as an integral part of the ground forces framework and could not be spared.[54]

During operations in the Mersing area in which No 95 Squadron took part thirteen terrorist camps were found and destroyed, eighty suspects were arrested, one wanted terrorist leader was killed and four terrorists were wounded. No 94 Squadron operating in the Rawang area where the terrorists were particularly active, killed three terrorists themselves and seven more in concert with other troops, as well as helping to find and destroy twelve large and nineteen small camps and arresting three terrorist agents.[55] No 94 Squadron was relieved at Rawang by No 93 Squadron from Seletar on 1 May 1950 and No 95 Squadron was withdrawn from Mersing for airfield defence duties at Tengah on 31 July 1950.[56] On 12 October 1950 No 93 Squadron at Rawang was relieved by No 91 Squadron from Changi and returned to Seletar to take over from No 94 Squadron which moved to Changi.[57]

During 1951 the operational squadrons of the RAF Regiment (Malaya) were deployed under the operational control of the 18th Brigade in the Rawang and Sungei Besi areas of Selangor. While on detachment in the Rawang area, No 91 Squadron killed one terrorist, captured another and wounded two others in the Ulau

Simpan area, besides discovering five camps, while its relief, No 94 Squadron, when it took over the same area in February 1951, was ambushed by a terrorist force which outnumbered it by three to one but fought back to such effect that it killed four terrorists for the loss of five of its own airmen.[58] Altogether No 94 Squadron made eleven contacts with the terrorists during its tour of duty, killed five of them and destroyed twelve camps for the loss of five of its own force killed and eight wounded. On 17 July 1951 No 94 Squadron returned to Tengah from Rawang to take over from No 95 Squadron which took up the Regiment's operational commitment at Sungei Besi.[59] No 95 Squadron were relieved on 1 December 1951 by No 92 Squadron and returned to Tengah without loss to themselves and with a tally of three terrorists killed, including one District Committee Member, five wounded, two captured and seventeen camps and twenty-three food dumps found and destroyed.[60]

On 1 April 1952 the RAF Regiment (Malaya) Wing was formed to administer the Headquarters and Depot at Changi and the five squadrons then in existence.[61] By this time all five squadrons had completed at least one, and in most cases two, tours in the jungle and had become as experienced as any other unit in operations against the terrorists. No 92 Squadron continued to operate in the Sungei Besi area of Selangor until the end of the tour but its relief, No 91 Squadron, which took over the operational commitment in April 1952, moved to a new area in the Bukit Cherakah Forest Reserve, with a base camp at Bukit Darah.[62] This area, which the squadrons of the RAF Regiment (Malaya) were to remain responsible for until January 1954, proved fairly productive during the early stages of operations there and both No 91 Squadron and No 93 Squadron, which took over on 1 September 1952, achieved several kills.[63] After No 95 Squadron had relieved No 93 Squadron in June 1953, however, this area became singularly quiet, possibly due to constant patrolling, and remained so when No 92 Squadron from Seletar took over operational duties on 12 May 1953.[64] When No 94 Squadron relieved No 92 Squadron in September 1953, therefore, it was decided to change the location of the Regiment's operational area. The Director of Operations arranged for the Regiment to take over operations in the Kuala Langat Forest Reserve area of Selangor, with base camps at Sepang, Sungei Manggis and Klang. No 94 Squadron moved from Bukit Darah to Klang on 3 December 1953 and this move soon achieved results as No 91 Squadron, which took over operations on 5 January 1954, killed two terrorists and wounded four others during the early stages of their six months tour of duty.[65] In July 1954 No 95 Squadron relieved No 94 Squadron at Klang but moved on to the Pasangan area of the Kuala Selangor district on 17 November 1954 to take part in Operation 'Inswinger'.[66] This area, north of the Sungei Selangor, is mostly jungle swamp and from an operational aspect contains some of the most difficult terrain in Malaya. Most patrols were carried out through knee or waist deep swamp and camps on 'high' ground were frequently rendered untenable when the water level rose after rain had fallen. Despite these difficulties No 95 Squadron located and destroyed three camps and one food dump before they were relieved by No 92 Squadron in March 1955.[67]

In August 1955 No 93 Squadron took over operational duties from No 92 Squadron and returned to Rawang in Selangor where the RAF Regiment (Malaya) had last operated from in July 1951.[68] At the end of 1955, however, the Regiment ceased operations against the terrorists while it underwent a period of reorganization. A new squadron, No 96, was formed at Changi on 1 January 1956 in the light anti-aircraft role and No 93 Squadron was converted to a field role. In place of the five rifle squadrons that had existed in 1950 there were now three field squadrons, Nos 91, 93 and 94, and three light anti-aircraft squadrons, Nos 92, 95 and 96.[69]

The deployment of squadrons of the RAF Regiment (Malaya) on anti-terrorist operations recommenced on 1 July 1956 and from then onwards until they were finally withdrawn in 1959 each squadron was deployed for operational tours of six months.[70] With the concentration of hostilities in the north of the Federation No 94 Squadron was moved from Butterworth to the Regiment's new operational area in Southern Perak, based on a camp at Slim River, and operated under the control of the 1st Federal Division.[71] In September 1956 Operation 'Parchment' began, which embraced the whole of Southern Perak and was aimed at the destruction of the terrorist organization in No 5 MCP District by methods which included food rationing, the denial of food supplies, ambushes, constant patrolling and the destruction of terrorist cultivations.[72] Phase I, which ended in December 1956, was mainly concerned with the deployment of troops, including No 94 Squadron RAF Regiment (Malaya), and the general intensification of patrol and ambush activity. Phase II commenced on 1 January 1957 and coincided with the relief of No 94 by No 95 Squadron from Tengah, which came under the operational command of the 2nd Battalion The Malay Regiment. The Squadron was given as its main target the Besout Armed Work Cell which was known to exist in the squadron's main area of responsibility due west of the main road from Kuala Lumpur to Ipoh, from Slim River in the South to Sungkai in the north, an area of about 125 square miles which contained numerous 'kampongs', rubber and palm oil estates and swamp and jungle of all types. From 1 January 1957 to the end of the second phase of Operation 'Parchment' on 31 March 1957 forty personnel of No 95 Squadron were engaged on searching all vehicles and persons entering or leaving factories and estates in this area and numerous irregularities in the carriage of restricted food items were discovered. In addition ambushes were mounted on the approaches to unwired 'kampongs' and one flight was deployed in the jungle to prevent the terrorists from gaining access to their Min Yuen supporters. Flights of No 95 Squadron took part in several combined operations with the 2nd Battalion The Malay Regiment, following up air strikes, cordoning villages and carrying out house searches. No contacts were made in this phase of the operation, however, and there were few reports of terrorist movement in the area. Phase III of Operation 'Parchment' began on 1 April 1957 with a change in the deployment of the security forces involved. No 95 Squadron was placed under the operational command of the 1st Battalion The Rifle Brigade and its commander was given the control of an operational platoon of the Home Guard. Food control measures were reduced on a number of New Villages and only one, Slim River, remained the responsibility of No 95 Squadron, enabling a further flight to be released for jungle operations. For three months, from April to June 1957, three flights of No 95 Squadron, as well as elements of the Headquarters Flight, were more or less permanently in the jungle investigating rumours in lieu of specific information received from the Police Special Branch and carrying out combined operations with the Rifle Brigade. In April 1957 a further redeployment placed No 95 Squadron under the operational command of the 5th Battalion The Malay Regiment and the squadron returned to Tengah on 29 June on its relief by No 96 Squadron from Changi.[73] Two flights of No 96 Squadron were employed on jungle operations and one on gate checking and guard duties at the Slim River New Village but, although five food dumps were discovered, no contacts with the terrorists were made and it was assumed that the Besout Armed Work Cell had been withdrawn to the deep jungle area west of the unit's operational area. No 96 Squadron was withdrawn from Operation 'Parchment', therefore, on 14 December 1957 and its relief, No 92 Squadron from Seletar, was deployed in a more active operational area in the Batu

Gajah district of Perak.[74] Meanwhile the RAF Regiment (Malaya) had made a further contribution to anti-terrorist operations during 1957 by releasing one flight of No 93 Squadron at Kuala Lumpur for operations in Selangor and one flight of No 94 Squadron at Butterworth for operations in Kedah.[75] Although there were no large concentrations of terrorists in these areas these flights were useful in maintaining security force pressure where no other units were available.

Throughout 1958 the RAF Regiment (Malaya) continued to provide one complete squadron, as well as one flight from each of the two squadrons based at airfields in the Federation, for anti-terrorist operations in support of the Army, although this contribution was interrupted for a period of four months in the case of the squadron and for two months in the case of one of the flights to permit reorganization and retraining of the force.[76] At the squadron level No 92 Squadron was deployed at Kampar in Perak from 6 January to 15 July 1958, under the operational control of the 2nd Federal Infantry Brigade and the command of the 2nd Battalion The Royal Malay Regiment,* and took part in the highly successful Operation 'Bintang' in the area South-West of Ipoh during which all but 17 of the 70 terrorists in the area were eliminated.[77] As well as claiming ten kills themselves, No 92 Squadron made a valuable contribution to this operation by the constant patrolling and ambushing of courier routes and the destruction of food dumps. No 93 Squadron from Kuala Lumpur, which took over the squadron commitment at Kampar from No 92 Squadron on 17 November 1958, had previously provided one flight on a rotational basis for operations in Selangor under the command of the 1st Battalion The Royal Malay Regiment from 1 January to 26 September 1958 and had played an important part in reducing the number of terrorists in that state from 59 to 4. On taking over from No 92 Squadron at Kampar, No 93 Squadron, under the command of the 3rd Battalion The Royal Malay Regiment, participated in Operation 'Ginger' in the area east of Ipoh and on 20 November 1958 one of its patrols captured a leading terrorist. Apart from the flights provided by No 93 Squadron for operations in Selangor, No 94 Squadron also provided one flight on a rotational basis for operations in Central Kedah, under the command of the 6th Battalion The Royal Malay Regiment, until 1 November 1958 when it was withdrawn for retraining. During most of this period the squadron provided the only regular service unit in the area and their constant harassing of the terrorists in conjunction with Police and Home Guard units elicited valuable information on which later ground force operations were planned.[78]

By the beginning of 1959 the terrorist threat in Malaya had virtually been eliminated and it was decided that there was no longer an operational need for six squadrons of the RAF Regiment (Malaya). Authority was given to reduce their establishment and, following the amalgamation of the Regiment's Wing and its Depot on 1 September 1958, Nos 92 and 96 Squadrons were disbanded at the beginning of November 1959 and No 93 on 1 April 1960.[79] Because of this imminent reduction and the dislocation that arose from frequent postings between individual units it was found impracticable for the remaining squadrons of the RAF Regiment (Malaya) to continue operations against the few remaining terrorists after No 93 Squadron had returned to Changi in April 1959 and they were accordingly withdrawn from active service.[80]

---

* The Malay Regiment was granted the prefix 'Royal' on 8 April 1958.

Almost continuously for nearly eleven years, from the initial deployment of No 91 Squadron at Segamat in Johore on 23 June 1948 to the final withdrawal of No 93 Squadron from Kampar in Perak on 1 April 1959, the RAF Regiment (Malaya) played a valuable, if subsidiary, role in providing extra troops to assist the Security Forces in the innumerable tasks which arose in combined operations against the terrorists. The Regiment itself benefited from the experience gained at all levels of active service and, if allowance is made for the small number of their personnel that were engaged on anti-terrorist patrols at any one time and the low priority of many of their operational areas, the material results which they achieved compared favourably with those of other units. By June 1952 the RAF Regiment (Malaya) claimed to have killed sixteen terrorists, wounded thirteen others and captured a further thirty-two, at a cost to themselves of nine killed and thirteen wounded.[81] By December 1954, after five and a half years of participation in the campaign, the Regiment claimed to have killed twenty terrorists, wounded twelve others, captured a further forty-one and to have found and destroyed 262 camps and food dumps, at a cost to themselves of two officers killed, one British and one Malay, and two officers wounded, and eight Malayan airmen killed and two wounded.[82] The esteem in which the contribution of the RAF Regiment (Malaya) to the campaign was held was reflected in the awards made to its personnel at that date, which included one OBE, one MBE, three British Empire Medals, three Military Medals, forty-two Mentions in Despatches and seven Certificates of Good Conduct.[83] Towards the end of the Emergency, however, in common with the rest of the ground forces, they were compelled to expend a greater effort for less return and in the first nine months of 1958 personnel of the RAF Regiment (Malaya) spent 136,106 man hours in the jungle, laid 386 ambushes by day and 370 by night and made only two contacts with the enemy, wounding only one terrorist, apart from discovering sixteen terrorist camps, eight of their resting places and six of their food dumps.[84]

CHAPTER 7

SUMMARY OF THE AIR FORCES CONTRIBUTION TO OPERATION 'FIREDOG'

Introduction

During the whole of the Emergency the air forces in the Malayan theatre operated in support of the ground security forces in order to restore law and order to the country and defeat the menace of the Communist terrorists. In considering whether the best use was made of the available air forces and whether these resources were adequate, it should be appreciated that the support of civil and military forces in the enforcement of internal security in Malaya was only the tertiary role of AHQ (Malaya or No 224 Group)—the group that was primarily responsible for carrying out 'Firedog' operations. The principal role of this headquarters was air defence against a possible hot war attack by the military forces of China and to this end the main units in the group were designed as fighter squadrons and a considerable expenditure was diverted into radar equipment. The secondary role of the air forces in Malaya was the support of certain naval units and Army field forces and this direct support role also ensured that the equipment allocated to the group was not necessarily of the type that suited many of the tasks that arose in connection with its internal security role.

However, because the restoration of law and order in Malaya was considered important to the general stability of the area, the Chiefs of Staff temporarily departed from the normal policy for the Malayan Tactical Group and devoted a high proportion of the available manpower and effort to Emergency tasks, besides making certain modifications in their equipment planning in order to provide units that were more suitable for counter-insurgency tasks. Nevertheless, the maintenance of an adequate air defence organization in the Malayan theatre was always in the background and influenced both the re-equipment and the training programmes of the air forces to the detriment of their efficacy as an anti-terrorist unit.

The Role of the Air Forces in the Malayan Emergency

The role of the air forces during the Emergency was defined in Emergency Directive No 2, para 23 as follows:

'The RAF is also operating in support of the Civil Power. The primary task of the RAF is to operate in conjunction with and in support of the ground forces. This support may include offensive air strikes (bombing and ground strafing attacks), air supply, visual and photographic reconnaissance, survey photography and inter-communication.'

Towards the end of 1953, when AHQ Malaya became anxious to carry out independent action against the terrorists and to have a greater say in the tactical application of the overall strategic plan of action, this directive was rewritten as follows:

'. . . this support may include (i) offensive air strikes (bombing and ground strafing attacks) (ii) offensive air strikes in an independent role, with or without follow-up by ground, including airborne, security forces (iii) offensive or tactical air transportation and positioning of airborne or parachute forces (iv) air supply (v) visual air photographic reconnaissance (vi) survey photography (vii) inter-communication.'

Thus was official recognition given to the fact that the air forces could be, and of necessity had to be, used in a more independent role after the terrorists had withdrawn into the deep jungles of central Malaya, thereby reducing the chances of locating and engaging them with ground forces alone.

The Control of Air Force Operations

In the type of campaign that prevailed during the Malayan Emergency it was extremely important that there should be the closest possible co-ordination and liaison between the air forces and the ground forces. During the early phases of the campaign air support was called for on an *ad hoc* basis and was undoubtedly misused to some extent as well as being unable to operate with maximum efficiency. At a higher level the location of AHQ Malaya at Changi on Singapore Island, remote from the Director of Operations, the GOC Malaya and the Federal Police Headquarters, was both inefficient and confusing and its move to Kuala Lumpur early in 1954 was long overdue and considerably improved the effective direction of the air forces engaged on Emergency tasks. At a lower level State and District War Executive Committees planned, organized and mounted virtually all operations against the terrorists from 1951 onwards but it was not until 1953 that air force representatives were appointed to the Operations Sub-Committees of the SWECs in Kedah, Negri Sembilan, Perak, Pahang and Johore. This representation ensured a more effective use of the air resources by increasing the ground forces' awareness of their potential and by giving the air arm access to potential target information at a time when the withdrawal of the terrorists into jungle hideouts ensured that air action, used independently or in conjunction with airborne or paratroop forces, had the greatest chance of achieving success.

The most notable development in the liaison between the air and ground forces, on which the anti-terrorist campaign was fought and won, was the establishment of a Joint Operations and Intelligence Centre at GHQ Malaya in Kuala Lumpur. This centre was manned by a joint Army and RAF staff whose responsibility it was to evaluate all calls for air support and to ensure that the best use was made of the available air effort. The JOC in its final form did not evolve until 1953, but as a control mechanism for combined operations it proved to be a significant evolution in the general direction of anti-terrorist operations.

Deployment of the Air Forces in Malaya

The location of the air force units that were engaged on Emergency tasks was determined not by tactical considerations but by the availability of airfields. Before 1953 there was no airfield in the Federation of Malaya that was capable of operating either Lincoln medium bombers or jet aircraft and this ensured that nearly all offensive air support was mounted from Singapore Island. This deployment had certain domestic advantages but suffered from the over-riding disadvantage of remoteness from many operational areas. For example, Operation 'Sword', mounted in Kedah in November 1953, absorbed 340 offensive sorties, many of them by Lincolns operating from Tengah whose flying time could have been considerably reduced by having a suitable base in Northern Malaya, which would have enabled one squadron to do the work of two based on Singapore Island. The improvement of the east-west runway at Butterworth provided an adequate base for medium bomber and jet aircraft in Northern Malaya from 1954 onwards and considerably improved the efficiency of their operation.

Although offensive support aircraft suffered to some extent from the paucity of adequate airfields on the mainland of Malaya, there were sufficient airfields to operate medium range transport aircraft with reasonable efficiency while the network of grass airstrips that was developed throughout the Federation proved to be an essential and effective basis for the operation of light communication aircraft.

Offensive Air Support

From the point of view of offensive air support it is doubtful whether any modern air force has had to operate under more unsatisfactory conditions, from the point of view of targets and information on the results achieved, than that engaged in Emergency operations in Malaya. Offensive air action in terrain dominated by featureless jungle was handicapped by the lack of strategic targets, the absence of firm enemy lines of communication and enemy concentrations or strong points and the difficulty of establishing well demarcated bomb-lines. Target information was rarely adequate to permit the proper use of air striking power whose aims had to be modified with the following objects:

a. Driving the terrorists out of their areas into ambushes.
b. Moving the terrorists into country suitable for ground operations.
c. Dispersing large parties of terrorists and thus reducing their offensive potential.
d. Containing large parties of terrorists while ground forces swept an area.
e. Destroying terrorist camps and inflicting casualties.
f. Protecting an area or convoy route by air cover or flare dropping.
g. Harassing the terrorists and lowering their morale.
h. Deceiving the terrorists as to security force intentions and locations.

Most of these aims were achieved by pre-planned operations based on intelligence reports of likely terrorist concentrations. Demands for immediate air support of troops in contact with the enemy were rare, which meant that the delay in mounting air strikes that was imposed by the deployment of offensive squadrons, the need to obtain police clearance of the target area and the difficulties of navigation and target identification, was largely nullified.

The techniques that were developed for harassing attacks and area bombardments were improved throughout the campaign and were as effective as possible under the prevailing conditions. In retrospect the systematic bombardment of map squares achieved little but was justifiable in view of the lack of target intelligence and the inaccuracies of target maps that prevailed at the time. These handicaps were rectified by the increasing efficiency of the Police Special Branch in eliciting information of terrorist locations from surrendered enemy personnel and other informers and by the improvement in the coverage of Malaya by air photographs, both of which enabled 'pinpoint' attacks to be made which showed greater returns for less effort.

The most effective offensive support aircraft in use during the Malayan campaign were the Lincoln and the Hornet, both of which had a relatively long endurance and high firepower. Lincolns bore the brunt of the medium bomber tasks while

Hornets, being more manoeuvrable and able to attack in conditions of weather and terrain which often rendered attacks by medium bombers abortive, were largely used in a strafing and precision bombing role. Unfortunately the Hornet was obsolete and difficult to maintain by 1953 and its replacement by jet aircraft considerably affected the efficacy of the offensive air support force. Jet aircraft, whether fighters or light bombers, were too sophisticated for this type of campaign, having neither the range, the endurance or the ability to operate at low level which characterized the older, slower piston-engined aircraft. Sunderlands were also used occasionally in an offensive role but their utility was restricted because of their small bombload. In general, however, the offensive air support force was adequate to meet the tasks required of it as the introduction of jet aircraft into the Malayan theatre coincided with a decline in calls for this type of support.

From this point of view of tangible results the offensive air support provided during the Malayan campaign was hardly worthwhile but the incalculable effects which it had on weakening the terrorists' morale and reducing their ability to mount offensives or withstand security force pressure was considered to be an important factor in preventing the insurgents from progressing beyond the first stage of their campaign to the domination and control of selected areas. In any case, when the terrorists retired to deep jungle areas, air power was frequently the only method of maintaining some pressure against them and was therefore directly instrumental in shortening the duration of the campaign.

Air Transport Support

In a country like Malaya, with its paucity of surface communications, the need for air transport support is essential and it became the main role of the air forces during the Emergency. Without the mobility that was granted to the ground forces by a combination of air supply, troop lifts, paratroop operations, casualty evacuation and inter-communication by light aircraft, the campaign against the terrorists would have been much longer and considerably more expensive.

Supply Dropping. Of the various transport support roles, the tactical air supply of food, medicine, clothing, ammunition and equipment was the most important and, by enabling the ground forces to carry out deep penetration of the jungle and remain on patrol for extended periods, it proved to be indispensable to ultimate victory. The total amount of supplies that were dropped during the campaign exceeded 25,000 short tons—a task which required not more than eight medium range transport aircraft daily and usually averaged four. Three RAF transport squadrons took turns in bearing the brunt of the supply dropping commitment and it is a tribute to the skill of all the transport pilots and to the techniques which they evolved that less than $1\frac{1}{2}$ per cent of all the supplies that were dropped were not recovered by the ground forces.

Trooplifting. Next in order of importance to air supply in the air transport support role was the trooplifting task of the small helicopter force which gave valuable assistance to the ground forces from 1953 until the end of the campaign. With the arrival of a Naval squadron of S55 helicopters in Malaya in that year this role assumed increasing importance and gave a long-needed flexibility to ground force operations, at a time when a stalemate seemed likely, which was largely responsible for the systematic elimination of the terrorist threat during the later stages of the campaign. In May 1953 1,623 troops and 36,500 lb of equipment were lifted into jungle landing zones by medium helicopters during ten days of

Operation 'Commodore' alone and the value of this type of support was reflected in the subsequent increase in calls upon the available helicopter force. Throughout the campaign, however, demands for helicopters were always greater than the supply and further reinforcements, besides the RAF Whirlwind squadron which arrived in 1955, would have been welcome. However, it should be realized that helicopters were expensive and costly to maintain and operate in Malaya. Jungle operations are the most strenuous type of helicopter operations and afford a severe test of the aircraft and its equipment. Not surprisingly, the small helicopter force in this theatre was beset by recurring technical faults and while additional reinforcements would have helped to maintain a higher rate of serviceability, it is doubtful whether the cost of operating a much larger force would have been justified by the results it might have achieved.

Casualty evacuation. The major role of light helicopters during the campaign was casualty evacuation which assumed great importance in the Malayan theatre because of the difficult terrain over which ground force patrols operated, the need to free them from the task of evacuating their casualties (which frequently meant the abandonment of a patrol) and the need for early treatment of the more serious injuries. Light helicopters proved a fairly adequate answer to most requests for casualty evacuation and gave an immense fillip to the morale of the Security Forces who were operating in deep jungle areas. However, the limitations on the operation of these aircraft that were imposed by environmental conditions, such as altitude, terrain and turbulence, were all too often not fully appreciated. Nevertheless, light helicopters did as much as could be expected of them in the casualty evacuation role, assisted by medium helicopters when available, and the replacement of the original Dragonflies by Sycamores helped to improve their serviceability rate.

Paratrooping. Less important than the trooplifting role of the air transport support forces was the paratrooping commitment of the medium range transport squadrons. The problem of mounting paratroop operations in Malaya were considerable but techniques were evolved during the course of the campaign which enabled several successful operations to be carried out. These were of particular value in introducing troops quickly into operational zones while maintaining the element of surprise on which the success of the assault depended. However, although the possibilities of this form of attack were demonstrated, it was seldom employed during the campaign as helicopters proved capable of introducing a greater number of less specialized troops into jungle areas with greater speed and accuracy.

Communications. A minor but important role of the air transport support forces in Malaya was the maintenance of internal communications within the Federation. The route transport operations of the medium range transport force were invaluable in airlifting troops, freight and casualties between the major airfields when rapid deployment was considered important, especially over areas where ambushes were likely to occur. For maintaining communications between the numerous light aircraft strips of the Federation, which enabled commanders to move rapidly within their operational areas, the light liaison flights of No 656 AOP Squadron provided valuable support at the beginning of the campaign. Their strength and capabilities were inadequate for this purpose, however, and in any case they were needed for their primary role of tactical reconnaissance. Helicopters provided some assistance but were specialized aircraft that were only used when no other aircraft was suitable and when they were not required for more urgent tasks.

The answer to the problem of maintaining short range communications was provided by the small and hard-worked Pioneer force of No 267 (later No 209) Squadron which was introduced into Malaya in 1954 and which performed an invaluable service in ferrying troops, freight, police reinforcements and civil administrators into and out of grass airstrips in remote operational areas, notably those that were constructed adjacent to the deep jungle forts which served as bases for bringing the aboriginal population of Malaya under Government protection.

Psychological Warfare. One of the most useful weapons in the anti-terrorist campaign was psychological warfare, which made a major contribution to the slow erosion and ultimate collapse of the insurgents' morale that presaged their final defeat. Although the effectiveness of this type of warfare depended primarily on the overall military situation on the ground and it was necessarily directed through appeals by the civil government, its efficacy, both in inspiring public and undermining terrorist confidence in the ultimate outcome of the campaign, was largely reliant on the use of air support for the transmission of messages. Medium range transport aircraft dropped nearly 500 million strategic and tactical leaflets during the course of the campaign while two Dakotas and three Austers, after some initial difficulties and the modification and improvement of their equipment, carried out over 4,000 hours of aerial broadcasting. As in the case of offensive air support the tangible results of this campaign cannot be assessed but the number of terrorists who claimed to have surrendered wholly or partly as a result of hearing or reading one of these messages broadcast from the air fully justified the effort which it entailed.

Crop Spraying. After the terrorists withdrew into deep jungle hideouts a food denial campaign was mounted to deny them essential foodstuffs in order to starve them into submission. Part of this campaign was directed against the jungle cultivations on which the terrorists relied heavily for their basic sustenance. Tests proved that crops growing in these jungle clearings could be successfully destroyed by a chemical spray delivered by helicopters. A series of operations mounted in 1953 and 1954 verified this claim but this practice was not extended into a regular commitment as the area where this type of garden clearing was most frequently found coincided with the area inhabited by the aboriginal population of Malaya and it proved difficult to differentiate between their cultivations and those of the terrorists. Moreover, such clearings were not easy to locate and the tactical reconnaissance effort required was not often available owing to the claims of tasks with a higher priority. In any case there was little to be gained from searching for these clearings when the necessary helicopter effort was not available to destroy them and consequently the practice of crop spraying fell into abeyance during the final years of the campaign.

Air Reconnaissance

Visual. Tactical reconnaissance was accepted by the air forces as a regular commitment from the start of the Emergency and was carried out mainly by the Austers of No 656 AOP Squadron, which devoted 60 per cent of its total effort to this task. For most of the Emergency this squadron was administratively controlled by AHQ Malaya but was operationally controlled by the Army formations to which its flights were detached. Because of the state basis of operational planning, combined with the type of anti-terrorist operation and the nature of the enemy's activity, this method of control of tactical reconnaissance was acceptable. The total available effort was barely adequate, however, and the aircrew and maintenance staff of No 656 Squadron were overworked in maintaining an average of nearly 1,500 sorties a month for most of the Emergency. For tactical reconnaissance over jungle areas the helicopter, with its ability to hover, was a superior aircraft to the Auster but was rarely used for this purpose as it was required for more urgent tasks. Nevertheless, tactical reconnaissance proved invaluable in locating terrorist camps and concentrations in featureless jungle and in improving the general intelligence of their movements—the deficiency of which was the greatest hindrance to mounting security force offensives at the start of the campaign.

Photographic. Throughout the campaign photographic reconnaissance was carried out by No 81 Squadron. Apart from the systematic 'Block Cover' of the country, from which maps at a scale of 1 : 63,360 were prepared which helped to remedy the paucity and inaccuracies of current topographical maps of Malaya, vertical and oblique photographs at a scale of 1 : 10,000 or larger were produced for tactical purposes in specific operational areas. Small mosaics showing target areas were in general use for briefing aircrews while ground force commanders used them as basic operational maps in the field. The photographic reconnaissance effort, and the photographic interpretation by detachments of JAPIC (FE) and No 103 APIS, proved adequate for the provision of up-to-date cover for specific ground and air operations but it should be noted that the value of this type of support during the Malayan campaign was considerably reduced by the nature of the terrain and the use that was made of it by the terrorists in camouflaging their camps and gardens.

ANNEXES

NOTE: Certain of the annexes are incomplete. This is due to lack of supporting documents giving the necessary statistical information and is denoted by blanks in the various columns

Annex A

COMMUNIST TERRORIST ORGANIZATION—STRENGTH BY STATES, 1948–1960

State	1948 (Jul)	1949 (Mar)	1950	1951	1952	1953	1954	1955	1956 (Jan)	1957 (Jan)	1957 (Dec)	1958 (Dec)	1959 (Sep)	1960 (Jan)	1960 (Jul)	Total Strength of MCP 1947 (Feb)
(S Thailand)											183	485	455	495	488	
Kedah/Perlis	350	520							}295	304	91	58	53	—	—	560
Penang									49	42	40	23	9	4	—	535
Kelantan	200	50							147	140	108	8	—	—	—	200
Trengganu		120							17	29	22	9	8	8	8	250
Perak	500	440							906	778	774	237	155	100	65	1,990
Pahang	300	230							139	44	42	34	20	16	3	1,920
Selangor	300	580							167	101	59	4	—	—	—	2,000
Negri Sembilan	}150	210							220	117	55	2	—	—	—	795
Malacca									102	59	13	—	—	—	—	385
Johore	500	400							524	452	294	8	4	—	—	2,990
(Singapore)	—	—							—	—	—	—	—	—	—	965
TOTAL	2,300*	2,550*	3,923	7,292	5,765	4,373	3,402	2,798	2,566	2,066	1,681	868	704	623	564	12,590

* Estimated totals
MCP = Malayan Communist Party

Annex B

MALAYAN RACES LIBERATION ARMY (MRLA)—CHAIN OF COMMAND

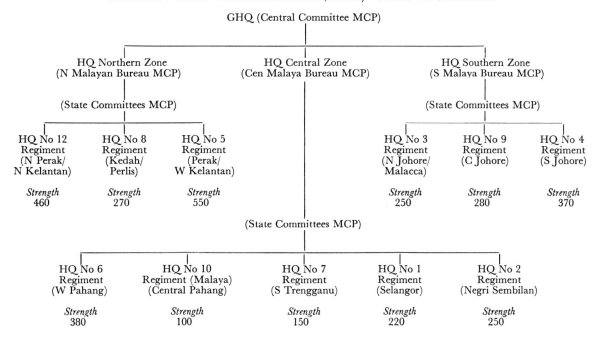

Note: This Order of Battle includes only formations from GHQ level down to Regiment level. The larger Regiments were divided into Military Sub-Districts, Battalions or Companies, while the smaller Regiments were divided into Platoons. The strength of individual units at the same level varied considerably. Approximate strengths of Regiments shown above were for the period January to August 1951.

Annex C

EXAMPLE OF THE COMPOSITION OF A MRLA* REGIMENT

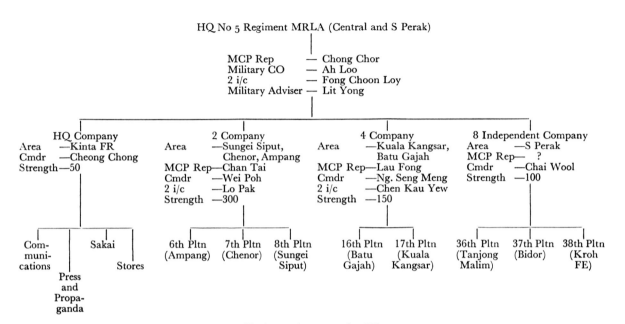

HQ No 5 Regiment MRLA (Central and S Perak)

MCP Rep — Chong Chor
Military CO — Ah Loo
2 i/c — Fong Choon Loy
Military Adviser — Lit Yong

HQ Company
Area — Kinta FR
Cmdr — Cheong Chong
Strength — 50

Communications
Sakai
Press and Propaganda
Stores

2 Company
Area — Sungei Siput, Chenor, Ampang
MCP Rep — Chan Tai
Cmdr — Wei Poh
2 i/c — Lo Pak
Strength — 300

6th Pltn (Ampang)
7th Pltn (Chenor)
8th Pltn (Sungei Siput)

4 Company
Area — Kuala Kangsar, Batu Gajah
MCP Rep — Lau Fong
Cmdr — Ng. Seng Meng
2 i/c — Chen Kau Yew
Strength — 150

16th Pltn (Batu Gajah)
17th Pltn (Kuala Kangsar)

8 Independent Company
Area — S Perak
MCP Rep — ?
Cmdr — Chai Wool
Strength — 100

36th Pltn (Tanjong Malim)
37th Pltn (Bidor)
38th Pltn (Kroh FE)

Total approximate strength—600

* Malayan Races Liberation Army

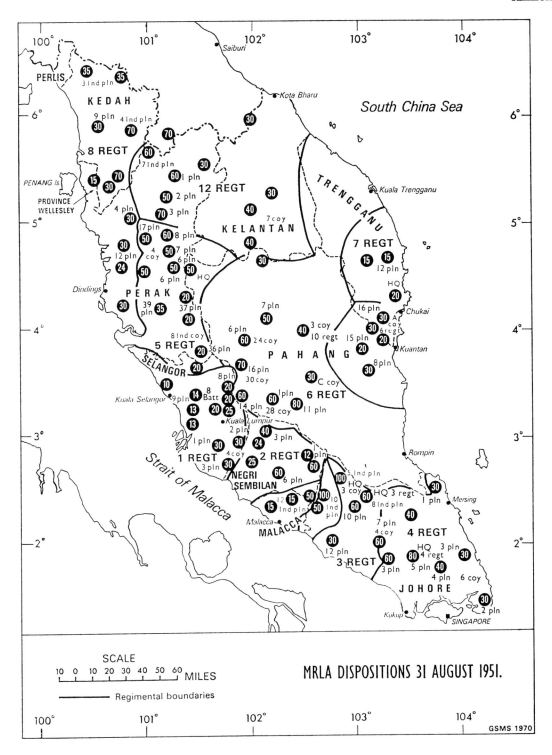

MRLA DISPOSITIONS 31 AUGUST 1951.

SCALE

10 0 10 20 30 40 50 60 MILES

———— Regimental boundaries

GSMS 1970

Annex E

GROUND FORCES ORDER OF BATTLE, 1948–1957

Strength and Composition of the Army and the Police

THE ARMY	Jun 1948	Jan 1949	Oct 1950	Aug 1951	Jun 1952	Jan 1953	Jun 1954	Jan 1955	Jan 1956	Jan 1957	Aug 1957
Armoured Car Regiments	—	1	2	2	2	2	2	2	2	2	1
Armoured Car Squadrons	—	—	—	—	—	1	1	1	1	1	2
Field Regiments	—	—	—	—	—	—	—	—	1	1	1
Field Batteries	—	—	1	1	1	1	2	2	1	2	2
HAA Batteries	—	—	—	—	—	—	1	1	1	1	1
Field Engineer Regiments	—	—	—	—	—	—	1	2	2	2	2
Infantry Battalions	10	15	19	19	21	23	22	22	23	23	21
Commando Brigade	—	—	1	1	—	—	—	—	—	—	—
Malayan Scouts	—	—	1	1	1	—	—	—	—	—	—
22nd SAS Regiment (3 Squadrons)	—	—	—	—	—	1	1	1	1	1	1
NZ SAS Squadron	—	—	—	—	—	—	—	—	1	1	1
Squadron, The Parachute Regiment	—	—	—	—	—	—	—	—	1	1	—

THE POLICE	Jun 1948	Jan 1949	Jan 1950	Jan 1951	Jan 1952	Jan 1953	Jan 1954	Jan 1955	Jan 1956	Jan 1957	Aug 1957
Regular Police	c9,000	12,767	16,220	16,814	22,187	36,737	24,427	19,659*	16,840		22,365*
Special Constabulary	—	33,610	29,987	43,475	44,878	33,570	27,208	23,238	23,238		22,409
Home Guard (average strength for year)	—	—	—	200,000	c250,000	210,000	172,500	152,000	132,000		

* Includes 2,819 and 2,915 Police Field Force

EMERGENCY COMMAND STRUCTURE

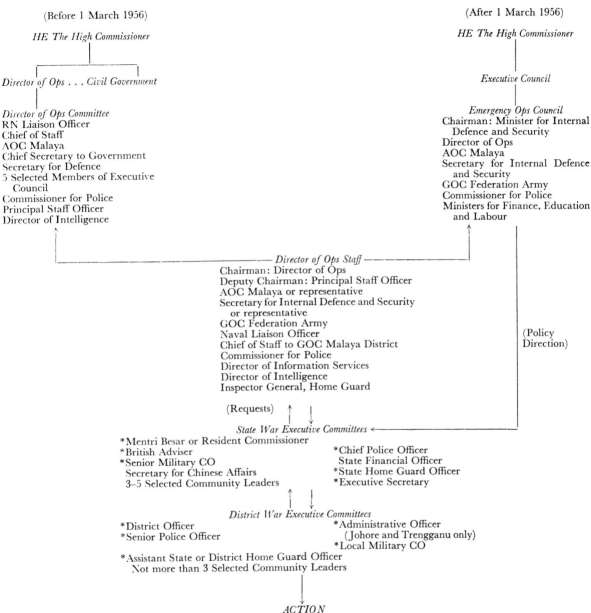

(Before 1 March 1956)

HE The High Commissioner

Director of Ops . . . Civil Government

Director of Ops Committee
RN Liaison Officer
Chief of Staff
AOC Malaya
Chief Secretary to Government
Secretary for Defence
5 Selected Members of Executive
  Council
Commissioner for Police
Principal Staff Officer
Director of Intelligence

(After 1 March 1956)

HE The High Commissioner

Executive Council

Emergency Ops Council
Chairman: Minister for Internal
  Defence and Security
Director of Ops
AOC Malaya
Secretary for Internal Defence
  and Security
GOC Federation Army
Commissioner for Police
Ministers for Finance, Education
  and Labour

———— *Director of Ops Staff* ————————
Chairman: Director of Ops
Deputy Chairman: Principal Staff Officer
AOC Malaya or representative
Secretary for Internal Defence and Security
  or representative
GOC Federation Army
Naval Liaison Officer
Chief of Staff to GOC Malaya District
Commissioner for Police
Director of Information Services
Director of Intelligence
Inspector General, Home Guard

(Policy
Direction)

(Requests)

State War Executive Committees ←————
*Mentri Besar or Resident Commissioner
*British Adviser   *Chief Police Officer
*Senior Military CO   State Financial Officer
  Secretary for Chinese Affairs   *State Home Guard Officer
  3–5 Selected Community Leaders   *Executive Secretary

District War Executive Committees
*District Officer   *Administrative Officer
*Senior Police Officer   (Johore and Trengganu only)
               *Local Military CO
*Assistant State or District Home Guard Officer
  Not more than 3 Selected Community Leaders

ACTION

*Members of State or District Operations Sub-Committees
Note : *Before 1 March 1956* Direction went from Director of Ops Committee to Director of Ops Staff and Requests in the Reverse
    Direction.

    After 1 March 1956 Direction went from Emergency Ops Council to State War Executive Committees and Requests from
    Director of Ops Staff up to the Emergency Ops Council.

Annex G

OFFICERS ADMINISTERING THE GOVERNMENT AND THE ARMED FORCES IN MALAYA DURING THE EMERGENCY

Date of Appointment

HE The High Commissioner of the Federation of Malaya

Sir Edward Gent	1 February 1948–4 July 1948 (killed)
Sir Henry Gurney	6 October 1948–6 October 1951 (killed)
General Sir Gerald Templer	5 February 1952
Sir Donald MacGillivray	31 May 1954

Director of Operations, Malaya

Lieutenant-General Sir Harold Briggs	1 April 1950
General Sir Rob Lockhart	3 December 1951
General Sir Gerald Templer	5 February 1952
Lieutenant-General Sir Geoffrey Bourne	1 June 1954
Lieutenant-General Sir Roger Bower	19 May 1956
Lieutenant-General Sir James Cassels	17 September 1957

General Officer Commanding, Malaya

Major-General D. A. L. Wade	1 October 1948
Major-General C. H. Boucher (later Sir Charles H.)	—1948
Major-General R. E. Urquhart	27 Februar 1950
Major-General Sir Hugh Stockwell	11 June 1952
Lieutenant-General Sir Geoffrey Bourne	7 April 1954
Lieutenant-General Sir Roger Bower	19 May 1956

The Air Officer Commanding, Air Command Far East (Far East Air Force after 1 June 1949)

Air Marshal Sir Hugh P. Lloyd	18 November 1947
Air Marshal F. J. Fogarty (later Sir Francis J.)	26 November 1949
Air Marshal A. C. Sanderson (later Sir A. Clifford)	11 June 1952
Air Marshal F. J. Fressanges (later Sir Francis J.)	12 November 1954
Air Marshal The Earl of Bandon	13 July 1957
Air Marshal A. D. Selway (later Sir Anthony D.)	30 June 1960

The Air Officer Commanding, Malaya (No 224 Group after 31 August 1957)

Air Vice-Marshal A. C. Sanderson	28 May 1948
Air Vice-Marshal F. J. Mellersh (later Sir Frank J.)	13 May 1949
Air Vice-Marshal R. S. Blucke	21 January 1951
Air Commodore J. L. F. Fuller-Good	17 August 1951
Air Vice-Marshal G. H. Mills	14 February 1952
Air Vice-Marshal F. R. W. Scherger	1 January 1953
Air Vice-Marshal W. H. Kyle	14 January 1955
Air Vice-Marshal V. E. Hancock	11 June 1957
Air Vice-Marshal R. A. Ramsey Rae	10 June 1959

Annex H

EMERGENCY STATISTICS—ANNUAL, 1948–1960

Year	No of Contacts Between SF and CT	No of CT Inspired Incidents					No of CTs Eliminated				No of SF Casualties			No of Civilian Casualties			
		Total (Major and Minor)	Major	Minor	Thousands of Rubber Trees Slashed	Attacks on Railways	Total	Killed	Captured	Surrendered	Total	Killed	Wounded	Total	Killed	Wounded	Missing
*1948		1,274					693	374	263	56	360	149	211	554	315	149	90
1949		1,442					1,207	619	337	251	476	229	247	694	334	200	160
1950	983	4,739	1,744	2,995	1,131·00		942	648	147	147	889	393	496	1,161	646	409	106
1951	1,911	6,082	2,333	3,749	450·00	29	1,399	1,077	121	201	1,195	504	691	1,024	533	356	135
1952	1,868	3,727	1,389	2,338	3·74	16	1,527	1,148	123	256	664	263	401	632	343	158	131
1953	1,407	1,170	258	912	1·78	18	1,392	947	73	372	209	92	117	143	85	15	43
1954	993	1,077	293	784	119·82	13	971	709	51	211	241	87	154	185	97	31	57
1955	565	781	206	575	1·48	12	709	406	54	249	182	79	103	143	62	24	57
1956	486	435	102	333			473	287	52	134	126	47	79	92	30	36	26
1957																	
1958																	
1959																	
†1960																	

* 6 months   † 7 months

Annex J

EMERGENCY STATISTICS—MONTHLY AVERAGES, 1948–1960

Year	No of Contacts Between SF and CT	No of CT Inspired Incidents					No of CTs Eliminated				No of SF Casualties			No of Civilian Casualties			
		Total (Major and Minor)	Major	Minor	Thousands of Rubber Trees Slashed	Attacks on Railways	Total	Killed	Captured	Surrendered	Total	Killed	Wounded	Total	Killed	Wounded	Missing
*1948		106					115	62	44	9	60	25	35	92	52	25	15
1949		120					100	51	28	21	40	19	21	58	28	17	13
1950	82	395	145	250	94·29		78	54	12	12	74	33	41	97	54	34	9
1951	159	506	194	312	37·62	2·5	117	90	10	17	100	42	58	86	44	30	12
1952	156	311	116	195	·31	1·3	127	96	10	21	55	22	33	53	29	13	11
1953	117	97	21	76	·15	1·5	116	79	6	31	18	8	10	12	7	1	4
1954	83	89	24	65	9·99	1·1	81	59	4	18	20	7	13	16	8	3	5
1955	47	65	17	48	·12	1·0	60	34	5	21	16	7	9	12	5	2	5
1956	41	36	8	28			39	24	4	11	10	4	6	8	3	3	2
1957																	
1958																	
1959																	
†1960																	

* 6 months   † 7 months

164

MAP OF 'WHITE AREAS' IN MALAYA, 1955–1959

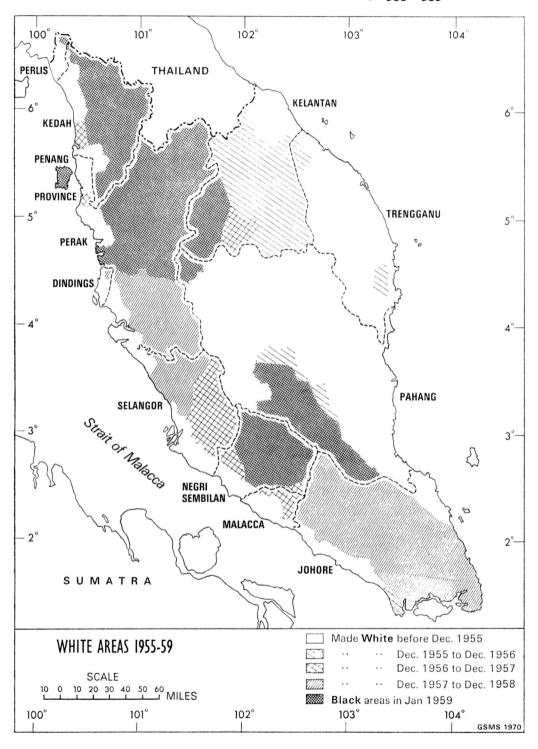

WHITE AREAS 1955-59

SCALE

10 0 10 20 30 40 50 60
MILES

	Made **White** before Dec. 1955
	,, ,, Dec. 1955 to Dec. 1956
	,, ,, Dec. 1956 to Dec. 1957
	,, ,, Dec. 1957 to Dec. 1958
	Black areas in Jan 1959

GSMS 1970

AIR FORCES ORDER OF BATTLE—SQUADRONS AVAILABLE 1948–1960

Type of Support	Type of Aircraft	Jun 1948	Sep 1949	Jul 1950	Aug 1951	Dec 1952	Dec 1953	Dec 1954	Dec 1955	Dec 1956	Dec 1957	Dec 1958	Dec 1959	Jul 1960
Offensive	Single Engined	1	2	2	1¼	1	1	1	3	3	2	1	2	3
	Twin Engined	—	1	2	2¾	3	2	2	1	—	1	2	3	3
	Four Engined	—	—	2	1	1	2	1½	—	1	1	—	—	—
	Flying Boat (at call)	1	1	2	1½	1½	1½	2	1	1	1	—	—	—
Transport	Single Engined	—	—	—	—	—	—	1 Flt	1 Flt	1 Flt	1 Flt	1 Flt	1 Flt	1 Flt
	Twin Engined	1	1	1	1	1	1	Detachment from FE Transport Wing equivalent to 1 Flt						
	Light Helicopter	—	—	2 h/c	2 h/c	5 h/c	1	1	1	1	1	1	—	—
	Medium Helicopter	—	—	—	—	—	1	2	2	1	1	1	1 Flt	1 Flt
Communications (including voice aircraft)	Various	1	1	1	1	1	1	1½	1½	1½	1½	1½	1½	1½
Reconnaissance	Various (PR)	1	1	1	1	1	1	1	1	1	1	1	1	1
									(plus Bomber Command detachment)					
	Auster (VR)	1	1	1	1	1	1	1	1	1	1	1	1	1
									(plus MAAF at call)					

Annex M

SQUADRONS AVAILABLE FOR OPERATION 'FIREDOG' 1948–1960

(Operational types only)

Squadron	Role	Aircraft	Maximum Unit Establishment	Location (Detachments)	Period From	Period To
OFFENSIVE AIR SUPPORT No 1 RAAF	MB	Lincoln B30A	8	Tengah	16 Jul 1950	31 Jun 1958
No 2 (B) RAAF	LB	Canberra B1	9	Butterworth	1 Jul 1958	after 1 Jul 1960
No 3 (F) RAAF	DF/GA	Sabre 32	16	Butterworth	11 Nov 1958	after 1 Jul 1960
No 14 RNZAF	DF/GA	Venom FB1	16	Tengah	10 Apr 1955	1 Sep 1958
No 28 RAF	DF/GA–FR	Spitfire 18	9	Tengah Sembawang (Kuala Lumpur)	prior to 1 Jan 48 26 Jan 1948	26 Jan 1948 11 May 1949
No 33 RAF (amalgamated with No 45 RAF on 31 Mar 1955. Number plate to 2nd TAF on 15 Oct 1955)	DF/GA–FR	Tempest F2 Hornet F3/4	16 16	Changi (Kuala Lumpur) Tengah (Butterworth) Butterworth	8 Aug 1949 17 Mar 1950 1 Aug 1952	17 Mar 1950 1 Aug 1952 31 Mar 1955
No 45 RAF (amalgamated with No 33 RAF on 31 Mar 1955)	LB–DF/GA	Beaufighter 10 Brigand B1 Hornet F3 Venom FB1 Canberra B2	8 10 16 16 8	Kuala Lumpur Tengah (Kuala Lumpur) Tengah (Kuala Lumpur) Butterworth Tengah	1 May 1949 6 Dec 1949 31 Jan 1952 15 Oct 1955 15 Nov 1957	6 Dec 1949 31 Jan 1952 31 Mar 1955 15 Nov 1957 after 1 Jul 1960
No 45/33 RAF (renumbered No. 45 RAF on 15 Oct 1955)	DF/GA	Hornet F3/4 Vampire FB9 Venom FB1	20 16 16	Butterworth Butterworth Butterworth	31 Mar 1955 1 Jun 1955 15 Sep 1955	1 Jun 1955 15 Sep 1955 15 Oct 1955
No 60 RAF	DF/GA	Spitfire 18 Vampire FB5/9 Venom FB1/4	17 16 16	Tengah Sembawang (Kuala Lumpur) Tengah (Kuala Lumpur) Tengah (Kuala Lumpur) Tengah (Kuala Lumpur)	prior to 1 Jan 48 26 Jan 1948 25 Aug 1949 1 Dec 1950 15 Jan 1951 1 May 1955	26 Jan 1948 25 Aug 1949 1 Dec 1950 15 Jan 1951 1 May 1955 1 Oct 1959
	N/AWF	Meteor NF14	12	Tengah	1 Oct 1959	after 1 Jul 1960
No 75 RNZAF	LB	Canberra B2	8	Tengah	1 Jul 1958	after 1 Jul 1960
No 77 (F) RAAF	DF/GA	Sabre 32	16	Butterworth	11 Feb 1959	after 1 Jul 1960
No 84 RAF (reduced to cadre basis on 1 Feb 1953) Number plate to MEAF on 20 Feb 1953	LB	Beaufighter 10 Brigand B1	8 10	Changi Tengah (Kuala Lumpur) Tengah (Kuala Lumpur)	prior to 1 Jan 48 22 Mar 1948 9 Apr 1950	22 Mar 1948 11 Oct 1948 20 Feb 1953 (on detachment from MEAF)
No 88 RAF (disbanded on 1 Oct 1954)	LR/GR–MR	Sunderland GR5	5	Seletar (normally on attachment at Iwakuni, Japan)	1 Oct 1950	5 Apr 1954
No 205 RAF (amalgamated with No 209 RAF on 31 Dec 1954)	LR/GR–MR	Sunderland GR5 Sunderland GR5 Shackleton MR1	5 4 8	Seletar (Iwakuni, Japan) Seletar Changi	15 Sep 1949 1 Nov 1958 1 Nov 1958	13 Dec 1954 31 May 1959 after 1 Jul 1960

Squadron	Role	Aircraft	Maximum Unit Establishment	Location (Detachments)	Period	
					From	To
No 209 RAF (amalgamated with No 205 RAF on 31 Dec 1954. Number plate to SR/TPT role FEAF on 1 Nov 1958)	LR/GR–MR	Sunderland GR5	5	Seletar (Iwakuni, Japan)	prior to 1 Jan 48	31 Dec 1954
No 205/209 RAF (renumbered No 205 RAF on 1 Nov 1958)	LR/GR–MR	Sunderland GR5 Shackleton MR1	8 2	Seletar Changi	31 Dec 1954 26 Feb 1958	1 Nov 1958 1 Nov 1958
MALAYAN AUXILIARY AIR FORCE (MAAF) Malaya/Penang Sqn	Auxiliary Fighter (changed to LL/Recce on 3 Apr 1957)	DH82A (Tiger Moth) Harvard 2B Chipmunk	4 4 4	Butterworth	1 Mar 1950 1 Feb 1951 Jan/Mar 1957	Jan/Mar 1957 Jan/Mar 1957 3 Apr 1957
Singapore Sqn		DH82A (Tiger Moth) Harvard 2B Spitfire F24 Chipmunk	4 6 3 4	Tengah	1 Mar 1950 1 Feb 1951 1 Jul 1951 27 Feb 1957	27 Feb 1957 27 Feb 1957 15 Apr 1953 3 Apr 1957
Kuala Lumpur Sqn		DH82A (Tiger Moth) Harvard 2B Chipmunk	4 4 4		1 Dec 1951 1 Feb 1951 Jan/Mar 1957	Jan/Mar 1957 Jan/Mar 1957 3 Apr 1957
AIR TRANSPORT SUPPORT No 38 RAAF	MR/TPT	Dakota C47B	4	Changi (Kuala Lumpur)	1 Jun 1950	30 Nov 1952
No 41 RNZAF	MR/TPT	Dakota C3 Bristol Freighter	5 4	Changi (Kuala Lumpur) Changi (Kuala Lumpur)	1 Sep 1949 1 Jul 1955	30 Nov 1951 after 1 Jul 1960
No 48 RAF	MR/TPT	Dakota C4 Valetta C1 Hastings C1/2 Beverley C1	8 8 8 4	Changi (Kuala Lumpur) Changi (Kuala Lumpur) Changi (Kuala Lumpur) Changi (Kuala Lumpur)	prior to 1 Jan 48 1 Apr 1951 1 May 1957 1 Jun 1959	1 Apr 1951 1 May 1957 after 1 Jul 1960 after 1 Jul 1960
No 52 RAF	MR/TPT	Dakota C4 Valetta C1	8 10	Changi (Kuala Lumpur) Changi (Kuala Lumpur) Kuala Lumpur	prior to 1 Jan 48 3 Sep 1951 1 Oct 1959	3 Sep 1951 1 Oct 1959 after 1 Jul 1960
No 110 RAF (disbanded on 31 Dec 1957. Number plate to SR/TPT role, FEAF on 3 Jun 1959)	MR/TPT SR/TPT	Dakota C4 Valetta C1 Whirlwind H/C HAR4 Sycamore H/C HR14	8 8 5 13	Changi (Kuala Lumpur) Changi (Kuala Lumpur) Kuala Lumpur Butterworth (Whirlwinds at Kuala Lumpur, Sycamores non-operational at Seletar)	prior to 1 Jan 48 24 Oct 1951 3 Jun 1959 1 Sep 1959	23 Nov 1951 31 Dec 1957 1 Sep 1959 after 1 Jul 1960

Annex M—continued

Squadron	Role	Aircraft	Maximum Unit Establishment	Location (Detachments)	Period From	Period To
No 155 RAF (disbanded on 3 Jun 1959. Aircraft to No 194 RAF)	SR/TPT	Whirlwind H/C HAR 2/4	17	Kuala Lumpur (Kluang, Seletar)	1 Sep 1955	3 Jun 1959
No 194 RAF (renumbered No 110 RAF on 3 Jun 1959)	SR/TPT	Dragonfly H/C 2/4	9	Sembawang (Kuala Lumpur)	2 Feb 1953	1 May 1953
				Kuala Lumpur (Ipoh, Kluang, Benta)	1 May 1953	1 Oct 1956
		Sycamore H/C, HR 14	14	Kuala Lumpur (Ipoh, Kluang, Benta)	1 Apr 1954	3 Jun 1959
No 209 RAF	SR/TPT	SE Pioneer CC1	9	Kuala Lumpur	1 Nov 1958	1 Oct 1959
				Seletar (Kuala Lumpur)	1 Oct 1959	after 1 Jul 1960
		TE Pioneer CC1	5	Kuala Lumpur	18 Mar 1959	1 Oct 1959
				Seletar (Kuala Lumpur)	1 Oct 1959	after 1 Jul 1960
		Pembroke C1	5	Kuala Lumpur	1 Nov 1958	1 Oct 1959
				Seletar	1 Oct 1959	15 Dec 1959
		Dakota C4	3	Kuala Lumpur (Bayan Lepas)	1 Nov 1958	1 Oct 1959
		Auster 6/7	2	Kuala Lumpur	1 Nov 1958	18 Mar 1959
No 267 RAF (renumbered No 209 RAF on 1 Nov 1958)	SR/TPT	SE Pioneer CC1 (Support Flight)	8	Kuala Lumpur	15 Feb 1954	1 Nov 1958
		Pembroke C1	5	Kuala Lumpur	15 Feb 1954	1 Nov 1958
		Auster 6/7	2		15 Feb 1954	1 Nov 1954
		Harvard 2B (Communications Flight)	2		1 Nov 1954	3 Dec 1956
		Dakota C4	3	Kuala Lumpur	20 Mar 1954	1 Nov 1958
		Auster 6/7	2		20 Mar 1954	1 Nov 1958
No 848 Naval Air (withdrawn from operations on 10 Dec 1956)	SR/TPT	S55 H/C	10	Sembawang (Kuala Lumpur)	23 Jan 1953	1 May 1953
				Kuala Lumpur	1 May 1953	26 Mar 1956
				Sembawang (Kluang)	26 Mar 1956	12 Nov 1956
No 1311 Transport Flight, No 303 Helicopter Wing (became Support Flight No 267 RAF on 15 Feb 1954)	SR/TPT	SE Pioneer CC1	4	Kuala Lumpur	1 Sep 1953	15 Feb 1954
HQ Far East Transport Wing (1 Flight—became Voice Flight, No. 267 RAF on 15 Feb 1954)	SR/TPT	Valetta C1	2	Changi (Kuala Lumpur)	1 Jul 1953	20 Mar 1954
Far East Communications Squadron	Comm	Dakota C4	6	Changi (Kuala Lumpur, Butterworth)	prior to 1 Jan 48	16 Nov 1951
		Valetta C1/2	4		1 Jul 1951	after 1 Jul 1960
		York C1	1		prior to 1 Jan 48	1 Dec 1956
		Hastings C1/4	2		1 Jan 1953	after 1 Jul 1960
		Devon C1	2		1 Dec 1948	15 Feb 1954
		Pembroke C1	3		15 Apr 1954	1 May 1960
		Anson 19	5		prior to 1 Jan 48	16 Dec 1950
		Harvard 2B	12		prior to 1 Jan 48	3 Feb 1956

Squadron	Role	Aircraft	Maximum Unit Establishment	Location (Detachment)	Period From	Period To
Far East Communications Squadron—*contd.*		Auster 6/7 Vampire FB9 Venom FB1 Meteor T7	2 2 1 3		1 Jul 1948 1 Nov 1954 1 Jul 1956 3 Feb 1956	1 Dec 1956 30 Sep 1958 30 Sep 1958 16 Nov 1959
No 81 RAF	PR	Spitfire F18–PR19	5	Changi Tengah (Kuala Lumpur) Seletar (Kuala Lumpur)	prior to 1 Jan 48 1 Feb 1948 16 Mar 1950	1 Feb 1948 16 Mar 1950 15 Oct 1953
		Mosquito PR34/34a	8	Changi Tengah (Kuala Lumpur) Seletar (Kuala Lumpur)	prior to 1 Jan 48 1 Feb 1948 16 Mar 1950	1 Feb 1948 16 Mar 1950 31 Dec 1955
		Harvard 2B	1	Changi Tengah	prior to 1 Jan 48 1 Feb 1948	1 Feb 1948 1 Jun 1948
		Anson 19	1	Tengah Seletar	31 Oct 1949 16 Mar 1950	16 Mar 1950 1 Jun 1951
		Meteor PR10	6	Seletar (Kuala Lumpur) Tengah	15 Oct 1953 1 Apr 1958	1 Apr 1958 after 1 Jul 1960
		Pembroke C(PR)1	4	Seletar Tengah	1 Dec 1955 1 Apr 1958	1 Apr 1958 13 Jan 1960
		Canberra PR7	3	Tengah	13 Jan 1960	after 1 Jul 1960
No 656 RAF (became No 656 Army Air Corps on 1 Sep 1957)	AOP (changed to AOP/LL on 1 May 1952)	Auster 5/6/7/9	31	Sembawang (Kuala Lumpur, (Taiping, Seremban, Kluang) Changi (Kuala Lumpur, Taiping, Seremban, Temerloh, Benta, Sembawang) Kuala Lumpur (Taiping, Seremban, Temerloh, Benta, Sembawang, Ipoh, Port Dickson)	15 Jul 1948 17 Aug 1949 1 Aug 1951	17 Aug 1949 1 Aug 1951 after 1 Jul 1960
MAAF Penang Sqn (disbanded on 31 Dec 1958)	LL/ Recce	Chipmunk	4	Butterworth	3 Apr 1957	31 Dec 1958
Kuala Lumpur Sqn (disbanded on 31 Dec 1958)		Chipmunk	4	Kuala Lumpur	3 Apr 1957	31 Dec 1958
Singapore Sqn		Chipmunk	4	Tengah Seletar	3 Apr 1957 1 Apr 1958	1 Apr 1958 after 1 Jul 1960
Casualty Evacuation Flight, FEAF (absorbed by No 194 RAF on 2 Feb 1953)	SR/TPT	Dragonfly H/C 2/4	9	Changi (Kuala Lumpur, Butterworth)	1 May 1960	2 Feb 1953

Appendix I to Annex M

TEMPORARY DETACHMENTS OF UK BASED UNITS AVAILABLE FOR 'FIREDOG' OPERATIONS

Operation	Squadron No	Aircraft		Location	Period	
					From	To
'Musgrave'	57	Lincoln 2B (4A)	8	Tengah	20 Mar 1950	29 Mar 1951
	100	Lincoln 2B (4A)	8	Tengah	20 Mar 1950	29 Mar 1951
	61	Lincoln 2B (4A)	8	Tengah	20 Mar 1950	29 Mar 1951
'Bold'	83	Lincoln 2B (4A)	8	Tengah	1 Sep 1953	1 Mar 1955
	7	Lincoln 2B (4A)	8	Tengah	1 Sep 1953	1 Mar 1955
	148	Lincoln 2B (4A)	8	Tengah	1 Sep 1953	1 Mar 1955
'Mileage'	101	Canberra B6	6/8	Butterworth	1 Mar 1955	31 Aug 1956
	617	Canberra B6	8	Butterworth	1 Mar 1955	31 Aug 1956
	12	Canberra B6	8	Butterworth	1 Mar 1955	31 Aug 1956
	9	Canberra B6	8	Butterworth	1 Mar 1955	31 Aug 1956
'Profiteer'*	214	Valiant B1 and	2/4	Changi	31 Oct 1957	27 Mar 1958
	90	Vulcan B1		Butterworth	6 Jun 1958	26 Jun 1960
	148					
	and others					
'Planters Punch'	542	Canberra PR7	2	Changi	13 May 1955	31 Oct 1959
	540	Canberra PR7	2	Changi	13 May 1955	31 Oct 1959
	82	Canberra PR7	2/4	Changi	13 May 1955	31 Oct 1959
	58	Canberra PR7	2/4	Changi	13 May 1955	31 Oct 1959

* Intermittent detachments of 'V' bombers for 2 weeks every 3 months

MONTHLY AIRCRAFT SERVICEABILITY—1949 to 1952

(**In Percentages**)

Month	Medium Bombers	Light Bombers	Fighters		Medium Range Transports		Austers	Flying Boats	Helicopters
1949									
April	—	42·5	44·7		66·9		58·1	51·3	—
May	—	41·5	50·5		75·7		68·5	51·3	—
June	—	28·4	45·4		69·1		63·7	51·3	—
July	—	38·9	52·2		67·3		56·2	40·6	—
August	—	38·5	44·8		73·2		73·5	36·6	—
September	—	38·2	56·5		68·3		60·2	56·5	—
October	—	33·4	49·1		74·3		76·6	42·3	—
November	—	29·2	50·0		77·3		61·4	50·1	—
December	—	34·8	45·6		73·2		67·9	35·5	—
1950									
January	—	34·9	39·5		68·9		62·3	44·2	—
February	—	46·3	50·0		72·1		62·3	41·9	—
March	61·2	46·9	51·9		72·3		63·8	40·8	—
April	67·0	66·8	46·6		73·1		70·7	44·4	—
May	77·9	58·0	55·2		74·5		66·7	53·1	—
June	83·6	63·9	60·0		65·7		55·0	55·5	—
July	94·3	56·6	55·8		68·5		66·3	67·8	—
August	85·8	59·7	59·1		71·6		67·8	62·0	—
September	85·2	56·8	55·7		71·5		56·4	57·9	—
October	79·6	56·7	54·4		66·8		64·8	60·0	—
November	76·0	54·9	57·5		59·6		64·7	60·1	—
December	81·5	54·2	57·9		71·6		77·7	62·3	—
1951									
January	78·0	63·4	63·1		64·8		69·9	67·0	37·0
February	71·2	56·8	57·1		69·1		62·5	57·3	38·8
March	62·0	51·0	55·7		71·2		63·3	64·5	47·3
April	68·5	53·5	54·9		81·5		64·0	63·0	64·0
May	54·7	60·5	48·9		79·4		50·4	64·0	54·0
June	71·0	67·1	53·9		79·4		60·9	63·1	37·3
July	66·1	26·9	53·7		75·0		57·9	60·1	57·6
August	70·1	48·5	53·1		74·2		63·2	63·6	64·1
			Hornet	*Vampire*	*Dakota*	*Valetta*			
September	72·5	49·8	57·8	46·8	68·4	51·2	61·7	62·9	52·0
October	65·4	53·4	58·9	70·6	73·5	51·7	71·4	68·7	42·8
November	70·5	56·1	67·3	72·3	88·2	49·0	65·7	63·5	23·0
December	65·3	57·5	57·3	61·9	82·5	54·8	67·4	68·0	40·0
1952									
January	71·7	65·5	59·1	54·5	83·2	58·3	67·0	74·0	65·0
February	81·2	62·1	51·1	54·3	93·5	52·1	61·9	62·7	77·3
March	80·0	60·0	50·0	43·3	—	53·7	51·6	56·5	63·3
April	67·0	59·0	58·3	52·9	—	61·3	55·3	59·9	46·7
May	48·0	64·4	47·6	54·4	—	58·5	70·6	59·3	59·5
June	66·2	50·0	60·0	64·4	—	55·1	68·6	60·9	58·0
July	67·8	48·0	53·1	73·1	—	55·5	74·8	63·5	67·5
August	78·6	51·0	46·3	59·4	—	54·6	75·8	54·7	51·3
September	76·2	51·0	46·3	59·4	—	54·5	75·8	54·7	51·3
October	68·8	35·0	45·8	61·3	—	54·6	75·2	66·2	65·0
November	72·0	43·0	43·0	65·8	—	54·8	80·1	55·9	68·0
December	73·4	34·2	44·4	65·0	—	61·4	78·4	54·6	52·0

Annex O

AIRCRAFT ACCIDENTS IN MALAYA 1948–1951

Date	Aircraft	Squadron No	Crash Location	No Killed
19 Aug 1948	Dakota KJ962	110	Near Batu Melintang	5
8 Oct 1948	Spitfire TP225	60	Near Raub	1
12 Nov 1948	Spitfire TP231	28	Near Serendah	1
12 Nov 1948	Dakota KM633	110	Near Rawang	5
11 Feb 1949	Beaufighter RD858	45	Near Butterworth	2
27 Jul 1949	Spitfire TP223	60		1
7 Sep 1949	Dakota KN536	52	Near Ipoh	3
27 Oct 1949	Auster TJ674	656	Near Temerloh	2
26 Nov 1949	Beaufighter RD866	45	Durian Tipis, near Seremban	2
17 Dec 1949	Spitfire TP195	60	Sungei Besi	1
22 Jan 1950	Spitfire TP219	60	Kampong Solok near Malacca	1
26 Mar 1950	Sunderland SZ573	209	Seletar (exploded during bombing-up)	2
6 Jul 1950	Brigand RH850	45	Kelantan	3
24 Jul 1950	Tempest PR786	33	Klian Intan, near Kroh	1
31 Jul 1950	Brigand RH815	84	Cameron Highlands	3
25 Aug 1950	Dakota KN630	52	Near Kampong Jendera, Kelantan	12
16 Nov 1950	Tempest PR895	33	Butterworth	—
11 Jan 1951	Brigand VS838	45	Cameron Highlands	3
15 Feb 1951	Brigand VS859	45	Negri Sembilan	2
1 Jun 1951	Brigand VS869	84	Tengah	3
15 Jun 1951	Brigand VS857	45	Near Tengah	1
19 Jun 1951	Brigand RH881	84		1
10 Aug 1951	Hornet WB870	33	Near Bedok	1

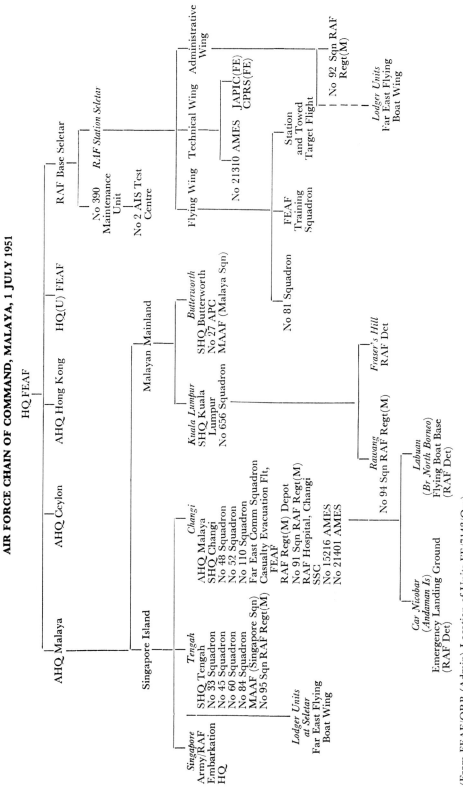

AIR FORCE CHAIN OF COMMAND, MALAYA, 1 JULY 1951

(From FEAF/ORB (Admin) Location of Units FE/7143/Org)

Annex Q

AIRFIELDS IN MALAYA, 1955

J	=	Johore	Pa	=	Pahang
K	=	Kedah	Pe	=	Penang
KT	=	Kelantan	PW	=	Province Wellesley
M	=	Malacca	S	=	Selangor
NS	=	Negri Sembilan	SI	=	Singapore Island
P	=	Perak	T	=	Trengganu

Suitable for Austers, Pioneers Beavers & Valettas		Suitable for Austers, Pioneers & Beavers		Suitable for Austers & Pioneers		Suitable for Pioneers only		Suitable for Helicopters only	
Alor Star	(K)	Bahau	(NS)	Airhouse, Singapore	(SI)	Fort Dixon	(Pa)	Langkap	(P)
Bayan Lepas	(Pe)	Batu Arang	(S)	Gemas	(NS)	Gambir	(P)	Kinrara	(NS)
Butterworth	(PW)	Batu Pahat	(J)	Fort Iskander or		Fort Kemar	(P)	Dabong	(Pa)
Changi	(SI)	Benta	(Pa)	Kampong Baapas	(Pa)	Fort Legap	(P)	Fort Chabai	(K)
Gong Kedah	(KT)	Bentong	(Pa)	Jerantut	(Pa)	Penggerang	(J)		
Ipoh	(P)	Bidor	(P)	Kampong Kuala Aur	(Pa)	Fort Shean	(Pa)		
Kallang	(SI)	Chukai	(T)	Kampong		Fort Telanok	(Pa)		
Kluang	(J)	Dungun	(T)	Kuala Medang	(Pa)				
Kota Bharu	(KT)	Grik	(P)	Kampong Kijal	(T)				
Kuala Lumpur (Main)	(S)	Gua Musang	(KT)	Kemayan	(P)				
Kuantan (Main)	(Pa)	Jenderata	(Pa)	Kota Tinggi	(J)				
Malacca (Main)	(M)	Johore Bahru	(J)	Kuala Kotil	(Pa)				
Seletar	(SI)	Kampong Lambor Karan	(P)	Kuala Kubu Bahru	(S)				
Sembawang	(SI)	Kangar Kahang	(Pa)	Kuala Lumpur (Noble-Field)	(S)				
Taiping	(P)	Kroh	(P)	Kuantan (Beserah Beach)	(Pa)				
Tengah	(SI)	Kuala Kangsar	(P)	Kulai Besar	(J)				
Trengganu (Main)	(T)	Kuala Krai	(P)	Lubok Kiap	(K)				
		Labis	(J)	Lukit Tin	(P)				
		Labu Kubong	(P)	Malacca (Padang)	(M)				
		Lima Blas	(S)	Muar (Town)	(J)				
		Machang	(KT)	Pekan	(Pa)				
		Mersing	(J)	Raub	(Pa)				
		Muar (Bakri)	(J)	Rompin (Beach)	(Pa)				
		Pontian	(J)	Seremban (Paroi)	(NS)				
		Port Dickson	(NS)	Slim River	(P)				
		Port Swettenham	(S)	Sungei Sawak	(P)				
		Segamat	(J)	Tanjong Malim	(S)				
		Sitiawan	(P)	Tampin	(M)				
		Sungei Patani	(K)	Titi	(P)				
		Sungei Tinggi	(S)	Trengganu (Island)	(T)				
		Temerloh	(Pa)						
		Triang	(Pa)						
		Ulu Bernam	(S)						

MAP OF AIRFIELDS IN MALAYA, 1955

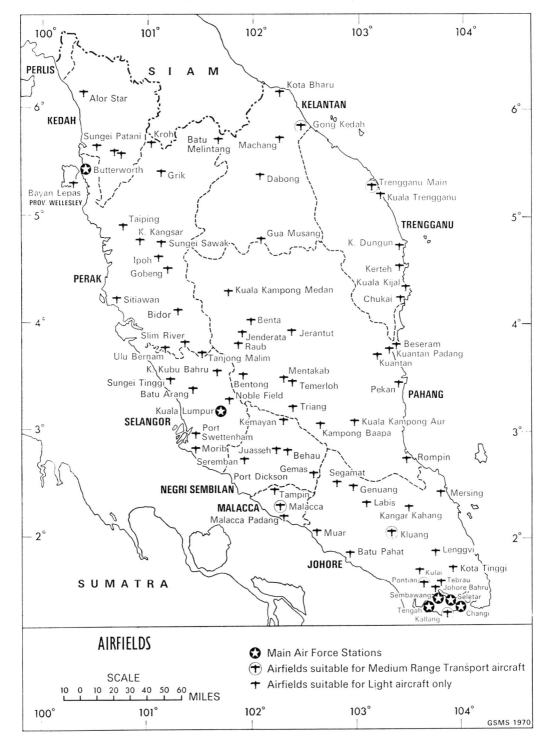

AIRFIELDS

⭐ Main Air Force Stations

✈ Airfields suitable for Medium Range Transport aircraft

✦ Airfields suitable for Light aircraft only

SCALE

10 0 10 20 30 40 50 60 MILES

GSMS 1970

Annex R

OPERATION 'FIREDOG', AIR EFFORT—ANNUAL, 1948–1960

	Jul 48 to Mar 49	Apr 49 to Dec 50	Jan 51 to Aug 51	Sep 51 to Feb 52	Mar 52 to Dec 52	1953	1954	1955	1956	1957	1958	1959	Jun 59 to Jul 60	Jan to Jul 60
Offensive Air Support No of strikes	95	1,017	745	394	551	298	426	300	139	49	47	2	—	—
No of sorties	403	6,011	3,278	1,871	3,132	2,303	2,055	1,831	790	373	926	31	—	—
Weight of bombs (short tons)	78	6,900	4,956	2,727	3,404	3,384	4,491	4,042	1,891	871	1,756	—	—	—
No of R/P	1,256	27,169	13,850	8,749	8,008	5,925	4,508	3,096	873	380	345		—	—
Thousands of rounds of ·303, ·5, 20 mm	207	2,371	1,403	848	1,806	1,195	968	668	186	46	111		—	—
Air Transport Support Total No of sorties	5,784	13,735	6,487	5,205	7,953								—	
Total No of troops and passengers	9,639	18,324	10,273	8,660	13,888	19,368	18,228	37,740	37,476	30,648	32,698	9,087	—	
Total freight (short tons)	423	3,518	1,716	773	1,535								—	
Supply drop sorties	99	1,581	741	372	791	1,346	2,080	2,065	1,553	1,361	1,265		—	
Supplies dropped (short tons)	118	2,798	1,423	567	1,246	2,231	3,396	3,888	2,995	2,398	2,671	1,426	—	696
Pioneers No of sorties	—	—	- -	—	—	—		4,691	7,527	6,574	3,201	—	—	
No of troops and passengers	—	—	—	—	—	—	1,486	5,393	7,936	6,805	3,607	—	4,555	
No of casualties	—	—	—	—	—			113		105	43	—	101	
Freight (short tons)	—	—	—	—	—	—	84	359	1,004	923	509	—	266	
Helicopters No of sorties	—	—						21,700	26,324	20,664	23,880	—		
No of troops and passengers	—	—				10,098 (May to Dec only)	11,892	32,294	29,668	22,627	29,453	—	7,123	
No of casualties	—	26	40	40	119	518	743	793	696	633	755	—	309	

	Jul 48 to Mar 49	Apr 49 to Dec 50	Jan 51 to Aug 51	Sep 51 to Feb 52	Mar 52 to Dec 52	1953	1954	1955	1956	1957	1958	1959	Jun 59 to Jul 60	Jan to Jul 60
Freight (short tons)	—	—				82 (May to Dec)	119	351	218	207	314	—	84	
Psychological warfare No of leaflets dropping sorties	99	229	261	237	288	184	240	365	333	308	293	—		
Thousands of leaflets		12,520	11,405	1,633	11,449	61,848	70,799	141,181	95,846	87,988	86,100	40,412	—	9,898
No of loud hailing sorties	—	—	—	—	—	327	666	922	776	821	685			
No of hours of aerial broadcasting	—	—	—	—	—		643	869	763	732	505	197		61
Reconnaissance Total No of sorties	1,339	3,606	2,199	2,490	5,494			9,116	7,261	6,471	4,639			
Photographic reconnaissance sorties	197	643	710	595	1,102	1,335	945	833	749	710	721			
Austers Total No of sorties							22,794	22,909	17,156	15,346	15,307			
Visual reconnaissance sorties							9,666	8,283	6,211	5,770	3,918			
Supply drop sorties							762	944	711	697	1,043			
Leaflet drop sorties							747	391	444	615	451			
AOP sorties									118	168	141			
Target marking sorties							88	264	136	130	209			
Communications and miscellaneous sorties							11,531	13,027	9,536	7,966	9,545			

Annex S

OPERATION 'FIREDOG', AIR EFFORT—MONTHLY AVERAGES, 1948–1960

	Jul 48 to Mar 49	Apr 49 to Dec 50	Jan 51 to Aug 51	Sep 51 to Feb 52	Mar 52 to Dec 52	1953	1954	1955	1956	1957	1958	1959	Jun 59 to Jul 60	Jan to Jul 60
Offensive Air Support No of strikes	10	48	92	65	55	25	35	25	12	4	4	—		—
No of sorties	44	286	409	311	313	192	171	153	66	31	88	3		—
Weight of bombs (short tons)	8	328	619	454	340	282	374	329	158	73	146			—
No of R/P	139	1,293	1,731	1,458	801	494	375	258	73	32	29			—
1000's of rounds of ·303, ·5, 20 mm	23	112	175	141	181	100	81	56	15	4	9			—
Air Transport Support Total No of sorties	642	654	810	867	795									
Total No of troops and passengers	1,071	872	1,284	1,443	1,389	1,614	1,519	3,145	3,123	2,554	2,725	757		
Total freight (short tons)	47	167	214	128	153									
Supply drop sorties	11	75	92	62	79	112	173	172	129	113	105			
Supplies dropped (short tons)	13	133	177	94	125	186	283	324	250	200	221	119		100
Pioneers No of sorties	—	—	—	—	—	—		391	627	548	266			
No of troops and passengers	—	—	—	—	—	—	124	449	661	567	300	—	325	
No of casualties	—	—	—	—	—	—		9		9	4	—	7	
Freight (short tons)	—	—	—	—	—	—	7	30	84	77	42	—	19	
Helicopters No of sorties	—	—						1,808	2,194	1,722	1,990	—		
No of troops and passengers	—	—				1,261 (May to Dec only)	991	2,791	2,472	1,887	2,454	—	594	
No of casualties	—	2	3	3	10	43	62	66	58	53	63	—	24	
Freight (short tons)	—	—				10 (May to Dec only)	10	29	18	17	26	—	7	

	Jul 48 to Mar 49	Apr 49 to Dec 50	Jan 51 to Aug 51	Sep 51 to Feb 52	Mar 52 to Dec 52	1953	1954	1955	1956	1957	1958	1959	Jun 59 to Jul 60	Jan to Jul 60
Psychological Warfare No of leaflet dropping sorties	11	10	32	39	29	15	20	30	28	26	24	—		
1000's of leaflets		596	1,425	272	1,145	5,157	5,900	11,765	7,987	7,332	7,175	3,368		1,414
No of loud hailing sorties	—	—	—	—	—	27	55	77	65	68	57	—		
No of hours of aerial broadcasting	—	—	—	—	—		54	72	64	61	42	16		5
Reconnaissance Total No of sorties	148	171	274	415	549			770	605	539	387			
Photographic reconnaissance sorties	16	30	89	99	110	111	79	69	62	59	60			
Austers Total No of sorties							1,899	1,909	1,430	1,279	1,292			
Visual reconnaissance sorties							805	690	518	481	326			
Supply drop sorties							63	79	69	58	87			
Leaflet drop sorties							62	33	37	51	38			
AOP sorties									10	14	12			
Target marking sorties							7	22	11	11	17			
Communications and miscellaneous sorties							961	1,086	795	664	796			

Annex T

OPERATION 'FIREDOG', OFFENSIVE AIR SUPPORT, 1948–1960

	No of Strikes	No of Sorties	1,000 lb	500 lb	350 lb Clusters	20 lb	R/P	20 mm	·5	·303
1948										
Jul	10	25								
Aug	15	64								
Sep	5	44								
Oct	8									
Nov	12			47			141	8,563	7,724	
Dec	20			16		32	157	11,645	13,358	
1949										
Jan	8	28	—	32	—	—	87	10,624	9,031	—
Feb	11	16	—	18	—	132	69	7,718	9,095	—
Mar	6	21	—	8	—	168	70	5,729	4,687	
Apr	17	56		3	—	641	2	11,345	17,679	
May	35	131		56	—	360	360	20,616	15,584	
Jun	21	81		33	—	475	199	20,203	15,583	
Jul	28	160		53	—	3,723	347	26,314	26,255	36,000
Aug	10	68		86	—	702	322	15,560	2,850	12,050
Sep	18	73		46	—	304	375	29,534	9,155	2,870
Oct	18	116								
Nov	34	185								
Dec	28	203								
1950										
Jan	58	258								
Feb	56	274								
Mar	40	514	8	137	—	—	567	21,109	27,420	—
Apr	46	567	70	780	—	1,536	2,384	125,875	102,760	18,350
May	58	411	682	201	—	564	2,156	122,987	53,342	—
Jun	68	328	1,066	259	—	6,258	1,538	61,551	38,050	46,970
Jul	58	448	1,184	394	—	615	2,164	100,785	50,670	—
Aug	81	524	1,091	739	—	804	1,929	109,873	78,657	—
Sep	106	504	964	1,505	—	626	2,055	126,750	67,527	—
Oct	88	443	1,212	298	—	235	2,180	121,329	46,181	—
Nov	78	338	1,305	427	—	323	1,936	84,114	36,339	10,100
Dec	71	329	635	749	—	395	2,157	96,119	63,663	2,135
1951										
Jan	83	369	418	1,710	—	332	1,730	88,118	38,886	2,135
Feb	75	392	447	1,917	—	592	1,606	98,145	80,927	—
Mar	92	442	660	2,416	—	—	1,841	8,176	72,211	—
Apr	65	276	336	942	—	1,320	1,271	26,142	30,166	34,150
May	89	378	76	1,348	—	3,016	1,907	36,608	39,030	76,050
Jun	118	572	42	2,049	14	6,536	2,418	119,141	97,706	132,950
Jul	153	473	230	887	112	7,004	1,575	86,776	71,501	160,430
Aug	71	332	611	492	174	2,432	1,421	31,740	44,465	47,900
Sep	54	210	444	372	14	3,298	784	18,652	33,370	61,700
Oct	65	291	788	464	—	4,044	1,208	14,210	45,280	59,950
Nov	85	471	584	1,214	—	3,676	2,512	44,966	52,914	87,850
Dec	52	290	444	498	70	2,368	1,688	36,325	37,229	40,800
1952										
Jan	46	281	300	602	134	1,560	2,355	35,852	38,572	25,800
Feb	74	308	415	974	56	3,730	202	70,520	59,530	83,819
Mar	65	286	370	725	288	3,704	1,075	76,800	77,232	82,250
Apr	59	214	346	610	—	1,552	1,283	59,330	62,221	31,700
May	47	201	140	714	48	2,305	353	63,558	47,512	36,610
Jun	53	255	52	1,129	70	1,659	—	83,269	76,406	34,000
Jul	69	438	34	1,232	56	1,272	32	110,607	68,008	13,120
Aug	71	435	24	1,438	23	1,416	643	112,864	59,396	31,350
Sep	34	243	94	878	—	2,161	955	66,559	38,805	29,600
Oct	56	344	281	883	—	1,792	1,129	94,700	58,038	27,250
Nov	58	434	198	877	—	1,920	1,627	147,705	37,863	31,650
Dec	44	260	164	544	—	2,230	832	89,266	30,680	35,600

	No of Strikes	No of Sorties	1,000 lb	500 lb	350 lb Clusters	20 lb	R/P	20 mm	·5	·303
1953										
Jan	34	191	299	716	—	800	492	65,688	37,885	7,400
Feb	32	211	244	590	—	640	516	73,151	22,585	12,000
Mar	8	52	12	104	—	160	184	19,847	2,950	3,000
Apr	23	158	315	477	—	1,960	227	32,417	38,640	12,000
May	12	204	87	180	—	400	669	80,867	7,980	5,100
Jun	5	44	48	255	—	160	93	15,307	15,070	300
Jul	19	101	247	604	—	160	530	70,582	31,550	2,850
Aug	29	157	116	405	—	320	522	57,793	14,050	5,200
Sep	25	209	323	877	—	—	432	42,325	25,633	—
Oct	37	247	443	522	—	2,400	701	59,776	39,797	43,250
Nov	33	478	582	1,242	—	4,080	1,072	53,278	65,715	69,170
Dec	41	241	416	747	—	2,720	487	29,156	69,700	63,460
1954										
Jan	57	238	552	1,047	—	2,080	428	25,045	51,874	28,428
Feb	29	108	238	705	—	620	130	10,139	31,057	6,200
Mar	61	150	206	1,330	—	—	126	13,366	57,303	—
Apr	30	79	190	680	—	400	64	5,291	41,474	10,000
May	23	143	328	869	—	—	176	17,188	38,796	—
Jun	25	163	301	766	—	—	292	30,657	35,541	—
Jul	26	213	589	418	—	1,025	537	28,094	17,585	16,500
Aug	22	90	236	612	—	—	121	13,697	43,956	—
Sep	24	171	433	776	—	600	551	28,330	34,677	18,700
Oct	43	252	328	1,389	—	1,182	521	59,350	57,795	35,550
Nov	57	298	35	1,742	—	560	627	49,480	47,698	25,000
Dec	29	150	36	659	—	700	334	24,693	39,565	24,600
1955										
Jan	65	458	384	1,882	—	1,120	1,160	91,535	84,462	26,500
Feb	26	115	524	461	—	420	117	14,096	31,875	6,800
Mar	33	169	860	296	—	—	245	18,142	17,241	—
Apr	18	140	552	342	—	—	107	22,117	14,757	—
May	20	177	294	718	—	280	345	37,710	16,043	—
Jun	50	294	376	1,058	—	300	693	84,863	43,349	—
Jul	31	154	509	590	—	—	117	29,222	34,419	—
Aug	24	119	626	250	—	—	82	24,365	31,531	—
Sep	1	4	56	—	—	—	—	—	—	—
Oct	—	—	—	—	—	—	—	—	—	—
Nov	5	33	197	56	—	—	—	464	4,480	—
Dec	27	168	800	52	—	560	230	30,160	4,030	—

Annex T—continued

	No of Strikes	No of Sorties	1,000 lb	500 lb	350 lb Clusters	20 lb	R/P	20 mm	·5	·303
1956										
Jan	13	57	57	122	—	—	138	14,886	8,701	—
Feb	18	164	871	206	—	—	151	26,743	12,269	—
Mar	6	38	283	—	—	—	32	5,454	800	—
Apr	7	31	122	70	—	140	—	—	—	—
May	10	39	34	112	—	—	—	2,336	2,520	—
Jun	22	264	427	792	—	690	505	44,081	19,363	—
Jul	16	38	102	292	—	429	—	1,948	4,140	—
Aug	7	15	44	63	—	570	—	850	—	—
Sep	16	64	178	250	—	380	47	5,779	13,549	—
Oct	13	55	150	280	—	382	—	2,909	9,310	—
Nov	8	20	126	96	—	760	—	1,212	5,300	—
Dec	3	15	180	—	—	—	—	3,700		—
1957										
Jan	8	41	284	56	—	380	40	3,316	1,930	—
Feb	—	—	—	—	—	—	—	—	—	—
Mar	4	12	8	112	—	—	—	—	—	—
Apr	3	8	26	70	—	190	—	960	3,380	—
May	4	31	202	—	—	—	—	1,001	—	—
Jun	2	12	24	—	—	—	—	—	—	—
Jul	11	107	368	154	—	—	304	13,201	—	—
Aug	1	5	70	—	—	—	—	—	—	—
Sep	1	14	84	42	—	—	—	—	—	—
Oct	4	26	59	112	—	—	36	2,529	—	—
Nov	8	110	74	432	—	1,032	—	18,375	—	—
Dec	3	7	6	8	—	190	—	834	—	—
1958										
Jan	7	141	386	60	—	546	—	32,254	—	—
Feb	5	23	218	41	—	156	—	—	—	—
Mar	9	244	194	1,112	—	750	284	29,803	—	—
Apr	6	209	236	991	—	—	—	31,570	—	—
May	5	108	458	212	—	—	—	13,676	—	—
Jun	2	37	99	252	—	—	—	2,720	—	—
Jul	6	75	90	324	—	—	—	—	—	—
Aug	1	9	8	30	—	—	—	1,060	—	—
Sep	2	34	138	—	—	—	61	—	—	—
Oct	1	5	30	—	—	—	—	—	—	—
Nov	2	18	—	108	—	—	—	—	—	—
Dec	1	23	16	90	—	—	—	—	—	—
1959										
Aug	2				—			—	—	—
1960	—	—	—	—	—	—	—	—	—	—

OPERATION 'FIREDOG', MEDIUM RANGE TRANSPORT SUPPORT (AIR SUPPLY) 1948–1960

Month	No of Air Supply Sorties	Weight Dropped (lb)	Month	No of Air Supply Sorties	Weight Dropped (lb)
1948			*1952*		
Jul	3	c2,000	Aug	86	278,055
Aug	10	c30,500	Sep	94	300,918
Sep	5	c6,000	Oct	101	337,144
Oct	3	c3,500	Nov	75	228,631
Nov	3	c11,500	Dec	79	252,609
Dec	7	c9,200			
			1953		
1949			Jan	90	306,199
Jan	24	41,392	Feb	71	232,677
Feb	29	29,685	Mar	95	326,798
Mar	26	56,481	Apr	85	279,245
Apr	44	115,910	May	109	383,164
May	96	204,929	Jun	103	322,868
Jun	70	223,653	Jul	91	313,967
Jul	69	166,558	Aug	90	283,650
Aug	48	132,461	Sep	101	303,317
Sep	75	227,520	Oct	136	464,688
Oct	206	425,385	Nov	223	752,518
Nov	130	245,107	Dec	152	492,904
Dec	58	175,484			
			1954		
1950			Jan	144	460,866
Jan	108	145,496	Feb	123	395,558
Feb	71	133,331	Mar	159	497,551
Mar	103	296,362	Apr	140	459,817
Apr	160	410,155	May	159	522,118
May	90	214,512	Jun	142	468,762
Jun	125	308,368	Jul	197	653,413
Jul	126	369,385	Aug	184	613,882
Aug	126	391,328	Sep	181	613,698
Sep	110	325,852	Oct	219	721,270
Oct	122	366,365	Nov	224	724,230
Nov	141	371,037	Dec	208	661,977
Dec	130	392,267			
			1955		
1951			Jan	173	600,841
Jan	179	468,694	Feb	168	612,914
Feb	165	479,780	Mar	218	808,035
Mar	162	423,753	Apr	187	673,625
Apr	155	421,399	May	191	687,773
May	159	402,167	Jun	189	697,220
Jun	117	317,008	Jul	184	698,845
Jul	64	215,113	Aug	162	588,255
Aug	52	126,870	Sep	154	609,204
Sep	59	174,312	Oct	164	656,383
Oct	74	186,077	Nov	147	613,423
Nov	50	145,181	Dec	128	530,129
Dec	53	104,385			
			1956		
1952			Jan	158	636,350
Jan	84	219,830	Feb	145	600,037
Feb	117	306,511	Mar	117	449,334
Mar	69	248,246	Apr	104	404,965
Apr	68	182,111	May	118	373,856
May	66	182,087	Jun	129	517,351
Jun	68	194,415	Jul	128	524,086
Jul	81	281,985	Aug	123	479,823

Annex U—continued

Month	No of Air Supply Sorties	Weight Dropped (lb)	Month	No of Air Supply Sorties	Weight Dropped (lb)
1956			*1958*		
Sep	135	507,222	Sep	114	513,400 (41,430)
Oct	158	526,152	Oct	103	468,020 (35,980)
Nov	126	442,316	Nov	118	456,545 (33,670)
Dec	112	529,333	Dec	88	368,016 (22,735)
1957			*1959*		
Jan	124	462,028	Jan	69	246,698
Feb	115	473,895	Feb		216,744
Mar	130	464,394	Mar		267,952
Apr	119	500,331	Apr		224,707
May	120	409,679	May		258,649
Jun	93	310,973	Jun		190,438
Jul	128	457,818	Jul		220,747
Aug	107	408,743 (24,800)	Aug		183,045
Sep	86	311,047 (19,090)	Sep		197,641
Oct	111	368,853 (22,590)	Oct		228,068
Nov	112	407,496 (24,470)	Nov		319,940
Dec	116	331,040 (18,910)	Dec		297,779
1958			*1960*		
Jan	105	423,670 (25,260)	Jan		217,807
Feb	108	409,095 (24,855)	Feb		161,435
Mar	113	466,752 (27,030)	Mar		245,000
Apr	92	414,702 (25,400)	Apr		232,350
May	113	477,792 (29,350)	May		199,136
Jun	84	347,401 (21,020)	Jun		216,246
Jul	115	489,370	Jul		251,728
Aug	112	502,930 (31,900)			

Note: Figures in brackets show weight of parachutes included in total weight dropped.

OPERATION 'FIREDOG', SHORT RANGE TRANSPORT SUPPORT (AUSTER), 1954–1958

Number of Sorties

Month	No of Hours	Total	Airstrike Target Marking	Visual Reconnaissance	Air Observation Post	Supply Dropping	Communication	Leaflet Dropping	Miscellaneous
1954									
Jun	1,827·00	1,821		691		41	644	70	375
Jul	2,065·30	1,839	50	926		38	547	68	210
Aug	1,793·00	1,853		879		53	546	17	358
Sep	2,154·20	2,192	24	976		38	578	60	516
Oct	1,856·20	1,925	9	727		78	665	45	401
Nov	2,147·00	2,330	1	935		99	838	58	399
Dec		2,318	4	1,347		119	497	70	281
1955									
Jan	2,206·35	2,619	29	1,469		82	571	49	419
Feb	2,067·25	1,839	23	851		71	759		135
Mar	2,438·40	2,553	47	942		120	1,112	61	271
Apr	1,976·55	2,197	22	644		108	697	63	663
May	2,185·55	2,595	20	847		134	986	53	555
Jun	2,247·40	2,681	68	783		127	953	46	704
Jul		1,117	22	390		37	222	23	423
Aug	591·15	861	14	346		21	82	6	392
Sep	1,182·10	1,538		310		43	266	86	833
Oct	1,548·40	1,520		645		75	723	36	41
Nov	1,698·35	1,624		523		76	567	11	547
Dec	1,677·40	1,925	19	533	18	50	974	20	311
1956									
Jan	1,663·25	1,726	4	715	9		613	44	341
Feb	1,510·20	1,443	14	570	20	44	731	9	54
Mar	1,777·10	1,878	4	701	15	76	916	23	143
Apr	1,672·05	1,679		591	12		858	10	208
May	1,754·05	1,716		555	14		997	21	129
Jun	1,328·30	1,428	37	459	8	118	767	20	19
Jul	1,170·30	1,239	23	456	7	81	639	42	7
Aug	1,119·25	1,574	7	356	17	84	779	68	263
Sep	1,192·55	1,210		452	5	47	622	55	
Oct	1,308·45	1,267	19	509	7	99	576	56	1
Nov	1,102·40	1,045	18	459	4	49	431	34	
Dec	962·05	967	10	388	2	63	442	62	
1957									
Jan	1,289·40	1,309	22	491	10	77	687	22	
Feb	1,204·25	1,304	13	549	8	61	653	20	
Mar	1,323·15	1,353	9	555	16	61	660	55	
Apr	1,097·35	1,138	12	441	36	40	567	41	
May	1,150·10	1,277	27	492	6	48	680	24	
Jun	1,248·35	1,397	13	536	14	53	767	14	
Jul	1,172·00	1,403	31	519	18	91	711	33	
Aug	1,204·20	1,311	3	452	15	32	775	34	
Sep	1,089·55	1,355	5	369	15	101	754	111	
Oct	1,200·50	1,250	18	519	16	36	584	77	
Nov	1,027·00	1,135	15	402	3	59	589	67	
Dec	1,112·40	1,155	5	445	11	38	539	117	
1958									
Jan	1,237·40	1,273	19	453	3	52	693	53	
Feb	1,112·50	1,018	22	374	15	46	535	26	
Mar	1,138·28	1,118	60	433	9	59	548	9	
Apr	917·20	875	36	280	5	47	453	53	
May	1,039·25	993	15	363	24	47	510	34	
Jun	1,209·45	1,409	12	369	20	126	867	15	
Jul		1,587	11	340	5	116	806	9	
Aug	1,263·00	1,477	1	350	8	73	1,018	27	
Sep	1,227·20	1,618	8	23	1	128	1,366	92	
Oct	1,131·35	1,364	15	299	9	164	847	30	
Nov	1,167·00	1,503	2	360	18	100	952	71	
Dec	1,112·15	1,372	7	274	24	85	950	32	

Annex W

OPERATION 'FIREDOG', SHORT RANGE TRANSPORT SUPPORT (PIONEER), 1954–1960

Month	Sorties	Hours Flown	Troops Lifted	Passengers Carried	Casualties Evacuated	Freight Carried (lb)
1954						
May				93	—	3,380
Jun	164			156	8	2,830
Jul	223			286	6	26,530
Aug	124			161	4	6,265
Sep	115			107	6	3,035
Oct	176			291	3	18,935
Nov	139			172	—	11,330
Dec	181			240	5	11,315
1955						
Jan	170	91·45		256	8	14,655
Feb	177			130	12	8,190
Mar	221	133		292	3	10,440
Apr	342	162		501	16	45,152
May	376	229		409	12	25,510
Jun	459	250		653	13	41,061
Jul	430	232		470	10	31,825
Aug	494	290		648	14	38,015
Sep	681	251		574	—	23,995
Oct	443	285		504	15	28,465
Nov	532	304		701	9	57,460
Dec	366	256·15		255	1	33,880
1956						
Jan	479			508	9	42,030
Feb	482		268	269	4	54,115
Mar	579			616	6	94,556
Apr	633			623		100,182
May	533		263	284	11	85,355
Jun	693	434·45	358	354		111,297
Jul	616	389·05	357	352		78,879
Aug	806	501·40	348	434		87,191
Sep	647	391·55	444	363		80,118
Oct	803	425·00	601	290		101,105
Nov	606	349·50	286	287		76,084
Dec	649	358·00	387	244		92,981
1957						
Jan	686	383·20	344	341	11	91,572
Feb	490	287·05	330	220	7	59,710
Mar	568	364·15	232	282	9	83,148
Apr	523	289·15	388	226	5	58,588
May	689	408·00	402	278	14	85,996
Jun	559	306·20	214	216	12	87,405
Jul	608	383·10	467	239	9	89,934
Aug	418	256·40	289	194	11	50,581
Sep	433	250·50	272	183	7	72,685
Oct	531	314·00	353	201	9	74,682
Nov	688	381·30	530	213	8	112,544
Dec	381	260·45	221	166	3	56,123

Month	Sorties	Hours Flown	Troops Lifted	Passengers Carried	Casualties Evacuated	Freight Carried (lb)
1958						
Jan	532	331·10	438	146	2	86,355
Feb	370	214·00	338	127	6	41,112
Mar	55	33·05	—	38	1	4,326
Apr	16	16·30	—	12	—	175
May	180	101·10	212	67	6	15,000
Jun	272	160·50	201	82	8	49,468
Jul	199	177·00	69	90	3	24,001
Aug	437	239·55	432	107	5	83,210
Sep	280	149·00	103	58	3	55,561
Oct	497	247·05	540	89	4	87,936
Nov	259	143·05	183	53	5	46,582
Dec	114	54·05	187	35	—	15,223
1959						
Jan						
Feb						
Mar						
Apr						
May						
Jun			482	78	6	58,132
Jul			108	93	14	27,031
Aug			392	91	7	54,790
Sep			162	68	7	40,862
Oct			}			
Nov			} 213	97	7	46,781
Dec			}			
			} 393	72	9	56,420
1960			}			
Jan			}			
Feb			} 358	35	4	37,490
Mar			}			
Apr			} —	2	—	2,897
May			}			
Jun			} 79	11	—	5,790
Jul			}			

Annex X

OPERATION 'FIREDOG', SHORT RANGE TRANSPORT SUPPORT (HELICOPTER), 1950–1960

Month	No of Sorties	No. of Casualties Evacuated (Sorties in Brackets)	No of Troops Lifted	No of Passengers Carried on Communication Flights	Freight Carried (lb)
1950					
Jun		3	—	—	—
Jul		4	—	—	—
Aug		4	—	—	—
Sep		2	—	—	—
Oct		1	—	—	—
Nov		5	—	—	—
Dec		7	—	—	—
1951					
Jan		2	—	—	—
Feb		3	—	—	—
Mar		12	—	—	—
Apr		5	—	—	—
May		3	—	—	—
Jun		3	—	—	—
Jul		11	—	—	—
Aug		1	—	—	—
Sep		9	—	—	—
Oct		5	—	—	—
Nov		—	—	—	—
Dec		1	—	—	—
1952					
Jan		2			
Feb		23			
Mar		21			
Apr		1			
May		4			
Jun		13 (11)			
Jul		35 (33)			
Aug		11 (10)			
Sep		16 (12)			
Oct		3 (3)			
Nov		8 (5)			
Dec		7 (6)			
1953					
Jan		4 (4)			
Feb		12 (7)			
Mar		34 (19)			
Apr		15 (9)	540		
May		39 (29)	1,902		42,160
Jun		55 (23)	1,087		22,504
Jul		49 (33)	584		10,805
Aug		59 (39)	786		12,545
Sep		36 (25)	1,674		24,900
Oct		64 (36)	1,613		15,940
Nov		85 (63)	1,155		21,025
Dec		66 (56)	757		13,940
1954					
Jan		53 (34)	914	149	8,710
Feb		38 (24)	729	149	17,206
Mar		78	652	191	13,040

Month	No of Sorties	*Light H/C*	*Medium H/C*	*Light H/C*	*Medium H/C*	*Light H/C*	*Medium H/C*	*Light H/C*	*Medium H/C*
Apr		62	10	—	511	176	64	640	16,435
May		51	31	—	1,600	72	129	745	28,860
Jun		32	30	—	950	207	92	6,105	35,380
Jul		26	25	—	950	194	62	3,480	22,000
Aug		20	40	—	1,026	132	108	2,145	5,830
Sep		48	14	—	480	149	82	6,870	22,000
Oct		45	17	—	191	107	27	4,495	12,940
Nov		44	19	—	158	316	153	8,495	9,750
Dec		43	17	—	668	236	238	2,655	9,786

Month	No of Sorties			No of Casualties Evacuated			No of Troops Lifted			No of Passengers Carried on Communication Flights			Freight Carried (lb)		
	Light H/C	Medium H/C (a)	(b)	Light H/C	Medium H/C (a)	(b)	Light H/C	Medium H/C (a)	(b)	Light H/C	Medium H/C (a)	(b)	Light H/C	Medium H/C (a)	(b)
1955 Jan	303	563	258	48	8		73	1,212		362	80		11,026	33,168	
Feb	264	522	246	18	20		—	1,276		239	168		5,980	33,333	
Mar	339	694	669	34	34		—	2,395		309	243		7,590	65,619	
Apr	395	443	359	47	11		—	1,527		266	84		5,670	37,209	
May	531	511	820	54	21		—	2,168		372	191		1,290	23,769	
Jun	416	593	1,134	54	11	12	—	1,130	1,458	124	109	63	5,302	28,714	18,790
Jul	635	412	1,391	39	79		—	1,094	2,367	293	19	41	12,780	17,740	36,545
Aug	564	60	1,423	43	12		—	226	2,213	219	4	223	7,705	2,430	33,426
Sep	565	223	861	43	1	5	—	464	1,293	227	4	93	8,185	30,035	45,881
Oct	503	388	1,395	39	6	19	—	945	2,335	178	16	40	7,755	15,435	5,584
Nov	380	522	1,440	36	5	38	—	906	2,448	124	22	38	3,125	21,355	27,134
Dec	192	354	1,115	14	22	20	—	458	1,889	79	16	141	3,630	17,785	19,076

Note: Light H/C = No 194 Squadron
Medium H/C — (a) = No 848 (Naval Air) Squadron
(b) = No 155 Squadron

Annex X—continued

Month	No of Sorties			No of Casualties Evacuated			No of Troops Lifted			No of Passengers Carried on Communication Flights			Freight Carried (lb)		
	Light H/C	Medium H/C		Light H/C	Medium H/C		Light H/C	Medium H/C		Light H/C	Medium H/C		Light H/C	Medium H/C	
		(a)	(b)		(a)	(b)		(a)	(b)		(a)	(b)		(a)	(b)
1956 Jan	431	353	862	41	12	5	—	408	1,227	173	58	74	6,317	8,510	13,237
Feb	475	543	1,076	47	8	14	—	581	1,716	154	136	48	5,755	23,269	16,017
Mar	457	474	1,084	48	4	20	—	585	1,541	181	67	56	14,047	7,010	18,098
Apr	540	599	647	48	6	4	26	690	937	153	54	40	11,460	4,635	14,720
May	508	256	388	25	1	3	—	278	424	143	46	28	6,292	4,720	4,968
Jun	648	963	1,110	58	22	8	—	1,234	1,597	197	66	59	10,315	6,615	16,980
Jul	549	629	638	37	4	14	6	918	666	147	43	59	6,745	1,116	16,200
Aug	729	833	1,284	30	8	13	55	995	1,894	188	69	66	14,485	14,650	22,185
Sep	719	902	862	33	4	7	—	1,208	1,172	252	82	53	14,205	7,730	14,725
Oct	722	1,276	1,089	32	18	13	—	1,422	1,817	229	125	48	9,965	35,765	11,410
Nov	898	192	1,581	41	4	17	—	267	2,486	280	6	65	13,087	2,750	25,100
Dec	840	+	1,185	31	+	21	86	+	1,654	278	+	46	13,795	+	22,440

+ No 848 (Naval Air) Squadron disbanded

Month	No of Sorties		No of Casualties Evacuated		No of Troops Lifted		No of Passengers Carried on Communication Flights		Freight Carried (lb)	
	Light H/C	Medium H/C	Light H/C	Medium H/C	Light H/C	Medium H/C	Light H/C	Medium H/C	Light H/C	Medium H/C
1957										
Jan	1,054	899	48	3	177	1,650	290	24	19,675	7,747
Feb	776	193	46	1	160	296	223	5	10,240	2,310
Mar	841	613	58	4	13	890	296	21	16,459	27,590
Apr	856	774	40	8	146	1,385	244	24	13,609	12,645
May	790	1,397	55	27	142	2,177	213	30	16,970	24,390
Jun	870	1,620	61	9	250	2,439	218	66	16,890	16,745
Jul	941	1,529	53	7	371	2,417	219	42	17,340	37,145
Aug	773	983	48	5	151	1,667	211	34	9,770	30,015
Sep	692	574	34	3	269	719	148	25	22,745	29,345
Oct	868	602	27	2	490	915	116	25	11,325	6,479
Nov	696	655	37	17	351	1,042	160	28	10,141	12,538
Dec	855	812	29	10	370	1,265	171	42	16,501	26,330
1958										
Jan	673	870	35	2	203	1,275	156	53	10,125	13,025
Feb	811	804	30	5	393	1,287	182	67	10,379	46,639
Mar	933	822	53	4	316	1,769	188	53	12,740	26,335
Apr	855	957	31	5	252	1,427	243	94	19,059	30,465
May	1,092	936	58	10	451	1,419	251	62	31,720	30,633
Jun	1,211	984	58	7	574	1,756	246	93	35,903	55,297
Jul	1,538	1,193	70	32	1,090	1,727	183	103	18,065	82,100
Aug	1,034	1,241	36	25	781	2,069	150	68	15,515	46,691
Sep	966	1,341	42	31	685	2,157	98	88	17,985	33,786
Oct	1,448	1,243	47	20	1,437	2,156	65	45	18,128	26,457
Nov	489	744	31	42	288	1,355	54	54	7,230	11,635
Dec	783	712	44	34	642	1,258	57	56	17,078	12,220
1959										
Jan										
Feb										
Mar										
Apr										
May										
Jun*	—		—	14	—	133	—	29	—	9,507
Jul	—		—	33	—	326	—	77	—	12,170
Aug	—		—	13	—	179	—	35	—	6,128
Sep	—		—	22	—	157	—	51	—	10,285
Oct }										
Nov }	—		—	54	—	1,602	—	132	—	38,095
Dec }										
1960 }	—		—	57	—	997	—	108	—	45,714
Jan										
Feb }	—		—	34	—	1,149	—	95	—	13,405
Mar										
Apr }	—		—	39	—	1,192	—	100	—	21,827
May										
Jun }	—		—	43	—	695	—	66	—	10,908
Jul										

* 3 Jun 1959—No 194 Squadron merged with No 155 Squadron to become No 110 Squadron

Annex Y

OPERATION 'FIREDOG', SUPPORT FOR PSYCHOLOGICAL WARFARE CAMPAIGN, 1948–1960

Month	Thousands of Leaflets Dropped	No of Leaflet Dropping Sorties	Month	Thousands of Leaflets Dropped	No of Leaflet Dropping Sorties
1948			*1950*		
Jul		3	Oct		6
Aug		7	Nov		6
Sep			Dec		2
Oct					
Nov			*1951*		
Dec			Jan		21
			Feb		4
1949			Mar	3,750	15
Jan			Apr	1,500	44
Feb		1	May	300	22
Mar			Jun	2,250	106
Apr			Jul	900	27
May			Aug		22
Jun		8	Sep	750	
Jul		—	Oct	500	
Aug		—	Nov	55	
Sep	1,000	32	Dec	61	
Oct		8			
Nov		10	*1952*		
Dec	1,500	10	Jan	500	
			Feb	100	
1950			Mar	400	
Jan		4	Apr	1,034	
Feb		12	May	900	
Mar		12	Jun	1,220	6
Apr		4	Jul	760	8
May	1,404	40	Aug	3,276	14
Jun	4,000	35	Sep	405	5
Jul	1,000	7	Oct	778	7
Aug		16	Nov	1,411	7
Sep		24	Dec	1,635	6

Note: Leaflets were dropped by aircraft on air supply duties and, on occasion, by aircraft specially detailed. In addition, leaflets were sometimes dropped by offensive aircraft after the conclusion of air strikes.

Month	Thousands of Leaflets Dropped	No of Leaflet Dropping Sorties	No of Loudhailing Sorties		No of Hours of Broadcasting	
1953						
Jan	1,380	5	—		—	
Feb	4,426	14	—		—	
Mar	3,499	4	—		—	
Apr	4,039	21	3			
May	2,600	11	19			
Jun	2,670	12	31			
Jul	3,545	7	31		25·17	
Aug	4,843	15	43		62·20	
Sep	5,555	16	52		61·07	
Oct	19,536	51	52		55·38	
Nov	3,150	10	63		79·21	
Dec	6,615	18	33		38·07	
1954						
Jan	6,440	16	65		60·50	
Feb	4,680	16	44		74·04	
Mar	5,714	16	32		44·40	
Apr	2,240	16	39		45·20	
May	3,102	16	56		43·00	
			Dakota	*Auster*	*Dakota*	*Auster*
Jun	4,203	22	22	36	26·30	23·15
Jul	3,450	14	34	32	49·00	17·50
Aug	20,175	35	64	25	41·40	15·30
Sep	5,945	27	28	21	35·40	15·30
Oct	3,270	15	34	11	34·35	9·00
Nov	7,220	30	42	40	36·45	31·10
Dec	4,360	17	32	9	32·50	7·15
1955						
Jan	7,500	21	48	18	39·55	14·10
Feb	6,965	28	31	20	34·30	19·00
Mar	7,127	26	39	23	43·30	16·10
Apr	5,692	29	43	15	41·09	10·16
May	5,835	24	58	15	62·05	9·45
Jun	27,657	43	50	34	54·20	32·20
Jul	29,900	53	39	30	39·08	23·15
Aug	8,150	34	48	14	54·55	8·50
Sep	29,026	41	61	50	64·15	35·20
Oct	4,497	20	61	46	72·54	30·25
Nov	4,640	21	49	36	54·51	22·55
Dec	4,192	25	55	39	52·32	33·25

Annex Y—continued

Month	Thousands of Leaflets Dropped	No of Leaflet Dropping Sorties			No of Loudhailing Sorties		No of Hours of Broadcasting		No of Flying Hours on Loudhailing Sorties	
		Valetta	Bristol Freighter	Auster	Dakota	Auster	Dakota	Auster	Dakota	Auster
1956										
Jan	31,880	46			46	31	59·05	18·37		
Feb	3,726	17			29	13	29·40	7·35		
Mar	3,976	8	5	—	9	19	7·00	7·55		
Apr	4,961	17	3	—	36	13	34·25	5·20	104·15	20·55
May	3,184	14	—	1	33	20	42·15	12·55		
Jun	4,097	34	2	—	51	21	56·50	16·45	174·45	26·35
Jul	5,854	29	4	—	36	32	39·55	26·55	123·25	59·05
Aug	5,613	30	—	—	48	47	75·05	47·35	202·05	107·50
Sep	5,630	24	—	—	59	21	78·05	13·45	215·05	31·40
Oct	5,115	28	—	—	46	27	61·25	18·25	179·05	55·05
Nov	15,335	39	1	—	51	19	32·10	7·40	151·55	25·00
Dec	6,475	22	9	—	39	31	49·45	14·15	162·00	46·35
1957										
Jan	6,415	31	—	—	41	47	45·00	32·20	139·55	72·05
Feb	4,770	22	—	—	32	31	37·50	16·55	102·30	48·55
Mar	4,725	22	—	—	29	49	31·40	34·55	107·35	88·20
Apr	5,910	23	—	—	15	34	14·30	22·15	43·15	54·55
May	6,105	34	—	—	60	23	58·50	7·50	198·30	33·00
Jun	5,827	32	—	2	54	13	61·20	7·20	182·15	16·25
Jul	5,591	28	—	—	53	32	65·15	17·10	142·00	53·35
Aug	5,270	26	—	—	48	31	40·10	17·20	150·35	46·45
Sep	13,785	25	—	—	41	20	61·35	11·50	138·50	32·55
Oct	9,320	37	—	—	46	13	46·30	9·25	156·55	27·20
Nov	8,495	29	2	—	48	13	47·00	5·55	159·40	29·40
Dec	11,775	31	4	—	34	14	28·40	10·55	106·30	37·25
1958										
Jan	5,840	19	2	—	36	23	29·55	17·45	103·40	56·25
Feb	6,665	31	1	—	33	3	19·25	1·20	72·50	10·30
Mar	9,710	32	6	—	45	11	25·50	4·35	104·10	28·50
Apr	7,867	22	3	—	40	14	41·30	10·05	112·55	20·55
May	9,323	30	9	—	57	21	41·35	13·30	159·00	37·10
Jun	7,205	22	5	—	36	18	41·15	15·25	115·30	44·40
Jul	9,985	21	4	—	57	14	21·20	10·15	162·30	21·10
Aug	9,230	20	6	—	38	18	41·40	10·35	117·40	34·50
Sep	7,065	23	4	—	50	10	40·30	5·30	147·20	20·45
Oct	5,155	13	8	—	55	16	43·20	11·00	162·45	26·10
Nov	4,580	14	3	—	36	11	26·05	4·10	112·50	16·05
Dec	3,475	12	4	—	40	4	25·10	1·10	111·45	6·50
1959										
Jan	4,545						33·40			
Feb	6,072						20·55			
Mar	5,600						18·00			
Apr	3,735						10·55			
May	5,200						13·20			
Jun	3,220						11·45			
Jul	1,820						15·30			
Aug	2,675						28·55			
Sep	1,510						24·45			
Oct	2,910						12·10			
Nov	1,695						—			
Dec	1,430						6·45			
1960										
Jan	385						2·00			
Feb Mar	1,965						30·20			
Apr May	5,995						12·25			
Jun Jul	1,553						16·25			

OPERATION 'FIREDOG', PHOTOGRAPHIC RECONNAISSANCE, 1948–1958

Month	Number of Sorties					
	Total	Mosquito	Spitfire	Anson	Meteor	Pembroke
1948						
Jul	62	34	28	—	—	—
Aug	16	9	7	—	—	—
Sep	43	22	21	—	—	—
Oct	46	31	15	—	—	—
Nov	48	31	17	—	—	—
Dec	56	26	30	—	—	—
1949						
Jan	41	24	17	—	—	—
Feb	52	14	38	—	—	—
Mar	58	37	21	—	—	—
Apr	71	39	32	—	—	—
May	56	41	15	—	—	—
Jun	66	37	29	—	—	—
Jul	57	45	12	—	—	—
Aug	64	47	17	—	—	—
Sep	59	33	26	—	—	—
Oct			24	—	—	—
Nov			24	—	—	—
Dec		40		—	—	—
1950						
Jan	54				—	—
Feb	121	57	64	—	—	—
Mar	44	19	25	—	—	—
Apr	13				—	—
May		4			—	—
Jun		15		5	—	—
Jul		51		12	—	—
Aug		78			—	—
Sep		40		5	—	—
Oct		43		11	—	—
Nov		63		6	—	—
Dec		77			—	—
1951						
Jan	34				—	—
Feb	54	36	18	—	—	—
Mar	68	45	23	—	—	—
Apr	88	52	31	5	—	—
May	127	82	42	3	—	—
Jun	117	78	31	8	—	—
Jul	127	75	44	8	—	—
Aug	95	69	26	—	—	—
Sep	60	25	35	—	—	—
Oct	104	58	46	—	—	—
Nov	117	65	52	—	—	—
Dec	144	90	54	—	—	—
1952						
Jan	114	66	48	—	—	—
Feb	56	37	19	—	—	—
Mar	128	76	52	—	—	—
Apr	90	68	22	—	—	—
May	93			—	—	—
Jun	56			—	—	—
Jul	71	43	28	—	—	—
Aug	90	57	33	—	—	—
Sep	124	100	24	—	—	—
Oct	126	94	32	—	—	—
Nov	102	82	20	—	—	—
Dec	122	100	22	—	—	—

Annex Z—continued

Month	Number of Sorties					
	Total	Mosquito	Spitfire	Anson	Meteor	Pembroke
1953						
Jan	117	97	20	—	—	—
Feb	108	64	44	—	—	—
Mar	103	56	47	—	—	—
Apr	102	62	40	—	—	—
May	94	68	26	—	—	—
Jun	114	97	17	—	—	—
Jul	132	100	32	—	—	—
Aug	77	69	8	—	—	—
Sep	100	85	15	—	—	—
Oct	142	130	12	—	—	—
Nov	132	115	17	—	—	—
Dec	114	97	17	—	—	—
1954						
Jan	75			—		—
Feb	130			—		—
Mar	118			—		—
Apr	115	58	—	—	57	—
May	77	42	—	—	35	—
Jun	19	16	—	—	3	—
Jul	66	23	—	—	43	—
Aug	71	41	—	—	30	—
Sep	77	47	—	—	30	—
Oct	56	26	—	—	30	—
Nov	71	18	—	—	53	—
Dec	70	40	—	—	30	—
1955						
Jan	79	22	—	—	57	—
Feb	81	10	—	—	71	—
Mar	115	1	—	—	114	—
Apr	71	—	—	—	71	—
May	62	1	—	—	61	—
Jun	89	6	—	—	83	—
Jul	31	2	—	—	29	—
Aug	47	2	—	—	45	—
Sep	83	8	—	—	75	—
Oct	77	24	—	—	53	—
Nov	45		—	—		—
Dec	53	3	—	—	50	—
1956						
Jan	74	—	—	—	74	—
Feb	72	—	—	—	72	—
Mar	81	—	—	—	81	—
Apr	101	—	—	—	101	—
May	78	—	—	—	78	—
Jun	73	—	—	—	73	—
Jul	59	—	—	—	59	—
Aug	71	—	—	—	71	—
Sep	49	—	—	—	49	—
Oct	127	—	—	—	127	—
Nov	105	—	—	—	105	—
Dec	84	—	—	—	82	2
1957						
Jan	121	—	—	—	94	27
Feb	94	—	—	—	75	19
Mar	92	—	—	—	74	18
Apr	45	—	—	—	30	15
May	47	—	—	—	25	22
Jun	53	—	—	—	53	—
Jul	32	—	—	—	32	—
Aug	50	—	—	—	50	—
Sep	56	—	—	—	56	—
Oct	55	—	—	—	55	—
Nov	45	—	—	—	45	—
Dec	19	—	—	—	19	—

Month	Number of Sorties					
	Total	Mosquito	Spitfire	Anson	Meteor	Pembroke
1958						
Jan	96	—	—	—	95	1
Feb	65	—	—	—	65	—
Mar	48	—	—	—	48	—
Apr	42	—	—	—	42	—
May	46	—	—	—	42	4
Jun	66	—	—	—	66	—
Jul	25	—	—	—	25	—
Aug	89	—	—	—	89	—
Sep	62	—	—	—	62	—
Oct	61	—	—	—	59	2
Nov	65	—	—	—	65	—
Dec	60	—	—	—	60	—

MAIN SOURCES OF INFORMATION

Abbreviated Title	Description	AHB Reference
ACFE or FEAF/ORB	Operations Record Book, Air Command, Far East or Far East Air Force	
M or 224 Gp/ORB	Operations Record Book, Air Headquarters Malaya or No 224 Group	
ACFE or FEAF/MIS	Monthly Intelligence Summary issued by Air Command, Far East or Far East Air Force	
M/WSAO	Weekly Summary of Air Operations issued by Air Headquarters, Malaya— (*incorporated in SF/WIS after* 19 *Apr* 1953)	IIJ53/19
SF/WIS	Weekly Intelligence Summary issued by the Security Forces in Malaya	IIJ53/19
AOC (M or 224 Gp) Report	Reports on RAF Operations in Malaya issued approximately every year by the Air Officer Commanding, Malaya	IIJ53/16/2
FEAF/'Firedog'	Monthly Command Summary of RAF Contribution to Operation 'Firedog', issued by Headquarters, Far East Air Force	Form Stats 122
FEAF/Opsum	Weekly Summaries of Operations in Malaya, from Headquarters Air Command, Far East or Far East Air Force to the Air Ministry	IIJ50/140/1–5
FEAF/Air Attachés Conference	Report of Annual Meeting of Air Attachés in the Far East	
M/Training Summary	Monthly squadron training summaries issued by Air Headquarters Malaya or No 224 Group	
DO(M) Report	Report on the Emergency in Malaya from Apr 1951 to Nov 1951 by the Director of Operations, Malaya	IIJ53/18/1
DO(M) Review	Annual review of the Emergency Situation in Malaya by the Director of Operations, Malaya	IIJ53/18/(2–3)
L/A Warfare LL	Quarterly Liaison Letters on Land/Air Warfare issued by General Headquarters, Far East Land Forces	IIJ50/141/1/1
Malaya/CO Report	Annual Reports on the Federation of Malaya issued by the Colonial Office	
COI/Malaya	'The Fight against Communist Terrorism in Malaya', issued by the Central Office of Information in June 1951	

Abbreviated Title	*Description*	*AHB Reference*
Rand/'The Malayan Emergency'	Memorandum of the Malayan Emergency issued in July 1963 as part of a symposium on the role of airpower in counter-insurgency and unconventional warfare which was prepared for the United States Air Force Project Rand (Ref RM–3651–PR)	
M/Formations	List of formations in Malaya during the Emergency prepared by the Air Historical Branch 5	II/80/41
M/'Musgrave'	Report on Operation 'Musgrave' from Jun to Dec 1950	IIJ53/24/1
AM/ACAS(P)	File of the Assistant Chief of Air Staff (Policy) entitled 'Malaya', 11 May 1945 to 24 Sep 1958	ID6/618/(1–15)
AM/CAS	Files of the Chief of Air Staff entitled:	
	'Malaya, Internal Security', 26 Jun 1948 to 2 Oct 1950	ID3/1697/(1–3)
	'Establishment of Communications Aircraft for Malaya' 23 Jan 1953 to 13 Jan 1959	ID3/906/6
AM/VCAS	Files of the Vice Chief of Air Staff entitled:	
	'Malaya, Internal Security' 13 Nov 1950 to 16 Dec 1957	ID9/621/1(1–5)
	'Malaya, Command Organization' 14 Nov 1950 to 15 Dec 1953	ID9/621/2(1–2)
	'Malaya, Air Effort' 8 Mar 1951 to 13 Apr 1956	ID9/621/5(1–2)
	'Malaya Emergency. Higher Direction' 29 Jan 1952 to 15 May 1954	ID9/621/4(1)
	'Malaya. Helicopters' 27 Nov 1951 to 20 Dec 1955	ID9/621/12(1–4)
	'Airfields in Malaya' 2 Jan 1953 to 18 Oct 1957	ID9/621/14(1–4)
	'Deployment of Squadrons in Malaya' 16 Mar 1951 to 22 Dec 1955	ID9/906/4(1–3)
	'Policy in Malaya' 11 May 1945 to 13 Feb 1951	ID9/515/(1–5)
	'Progress Report on Emergency in Malaya' 11 Oct 1951 to 6 May 1958	ID9/621/11(1–2)
	'Policy for Employment of Malay Regiment' 22 Nov 1950 to 9 Dec 1952	ID9/621/3(1)
	'Malaya. Potential of the Communist Party' 18 Nov 1950	ID9/621/6(1)
	'Malaya. Political and Economic Background' 15 Nov 1950 to 14 Nov 1957	ID9/621/7(1–7)

Abbreviated Title	*Description*	*AHB Reference*
AM/VCAS	'Far East Policy' 1 Nov 1951 to 19 Aug 1958	ID9/6/1(1–2)
	'Operational Requirements—Helicopters—General' 27 Aug 1954 to 17 Sep 1958	IIJ53/16/2/6 Pt 1
	'Aircraft Requirements. Malaya' 5 Jun 1954 to 1 Feb 1955	IIJ53/16/2/3
	'Role of RAF in the Present Emergency' 10 Feb 1953 to 14 Jan 1954	IIJ53/16/2/2

REFERENCES

KEY

ACAS	Assistant Chief of Air Staff
ACFE	Air Command, Far East
Admin	Administrative Wing
AM	Air Ministry
AS	Air Staff
CAI	Command Administrative Instruction
CAS	Chief of Air Staff
COI	Command Operational Instruction
COI/Malaya	Central Office of Information, Malaya
COM	Command Organization Memorandum
COO	Command Operational Order
COS	Chiefs of Staff
DO(M)	Director of Operations, Malaya
FARELF	Far East Land Forces
FEAF	Far East Air Force
FO	Foreign Office
GAI	Group Administrative Instruction
GOI	Group Operational Instruction
GOM	Group Organization Memorandum
GOO	Group Operational Order
GSI	Group Signals Instruction
Gp	Group
L/A	Land/Air
LL	Liaison Letter
M	Air Headquarters, Malaya
Malaya/CO Report	Malaya/Colonial Office Report
MIS	Monthly Intelligence Summary
ORB	Operations Record Book
SACSEA	Supreme Allied Command, South East Asia
SEACOS	South East Asia, Chiefs of Staff
SF	Security Forces
Tech	Technical Wing
VCAS	Vice Chief of Air Staff
WIS	Weekly Intelligence Summary
WSAO	Weekly Summary of Air Operations

INTRODUCTION

[1] M/ORB(AS) Jul 1951, Appendix, FEAF Operational Research Report No 1; Rand/The Malayan Emergency', p 2

CHAPTER 1

[1] Details from Malaya/CO Reports, 1948–1956, *passim*; DO(M) Review, 1948–1957, p 3. (IIJ53/18/3); COI/Malaya, Jun 1951 pp 4–6

[2] VCAS file 'Policy in Malaya', COS JP(45)121, 7 Jun 1945 (ID9/515/Pt 1)

[3] ibid, SEACOS 393, 11 May 1945, 394, 12 May 1945 (ID9/515/Pt 1)

[4] M/ORB(AS) Apr 1948; VCAS file 'Policy in Malaya', COS JP(45)121, 7 Jun 1945, COS (45) 586 (0), 24 Sep 1945 (ID9/515/Pt 1)

[5] ibid, SEACOS 394, 12 May 1945 (ID9/515/Pt 1)

[6] ibid, SACSEA to FO/434, 3 Sep 1945 (ID9/515/Pt 1)

[7] Details from Malaya/CO Reports, 1948 to 1956, *passim*; DO(M) Review, 1948 to 1957, pp 3–5 (IIJ53/18/3); DO(M) Review 1955 pp 2, 3, and 1956, pp 1–3 (IIJ53/18/2); COI/Malaya, Jun 1951, pp 4–9; AOC(M) First Report, Jun 1948 to Mar 1949, pp 2, 3, Second Report, Apr 1949 to Dec 1950, pp 6, 7, and Third Report, Jan to Aug 1951, pp 3, 4 (IIJ53/16/2)

[8] Malaya/CO Report, 1952, p 5

[9] ibid, 1949, p 203; AOC(M) Second Report, Apr 1949 to Dec 1950, p 6 (IIJ53/16/2)

[10] ibid, Third Report, Jan to Aug 1951, Annexure 3 to Appendix A (IIJ53/16/2)

[11] ibid, Third Report, Jan to Aug 1951, pp 3, 4 (IIJ53/16/2)

[12] ibid, Third Report, Jan to Aug 1951, p 3 (IIJ53/16/2)

[13] DO(M) Review, 1948 to 1957, p 4 (IIJ53/18/3)

[14] Details from Malaya/CO Reports, 1948 to 1956, *passim*; DO(M) Review, 1948 to 1957, pp 19–21, (IIJ53/18/3); DO(M) Reviews, 1955 pp 9–19, and 1956, Appendices F–J (IIJ53/18/2); COI/ Malaya, Jun 1951, pp 10–11; AOC(M) Second Report, Apr 1949 to Dec 1950, pp 8, 9 and Third Report, Jan to Aug 1951, pp 5–7 (IIJ53/16/2)

[15] Malaya/CO Reports, 1949 p 209, 1950 p 7, and 1954 p 411

[16] ibid, 1951 p 8; AOC(M) Third Report, Jan to Aug 1951, p 6 (IIJ53/16/2)

[17] DO(M) Review, 1955, p 10 (IIJ53/18/2)

[18] ibid, 1948–1957, Appendix B, Table I (IIJ53/18/3)

[19] AOC(M) Second Report, Apr 1949 to Dec 1950, p 8 (IIJ53/16/2); Malaya/CO Report, 1949. p 209

[20] DO(M) Review, 1956, Appendix G, p 1 (IIJ53/18/2)

[21] ibid, 1948 to 1957, Appendix C, (IIJ53/18/2); ACFE–FEAF/ORB (AS) Orders of Battle, 1948 to 1960 *passim*

[22] DO(M) Review, 1948 to 1957, p 19 (IIJ53/18/2); Malaya/CO Reports, 1948 to 1956 *passim*

[23] ibid, 1948 to 1956, *passim*; DO(M) Review, 1948 to 1957, pp 13–15 (IIJ53/18/2); DO(M) Review. 1956, p 4 (IIJ53/18/3)

[24] Details from VCAS file 'Policy in Malaya', COS (50) 216, 27 Jun 1950 (ID9/515/Pt 4); Malaya/ CO Report, 1950, pp 3–13; DO(M) Review, 1948 to 1957, pp 9, 16–19 (IIJ53/18/2); AOC(M) Second Report, Apr 1949 to Dec 1950, p 7 and Third Report, Jan to Aug 1950, pp 4, 5 (IIJ53/16/2). DO(M) Report, 1950/1951, pp 6–10 (IIJ53/18/1)

[25] As for (24) plus VCAS file 'Policy in Malaya', SEACOS 242, GHQ FARELF to Min of Defence, 15 Nov 1951 (ID9/515/Pt 5)

[26] Malaya/CO Report, 1949, p 209

[27] DO(M) Review, 1948–1957, p 17 (IIJ53/18/2)

[28] Malaya/CO Report, 1950, p 13

[29] ibid, 1949 p 210, 1950 p 13, 1951 p 16 and 1952 p 16

[30] ibid, 1949, p 209

[31] DO(M) Review, 1948 to 1957, p 17 (IIJ53/18/2)

[32] M/ORB (AS) Aug 1953, Appendix 161; L/A Warfare LL No 7, Jan/Jun 1953, p 4 (IIJ50/141/1/1)

[33] DO(M) Review, 1956, p 8 (IIJ53/18/3)

[34] VCAS file 'Policy in Malaya', ACFE to AM/CCX172, 24 Jul 1948, Commissioner General SE Asia to Sec of State Colonies/93, 26 Jun 1948 (ID9/515/Pt 2); DO(M) Review, 1948 to 1957, p 13 (IIJ53/18/2)

[35] ibid, 1948 to 1957, p 15 (IIJ53/18/2); Malaya/CO Report, 1954, p 402

[36] ibid, 1948 to 1956 *passim*; DO(M) Review, 1956, Appendix C, p 2 (IIJ53/18/3); ACFE–FEAF/ MIS 1948 to 1960, *passim*

[37] Malaya/CO Report, 1952 p 7 and 1953 p 340

[38] VCAS file 'Policy in Malaya', GHQ FE to Min of Defence/SEACOS 853, 26 Jun 1948, Commissioner General SE Asia to Sec of State Colonies/93, 26 Jun 1948 (ID9/515/Pt 2)

CHAPTER 1

39 ibid, COS(50)216, 27 Jun 1950, DO(50)92, 24 Oct 1950 (ID9/515/Pt 4) ; M/ORB (AS) Aug 1950, AHQ(M)/S119/6/Air

40 Malaya/CO Report, 1950, p 7

41 M/ORB (AS) Aug 1950, AHQ(M)/S119/6/Air

42 Details from Malaya/CO Reports, 1948 to 1956 *passim*; DO(M) Review, 1948 to 1957, pp 8–11 (IIJ53/18/2) ; ACFE–FEAF/MIS and SF/WIS 1948 to 1958 *passim*; AOC(M) Reports 1 to 5, 9 and 10, Jun 1948 to Dec 1952 and 1957 to 1958 *passim*; VCAS files 'Malaya, Internal Security' (ID9/621/1/Pts 1–5)

43 M/ORB (AS) Apr 1948, GOO 12/48

44 AOC(M) First Report, Jun 1948 to Mar 1949, p 7 (IIJ53/1/62)

45 VCAS file 'Policy in Malaya', ACFE to AM/CCX 200, 14 Aug 1948, ACAS to VCAS, 5 Nov 1948 (ID9/515/Pt 2)

46 AOC(M) First Report, Jun 1948 to Mar 1949, p 12 (IIJ53/16/2) ; M/ORB (AS) Jan 1949

47 ibid, Second Report, Apr 1949 to Dec 1950, p 13, Appendix C pp 27–29 (IIJ53/16/2)

48 Malaya/CO Report, 1949, p 212

49 ibid, 1949, p 203

50 ibid, 1949, p 205; DO(M) Review, 1948 to 1957, p 9 (IIJ53/18/2)

51 Malaya/CO Report, 1950, p 1; FEAF/MIS Feb 1951, p 6

52 Malaya/CO Report, 1950, p 12; AOC(M) Second Report, Apr 1949 to Dec 1950, p 8 (IIJ53/16/2)

53 ibid, Second Report, Apr 1949 to Dec 1950, p 13, 14 (IIJ53/16/2) ; M/ORB (AS) Apr 1950

54 AOC(M) Second Report, Apr 1949 to Dec 1950, Appendix C pp 32–34 (IIJ53/16/2)

55 Malaya/CO Report, 1951, p 10

56 AOC(M) Third Report, Jan to Aug 1951, pp 10–13 (IIJ53/16/2)

57 ibid, Fourth Report, Sep 1951 to Feb 1952, pp 7, 8 (IIJ53/16/2) ; Malaya/CO Report, 1951, p 1 ; DO(M) Report, 1950/1951, p 30 (IIJ53/18/1)

58 AOC(M) Third Report, Jan to Aug 1951, p 10 and Annexure 1 to Appendix E, pp 37, 38 (IIJ53/16/2)

59 ibid, Third Report, Jan to Aug 1951, p 4 (IIJ53/16/2) ; Malaya/CO Report, 1951, p 6

60 AOC(M) Fifth Report, Feb to Dec 1952, p 1 (IIJ53/16/2), COI/Malaya, Jun 1951, p 7

61 DO(M) Review, 1948 to 1957, p 10 (IIJ53/18/2)

62 Malaya/CO Report, 1952, p 4

63 ibid, 1952, p 11; AOC(M) Fourth Report, Sep 1951 to Feb 1952, pp 9–11 and Fifth Report, Feb to Dec 1952, p 5 (IIJ53/16/2)

64 ibid, Fifth Report, Feb to Dec 1952, p 3 (IIJ53/16/2) ; Malaya/CO Report, 1952, p 11

65 ibid, 1952, p 16 and 1953, p 339

66 DO(M) Review, 1948 to 1957, p 10 (IIJ53/18/2)

67 L/A Warfare LL No 7, Jan/Jun 1953, pp 1–3 and No 8, Jul 1953/Mar 1954, pp 3–5 (IIJ50/141/1/1) ; Malaya/CO Report, 1953, pp 347–350

68 L/A Warfare LL No 8, Jul 1953/Mar 1954, pp 3, 4 (IIJ50/141/1/1)

69 ibid, No 8 Jul 1953/Mar 1954, p 7 (IIJ50/141/1/1) ; Malaya/CO Report, 1953, p 343 and 1954, p 405

70 ibid, 1954, p 405; DO(M) Review, 1948 to 1957, p 11 (IIJ53/18/2) ; L/A Warfare LL No 9, Apr/Sep 1954, p 1 (IIJ50/141/1/1)

71 ibid, No 8, Jul 1953/Mar 1954, p 5 (IIJ50/141/1/1) ; Malaya/CO Report, 1954, pp 412–417

72 ibid, 1954, p 401

73 ibid, 1954, p 401, DO(M) Review, 1955, p 10 (IIJ53/18/3)

74 Malaya/CO Report, 1955, p 432

75 ibid, 1955, p 432; M/ORB (AS) Sep 1955

76 DO(M) Review, 1955, p 2 (IIJ53/18/3)

77 ibid, 1955, p 4 (IIJ53/18/3), Malaya/CO Report, 1955, p 421 ; FEAF/Air Attachés' Conference 1956

78 Malaya/CO Report, 1956, p 437; DO(M) Review, 1956, p 7 (IIJ53/18/3)

79 ibid, 1956, Appendix H, p 1 (IIJ53/18/3) ; Malaya/CO Report, 1956, pp 443, 446; M/ORB (AS) Feb 1956

80 Malaya/CO Report, 1956, pp 446–449

81 DO(M) Review, 1956, p 8 (IIJ53/18/3) ; VCAS file 'Malaya, Internal Security', COS(56)33, 30 Aug 1956, Annexure to COS 1174, 21 Aug 1956 (ID9/621/1/Pt 3)

82 DO(M) Review, 1956, p 7 (IIJ53/18/3)

83 ibid, 1948 to 1957, p 22 (IIJ53/18/2) ; AOC (224 Gp) Ninth Report, Jan to Dec 1957, p 5 and Appendix A (IIJ53/16/2)

84 DO(M) Review, 1948 to 1957, p 22 (IIJ53/18/2)

85 ibid, 1948 to 1957, p 23 (IIJ53/18/2); AOC (224 Gp) Ninth Report, Jan to Dec 1957, p 2 (IIJ53/16/2)

86 ibid, Tenth Report, Jan to Dec 1958, p 1 (IIJ53/16/2)

87 ibid, Tenth Report, Jan to Dec 1958, pp 2, 3 (IIJ53/16/2)

CHAPTER 1

88 ibid, Tenth Report, Jan to Dec 1958, pp 1, 3 (IIJ53/16/2)
89 ibid, Tenth Report, Jan to Dec 1958, p 4 (IIJ53/16/2)
90 ibid, Tenth Report, Jan to Dec 1958, p 4 (IIJ53/16/2)
91 M/ORB (AS) Apr, Aug 1959
92 ibid, Apr, Nov 1959
93 VCAS file 'Malaya, Internal Security', DO for BDCC (FE), Appendix to COS/1027, 19 Jun 1951 (ID9/621/1 Pt 1); DO(M) Review, 1948 to 1957, pp, 6, 7 (IIJ53/18/2); Rand/'The Malayan Emergency', *passim*
94 DO(M) Review, 1948 to 1957, pp 6, 7 (IIJ53/18/2)
95 ibid, 1948 to 1957, p 6 (IIJ53/18/2)
96 ibid, 1948 to 1957, p 6 (IIJ53/18/2)
97 ibid, 1955, p 10 (IIJ53/18/3)
98 ibid, p 10 (IIJ53/18/3)

CHAPTER 2

1 M/224 Gp/ORB(AS) Appendices; periodic Directives of Command to AOC (M/224 Gp) from C in C FEAF
2 ACFE–FEAF/ORB(AS) Appendices; FE/33680/0/1/Org; FE/S7143/3/Org; FE/S7560/2/Org 1; FE/S7568/Org 1a
3 M/ORB(AS) Jul 1960, GAI 4/60
4 VCAS file 'Policy in Malaya', FEAF to AM/AX 638, 16 Jul 1950 (ID9/515/Pt 4)
5 M/Training Summaries, *passim*
6 M/ORB(AS) Aug 1950, AHQ(M)/352/10/Air
7 M/Training Summaries, *passim*
8 AOC(224 Gp) Ninth Report, Jan/Dec 1957. (IIJ53/16/2)
9 ACFE/ORB(AS) Apr 1948, COO1/48; M/ORB(AS) May 1948, GOO 13/48; M/ORB(AS) Apr 1948, GOO 14/48
10 M/ORB(AS) Apr 1948, GOO 12/48
11 ibid, Jun, Sep 1948, GOO 24/48, GOM 38/48; ACFE/ORB (Admin) Jul, Sep 1948, COM 42/48, COM 53/48
12 M/ORB(AS) Jul, Dec 1949, GOI 13/49, GAI 9/49
13 ibid, Apr 1950, GAI 8/50, FEAF/ORB (Admin) Mar 1950, CAI 5/50
14 FEAF/ORB (Admin) Apr 1948, Appendix 6/48, FE/33250/0/12/Org
15 M/ORB(AS) May 1948, Appendix 12/48
16 ibid, Apr 1955, Appendix 6/55
17 ibid, Jul 1955, Appendix 93/55, Joint Army/Air Instruction No 2
18 ibid
19 ibid, Jun 1949, GOM 13/49
20 VCAS file 'Policy in Malaya', FE/30021/Org, 1 Apr 1948 (ID9/515/Pt 2)
21 ibid
22 ibid, CIC (FE) 48/1, 6 Feb 1948. (ID9/515/Pt 2)
23 AOC(M) First Report, Jun 1948/Mar 1949, p 4 (IIJ53/16/2)
24 M/ORB(AS) Jun 1948, GOO 24/48, GAI 3/48
25 VCAS file 'Policy in Malaya', ACFE to AM/AOX 802, 1 Jul 1948 (ID9/515/Pt 2)
26 AOC(M) Second Report, Apr 1949/Dec 1950, p 10 (IIJ53/16/2)
27 M/ORB(AS) Nov 1949, GOO 23/49
28 ibid
29 ibid, Mar 1952, Feb 1943, GOM 5/52, 9/53; FEAF/ORB (Admin) Apr 1952, CAI 5/52
30 M/ORB(AS) Feb 1953, GAI 1/53, 6/53; Dec 1952, AHQ(M)/S3040/5/Org, Appendix 294
31 ibid, Apr 1953, GOM 14/53
32 ibid, Feb 1953, AHQ(M)/S3040/20/Org, Appendix 197; Jan 1954, GOM 1/54
33 FEAF/ORB(Admin) May 1957, COM 16/57; M/ORB Jun 1957, GAI 5/57
34 AOC (224 Gp) Ninth Report, Jan/Dec 1957, p 26 (IIJ53/16/2)
35 VCAS file 'Malaya, Internal Security', COS(56) 363, COS(57) 110, Annexes (ID9/621/1/Pt 3)
36 M/ORB(AS) Aug 1957, GOI 1/57
37 ibid, Jun 1957, GAI 5/57
38 FEAF/ORB(Admin) Sep 1957, COM 33/57
39 ibid, Nov 1957, COM 41/57, 56/57
40 ibid, Dec 1957, COM 49/57
41 ibid, Dec 1957, Jun 1958, COM 50/57, CAI 13/58

CHAPTER 2

42 ibid, Jul 1958, COM 19/58
43 ibid, May 1958, Feb 1959, CAI 9/58, COM 13/59
44 ibid, Feb, Jul 1959, COM 13/59, 63/59
45 ibid, May 1960, COM 13/60
46 ibid, Feb 1959, COM 14/59
47 ibid, Jun 1960, COM 85/60
48 ibid, Jun 1960, COM 82/60; M/ORB(AS) Jun 1960, GSI 2/1960

CHAPTER 3

1 VCAS file 'Malaya, Air Effort', FEAF(AS) note on 'The Air Aspect of Operations in Malaya', 4 Jan 1952 (ID9/621/5/Pt 1)
2 FEAF/MIS Nov 1949, p 7
3 VCAS file 'Malaya, Air Effort', FEAF(AS) note on 'Air Action in Malaya', Nov 1951 (ID9/621/5/Pt 1)
4 FEAF/MIS Nov 1949, p 7
5 M/ORB(AS) Aug 1951, GOI 2/51
6 ibid, Aug 1950, AHQ(M)/S119/6/Air, Minutes of meeting to discuss Army/Air co-operation in the Anti-Bandit Campaign, 14 Aug 1950
7 L/A Warfare LL No 7, Jan/Jun 1953, p 1 (IIJ50/141/1/1)
8 ibid, No 8, Jul 1953/Mar 1954, p 2 (IIJ50/141/1/1)
9 M/ORB(AS) Jan 1954, AHQ(M)/S307/6/AO Minutes of conference called to discuss air-strike action in the Malayan campaign, 22 Jan 1954
10 DO(M) Review, 1955, DEF/Y40/19A, p 15 (IIJ53/18/2)
11 AOC(224 Gp) Tenth Report, Jan/Dec 1958, p 6 (IIJ53/16/2)
12 M/ORB(AS) Jun 1952, AHQ(M)S307/6/AO Minutes of conference on air-strike action in Malaya 15 Jun 1952
13 ibid, Dec 1948, AIX 37, Appendix 46/48, 'Firedog Diary', Aug 1950, AHQ(M)/S119/6/Air, Minutes of meeting to discuss Army/Air co-operation in the Anti-Bandit Campaign, 14 Aug 1950
14 ibid, May 1952, AHQ(M)/S307/6/AO, Note on Ground to Air Communications, 22 May 1952
15 ibid
16 M/ORB(AS) GOO *passim*
17 ACFE–FEAF/ORB(AS) Orders of Battle, 1948–1960 *passim*, see Annex L
18 M/ORB(AS) Jun, Sep 1948, GOO 24/48, GOM 36/48, 37/48, ACFE/ORB (Admin) Jul 1948, COM 42/48
19 ACFE/ORB (Admin) Aug 1948, COM 63/48
20 ibid, Oct 1948, FE/33680/0/1/Org, Appendix 1
21 M/ORB(AS) May, Aug 1949, GOM 7/49, 24/49, 25/49, GOO 2/49
22 ibid, Aug 1949, GOM 30/49, GOO 16/49
23 ibid, Nov, Dec 1949, GOM 44/49, 46/49
24 ibid, Apr 1950, GAI 8/50; VCAS file 'Policy in Malaya', AM to FEAF/MSX 182, 21 Mar 1950 (ID9/515/Pt 3)
25 M/ORB(AS) Mar 1950, GOO 29/50; VCAS file 'Policy in Malaya', AM to BC/MSX 164, 8 Mar 1950 (ID9/515/Pt 3)
26 M/ORB(AS) Jan 1950, GOO 10/50; VCAS file 'Policy in Malaya', FEAF to AM/AX 29, AX 251, AX 364, 20 Jan, 1, 6 Feb 1950 (ID9/515/Pt 3)
27 VCAS file 'Policy in Malaya', DDOps (B) minute, 26 Jan 1950 (ID9/515/Pt 3)
28 ibid, ACAS(Ops) to VCAS, minute, 27 Jan 1950 (ID9/515/Pt 3)
29 M/ORB(AS) May 1950, GOM 10/50; FEAF/ORB (Admin) May 1950, CAI 12/50; VCAS file 'Policy in Malaya', FEAF to AM/AX 626, 8 Apr 1950, BC to FEAF/AO 139, 21 Apr 1950 (ID9/515/Pt 3)
30 VCAS file 'Policy in Malaya', AM to FEAF/MSX 148, AX 594, AX 759, 24, 27 Feb, 1 Mar 1950 (ID9/515/Pts 2 and 3)
31 M/ORB(AS) Apr, Oct 1950, GAI 8/50, 25/50; FEAF/ORB (Admin) Nov 1950, CAI 34/50
32 VCAS file 'Policy in Malaya', Sec of State for Colonies to Governor of Federation of Malaya/237, 17 Mar 1950; SEACOS (38) 50, 4 Apr 1950; FEAF to Melbourne/AX 750, 29 Jun 1950 (ID9/515/Pts 3 and 4)
33 ACFE/ORB (Admin) Apr 1948, ACFE/33250/0/12/Org
34 FEAF/ORB (Admin) Jun 1949, Appendix 6, Discussion of deployment of air forces in Malaya, 28 Jun 1949

CHAPTER 3

35 VCAS file 'Policy in Malaya', AM to FEAF/A 1407, 6 Apr 1951 (ID9/515/Pt 5)
36 ibid, AM to FEAF/A 1069, A 1208, 3, 10 Jan 1951 (ID9/515/Pt 5)
37 ibid, AM to FEAF/A 1069, 3 Jan 1951. (ID9/515/Pt 5); VCAS file 'Malaya, Internal Security', SEACOS (213) 50, BDCC (FE) to COS 30 Nov 1950 (ID9/621/1/Pt 1)
38 VCAS file 'Malaya, Air Effort', FEAF to AM/AX 527, 3 Aug 1950 (ID9/621/5/Pt 1)
39 ibid, AM to FEAF/A 1002, 1 Sep 1950 (ID9/621/5/Pt 1)
40 ibid, FEAF to AM/A 727, 16 Sep 1950 (ID9/621/5/Pt 1)
41 ibid, AM to FEAF/A 2160 ref: COSSEA (778), 26 Oct 1950 (ID9/621/5/Pt 1)
42 M/ORB(AS) Jan 1951, GOM 3/51; VCAS file 'Policy in Malaya', AM to FEAF/A 1208, A 2948, 10, 12 Jan 1951 (ID9/515/Pt 5)
43 M/ORB(AS) Oct, Nov 1950, Jan 1951, GOO 77/50, GOM 45/50, 2/51
44 ibid, Mar, Apr 1951, GOM 10/51, GOO 14/51
45 M/Training Summaries, *passim*; AOC(M) Third Report, Jan/Aug 1951, p 7 (IIJ53/16/2)
46 AOC(M) Third Report, Jan, Aug 1951, p 7 (IIJ53/16/2)
47 M/ORB(AS) Dec 1949, GOO 27/49
48 ibid, May 1950, GOO 40/50
49 ibid, May 1951, GAI 6/51
50 ibid, Dec 1951, GOM 39/51
51 ibid, Feb 1953, GOM 8/53
52 VCAS file 'Malaya Air Effort', FEAF to AM/A 429, 4 Apr 1953 (ID9/621/5/Pt 2)
53 ibid, AM to FEAF/A 2978, 9 Jun 1953; FEAF to AM/A 860, A 177, 15, 19 Jun 1953; AM file CMS/2266/53/ACAS(Ops), 11 Jun 1953 (ID9/621/5/Pt 2)
54 ibid, FEAF to AM/A 429, 23 Jun 1953; BC to AM/AO 989, 1 Dec 1953
55 M/ORB(AS) Mar 1955, GAI 2/55; FEAF/ORB (Admin) Oct 1955/Jun 1956, CAI 31/55, COO 8/55, COM 35/56
56 FEAF/ORB (Admin) Aug 1955, COM 26/55
57 DO(M) Review, 1955, DEF/Y40/19A, p 14 (IIJ53/18/2)
58 M/ORB(AS) Mar 1955 GAI 1/55
59 DO(M) Review, 1955, DEF/Y40/19A, p 14 (IIJ53/18/2)
60 FEAF/ORB (Admin) Dec 1956, COM 59/56
61 VCAS file 'Malaya, Air Effort', BF22/DDOps (B), 7 Feb 1956 (ID9/621/5/Pt 2)
62 FEAF/ORB (Admin) Sep 1957, COM 31/57
63 VCAS file 'Malaya, Air Effort', DO(M), DEF/Y/25/7, 3 Mar 1955 (ID9/621/5/Pt 1)
64 AOC (224 Gp) Tenth Report, Jan/Dec 1958, p 6 (IIJ53/16/2)
65 FEAF/ORB (Admin) Nov 1957, COM 45/57
66 ibid, Oct 1958, COM 45/58
67 ibid, Sep 1955, CAI 25/55, Jun, Jul, Nov 1958, COM 17/58, 19/58, 52/58; VCAS file 'Malaya, Internal Security', DC(56) 7, 2 Oct 1956. (ID9/621/1/Pt 3)
68 M/ORB(AS) Sep 1958, GOO 9/58, May 1959, GAI 4/59
69 FEAF/ORB (Admin) Jul 1958, COM 19/58, Jul 1959, COM 62/59
70 VCAS file 'Policy in Malaya', FEAF to AM/AOX 963, 17 Apr 1950. (ID9/515/Pt 3)
71 M/ORB(AS) Nov 1948, GOO 28/48; FEAF/ORB (Admin) Apr 1956, COM 22/46
72 VCAS file 'Malaya, Air Effort', Air Staff note on 'The Air Aspect of Operations in Malaya', Nov 1951 (ID9/621/5/Pt 1)
73 M/ORB(AS) Mar 1950, AHQ(M)/S307/5/Air. Minutes of conference on the capabilities of Lincoln bombers, 22 Mar 1950
74 VCAS file 'Malaya, Air Effort', FEAF to AM/A 385, 703; AO 159, 221, 634, 974; AX 434, 626, AOX 95, 270, 512, 729, 829, 963 (ID9/621/5/Pt 1)
75 Rand/'The Malayan Emergency', p 56 M/ORB Jul 1958, Air Staff Instruction Air/21
76 M/ORB(AS) Jul 1951, Appendix, FEAF Operational Research Report No 1
77 ibid, Jan 1950, Appendix, AAHQ(M)S50/Instr
78 ibid, Jan 1950, Appendix, AAHQ(M)S50/Instr
79 ibid, June 1950, Appendix, AHQ(M)/S119/3/Air
80 AOC(224 Gp) Ninth Report, Jan/Dec 1957, p 44 (IIJ53/16/2)
81 M/ORB(AS) Apr 1951, GOO 20/51; ibid, Jul 1951, Appendix, FEAF Operational Research Report No 1
82 VCAS file 'Policy in Malaya', AM to FEAF/AX 1349, 2 Feb 1950 (ID9/515/Pt 2)
83 M/ORB(AS) Jul 1951, Appendix FEAF Operational Research Report No 1
84 ibid, Dec 1953, GOI 1/53
85 M/ORB(AS) Jan 1954, GOI 1/54
86 ibid, May, Jun 1950, GOO 44/50, 52/50
87 AOC(224 Gp) Ninth Report, Jan/Dec 1957, p 48 (IIJ53/16/2)
88 M/ORB(AS) Jan 1950, GOO 2/50, ref Operations 'Flare Up I and II'; VCAS file 'Policy in Malaya', AM to FEAF/MSX 169, 10 Mar 1950 (ID9/515/Pt 3)
89 M/ORB(AS) Apr 1950, GOO 32/50

CHAPTER 3

⁹⁰ ibid, Sep 1950, GOO 634/50
⁹¹ VCAS file 'Policy in Malaya', AM to FEAF/MSX 169, 10 Mar 1950 (ID9/515/Pt 3)
⁹² L/A Warfare LL No 8, Jul 1953/Mar 1954, Appendix A, p 11 (IIJ50/141/1/1); M/ORB(AS) Apr 1951, Appendix, AHQ(M)/S302/11/Air/Ops, 13 Mar 1951
⁹³ L/A Warfare LL No 8, Jul 1953/Mar 1954, p 3
⁹⁴ FEAF/MIS, *passim*
⁹⁵ M/ORB(AS) Jul 1951, Appendix, FEAF Operational Research Report No 1
⁹⁶ ibid, Jan 1954, AHQ(M)/S307/5/Air, Review of air support given to Operation 'Firedog', 1 Jan 1954
⁹⁷ ibid, Jul 1951, Appendix, FEAF Operational Research Report No 1
⁹⁸ ibid, Aug 1950, AHQ(M)/S119/6/Air, Minutes of meeting to discuss Army/Air Co-operation in the Anti-Bandit Campaign, 14 Aug 1950
⁹⁹ AOC(M) First and Second Reports, Jun 1948/Dec 1950, *passim* (IIJ53/16/2)
¹⁰⁰ ibid
¹⁰¹ M/ORB(AS) Oct 1950, GOO 75/50
¹⁰² ibid, Jul 1955, Appendix 90/55, Joint Army/Air Instruction No 6, Appendix A
¹⁰³ ibid, Jul 1955, Appendix 90/55, Joint Army/Air Instruction No 6, Appendix B
¹⁰⁴ ibid, Nov 1956, Appendix, Operational Standing Order No 19
¹⁰⁵ AOC(M) Second Report, Apr 1949/Dec 1950, p 14 (IIJ53/16/2)
¹⁰⁶ M/ORB(AS) Nov 1950
¹⁰⁷ ibid, Aug 1955
¹⁰⁸ ibid, Nov 1956, Appendix, Joint Army/Air Operational Instruction No 13, 31 Oct 1956
¹⁰⁹ AOC(M) Third Report, Jan/Aug 1951, p 16 (IIJ53/16/2)
¹¹⁰ M/ORB(AS) Oct 1950, GOI 8/50 to 15/50
¹¹¹ ibid, Jul 1955, Appendix 91/55, Joint Army/Air/Police Standing Operational Instruction, No 1 5 May 1955
¹¹² ibid, Jul 1956, Appendix, Operational Standing Order No 12
¹¹³ ibid, May 1957, GAI 3/57
¹¹⁴ AOC(224 Gp) Ninth Report, Jan/Dec 1957, p 51 (IIJ53/16/2)
¹¹⁵ M/ORB(AS) Jan 1950, GOO 5/50
¹¹⁶ Rand/'The Malayan Emergency', p 67
¹¹⁷ M/ORB(AS) Mar 1950, Appendix 398; L/A Warfare LL No 9, Apr/Sep 1954, Appendix A, pp 1–3 (IIJ50/141/1/1)
¹¹⁸ L/A Warfare LL No 9, Apr/Sep 1954, Appendix A, pp 1–3 (IIJ50/141/1/1)
¹¹⁹ M/ORB(AS) Mar 1956, Appendix, Joint Army/Air Instruction No 13
¹²⁰ ibid, Oct 1957, Appendix, Joint Army/Air Instruction No 17
¹²¹ ibid, Jul 1956, Appendix 94/56, AHQ(M) 541/44/Air
¹²² ibid, Nov 1956, Appendix, Operational Standing Order No 19
¹²³ ibid, Jun 1956, GAI 3/56, GOO 7/56
¹²⁴ ibid, Mar 1957, GAI 1/57
¹²⁵ ibid, Jun 1956, Appendix, Joint Army/Air Instruction No 16
¹²⁶ AOC(224 Gp) Tenth Report, Jan/Dec 1958, p 8 (IIJ53/16/2)
¹²⁷ M/ORB(AS) Oct 1959, GAI 6/59
¹²⁸ AOC(224 Gp) Ninth Report, Jan/Dec 1957, p 13 (IIJ53/16/2)
¹²⁹ M/ORB(AS) Aug 1950, Appendix AHQ(M)/S119/6/Air
¹³⁰ ibid, Apr 1949, Appendix AHQ(M)/S50/Inf
¹³¹ AOC(224 Gp) Ninth Report, Jan/Dec 1957, p 11 (IIJ53/16/2)
¹³² M/ORB(AS) Jan 1954, AHQ(M)/S307/6/AO Minutes of conference called to discuss **air-strike** action in the Malayan campaign, 22 Jan 1954
¹³³ ibid, Mar 1950, Appendix 336, Note on air-strike tactics, 15 Mar 1950
¹³⁴ AOC(224 Gp) Ninth Report, Jan/Dec 1957, p 10 (IIJ53/16/2)
¹³⁵ ibid, Tenth Report, Jan/Dec 1958, p 9 (IIJ53/16/2)
¹³⁶ M/ORB(AS) Mar 1950, Appendix 336, Note on air-strike tactics, 15 Mar 1950
¹³⁷ AOC(224 Gp) Ninth Report, Jan/Dec 1957, p 9; ibid, Tenth Report, Jan/Dec 1958, p 9. (IIJ53/16/2)
¹³⁸ AOC(M) First Report, Jun 1948/Mar 1949, pp 5, 6. Except where otherwise stated, details of the offensive air support provided during the Malayan campaign are taken from the periodic reports of the AOC (Malaya or 224 Group) on RAF operations in Malaya (IIJ53/16/2) and from the monthly intelligence summaries and weekly summaries of air operations in Malaya issued by HQ ACFE or FEAF AHQ(M), HQ Malaya Command and HQ Federation of Malaya Police
¹³⁹ VCAS file 'Policy in Malaya', ACFE to AM/CCX 200, 14 Aug 1948. (ID9/515/Pt 2)
¹⁴⁰ M/ORB(AS) Oct 1949, Appendix 18, Intelligence Summary
¹⁴¹ ibid, Apr 1949, AHQ(M)/S50/Inf; Nov 1949, GOO 4/49
¹⁴² ibid, Jan 1950; 'Malaya Tribune', 12 Jan 1950
¹⁴³ AM/ORB Jun 1950, GOO 576/50

CHAPTER 3

144 M/ORB(AS) Mar 1950, GOO 29/50
145 AM/ORB Jul 1950, GOO 599/50
146 L/A Warfare LL No 7, Jan/Jun 1953, p 1 (IIJ50/141/1/1)
147 ibid, p 2 (IIJ50/141/1/1)
148 ibid, No 8, Jul 1953/Mar 1954, p 2 (IIJ50/141/1/1)
149 M/WSAO and SF/WIS, *passim*
150 L/A Warfare LL, No 8, Jul 1953/Mar 1954, p 2 (IIJ50/141/1/1)
151 ibid, No 8, Jul 1953/Mar 1954, p 2 (IIJ50/141/1/1)
152 ibid, No 8, Jul 1953/Mar 1954, pp 3, 4 (IIJ50/141/1/1)
153 ibid, No 9, Apr/Sep 1954, p 3 (IIJ50/141/1/1)
154 M/ORB(AS) 1954, *passim*
155 ibid, Aug 1954, Appendix 105/54
156 ibid, Sep 1955, Appendix 127/55
157 ibid, Oct 1955, Appendix 134/55
158 Malaya/CO Report, 1954, pp 412–416
159 M/ORB(AS) Aug 1955, Appendix 106/55
160 ibid, Sep 1955, Appendices 122–129/55
161 ibid, Nov 1955
162 ibid, Nov/Dec 1955
163 VCAS file 'Malaya, Air Effort', DEFY/25/7, 3 Feb 1956 (ID9/621/S/Pt 1)
164 Malaya/CO Report, 1956, p 443; FEAF/Air Attachés' Conference Jan 1957, p 60; VCAS file 'Malaya, Air Effort', DO(M) to C in C, BC/DO/5226, 21 Mar 1956 (ID9/621/5/Pt 1)
165 M/ORB(AS) 1956, *passim*
166 Malaya/CO Report, 1956, pp 446–450
167 M/ORB(AS) Jan 1957
168 ibid, Aug 1959
169 Rand/'The Malayan Emergency', p 60
170 M/ORB(AS) Nov 1952, AHQ(M)/S307/6/AO, 23 Sep 1952
171 FEAF/MIS Nov 1949, p 8
172 AOC(M) Second Report, Apr 1949/Dec 1950, Appendix L, p 37 (IIJ53/16/2)
173 ibid (IIJ53/16/2)
174 VCAS file 'Progress Report on the Emergency in Malaya', COS 733(52) (ID9/621/11/Pt 1)
175 M/ORB(AS) Nov 1952, AHQ(M)/S307/6/AO, 23 Sep 1952; VCAS file 'Malaya, Air Effort', Note on the effect of Air Action in Malaya, 18 Jun 1952 (ID9/621/5/Pt 1)
176 *See* ibid, AM to FEAF/A 2160, 26 Oct 1950, A 2390, 8 Nov 1950 (ID9/621/5/Pt 1)
177 Rand/'The Malayan Emergency', p 58

CHAPTER 4

1 ACFE–FEAF/ORB(AS), Air Orders of Battle, *passim*
2 M/ORB(AS) Nov 1951, GOM 35/51
3 FEAF/ORB (Admin) Feb 1959, COM 14/59
4 M/ORB(AS) Nov 1948, Movement Order 1/48, Appendix 40/48; ACFE/ORB (Admin) Nov 1948, COM 70/48
5 M/ORB(AS) Oct 1949, GOO 20/49
6 ibid, Dec 1949, GOM 44/49; AOC(M) Second Report, Apr 1949 to Dec 1950, p 11 (IIJ53/16/2)
7 VCAS file 'Policy in Malaya', FEAF to AM/OX 605, 28 Apr 1950 (ID9/515/Pt 3)
8 M/ORB(AS) Mar 1951, GOM 7/51, 10/51, Appendix 3102/3/Org
9 ibid, Jun, Nov 1951, GOM 28/51, 31/51, 32/51, 33/51
10 VCAS file 'Policy in Malaya', FEAF to AM/AX 827, 21 Mar 1950, AM to RNZAF/MSX 186, 23 Mar 1950, COS(50)55, 3 Apr 1950 (ID9/515/Pt 3)
11 ibid, FEAF to AM/OX 605, 28 Apr 1950 (ID9/515/Pt 3); AOC(M) Fourth Report, Sept 1951 to Feb 1952, p 5 (IIJ53/16/2)
12 M/ORB(AS) Apr 1951, GOM 50/51, Nov 1952, GOM 35/52
13 DO(M) Review, 1955, p 12 (IIJ53/18/3)
14 AOC (224 Gp) Ninth Report, Jan to Dec 1957, p 26 (IIJ53/16/2); FEAF/ORB (Admin) Dec 1957, COM 50/57
15 ibid, Dec 1956, COM 60/56, Dec 1957, COM 48/57
16 ibid, Oct 1957, COM 36/57
17 M/ORB(AS) Jul 1959, GOM 66/59
18 ibid, Jun 1959, GAI 5/59; AOC (224 Gp) Jan to Dec 1957, p 26 (IIJ53/16/2)
19 ibid, Fourth Report, Sep 1951 to Feb 1952, Annexure 2 to Appendix C p 20 (IIJ53/16/2)

CHAPTER 4

²⁰ L/A Warfare LL No 9, Apr/Sep 1954, p 6 (IIJ50/141/1/1)
²¹ ibid, No 9, Apr/Sep 1954, p 5 (IIJ50/141/1/1); M/ORB(AS) Oct 1950, GOO 75/50, Jul 1955 Appendix, Operational Standing Order No 5; FEAF/MIS Nov 1954, Pt II
²² ibid, Nov 1954, Pt II, Mar. 1949, pp 6, 7; M/ORB(AS) Aug 1953, Appendix 160, 'The Deep Jungle Forts of Malaya'
²³ ibid, Aug 1953, Appendix 160, 'The Deep Jungle Forts of Malaya', Mar 1953; L/A Warfare LL No 8, July 1953/Mar 1954, p 7 (IIJ50/141/1/1)
²⁴ VCAS file 'Malaya, Air Effort', COS(55)18, 25 Jan 1955 ID9 621/5/Pt 1); AOC (224 Gp) Ninth Report, Jan to Dec 1957, p 27, Tenth Report, Jan to Dec 1958, p 11 (IIJ53/16/2)
²⁵ FEAF/MIS Nov 1954, Pt II
²⁶ ibid, Mar 1949, pp 6, 7
²⁷ Rand/'The Malayan Emergency', p 28
²⁸ AOC(M) First Report, Jun 1948 to Mar 1949, p 12 (IIJ53/16/2)
²⁹ Rand/'The Malayan Emergency', p 31
³⁰ ibid, p 31
³¹ Details of supply dropping operations during the Malayan campaign are taken from the periodic reports of the AOC (Malaya or 224 Group) on RAF operations in Malaya (IIJ53/16/2), the monthly intelligence summaries and weekly summaries of air operations in Malaya issued by HQ ACFE or FEAF, AHQ(M), HQ Malaya Command and HQ Federation of Malaya Police, ACFE–FEAF and M/ORBs, FEAF Command Training Summaries and FEAF/RAF Contribution to Operation Firedog.
³² M/ORB(AS) Apr 1948, GOO 12/48
³³ ibid, Apr 1948, Jun 1948, GOO 24/48; ACFE/ORB (Admin) Jul 1948, COM 42/48
³⁴ ACFE/MIS Jul 1948, p 2; M/ORB(AS) Dec 1948, GOM 46/48, 'Firedog Diary'
³⁵ ACFE/MIS Jul 1948, p 2, Aug 1948, pp 4, 6; VCAS file 'Policy in Malaya', ACFE to AM/CCX 172, 24 Jul 1948 (ID9/515/Pt 2)
³⁶ ibid, ACFE to AM/CCX 200, 14 Aug 1948 (ID9/515/Pt 2); ACFE/MIS Aug 1948, p 6; M/ORB(AS) Dec 1948, GOM 46/48, 'Firedog Diary'
³⁷ VCAS file 'Policy in Malaya', ACAS to VCAS/'Situation in Malaya', 2 Nov 1948 (ID9/515/Pt 1); AOC(M) First Report, Jun 1948 to Mar 1949, p 11 (IIJ53/16/2); M/ORB(AS) Nov 1948
³⁸ AOC(M) Second Report, Apr 1949 to Dec 1950, p 26 and Appendix C (IIJ53/16/2)
³⁹ ibid, Second Report, Apr 1949 to Dec 1950, pp 27–29 (IIJ53/16/2); M/ORB(AS) Nov 1949, Appendix, Telegram to AM/AX 363
⁴⁰ M/ORB(AS) Apr 1950; AOC(M) Second Report, Apr 1949 to Dec 1950, p 31, Appendix C (IIJ53/16/2)
⁴¹ M/ORB(AS) Apr, Jun 1951, GOM 15/51, 25/51
⁴² AOC(M) Fourth Report, Sep 1951 to Feb 1952, p 11 (IIJ53/16/2), DO(M) Report, 1950/1951, p 27 (IIJ53/18/1)
⁴³ AOC(M) Fourth Report, Sep 1951 to Feb 1952, pp 9–11 (IIJ53/16/2)
⁴⁴ ibid, Fifth Report, Feb to Dec 1952, p 5 (IIJ53/16/2)
⁴⁵ L/A Warfare LL No 8, Jul 1953/Mar 1954, pp 4–6 (IIJ50/141/1/1)
⁴⁶ ibid, No 8, Jul 1953/Mar 1954, p 7 (IIJ50/141/1/1)
⁴⁷ ibid, No 9, Apr/Sep 1954, p 5 (IIJ50/141/1/1)
⁴⁸ ibid, No 9, Apr/Sep 1954, p 5 and Appendix D (IIJ50/141/1/1); M/ORB(AS) Jul 1955, Aug 1955, Appendix 105/55
⁴⁹ Malaya/CO Report, 1954, pp 412–417
⁵⁰ VCAS file 'Malaya, Air Effort', COS(55)18, 25 Jan 1955 (ID9/621/5/Pt 1); DO(M) Review, 1955, p 12 (IIJ53/18/3); FEAF/ORB(AS) Air Orders of Battle, *passim*
⁵¹ Malaya/CO Report, 1955, pp 432–434
⁵² ibid, 1956, pp 446–449; DO(M) Review, 1956, p 7 (IIJ53/18/3)
⁵³ Malaya/CO Report, 1956, p 448; AOC (224 Gp) Ninth Report, Jan to Dec 1957, Appendix A (IIJ53/16/2)
⁵⁴ ibid, Ninth Report, Jan to Dec 1957, p 26 (IIJ53/16/2)
⁵⁵ ibid, Tenth Report, Jan to Dec 1958, p 10 (IIJ53/16/2)
⁵⁶ ibid, Tenth Report, Jan to Dec 1958, p 11 (IIJ53/16/2)
⁵⁷ ibid, Ninth Report, Jan to Dec 1957, p 26 (IIJ53/16/2)
⁵⁸ ibid, Tenth Report, Jan to Dec 1958, p 3 (IIJ53/16/2)
⁵⁹ M/ORB (AS) Aug 1959, p 1
⁶⁰ ibid, Nov 1959, p 1
⁶¹ ibid, Nov 1959, p 1
⁶² ibid, Dec 1959, p 2
⁶³ ibid, Jun 1960, p 1
⁶⁴ ibid, Nov 1952, Appendix AHQ(M)/S307/6/AO
⁶⁵ L/A Warfare LL No 9, Apr/Sep 1954, Appendix B (IIJ50/141/1/1)
⁶⁶ ibid, No 9, Apr/Sep 1954, Appendix B (IIJ50/141/1/1)

CHAPTER 4

[67] ibid, No 9, Apr/Sep 1954, Appendices B and D (IIJ50/141/1/1)
[68] AOC (224 Gp) Ninth Report, Jan to Dec 1957, p 25 (IIJ53/16/2)
[69] ibid, Fourth Report, Sep 1951 to Feb 1952, pp 9–11, Fifth Report, Feb to Dec 1952, p 3 (IIJ53/16/2)
[70] ibid, Fifth Report, Feb to Dec 1952, p 3 (IIJ53/16/2); L/A Warfare LL No 6, Jul/Dec 1952, p 2 (IIJ50/141/1/1)
[71] M/ORB(AS) Feb 1953, GOM 3/53
[72] L/A Warfare, LL No 8, Jul 1953/Mar 1954, pp 3–4 (IIJ50/141/1/1)
[73] ibid, No 9, Apr/Sep 1954, p 5 (IIJ50/141/1/1); M/ORB(AS) Jul 1954, Aug 1955, Appendix 105/55
[74] ibid, Jul 1955, Appendix 90/55, Joint Standing Operational Instruction No 1, 5 May 1955
[75] ibid, Jun 1957; FEAF/MIS, Jun 1957, p 1
[76] AOC (224 Gp) Tenth Report, Jan to Dec 1958, pp 9–10 (IIJ53/16/2)
[77] M/ORB(AS) Jul 1955, Appendix 90/55, Joint Standing Operational Instruction No 2, 11 May 1955
[78] FEAF/ORB (Admin), Jun 1951
[79] ibid, Jun 1951; M/ORB(AS) Dec 1948, Appendix 46/48
[80] FEAF/MIS, Jun 1951, p 6
[81] ibid, Jun 1951, p 7
[82] Details from periodic reports of the AOC(M), FEAF/ORBs (Admin) and FEAF/MIS
[83] M/ORB(AS) May 1948, GOO 12/48; ACFE/MIS, May 1948, p 1
[84] AOC(M) First Report, Jun 1948 to Mar 1949, p 7 (IIJ53/16/2)
[85] M/ORB(AS) Aug 1948, AIX 417, Appendix 46/48
[86] AOC(M) First Report, Jun 1948 to Mar 1949, p 12 (IIJ53/16/2)
[87] M/ORB(AS) Sep 1950, Appendix 'Notes on RAF in Malaya'
[88] FEAF/MIS, Sep 1950, p 2
[89] ibid, Jun 1951, p 7; M/ORB(AS) Sep 1951
[90] FEAF/ORBs (Admin), *passim*
[91] AOC(M) Fourth Report, Sep 1951 to Feb 1952, pp 10, 11 (IIJ53/16/2)
[92] DO(M) Report, 1955, p 13 (IIJ53/18/3)
[93] AOC (224 Gp) Tenth Report, Jan to Dec 1958, p 10 (IIJ53/16/2)
[94] ibid, Third Report, Jan to Aug 1951, p 14 (IIJ53/16/2); M/ORB(AS) Jul 1955, Appendix 90/55, Joint Standing Operational Instruction No 2, 11 May 1955
[95] ibid, Jun 1948, GOM 29/48; ACFE/ORB (Admin) Feb, Jun, COM 5/48, 41/48
[96] ibid, Jul 1948, COM 43/48; M/ORB(AS) Dec 1948, GOM 30/48, 46/48; VCAS file 'Policy in Malaya', ACFE to AM, 28 Jun 1948, FARELF to WO/14118 5DZ 10 Mar 1948 (ID9/515/Pt 2)
[97] M/ORB(AS) Dec 1948, GOM 30/48
[98] ibid, Dec 1948, GOM 30/48
[99] ibid, Dec 1948, GOM 30/48, 46/48
[100] ibid, Dec 1948, GOM 38/48; ACFE/ORB (Admin) Sep 1948, COM 52/48
[101] ibid Jul 1949, COI 13/49; M/ORB(AS) Sep 1949, GOM 38/49
[102] ibid, Jun 1950, GOM 25/50
[103] ibid, May 1951, GOM 17/51
[104] ibid, Jul 1951, GOM 25/51, Mar 1952, GOM 8/52
[105] ibid, May 1952, GOM 20/52
[106] ibid, Dec 1952, GOM 40/52
[107] ibid, Feb 1953, GOM 7/53
[108] ibid, Oct 1953, GOM 22/53
[109] ibid, Feb 1954, GOM 1/54
[110] ibid, Aug 1955, GOM 26/55, Jun 1956, GOM 15/56
[111] ibid, Sep 1957, GOM 29/57
[112] FEAF/ORB (Admin) Sep 1957, COM 34/57, Joint Army/Air Instruction No 10 (Revised), 22 Sep 1956
[113] AOC (224 Gp) Tenth Report, Jan to Dec 1958, p 14 (IIJ53/16/2)
[114] FEAF/ORB (Admin) Sep 1957, COM 34/57, Joint Army/Air Instruction No 10 (2nd Revision) 18 Sep 1957
[115] AOC (224 Gp) Tenth Report, Jan to Dec 1958, p 15 (IIJ53/16/2)
[116] ibid, First Report, Jun 1948 to Mar 1949, p 8 (IIJ53/16/2)
[117] FEAF/ORB (Admin) Command Training Summaries, *passim*
[118] AOC (224 Gp) Ninth Report, Jun to Dec 1957, pp 44, 45 (IIJ53/16/2)
[119] Details from M/ORBs (AS), ACFE–FEAF/MIS, SF/WIS and FEAF/RAF Contribution to Operation 'Firedog'
[120] VCAS file 'Malaya, Air Effort', VCAS to FEAF/445, 16 Mar 1953, FEAF to AM/A330, 6 Feb 1953, AM to FEAF/1942/ACAS(P), 13 Apr 1954 (ID9/621/5/Pt 2)
[121] ibid, VCAS 187/C37745, 2 Nov 1952 (ID9/621/5/Pt 2)

CHAPTER 4

[122] M/ORB(AS) Aug 1953, Appendix 160; L/A Warfare LL No 9, Apr/Sep 1954, p 6 (IIJ50/141/1/1)
[123] ibid, No 9, Apr/Sep 1954, Appendix C (IIJ50/141/1/1)
[124] M/ORB(AS) Jan 1954, GOM 1/54, 5/54
[125] FEAF/ORB (Admin) Dec 1956, COM 56/56
[126] ibid, Oct 1959, COM 75/59
[127] Details from M/ORBs (AS), FEAF/MIS and SF/WIS
[128] AOC (224 Gp) Ninth Report, Jan to Dec 1957, p 27 (IIJ53/16/2)
[129] ibid, Ninth Report, Jan to Dec 1957, p 46 (IIJ53/16/2)
[130] ibid, Tenth Report, Jan to Dec 1958, pp 11, 19 (IIJ53/16/2)
[131] ibid, Tenth Report, Jan to Dec 1958, p 11 (IIJ53/16/2)
[132] FEAF/ORB (Admin) Oct 1958, COM 45/58
[133] M/ORB(AS) Jan 1959, p 1
[134] ibid, May 1959, p 1
[135] FEAF/MIS Jun 1959, Pt III, p 5
[136] M/ORB(AS) Aug 1959, p 2
[137] FEAF/ORB (Admin) Jul 1959, COM 57/59, Jun 1960, COM 48/60
[138] M/ORB(AS) Feb 1954, GOM 1/54; FEAF/ORB(AS) Dec 1954, Air Order of Battle; AOC(M) Second Report, Apr 1949 to Dec 1950, p 18 (IIJ53/16/2); VCAS file 'Malaya, Air Effort' VCAS 187/C37745, 2 Nov 1952, FEAF to AM/A330, 6 Feb 1953 (ID9/621/5/Pt 1)
[139] M/ORB(AS) Mar 1954, GOM 5/54
[140] ibid, Sep 1954, GOM 13/54; FEAF/ORB (Admin) Dec 1956, COM 56/56
[141] ibid, Dec 1956, COM 56/56, Air Orders of Battle, *passim*
[142] M/ORB(AS) Jun 1959, Appendix, Minutes of Meeting held in JOC on 16 Jun 1959
[143] AOC (224 Gp) Ninth Report, Jan to Dec 1957, p 29 (IIJ53/16/2)
[144] ibid, Tenth Report, Jan to Dec 1958, p 20 (IIJ53/16/2)
[145] VCAS file 'Malaya, Internal Security', Appendix A to CIC/FE55(2) Final, (ID9/621/1/Pt 3); ibid, 'Malaya, Helicopters', COS(52)442, 15 Sep 1952, COS(52)275, 20 May 1952 (ID9/621/12/Pt 1)
[146] ibid, 'Airfields in Malaya', paper by AHQ(M)/AS (ID9/621/14); ibid, 'Malaya, Helicopters', COS(54)71, DO Directive, Instruction No 18, 2 Mar 1954 (ID9/621/12/Pt 2)
[147] L/A Warfare LL No 7, Jan/Jun 1953, Appendix A (IIJ50/141/1/1)
[148] ibid, No 7, Jan/Jun 1953, Appendix A (IIJ50/141/1/1)
[149] ibid, No 7, Jan/Jun 1953, Appendix A (IIJ50/141/1/1)
[150] VCAS file 'Malaya, Helicopters', COS(54)71, 2 Mar 1954 (ID9/621/12/Pt 2)
[151] AOC (224 Gp) Ninth Report, Jan to Dec 1957, p 45 (IIJ53/16/2)
[152] FEAF/MIS Nov 1954, Pt II; L/A Warfare LL No 7, Jan/Jun 1953, Appendix A (IIJ50/141/1/1)
[153] ibid, No 8, Jul 1953/Mar 1954, p 7 (IIJ50/141/1/1)
[154] VCAS file 'Airfields in Malaya', GHQ FEAF to MOD/CIC(FE)55(2) Final, 11 Oct 1956 (ID9/621/14/Pt 1)
[155] AOC (224 Gp) Ninth Report, Jan to Dec 1957, p 28 (IIJ53/16/2)
[156] ibid, Ninth Report, Jan to Dec 1957, p 46 (IIJ53/16/2)
[157] L/A Warfare LL No 8, Jul 1953/Mar 1954, p 6 (IIJ50/141/1/1); VCAS file 'Malaya, Helicopters', COS(54)71, 2 Mar 1954 (ID9/621/12/Pt 2)
[158] L/A Warfare LL No 7, Jan/Jun 1953, p 8 (IIJ50/141/1/1); FEAF/MIS Nov 1954, Pt II
[159] M/ORB(AS) Sep 1956, Joint Army/Air Instruction No 14; ibid, Jan 1951, GOO 1/51
[160] ibid, Apr 1950, GOM 19/50; FEAF/ORB (Admin) Aug 1950, COO 36/50
[161] VCAS file 'Malaya, Helicopters', COS(52)442, 15 Sep 1952 (ID9/621/12/Pt 2); M/ORB(AS) Feb, Aug, 1952, GOM 7/52, 12/52, 26/52
[162] ibid, Jan 1953, GOM 5/53
[163] ibid, Oct 1952, GOM 32/52
[164] ibid, Oct 1952, GOM 32/52
[165] No 194 Sqn ORB Feb 1953
[166] No 303 Wing ORB Feb 1953
[167] M/ORB(AS) Jan 1953, GOM 4/53 and Feb 1953 AHQ Malaya Operation Order No 2/53
[168] M/ORB(AS) Jan 1953, GOM 4/53; L/A Warfare LL No 7, Jan/Jun 1953, p 6 (IIJ50/141/1/1)
[169] M/ORB(AS) Apr 1953, GOM 13/53, Jan 1954, GOM 1/54
[170] FEAF/MIS Nov 1954, Pt II
[171] VCAS file 'Malaya, Helicopters', COS(52)275, 20 May 1952, COS(54)71, 2 Mar 1954 (ID9/621/12/Pt 2)
[172] ibid, COS(54)71, 2 Mar 1954 (ID9/621/12/Pt 2)
[173] ibid, COS(54)71, 2 Mar 1954 (ID9/621/12/Pt 2)
[174] ibid, COS(54)71, 2 Mar 1954 (ID9/621/12/Pt 2)
[175] ibid, COS(54)71, 2 Mar 1954, COS(54)102, 5 Apr 1954 (ID9/621/12/Pt 2)
[176] ibid, DO to COS/MA/DOO/50 and C47957/D Ops/3/684 (ID9/621/12/Pt 2)

CHAPTER 4

177 ibid, COS(54)102, 5 Apr 1954 (ID9/621/12/Pt 2)
178 ibid, COS(54)376, Appendix, 7 Dec 1954 (ID9/621/12/Pt 2)
179 ibid, 'Airfields in Malaya', Aide Memoire 2265/6/59/65, 1 Nov 1955 (ID9/621/14/Pt 2)
180 ibid, 'Malaya, Helicopters', COS(55)86, 20 Oct 1955, COS(55)89, 21 Oct 1955 (ID9/621/12/Pt 2); ibid, 'Malaya, Internal Security', COS(56)434, 10 Dec 1956 (ID9/621/1/Pt 3); FEAF/ORB (Admin) Dec 1956, COM 60/56
181 VCAS file 'Malaya, Internal Security', CIC(FE)55(2), Joint Army/Air Operational Instruction No 3, 19 May 1955 (ID9/621/1/Pt 3)
182 FEAF/ORB (Admin) Apr 1956, COM 23/56; DO(M) Review, 1956, Appendix H (IIJ53/18/3)
183 FEAF/ORB (Admin) Dec 1956, COM 54/56, 55/56; VCAS file 'Malaya, Internal Security', DC(56)7, 2 Oct 1956 (ID9/621/1/Pt 3)
184 FEAF/ORB (Admin) May 1957, COM 14/57
185 ibid, Dec 1957, COM 56/57
186 AOC (224 Gp) Tenth Report, Jan to Dec 1958, pp 12, 19 (IIJ53/16/2)
187 M/ORB(AS) Jun 1958, GOO 7/58, 8/58
188 ibid, Jul 1958, p 1
189 ibid, Aug 1958, GOO 8/58
190 ibid, Jun 1958, GOO 7/58, Aug 1958, GOO 8/58; AOC(M) Tenth Report, Jan to Dec 1958, p 13 (IIJ53/16/2)
191 FEAF/ORB (Admin) Jun 1959, COM 54/59
192 ibid, Sep 1959, COM 57/59, 69/59
193 M/ORB(AS) Jul 1959, p 1 Jan 1960, p 2
194 ibid, Nov 1959, p 1
195 Details from periodic reports of AOC(M) or 224 Gp, FEAF/MIS, SF/WIS, FEAF/RAF Contribution to Operation 'Firedog' and Monthly Command Training Summaries
196 M/ORB(AS) Aug 1950, GOO 64/50, Jan 1951, GOO 1/51, Jun 1950, GOM 19/50
197 ibid, Jan 1951, GOO 1/51
198 FEAF/MIS Nov 1954, Pt II
199 ibid, Jun 1950, p 1
200 'Straits Times', 20 Jun 1950
201 FEAF/MIS Oct 1950, pp 4, 5
202 M/ORB(AS) Oct 1951, p 1
203 ibid, Mar 1952, GOM 7/52, May 1952, GOM 12/52, Jun 1952, GOM 26/52, Oct GOM 32/52
204 FEAF/MIS Feb 1952, p 4
205 ibid, Nov 1953, para 50; L/A Warfare LL No 8, Jul 1953/Mar 1954, pp 4, 5 (IIJ50/141/1/1)
206 VCAS file 'Malaya, Helicopters', COS(54)71, 2 Mar 1954 (ID9/621/12/Pt 2)
207 M/ORB(AS) Nov 1952, GOO 29/52
208 AOC(M) Fourth Report, Sep 1951 to Feb 1952, pp 8, 12 (IIJ53/16/2)
209 VCAS file 'Malaya, Helicopters', COS(55)275, 8 May 1955 (ID9/621/12/Pt 2)
210 L/A Warfare LL No 7, Jan/Jun 1953, pp 1, 2 (IIJ50/141/1/1)
211 ibid, No 7, Jan/Jun 1953, pp 1, 2 (IIJ50/141/1/1)
212 ibid, No 8, Jul 1953/Mar 1954, pp 4, 5 (IIJ50/141/1/1)
213 ibid, No 9, Apr/Sep 1954, Appendix D (IIJ50/141/1/1); M/ORB(AS) Aug 1955, Appendix 105/55
214 L/A Warfare LL No 9, Apr/Sep 1954, p 3 (IIJ50/141/1/1)
215 DO(M) Review, 1955, p 13 (IIJ53/18/3)
216 ibid, 1956, Appendix H (IIJ53/18/3); FEAF/ORB (Admin) Apr 1956, COM 23/56
217 Malaya/CO Report, 1956, p 447; DO(M) Review, 1956, Appendix H (IIJ53/18/3)
218 FEAF/Air Attachés' Conference, 1957, p 64
219 AOC (224 Gp) Tenth Report, Jan to Dec 1958, p 12 (IIJ53/16/2); M/ORB(AS) Aug 1958, GOO 8/58
220 ibid, Oct 1958, p 2
221 ibid, Feb 1959, p 1; FEAF/MIS Feb 1959, p 2
222 ibid, Nov 1959, p 23; M/ORB(AS) Oct 1959, p 2
223 ibid, Oct 1959, p 2
224 ibid, May 1960, p 1, Jun 1960, p 1
225 AOC (224 Gp) Ninth Report, Jan to Dec 1957, p 37 (IIJ53/16/2)
226 M/ORB(AS) Dec 1951, p 2
227 VCAS file 'Policy in Malaya', AM to FEAF/MSX 169, 10 Mar 1950 (ID9/515/Pt 3)
228 M/ORB(AS) Mar 1951, AHQ(M)/S307/11/Air Ops
229 ibid, Mar 1951, AHQ(M)/S307/11/Air Ops; FEAF/MIS Nov 1954, Pt II
230 L/A Warfare LL No 8, Jul 1953/Mar 1954, Appendix A, pp 12, 13 (IIJ50/141/1/1)
231 M/ORB(AS) Oct 1953, pp 1, 2
232 VCAS file 'Malaya, Helicopters', COS(54)71, 2 Mar 1954 (ID9/621/12/Pt 2)
233 FEAF/MIS Nov 1954, Pt II

CHAPTER 4

234 ibid, Sep 1954, Pt II
235 ibid, Sep 1954, Pt II
236 AOC(M) Fifth Report, Feb to Dec 1952, p 6 (IIJ53/16/2)
237 ibid, Fifth Report, Feb to Dec 1952, p 6 (IIJ53/16/2); L/A Warfare LL No 6, Jul/Dec 1952, p 4; ibid No 7, Jan/Jun 1954, p 4 (IIJ50/141/1/1); FEAF/MIS May 1953, Pt I
238 ibid, Sep 1954, Pt I, Dec 1953, Pt I; L/A Warfare LL No 8, Jul 1953/Mar 1954, p 8 (IIJ50/141/1/1); M/ORB(AS) Feb 1954, GOI 3/54
239 ibid, Feb 1954, GOI 3/54; FEAF/MIS Sep 1954, Pt I, Jan 1954, Pt I; L/A Warfare LL No 8, Jul 1953/Mar 1954, p 8 (IIJ50/141/1/1)
240 M/ORB(AS) Feb 1954, GOI 3/54; FEAF/MIS Feb 1954, Pt I
241 M/ORB(AS) Mar 1954, GOM 5/54, Nov 1954, GOM 13/54
242 FEAF/ORB (Admin) Oct 1958, COM 45/58
243 M/ORB(AS) Oct 1958, p 1
244 ibid Jan 1959, p 1
245 ibid, Oct 1959, GAI 9/59; FEAF/ORB (Admin) Oct 1959, COM 83/59
246 FEAF/MIS Sep 1954, Pt II
247 ibid, Sep 1954, Pt II; M/ORB(AS) Jul 1955, Standing Operational Order No 6
248 FEAF/MIS Apr 1954, Pt I
249 ibid, Sep 1954, Pt II; M/ORB(AS) Jul 1955, Standing Operational Order No 6
250 AOC (224 Gp) Ninth Report, Jan to Dec 1957, p 38 (IIJ53/16/2)
251 Details from M/ORBs (AS), FEAF/MIS, SF/WIS, FEAF/RAF Contribution to Operation 'Firedog'
252 Malaya/CO Report, 1949, p 207; FEAF/MIS Sep 1949, p 2
253 Malaya/CO Report, 1951, p 10; AOC(M) Third Report, Jan to Aug 1951, p 14 (IIJ53/16/2)
254 ibid, Third Report, Jan to Aug 1951, p 11 (IIJ53/16/2); FEAF/MIS Jun 1951, p 3
255 AOC(M) Fourth Report, Sep 1951 to Feb 1952, p 11 (IIJ53/16/2)
256 FEAF/Command Training Summary, Aug 1952
257 L/A Warfare LL No 8, Jul 1953/Mar 1954, p 8 (IIJ50/141/1/1)
258 ibid, No 9, Apr/Sep 1954, p 8 (IIJ50/141/1/1); Malaya/CO Report 1954, p 413
259 FEAF/RAF Contribution to Operation 'Firedog', *passim*
260 FEAF/MIS Aug 1954, Pt I; M/ORB(AS) Aug 1954, p 1
261 FEAF/MIS Sep 1955, Pt I; Malaya/CO Report, 1955, p 430
262 DO(M) Review, 1955, p 20 (IIJ53/18/3); M/ORB(AS) Aug 1955, Appendix 125/55
263 ibid, Aug 1955, Appendix 125/55
264 Malaya/CO Report, 1956, p 440; DO(M) Review, 1956, Appendix L p 2 (IIJ53/18/2)
265 ibid, 1956, Appendix L p 2 (IIJ53/18/2); Malaya/CO Report, 1956, p 440
266 ibid, 1956, p 440; DO(M) Review, 1956, Appendix L p 2 (IIJ53/18/2)
267 ibid, 1956, Appendix H p 2 (IIJ53/18/2); Malaya/CO Report, 1956, p 443
268 ibid, 1956, p 440
269 AOC (224 Gp) Ninth Report, Jan to Dec 1957, pp 32, 33 (IIJ53/16/2)
270 ibid, Ninth Report, Jan to Dec 1957, pp 32, 34 (IIJ53/16/2)
271 ibid, Ninth Report, Jan to Dec 1957, p 33 (IIJ53/16/2)
272 ibid, Ninth Report, Jan to Dec 1957, p 34 (IIJ53/16/2); FEAF/MIS Feb 1957, p 1
273 AOC (224 Gp) Ninth Report, Jan to Dec 1957, p 21 (IIJ53/16/2); M/ORB(AS) p 1
274 ibid, Jan 1957, p 1; FEAF/MIS Jun 1957, p 2
275 M/ORB(AS) Jul 1957, p 1
276 DO(M) Review, 1948–1957, p 23 (IIJ53/18/2); AOC (224 Gp) Tenth Report, Jan to Dec 1958, p 17 (IIJ53/16/2)
277 ibid, Tenth Report, Jan to Dec 1958, p 17 (IIJ53/16/2)
278 ibid, Tenth Report, Jan to Dec 1958, p 16 (IIJ53/16/2)
279 ibid, Tenth Report, Jan to Dec 1958, p 16 (IIJ53/16/2)
280 ibid, Tenth Report, Jan to Dec 1958, p 17 (IIJ53/16/2)
281 ibid, Tenth Report, Jan to Dec 1958, p 17 (IIJ53/16/2)
282 ibid, Tenth Report, Jan to Dec 1958, p 17 (IIJ53/16/2)
283 ibid, Tenth Report, Jan to Dec 1958, p 17 (IIJ53/16/2); M/ORB(AS) 1958, *passim*
284 AOC (224 Gp) Tenth Report, Jan to Dec 1958, p 17 (IIJ53/16/2)
285 ibid, Tenth Report, Jan to Dec 1958, p 17 (IIJ53/16/2); M/ORB(AS) Dec 1958, p 1, Jan 1959, p 1; FEAF/ORB (Admin) Feb 1959, COM 14/59
286 FEAF/MIS Dec 1959/Jan 1960, p 33
287 ibid, Jun/Jul 1960, p 24
288 AOC(M) Third Report, Jan to Aug 1951, p 14 (IIJ53/16/2); Malaya/CO Report, 1951, p 11
289 FEAF/MIS Nov 1959, p 24
290 AOC(M) Second Report, Apr 1949 to Dec 1950, p 16 (IIJ53/16/2); Malaya/CO Report, 1949, p 203
291 FEAF/MIS May 1953, para 40, Jun 1953, para 26

CHAPTER 4

[292] DO(M) Review, 1955, p 14 (IIJ53/18/3)
[293] FEAF/MIS Sep 1954, Pt II

CHAPTER 5

[1] M/ORB (AS) Mar 1948, Appendix AHQ(M)/6257/Org; ACFE/ORB (Admin) Jul 1948, COM 42/48
[2] M/ORB (AS) Jun 1948, GOM 38/48; ACFE/ORB (Admin) Sep 1948, COM 53/48
[3] M/ORB (AS) Jun 1949, GOM 12/49; FEAF/ORB (Admin) Oct 1949, COM 39/49
[4] M/ORB (AS) Mar 1950, GOM 9/50; ibid, Mar 1950, GOM 10/50, GAI 8/50; FEAF/ORB (Admin) Mar 1950, COM 12/50
[5] M/ORB (AS) Aug 1950, GOO 68/50
[6] ibid, Nov 1950, GOM 43/50
[7] FEAF/ORB (Admin) Jan 1956, 1957, Appendix FE/S7143/3/Org
[8] ibid
[9] ibid, Feb, Mar, 1958, COM 2/58, 7/58
[10] M/ORB (AS) Jul, Oct, 1959, GAI 4/59, GOM 83/59
[11] FEAF/ORB (Admin) Aug 1955, Jun 1956, CAI 22/55, COM 19/56; VCAS file 'Malaya, Air Effort', BF22/DDOps(B), 7 Feb 1956 (ID9/621/5/Pt 1)
[12] FEAF/MIS, Aug 1952, pp 8, 9; AOC(M) First Report, Jun 1948/Mar 1949, p 8 (IIJ53/16/2)
[13] FEAF/MIS, Aug 1952, p 8
[14] AOC(M) First Report, Jun 1948/Mar 1949, p 9 (IIJ53/16/2)
[15] ibid, Tenth Report, Jan/Dec 1958, p 14. In 1957 experiments were carried out with infra-red film to try and improve the clarity of the detail shown on air photographs under variable lighting conditions but the ordinary panchromatic film already in use was found to give better results. AOC(M) Ninth Report, Jan/Dec 1957, p 36 (IIJ53/16/2)
[16] M/ORB (AS) Sep 1950, GOO 68/50
[17] AOC (M) First Report, Jun 1948/Mar 1949, p 8 (IIJ53/16/2)
[18] L/A Warfare LL No 9, Apr/Sep 1954, p 8 (IIJ50/141/1/1)
[19] ibid, p 8 (IIJ50/141/1/1)
[20] M/ORB (AS) Apr 1948, GOO 12/48
[21] FEAF/MIS Aug 1952, p 8; M/ORB (AS) Nov 1949, AAHQ(M) to AM/AX 363, 5 Nov 1949
[22] AOC(M) First Report, Jun 1948/Mar 1949, p 9 (IIJ53/16/2)
[23] ibid, Second Report, Apr 1949/Dec 1950, p 12 (IIJ53/16/2)
[24] FEAF/MIS Aug 1952, p 9
[25] AOC(M) Fourth Report, Sep 1951/Feb 1952, p 11 (IIJ53/16/2)
[26] Malaya/CO Report, 1953, p 346
[27] VCAS file 'Malaya, Air Effort'. 'An Appreciation of the Air Requirements for the Malayan Emergency', by the DO(M) and AOC(M), DEFY 40/10, Appendix to COS (54)237, 20 Jul 1954 (ID9/621/5/Pt 1)
[28] AOC(M) Tenth Report, Jan/Dec 1958, p 14 (IIJ53/16/2)
[29] FEAF/ORB (Admin) Oct 1956, Appendix FE/S7143/3 Org
[30] *See* Chapter 4
[31] FEAF/MIS Aug 1955, Appendix to Pt I
[32] *See* Chapter 4 for flight locations during the Malayan Campaign
[33] FEAF/MIS Aug 1955, Appendix to Pt I
[34] M/ORB (AS) Mar 1956
[35] FEAF/MIS Oct 1951, pp 3, 4
[36] ibid
[37] ibid, Aug 1955, Appendix to Pt I
[38] M/ORB(AS) Aug 1954
[39] FEAF/MIS Aug 1955, Appendix to Pt I
[40] L/A Warfare LL No 9, Apr/Sep 1954, p 6 (IIJ50/141/1/1)
[41] M/ORB (AS) Jun 1948, GOO 23/48
[42] AOC(M) First Report, Jun 1948/Mar 1949, p 12 (IIJ53/16/2)
[43] M/ORB(AS) May 1951, GOO 23/51
[44] ibid, Apr 1948, GOO 12/48
[45] AOC(M) First Report, Jun 1948/Mar 1949, p 8 (IIJ53/16/2)
[46] M/ORB(AS) Jun 1948, GOO 22/48, Dec 1948, 'Firedog Diary', Appendix 46/48
[47] ibid, Jun 1948, GOO 23/48
[48] ibid, Jul 1948, GOO 25/48

CHAPTER 5

[49] ibid, Dec 1948, 'Firedog Diary', Appendix 46/48
[50] AOC(M) First Report, Jun 1948/Mar 1949, p 8 (IIJ53/16/2)
[51] ibid
[52] M/ORB(AS) Dec 1948, 'Firedog Diary', Appendix 46/48
[53] AOC(M) Third Report, Jan/Aug 1951, p 14 (IIJ53/16/2)
[54] ibid, Fourth Report, Sep 1951/Feb 1952, p 12 (IIJ53/16/2)
[55] L/A Warfare LL No 6, Jul/Dec 1952, p 3 (IIJ50/141/1/1)
[56] ibid
[57] FEAF/MIS, Oct 1953; L/A Warfare LL Nos 7, 8, Jan 1953/Mar 1954, pp 4, 7 (IIJ50/141/1/1)
[58] VCAS file 'Malaya, Air Effort', 'An Appreciation of the Air Requirements in the Malayan Emergency', by the DO(M) and AOC(M) DEFY 40/10, Appendix to COS(54)237, 20 Jul 1954 (ID9/621/5/Pt 1)
[59] L/A Warfare LL No 8, Jul 1953/Mar 1954, p 7 (IIJ50/141/1/1)
[60] DO(M), 1955 Report, DEFY 40/19/A, p 14 (IIJ53/18/2)
[61] ibid
[62] ibid
[63] FEAF/MIS Aug 1955, Appendix to Pt I
[64] DO(M) 1956 Report, Appendix H to D Ops S25/2, 12 Feb 1957, p 2 (IIJ53/18/2)
[65] FEAF/ORB (Admin) Sep 1957, COM 34/57; (AOCM) Tenth Report, Jan/Dec 1958 p, 14 (IIJ53/16/2)
[66] ibid, p 15 (IIJ53/16/2)
[67] FEAF/MIS, Aug 1955, Appendix to Pt I
[68] DO(M), 1956 Report, Appendix H to D Ops S25/2, 12 Feb 1957, p 2 (IIJ53/18/2)
[69] L/A Warfare LL No 7, Jan/Jun 1953, p 4 (IIJ50/141/1/1)

CHAPTER 6

[1] ACFE/ORB (Admin), Jan 1949, Order of Battle; M/Formations (II/80/41)
[2] AOC(M) Third Report, Jan/Aug 1951, Annexure 3 to Appendix C, p 26; M/ORB(AS) Feb 1950, GOM4/50
[3] VCAS file 'Policy in Malaya', FEAF to AM/AX 3509, 13 Jul 1950 and AX 638, 16 Jul 1950 (ID9/515/Pt 1)
[4] AOC(M) Third Report, Jan/Aug 1951, Annexure 3 to Appendix C, p 26 (IIJ53/16/2)
[5] ibid (IIJ53/16/2)
[6] ibid, Fourth Report, Sep 1951/Feb 1952, Annexure 1 to Appendix C, p 19 (IIJ53/16/2)
[7] M/ORB(AS) Jan 1951, GOM 1/51, Dec 1951, GOM 40/51, Apr 1952, GOM 11/52
[8] ibid, Feb 1950, GOM 4/50
[9] AOC(M) Third Report, Jan/Aug 1951, Annexure 3 to Appendix C, p 26 (IIJ53/16/2)
[10] ibid, Fourth Report, Sep 1951/Feb 1952, Annexure 1 to Appendix C, p 19 (IIJ53/16/2); M/ORB(AS) Jan 1954, 'Review of the MAAF Mar to Dec 1953', AHQ(M)/955/RF
[11] FEAF/ORB (Admin) Aug 1955, COM 38/55
[12] M/ORB(AS) Dec 1952, GOM 39/52
[13] ibid, Apr 1954, GOM 14/54; FEAF/ORB (Admin) Aug 1955, COM 38/55
[14] ibid, Apr 1957, COM 38/55 Amendment, Mar 1958, COM 10/58
[15] ibid, Mar 1958, COM 9/58
[16] AOC(M) Fourth Report, Sep 1951/Feb 1952, Annexure 1 to Appendix C, p 19 (IIJ53/16/2)
[17] ibid, Fourth Report, Sep 1951/Feb 1952, Annexure 1 to Appendix C, p 19; Fifth Report, Feb/Dec 1952, Appendix F (IIJ53/16/2)
[18] M/ORB(AS) Jan 1954, Review of the MAAF Mar to Dec 1953 AHQ(M)/955/RF
[19] FEAF/ORB (Admin) Dec 1958, COM 60/58
[20] AOC(M) Fifth Report, Feb/Dec 1952, Appendix F; FEAF/'Firedog', *passim* (IIJ53/16/2)
[21] FEAF/ORB (Admin) May 1958, CAI 9/58
[22] ibid
[23] AOC (224 Gp) Tenth Report, Jan/Dec 1958, p 13 (IIJ53/16/2)
[24] FEAF/ORB (Admin) Jun 1960, COM 48/60, Aug 1960, COM 69/60
[25] M/ORB(AS) Sep 1959, p 1
[26] M/ORB(AS) Jan to Apr 1960, *passim*
[27] ibid
[28] ibid, Jul 1960, p 1
[29] VCAS file 'Policy in Malaya', AC58(48) 28 Oct 1948 (ID9/515/Pt 1); 'Straits Times', 1 Apr 1950
[30] FEAF/ORB (Admin) Mar 1950, CAI 6/50

CHAPTER 6

31 ibid
32 FEAF/MIS Dec 1954, Pt II
33 ibid, May 1948, p 4; M/ORB(AS) May 1948, GOI 21/48
34 ibid, Dec 1948, GOI 28/48, GOM 39/48
35 ibid, May 1948, GOO 14/48
36 FEAF/MIS Jun 1952, Sect II, pp 7–10
37 ibid
38 ibid, Dec 1954, Pt II
39 M/ORB Apr 1948, GOI 14/48, 17/48
40 FEAF/MIS Jun 1952, Sect II, pp 7–10
41 DO(M) Review, 1955, Appendix C (IIJ53/18/2)
42 M/ORB(AS) Apr 1948, GOO 15/48
43 ibid, Apr 1948 GOO 14/48, Jul 1948, GOM 38/48
44 ibid, Dec 1948 'Firedog Diary', Appendix 46/48; AOC(M) First Report, Jun 1948/Mar 1949, Appendix J, p 38 (IIJ53/16/2)
45 ibid, First Report, Jun 1948/Mar 1949, Appendix J, p 38 (IIJ53/16/2)
46 ibid (IIJ53/16/2)
47 ibid (IIJ53/16/2)
48 M/ORB(AS) Dec 1948, 'Firedog Diary', Appendix 46/48
49 AOC(M) First Report, Jun 1948/Mar 1949, Appendix J, p 38 (IIJ53/16/2)
50 M/ORB(AS) May 1949, GOI 6/49, Jul 1949, GOI 13/49
51 ibid, Jun 1949, GOM 21/49
52 ibid, Jul 1949, GOI 13/49
53 ibid, Mar 1950, GOM 12/50
54 AOC(M) Second Report, Apr 1949/Dec 1950, p 9 (IIJ53/16/2)
55 ibid (IIJ53/16/2)
56 M/ORB(AS) Sep 1950, GOO 73/50
57 ibid
58 ibid, Jan 1951, GOM 9/51; AOC(M) Third Report, Jan/Aug 1951, pp 6, 9 (IIJ53/16/2)
59 M/ORB(AS) Jul 1951, GOM 25/51
60 ibid, Nov 1951, GOO 39/51; AOC(M) Fourth Report, Sep 1951/Feb 1952, pp 5, 6 (IIJ53/16/2)
61 M/ORB(AS) Mar 1952, GOM 6/52
62 FEAF/MIS Dec 1954, Pt II
63 M/ORB(AS) Jul 1952, GOM 28/52
64 ibid, Mar 1953, GOM 12/53, May 1953, GOM 15/53; FEAF/MIS Dec 1954, Pt II
65 ibid, Dec 1954, Pt II; M/ORB(AS) Dec 1953, GOM 25/53
66 ibid, Mar 1954, GOM 17/54; FEAF/MIS Dec 1954, Pt II
67 ibid, Dec 1954, Pt II; M/ORB(AS) Jan 1955, GOM 7/55
68 FEAF/ORB (Admin) Orders of Battle, *passim*
69 ibid, Dec 1955, COM 51/55
70 ibid, May 1956, COM 27/56
71 ibid
72 AOC (224 Gp) Ninth Report, Jan/Dec 1957, p 40 (IIJ53/16/2)
73 ibid, Ninth Report, Jan/Dec 1957, p 42 (IIJ53/16/2)
74 ibid, Ninth Report, Jan/Dec 1957, p 43 (IIJ53/16/2)
75 ibid (IIJ53/16/2)
76 ibid, Tenth Report, Jan/Dec 1958, p 25 (IIJ53/16/2)
77 ibid
78 ibid
79 FEAF/ORB (Admin) Aug 1958, COM 26/58, Oct 1959, COM 76/59, Feb 1960, COM 32/6o
80 ibid, Apr 1959, COM 16/59; AOC (224 Gp) Tenth Report, Jan/Dec 1958, p 26 (IIJ53/16/2)
81 FEAF/MIS Jun 1952, Sect II, pp 7–10
82 ibid, Dec 1954, Pt II
83 ibid
84 AOC (224 Gp) Tenth Report, Jan/Dec 1958, p 25 (IIJ53/16/2)

ANNEXES

A AOC (M and 224 Gp) Reports, First—Jun 1948/Mar 1949, Appendix A p 16, Second—Apr 1949/Dec 1950, Appendix B p 23, Third—Jan/Aug 1951, Annexure 2 to Appendix A p 19, Fourth—Sep 1951/Feb 1952, Appendix A p 14, Ninth—Jan/Dec 1957, p 6, Tenth—Jan/Dec 1958, p 4 (IIJ53/16/2); DO(M) Reviews, 1955—Appendix C, 1956—Appendix C, 1948 to 1957 —Appendix D (IIJ53/18/2, 3)

B AOC (M) Second Report—Apr 1949/Dec 1950, Annexure 1 to Appendix B, p 24, ibid, Third Report, Jan/Aug 1951, Appendix A, p 16 (IIJ53/16/2)

C ibid, Third Report, Jan/Aug 1951, Annexure 1 to Appendix A (IIJ53/16/2)

D ibid, Third Report, Jan/Aug 1951, Annexure 3 to Appendix A p 20 (IIJ53/16/2)

E DO(M) Review, 1948 to 1957, Appendix B (IIJ53/18/2)

F ibid, 1956, Appendices D and E (IIJ53/18/3)

G Malaya/CO Reports, 1948–1957 *passim*; Army and Air Force Lists, 1948–1960, *passim*

H DO(M) Review, 1956, Appendix B (IIJ53/18/3)

J ibid

K ibid, 1955 Appendix B, 1948–1957, Appendix D (IIJ53/18/2, 3); AOC (224 Gp) Ninth Report, Jan/Dec 1957, Appendix B, Tenth Report Jan/Dec 1958, Appendix B (IIJ53/16/2)

L DO(M) Review, 1948–1957, Appendix C (IIJ53/18/2); FEAF/ORB (Admin) Orders of Battle 1948–1960, *passim*

M ibid, M/Formations, *passim*; FEAF/ORBs (Admin) and M/ORBs (AS), 1948–1960, *passim*

N M/ORB(AS) Training Summaries 1949–1952, *passim*; AOC(M) Second Report, Apr 1949/Dec 1950, Appendix N p 40, Third Report, Jan/Aug 1951, Annexure 1 to Appendix C p 24, Fourth Report, Sep 1951/Feb 1952, Annexure 2 to Appendix C p 20. Fifth Report, Feb/Dec 1952, Appendix D (IIJ53/16/2)

O ibid, First Report, Jun 1948/Mar 1949, Appendix O pp 42, 43, Second Report, Apr 1949/Dec 1950, Annexure to Appendix O pp 42–44, Third Report, Jan/Aug 1951, Annexure 1 to Appendix L pp 47–48, Fourth Report, Sep 1951/Feb 1952, Annexure 1 to Appendix B p 16 (IIJ53/16/2)

P FEAF/ORB (Admin) Location of Units 1 Jul 1951

Q M/ORB(AS) Jul 1955, Appendix 90/55, Joint Army/Air Instruction No 2, 11 May 1955; AOC(M) Second Report, Apr 1949/Dec 1950, Appendix Q; RAF Aeronautical Chart, 1 : 1,000,000, Malaya, Dir Survey and War Office, Jul 1960

R Information taken from AOC(M or 224 Gp) periodic reports; FEAF/MIS: M/WSAO, SF/WIS,
to FEAF/'Firedog' Summaries, FEAF and M/ORBs, *passim*
Z

INDEX

(The suffix letter 'n' denotes a footnote)

234 *Index*

Trek: Operation, 17
Trengganu: 17, 65, 88, Annex B; airfield in, 88, Annex Q; part declared 'White', 91; airstrips in, 92; reconnaissance, 131, 132; strength of CTO in, Annex A
Triang: 22, 55, 68; airfield at, Annex Q
Triangle: Operation, 15, 16
Triumph: HMS, 46
Trolok: 62–3
Tunku Abdul Rahman: Chief Minister of the Federation, 23

Ula Bernam: 64, 109; airfield at, Annex Q
Ulav Simpan: 141–2
United States Aid Scheme: 95, 104
Urquhart: Major General R E, GOC Malaya, Annex G

Valetta aircraft: 31, 76, 84, 90, Annex M; rate of serviceability, 31, 76, 77, 91, 115; and supply drops, 82, 83, 84; and paratrooping, 87; and ambulance role, 88; and communications, 90, 91, 95; and leaflet drops, 115, 117, 118, 119, 120; and aerial broadcasting, 115; airfields suitable for, Annex Q
Valiant aircraft: 47, Annex M
Valiant: Operation, 21, 82, 103, 107, 109
Vampire aircraft: 31, 45, 46, 47, 48, 49, 64, 66, 136, Annex M; rate of serviceability, 31; cost comparison with bombs, 45; armament faults, 45
Venom aircraft: 31, 47, 48, 49, 68, 70, Annex M; rate of serviceability, 31

VHF: inauguration of, 56
Villages: and terrorist groups, 74; defence of, 5, 8, 17; resettlement of Chinese squatters, 8, 9, 17, 19; new villages, 8, 9, 19, 24, 143; cost of resettlement, 9
Vulcan aircraft: Annex M
Vulture: Operation, 55

Wade: Major-General D A L, GOC Malaya, Annex G
Walkover: Operation, 17
Warbler: Operation, 18, 63, 117
Warrior: HMS, 46
Washington aircraft: 44
Wellington II: Operation, 21, 109
Wessex S58 helicopter: 102
Whirlwind helicopter: 31, 32, 100, 101, 102, 104, 105, 108, 110, 111, 112, 114, 151, Annex M; *S 55*, 31, 100, 101, 102, 103, 104, 107, 108, 109, 110, 112, 114, 150, Annex M
Widgeon: Operation, 15, 81
Wings:
No 90 (Composite) RAAF, 38
No 303 (Helicopter), 96, 103, Annex M
Far East Flying Boat, 35–6, 48, 131, Annex P
Far East Transport, 36, 75, 76, 82, 83, 87, 88, 118, Annex M

Yang Kwo: Vice Secretary General of the MCP, 68
Yeong Kwo: Deputy Secretary General of the MCP, killed, 23
York aircraft: 31, Annex M

Printed in the United Kingdom for HMSO
Dd 294707 7/92 C15 531/3 12521